DECOLONIZING JOSIAH

The Bible in the Modern World, 5

Series Editors
J. Cheryl Exum, Jorunn Økland, Stephen D. Moore

Editorial Board
Alison Jasper, Tat-siong Benny Liew, Hugh Pyper, Yvonne Sherwood,
Caroline Vander Stichele

Decolonizing Josiah

Toward a Postcolonial Reading of the Deuteronomistic History

Uriah Y. Kim

Sheffield Phoenix Press

2005

Copyright © 2005, 2006 Sheffield Phoenix Press

First published in hardback, 2005
First published in paperback, 2006

Published by Sheffield Phoenix Press
Department of Biblical Studies, University of Sheffield
Sheffield S10 2TN

www.sheffieldphoenix.com

All rights reserved.
No part of this publication may be reproduced or transmitted in any form or by any means, electronic or mechanical, including photocopying, recording or any information storage or retrieval system, without the publishers' permission in writing.

A CIP catalogue record for this book
is available from the British Library

Typeset by Forthcoming Publications
Printed by Lightning Source

ISBN 1-905048-13-0 (hardback)
ISBN 1-905048-72-6 (paperback)
ISSN 1747-9630

Dedicated to Crystal (Kyong-Mee)
and our wonderful children Hope and Adam

Contents

Foreword	ix
List of Abbreviations	xi

Chapter 1
INTRODUCTION: THE POLITICS OF INTERPRETATION
AND IDENTITY   1

Chapter 2
POSTCOLONIAL CRITICISM AND BIBLICAL STUDIES   18

Chapter 3
WHOSE HISTORY IS IT ANYWAY?   48

Chapter 4
WHOSE SPACE IS IT ANYWAY?   114

Chapter 5
THE *REALPOLITIK* OF LIMINALITY IN JOSIAH'S KINGDOM   182

REFLECTIONS   244

Bibliography	246
Index of References	262
Index of Authors	263

Foreword

My interest in King Josiah began in my first semester of the doctoral program while taking Dr Jeffrey Kuan's seminar on history of ancient Israel and Judah at the Graduate Theological Union in Berkeley in 1998. I was most intrigued by the somewhat cryptic account of Josiah's death in 2 Kgs 23.29-30 and why Josiah went up to Megiddo to 'meet' with Necho II. My investigation focused on the question, 'What happened at Megiddo?' I quickly realized that to solve this mystery the key was not in the texts that describe Josiah's death but in the historical context of Josiah's time. Additionally, I realized that it was almost impossible to avoid reading the story of Josiah outside of the Deuteronomistic History Hypothesis. Although I did not include a bulk of research on Josiah's death in my dissertation, it has served as a catalyst for my work on Josiah and the Deuteronomistic History.

During my research for the dissertation I was quite surprised by the failure of biblical studies to come to terms with its colonialist legacy in understanding the Deuteronomistic History. Biblical scholars have understood the Deuteronomistic History as history writing in the likeness of Western history and Josiah's kingdom as a nation in the likeness of the modern nation-state without taking into account of the fact that modern history and nation are Western projects that emerged within the context of the Western imperialism and colonialism that produced two enduring metanarratives—Orientalism and nationalism. Scholars continue to appeal to the identity discourse of the West, thereby continuing the West's intellectual habit of construing the rest of the world as inferior. What goes unnoticed in the politics of interpretation is that scholars have been engaged in politics of identity; their interpretations legitimate the West, but not the rest.

I asked myself: How is it possible, given the all-encompassing sway of the colonialist reading of the Bible, to understand the Deuteronomistic History in other than colonialist terms? The historical imagination, while making undiminished use of the tools of the critical historian, must be informed by the critical use of the experience of those who have lived as the other, as the colonized, as not at home in their own land—in my case, the experience of being Asian American. I read the story of Josiah intercontextually with the experience of Asian Americans from the space of liminality. It is my attempt to decolonize Josiah and his people and to understand the Deuteronomistic History not as a history in the likeness of the West, but as 'a history of their own'.

I am grateful to those who served on my dissertation committee: Dr Jeffrey Kuan, Dr Robert Coote, Dr Anne Kilmer, and Dr Timothy Tseng. Dr Kuan was my adviser from the beginning of my program, and he has stood by me with his constant support throughout my entire program. I cannot imagine a better adviser for me. Dr Coote was especially helpful in formulating my thoughts during the writing stage, and I thoroughly enjoyed his wisdom, sprinkled with his dry humor and warm humanity. I am also grateful to Sheffield Phoenix Press for accepting to publish my work and Professor Keith Whitelam for encouraging me to speak with my own voice.

Uriah Y. Kim
January 2005

ABBREVIATIONS

ABD	David Noel Freedman (ed.), *The Anchor Bible Dictionary* (New York: Doubleday, 1992)
ABR	*Australian Biblical Review*
ARAB	D.D. Luckenbill, *Ancient Records of Assyria and Babylonia* (2 vols; Chicago: Univeristy of Chicago Press, 1926–27)
ARW	*Archiv für Religionswissenschaft*
BA	*Biblical Archaeologist*
BARev	*Biblical Archaeology Review*
BASOR	*Bulletin of the American Schools of Oriental Research*
Bib	*Biblica*
BibInt	*Biblical Interpretation*
BRev	*Bible Review*
BZAW	Beihefte zur *Zeitschrift für die alttestamentliche Wissenschaft*
CBQ	*Catholic Biblical Quarterly*
CurBS	*Currents in Research: Biblical Studies*
DH	The Deuteronomistic History
Dtr	The Deuteronomist
EI	*Eretz Israel*
ETL	*Ephemerides Theologicae Lovanienses*
HTR	*Harvard Theological Review*
HUCA	*Hebrew Union College Annual*
HSM	Harvard Semitic Monographs
HSS	Harvard Semitic Studies
IEJ	*Israel Exploration Journal*
Int	*Interpretation*
JANES	*Journal of the Ancient Near Eastern Society of Columbia University*
JAOS	*Journal of the American Oriental Society*
JARCE	*Journal of the American Research Center in Egypt*
JBL	*Journal of Biblical Literature*
JETS	*Journal of the Evangelical Theological Society*
JNES	*Journal of Near Eastern Studies*
JSOT	*Journal for the Study of the Old Testament*
JSOTSup	*Journal for the Study of the Old Testament*, Supplement Series
JSS	*Journal of Semitic Studies*
JTS	*Journal of Theological Studies*
LCL	Loeb Classical Library
LXX	Septuagint
NEA	*Near Eastern Archaeology*
PEQ	*Palestine Exploration Quarterly*
Or	*Orientalia*
OTL	Old Testament Library

RelSRev	*Religious Studies Review*
SAK	*Studien zur Altägyptischen Kultur*
SBLMS	Society of Biblical Literature Monograph Series
SJOT	*Scandinavian Journal of the Old Testament*
Them	*Themelios*

1

INTRODUCTION: THE POLITICS
OF INTERPRETATION AND IDENTITY

The account of Josiah, king of Judah from 640 to 609 BCE, in 2 Kings 22–23 in the Hebrew Bible/Old Testament has played an extremely important role in the development of modern biblical scholarship in the nineteenth century. The discovery of the 'book of the law' and the subsequent 'reform' in the narrative of Josiah have captured the imagination of several generations of biblical scholars, thereby helping to construct a biblical discourse on the history and religion of ancient Israel. The account has been used as the linchpin that held together the dating of the sources (JEDP) in the Pentateuch. It has been used as a description of the context in which the pre-exilic redactional layers in many biblical books have been constructed. It has been used as crucial data for the development of religion of ancient Israel and for the reconstruction of the history of ancient Israel. Since Martin Noth suggested in the mid-twentieth century what is known now as the 'Deuteronomistic History Hypothesis' to describe the corpus of works from Deuteronomy to 2 Kings as a self-contained history, it has become standard to read the story of Josiah as part of the Deuteronomistic History (henceforth DH).[1] Even though some elements of Noth's theory, such as his explanation for the

---

1. Martin Noth, *The Deuteronomistic History* (JSOTSup, 15; Sheffield: JSOT Press, 1981). I do not want to add another review of the recent scholarship on the Deuteronomistic History, which has been done umpteen times. What follows is not a survey of the recent scholarship on DH, but a portrayal of the 'divided kingdom' in the scholarship on DH. For a comprehensive review of the history of research and debated issues before and after Martin Noth, see Thomas Römer and Albert de Pury, 'Deuteronomistic Historiography (DH): History of Research and Debated Issues', in Albert de Pury, Thomas Römer and Jean-Daniel Macchi (eds.), *Israel Constructs its History* (JSOTSup, 306; Sheffield: Sheffield Academic Press, 2000), pp. 24-141; for a concise review in relationship to Josiah, see Erik Eynikel, *The Reform of King Josiah and the Composition of the Deuteronomistic History* (Leiden: E.J. Brill, 1995), pp. 7-31; for the impact of Martin Noth on the scholarship on DH, see Steven L. McKenzie and M. Patrick Graham (eds.), *The History of Israel's Traditions* (JSOTSup, 182; Sheffield: Sheffield Academic Press, 1994); see also Thomas Römer (ed.), *The Future of the Deuteronomistic History* (Leuven: Leuven University Press, 2000).

purpose of DH, the sixth-century dating, and the redactional history of DH, have been challenged, his suggestion that the corpus of works from Deuteronomy to 2 Kings was a continuous, chronological narrative—in short, a history—has remained firmly rooted in the field of biblical studies. Thus, the figure of Josiah is also firmly rooted in DH.

For a long time after Noth's work, the only real problem in the scholarship on DH was the choice between following F.M. Cross, who argued for an original pre-exilic edition of DH during the reign of Josiah, and Rudolf Smend, who maintained Noth's position of an original exilic edition but argued for additional editors.[2] It was Frank Cross who divided Noth's 'kingdom' into two when he moved the dating of DH from the exile to the pre-exilic period, to Josiah's reign. Cross introduced more than a different dating; he changed the nature and purpose of DH. Cross argued that there were two themes operating in the Josianic edition of DH: (1) 'the sin of Jeroboam', namely, the establishment of a countercultus in Bethel and Dan (1 Kgs 13.2-5), which was the cause of the fall of Israel in 722 BCE (2 Kgs 17.1-23); and (2) the faithfulness of David, which offers the possibility of salvation and reunification of the divided kingdom. The latter theme climaxes in Josiah, the new David, and his reformation (2 Kgs 22.1–23.25). Therefore, Cross argued that the purpose of the Josianic edition of DH was to support Josiah's reform: to centralize the cult in Jerusalem in order to unify the divided kingdom. The Josianic edition gave purpose and meaning to DH as a triumphalist vision of salvation in Josiah and in his reformation.

Steven L. McKenzie describes the division in scholarship on DH as follows:

> In the beginning was the Deuteronomistic History. It was not *tohu wabohu* but a well ordered creation by one author who had access to Israel's traditions. We knew not his name, though scoffers say it was Martin Noth. We called him simply 'Dtr'. And it was good. But as scholars multiplied on the DH so did

---

2. F.M. Cross, *Canaanite Myth and Hebrew Epic* (Cambridge, MA: Harvard University Press, 1973), pp. 274-89 (the chapter is titled 'The Themes of the Book of Kings and the Structure of the Deuteronomistic History'). Rudolf Smend, 'The Law and the Nations: A Contribution to Deuteronomistic Traditional History', in Gary N. Knoppers and J. Gordon McConville (eds.), *Reconsidering Israel and Judah: Recent Studies on the Deuteronomistic History* (Winona Lake, IN: Eisenbrauns, 2000), pp. 95-110. The first thing people asked me when they found out that I was working on Josiah was whether I was going to follow Cross or Smend. It reminded me of when I came to the United States in 1976 and my cousins pressured me to decide whether I was for the Yankees or the Mets; they made it sound as if this was the most important decision of my life. I had no idea that they were baseball teams in New York. I chose 'Yankees' because it was easier to pronounce than 'Mets'. I had no idea that there were more than 30 teams in Major League Baseball; I was given only two choices. I have remained a die-hard Yankees fan for 28 years because of that fateful decision.

Dtrs. Soon, there arose a great division in the earth. Those in the North—of America—followed Cross while those across the Sea went after Smend. Each faction did what was right in its own eyes, and there was little interaction between them.[3]

The divergence between the two 'kingdoms' in scholarship on DH may have something to do with the difference in the starting point of investigation between Cross and Smend: Cross started out his investigation with the book of Kings, and Smend started out his investigation with Joshua and Judges. The difference may also have to do with the difference in their faith traditions, as suggested by Römer and de Pury: American Puritanism and German Protestantism (Lutheran).[4] Whatever the reason behind the division between these two schools, they have dominated the scholarship on DH for some time now. Although there are those who have been trying to combine both theories, like Antony Campbell and Mark O'Brien, the interaction and cooperation between the two schools has been minimal.[5] The reunification of the 'kingdom' founded by Noth seems unlikely.

3. S.L. McKenzie, 'The Divided Kingdom in the Deuteronomistic History and in Scholarship on It', in Römer (ed.), *The Future of the Deuteronomistic History*, pp. 135-45 (135).
4. Römer and de Pury suggest that Cross's faith tradition may have something to do with this view: 'We cannot refrain from questioning the role played in the genesis of the Anglo-Saxon model by the great admiration that Cross clearly has for King Josiah and his reform projects. It is almost a fascination, and we perceive in his work an optimistic theology, not so distant, after all, from the spirit of American puritanism. The approach to the texts is positivist: Cross and his students consider that, with only some exceptions, the Book of Kings relates events that are really historical. On the methodological level, literary criticism does not play an important role, and the arguments from which the theory is constructed are most often of a thematic order' ('Deuteronomistic Historiography', p. 73). They also suggest that there is a remarkable similarity between the Documentary Hypothesis and the Smend School's theory, which may be rooted in Protestant faith: 'The description of DH according to the stages DtrH–DtrP–DtrN implies the chronological sequence "History–Prophecy–Law", a sequence that surprisingly resembles the Wellhausenian idea of the religious evolution of Israel through its Old Testament history, and we can even ask whether Smend's model does not attempt, without realizing it, to apply the Pentateuchal documentary theory to the historical books… The "J" historian of the classical documentary theory would correspond quiet well to the DtrH of Smend. "E", whose relationship with the prophetic movement has been emphasized, would have its counterpart in DtrP, and "D" and "P", whose legalism Protestant exegesis always liked to stress, would find their parallel in the legalism of DtrN' ('Deuteronomistic Historiography', pp. 73-74).
5. Antony Campbell remarks: 'Despite myriad studies, it is surprising how little has been done to compare or integrate the insights of the Cross and Smend schools' (A.F. Campbell, 'Martin Noth and the Deuteronomistic History', in S.L. McKenzie and M.P. Graham [eds.], *The History of Israel's Traditions: The Heritage of Martin Noth* [JSOTSup, 182; Sheffield: Sheffield Academic Press, 1994], pp. 31-62 [53]).

However, these two schools, even with differences, have collaborated in shaping and dictating the discourse on DH as merely a choice between original pre-exilic edition(s) and the exilic edition(s). Although there have been serious challenges in recent years, their bipartisan rhetoric continues to dominate the politics of interpretation of DH.[6] More recent works continue to follow essentially the same trends of scholarship from the past, dealing essentially with the same issues and asking the same set of questions.[7] Schniedewind, somewhat dissatisfied with the status quo of scholarship on DH in recent years, comments that 'although a few studies apply newer

---

6. McKenzie comments that 'though the Smendites and Crossites have dominated the land, scholars and theories have continued to multiply. Of late, some have arisen among the faithful who no longer believe in the one History' ('The Divided Kingdom', pp. 144-45). For example, J. Gordon McConville advocates the book model of composition that sees each book as being edited in a distinctive way ('The Old Testament Historical Books in Modern Scholarship', *Them* 22 [1997], pp. 3-13); W. Boyd Barrick summarizes concisely the problem with the 'Deuteronomistic History Hypothesis' in his *The King and the Cemeteries: Toward a New Understanding of Josiah's Reform* (Leiden: E.J. Brill, 2002), especially pp. 10-16; Gary Knoppers divides the challenge to the Deuteronomistic History hypothesis in three ways: as books, as unrelated blocks of writing, and as a collection of blocks of writing edited fairly late in the editorial process ('Is there a Future for the Deuteronomistic History?', in Römer [ed.], *The Future of the Deuteronomistic History*, pp. 119-34). Another camp wants to go back to Noth: to view DH as one unified work of an author-historian with later additions, rather than to view DH as a work with multiple redactors (whether pre-exilic or exilic)—for example, John Van Seters, *In Search of History: Historiography in the Ancient World and the Origins of Biblical History* (New Haven: Yale University Press, 1983; repr., Winona Lake, IN: Eisenbrauns, 1997). Ironically, it is the literary critics who are using Noth's basic thesis of DH as a product of a single author-historian: by opting for the literary-critical approach to reading DH, it provides an option of going around the whole issue of the editing process by focusing on the final form—for example, R. Polzin, *Moses and the Deuteronomist: A Literary Study of the Deuteronomistic History—Part One: Deuteronomy, Joshua, Judges* (Bloomington: Indiana University Press, 1980), and *idem, Samuel and the Deuteronomist: A Literary Study of the Deuteronomistic History* (San Francisco: Harper & Row, 1987).

7. Two reviewers of recent works on DH have made such observations: McConville, 'The Old Testament Historical Books', and William Schniedewind, 'The Problem with Kings: Recent Study of the Deuteronomistic History', *RelSRev* 22 (1995), pp. 22-27. Schniedewind reviewed the following books: Iain W. Provan, *Hezekiah and the Book of Kings: A Contribution to the Debate about the Composition of the Deuteronomistic History* (BZAW, 172; Berlin: W. de Gruyter, 1988); Mark A. O'Brien, *The Deuteronomistic History Hypothesis: A Reassessment* (Orbis biblicus et orientalis, 92; Göttingen: Vandenhoeck & Ruprecht, 1989); Steven L. McKenzie, *The Trouble with Kings: The Composition of the Book of Kings in the Deuteronomistic History* (Leiden: E.J. Brill, 1991); Gary N. Knoppers, *Two Nations under God: The Deuteronomistic History of Solomon and the Dual Monarchies* (2 vols.; Atlanta: Scholars Press, 1993–94); Ernst Würthwein, *Studien zum deuteronomistischen Geschichtswerk* (Berlin: W. de Gruyter, 1994). McConville gives a summary of recent developments in scholarship on DH.

1. *Introduction* 5

literary approaches to the study of the DtrH...the DtrH has for the most part resisted this type of approach, and consequently the books presently under review follow previous trends in research'.[8] Schniedewind concludes that 'the current studies do little more than refine the traditional debate'.[9] However, McConville approves the fact that the contemporary debate on DH revolves around a set of basic themes that have been treated since Noth. He asserts that serious contributions to scholarship on DH have to address all or most of the themes and questions of previous generations of scholars. The bipartisan discourse has constructed a landscape in which every statement, inquiry, discourse, or 'knowledge' on DH has to be presented according to the rules and regulations of this discourse and has to be approved by it in order to be a legitimate or 'serious' contribution to scholarship on DH.

What goes unnoticed in their politics of interpretation is that they have been engaged in politics of identity. One of the more enduring legacies of Noth is the idea that the Deuteronomist (henceforth Dtr) was a historian in the likeness of modern historians, and, thus, DH is understood as history in the likeness of Western history. Although Noth and Cross differ significantly in their views of the function of Josiah in DH, they both collaborate in placing the discussion of Josiah within the discourse of history. But the fact that modern history is a Western project that emerged within the context of Western colonialism, which produced two enduring metanarratives—Orientalism and nationalism—is seldom noted in biblical studies. Modern history as it was developed in Germany in the nineteenth century and exported to the world served as an instrument of European racial nationalism. History is no more than an identity discourse of the West; it legitimates the West. In narrating the West's identity through history, it sees the West as the subject of history, and other peoples' histories as no more than footnotes in its narrative. Thus, while DH is understood as a historical account of ancient Israel's past (which is problematic in its own right), a prevailing tendency also construes it as the wellspring and touchstone of Western civilization. Such a view imagines DH as a narration of the original model of the nation, which the West has imitated and fulfilled. This tendency, thereby, makes the West the subject of DH. DH is thus viewed as the first and archetypical Western history. It describes the creation of an all-Israel state in Palestine, as the bringer of proper civilization to the region. This establishes a rightful hegemonic culture before which all must yield as being 'other', or 'less than', or, as Homi Bhabha puts it, 'unhomely'—not at home in one's own land. An understanding of Josiah and his kingdom that is framed within history that narrates the identity of Western civilization is still affected by the legacy of Orientalism. Such an understanding is complicit in the politics of identity that

8. Schniedewind, 'The Problem with Kings', p. 22.
9. Schniedewind, 'The Problem with Kings', p. 25.

only legitimates the experience, history, destiny, and aspirations of the West. Such politics of identity in interpreting Josiah need to be both recognized and put to critique.

We must recognize the persistent tendency among biblical scholars to appeal to the metanarrative of nationalism in their interpretation of Josiah. Nationalism narrates the identity of the West more directly than Orientalism, which is also about the identity of the West through the (mis)representation of the East. Orientalism and nationalism are two sides of Western imperialism. The rise of nationalism and nations is a historical event that had no precedent before the West imagined and experienced it. It is hard to believe that concepts such as 'nations' and 'nationalism' are rather recent inventions when they seem so firmly fixed in the contemporary imagination and seem so self-evident and timeless. Benedict Anderson comments that 'nation' is 'the most universally legitimate value in the political life of our time'.[10] Ernest Gellner comments that 'a man must have a nationality as he must have a nose and two ears… Having a nation is not an inherent attribute of humanity, but it has now come to appear as such.'[11] Tom Nairn describes nationalism as 'the pathology of modern developmental history, as inescapable as "neurosis" in the individual…rooted in the dilemmas of helplessness thrust upon most of the world…and largely incurable'.[12] However, Ernest Renan recognized the novelty of nations about a century ago:

> Nations…are something fairly new in history. Antiquity was unfamiliar with them; Egypt, China and ancient Chaldea were in no way nations. They were flocks led by a Son of the Sun or by a Son of Heaven. Neither in Egypt nor in China were there citizens as such. Classical antiquity had republics, municipal kingdoms, confederations of local republics and empires, yet it can hardly be said to have had nations in our understanding of the term.[13]

The modern understanding of the term 'nation' is based on the principle that a particular culture/people and a particular polity/state belong to each other from primordial time. This represents a congruence of state and people. The state has a centralized government and defined borders within which it has a monopoly of legitimate force. The people are defined by identity markers like race, ethnicity, history, and culture. The people have the legitimacy to occupy and to exercise ownership of the state. But the correspondence between a political state and a particular group of people is historically contingent. That is to say, peoples and nations emerge independently of each

---

10. Benedict Anderson, *Imagined Communities: Reflections on the Origin and Spread of Nationalism* (New York: Verso, 1991), p. 12.
11. Ernest Gellner, *Nations and Nationalism* (Ithaca, NY: Cornell University Press, 1983), p. 6.
12. Tom Nairn, quoted in Anderson, *Imagined Communities*, p. 5.
13. Ernest Renan, 'What is a Nation?', in H.K. Bhabha (ed.), *Nation and Narration* (London: Routledge, 1990), pp. 8-22 (9).

1. Introduction

other, and are not necessarily destined for each other. Gellner summarizes this point as follows:

> Nations, like states, are a contingency, and not a universal necessity. Neither nations nor states exist at all times and in all circumstances. Moreover, nations and states are not the *same* contingency. Nationalism holds that they were destined for each other; that either without the other is incomplete, and constitutes a tragedy. But before they could become intended for each other, each of them had to emerge, and their emergence was independent and contingent.[14]

According to the modernist view—championed by Hobsbawn, Gellner, and Anderson—the nation emerged with modernity. Gellner argues that the emergence of nations was a recent historical phenomenon that became possible only in an industrial society. Gellner explains that the congruence of culture and polity, the most important feature of nationalism, was nearly impossible in agrarian society, but became possible in industrial society when the relationship between culture and polity changed radically:

> What happens when a social order is accidentally brought about in which the clerisy does become, at long last, universal, when literacy is not a specialism but a precondition of all other specialisms, and when virtually all occupations cease to be hereditary? …In an age of universalized clerisy…a high culture pervades the whole of society, defines it, and needs to be sustained by the polity. *That* is the secret of nationalism.[15]

Nationalism justifies the nation as the legitimate force and cultural expression of the unification of the people/culture—out of many one—with the state/land. But Gellner maintains that 'nationalism is not what it seems, and above all it is not what it seems to itself. The cultures it claims to defend and revive are often its own inventions, or are modified out of all recognition.'[16] He summarizes how this happens:

> The basic deception and self-deception practiced by nationalism is this: nationalism is, essentially, the general imposition of a high culture on society, where previously low cultures had taken up the lives of the majority, and in some cases of the totality, of the population. It means that generalized diffusion of a school-mediated, academy-supervised idiom, codified for the requirements of reasonably precise bureaucratic and technological communication. It is the establishment of an anonymous, impersonal society, with mutually substitutable atomized individuals, held together above all by a shared culture of this kind, in place of a previous complex structure of local groups, sustained by old cultures reproduced locally and idiosyncratically by the micro-groups themselves. That is what *really* happens.[17]

---

14. Gellner, *Nations and Nationalism*, p. 6.
15. Gellner, *Nations and Nationalism*, p. 8.
16. Gellner, *Nations and Nationalism*, p. 56.
17. Gellner, *Nations and Nationalism*, p. 57.

However, Gellner reminds us that the nationalist principle, although showing its fragility at times and inherently unstable, has very deep roots in the current condition of the world. Gellner argues that the universality of literacy made it possible for the nationalist principle of congruence of polity and culture to be part of our reality, a principle that cannot be easily denied in our condition.

Benedict Anderson's now classic work about the origin and spread of nationalism argues that the nation is 'an imagined political community' that emerged by means of 'print-language capitalism'—the wide-ranging effects of the printing press and the establishment of language used in printing as an 'official' language of the people. Although Anderson acknowledges in a number of places that changes in technology and means of production are forces that shape the condition in which nations can be imagined, he argues that the imagination of the nation was really disseminated by the novel and the newspaper, which provided 'the technical means for "re-presenting" the *kind* of imagined community that is the nation'.[18] He suggests that these print-languages laid the bases for thinking about nations as imagined communities in three distinct ways:

> First and foremost, they created unified fields of exchange and communication below Latin and above the spoken vernaculars... These fellow-readers, to whom they were connected through print, formed, in their secular, particular, visible invisibility, the embryo of the nationally imagined community. Second, print-capitalism gave a new fixity to language, which in the long run helped to build that image of antiquity so central to the subjective idea of the nation... Third, print-capitalism created languages-of-power of a kind different from the older administrative vernaculars. Certain dialects inevitably were 'closer' to each print-language and dominated their final forms.[19]

Therefore, Anderson argues that the idea of unisonance—for example, singing national anthems together with fellow nationals who are actually strangers—captures how the nation as the imagined community connects its members: 'For it shows that from the start the nation was conceived in language, not in blood, and that one could be "invited into" the imagined community. Thus today, even the most insular nations accept the principle of *naturalization* (wonderful word!), no matter how difficult in practice they may make it.'[20]

Anderson's argument shifts the emphasis on the development of nations and nationalism from an ideology to a form of cultural expression. Anderson points out that 'nationality, or, as one might prefer to put it in view of that word's multiple significations, nation-ness, as well as nationalism, are cultural

18. Anderson, *Imagined Communities*, p. 25.
19. Anderson, *Imagined Communities*, p. 45.
20. Anderson, *Imagined Communities*, p. 145.

artefacts of a particular kind'.[21] Therefore, he proposes that 'nationalism has to be understood by aligning it, not with self-consciously held political ideologies, but with the large cultural systems that preceded it, out of which —as well as against which—it came into being'.[22] He suggests that nations were communities imagined through cultural expressions that eventually replaced two cultural systems—the religious community and the dynastic realm. Therefore, Anderson comments that:

> No surprise then that the search was on, so to speak, for a new way of linking fraternity, power and time meaningfully together. Nothing perhaps more precipitated this search, nor made it more fruitful, than print-capitalism, which made it possible for a rapidly growing number of people to think about themselves, and to relate themselves to others, in profoundly new ways.[23]

The change in the way people were relating to themselves engendered the need for a narrative of identity. Nations as imagined communities need narratives to tell the story of their birth, growth, their destiny and aspirations. To write a narrative that can give a national identity to an imagined community of strangers, there needs to be selective remembering or forgetting of past events, but always as long as these events are considered to be 'our own'. The selected events in the past are related to the nation as part of 'our own' history in order to narrate an identity of an imagined community. Anderson states that 'all profound changes in consciousness, by their very nature, bring with them characteristic amnesias. Out of such oblivion, in specific historical circumstances, spring narratives.'[24] Anderson compares these narratives to biographies that give identity to persons. However, Anderson points out a significant difference between narratives of person and nation:

> In the secular story of the 'person' there is a beginning and an end. She emerges from parental genes and social circumstances onto a brief historical stage, there to play a role until her death. After that, nothing but the penumbra of lingering fame or influence... Nations, however, have no clearly identifiable births, and their deaths, if they ever happen, are never natural.[25]

Anderson continues that because the nation has no parents 'the nation's biography can not be written evangelically, "down time", through a long procreative chain of begetting'.[26] He notes that the only alternative is to narrate the nation's biography 'up time': the present begets World War II, World War II begets World War I, and so on, and that this inverts the conventional

21. Anderson, *Imagined Communities*, p. 4.
22. Anderson, *Imagined Communities*, p. 12.
23. Anderson, *Imagined Communities*, p. 36.
24. Anderson, *Imagined Communities*, p. 204.
25. Anderson, *Imagined Communities*, p. 205.
26. Anderson, *Imagined Communities*, p. 205.

genealogy. Using an inverted genealogy, the past events are remembered or forgotten as 'our own'. The writing of national histories fulfilled the need for a narration of identity among the emerging nations of the West.

This is not to deny that the origins of nations can be traced prior to modernity. There are those who argue—the so-called revisionists—that nation-formation and nationalism have nothing to do with modernity, that nations were a natural outcome for some ethnic communities.[27] I believe the confusion in the debate over when the nation was born has something to do with the use of the word 'nation'. It is used to designate the people as well as the state. Obviously, the 'nation' as a people, united primarily through ethnicity and religion, existed prior to modernity, according to the revisionist view. But, the 'nation' as a nation-state (the congruence of the people or 'nation' and the state) did not exist prior to modernity, as understood by modernists. For example, Adrian Hastings defines the term 'nation' as follows:

> A nation is a far more self-conscious community than an ethnicity. Formed from one or more ethnicities, and normally identified by a literature of its own, it possesses or claims the right to political identity and autonomy as a people, together with the control of specific territory, *comparable to that of biblical Israel* and of other independent entities in a world thought of as one of nation-states.[28]

This definition falls between that of the term 'people' (without the qualification of the control of specific territory) and the term 'nation', as I have been using it. Hastings describes the term 'nation-state' as follows:

> A nation-state is a state which identifies itself in terms of one specific nation whose people are not seen simply as 'subjects' of the sovereign but as a horizontally bonded society to whom the state in a sense belongs. *There is thus an identity of character between state and people...* In it, ideally, there is a basic equivalence between the borders and character of the political unit upon the one hand and a self-conscious cultural community on the other. In most cases this is a dream as much as a reality. Most nation-states in fact include groups of people who do not belong to its core culture or feel themselves to be part of a nation so defined. Nevertheless almost all modern states act on the bland assumption that they are nation-states.[29]

This description is identical to the definition of 'nation' as I have been using it. Hastings argues that, although the idea that a 'nation' (i.e. people) should have its own 'state' became central to Western political thinking in the nineteenth century, 'it existed as a powerful reality in some places long

---

27. Adrian Hastings, *The Construction of Nationhood: Ethnicity, Religion and Nationalism* (Cambridge: Cambridge University Press, 1997).
28. Hastings, *The Construction of Nationhood*, p. 3 (emphasis mine).
29. Hastings, *The Construction of Nationhood*, p. 3 (emphasis mine).

1. Introduction

before that'.[30] His prime example is Israel in the Bible. In Israel, Hastings sees 'a nation—a unity of people, language, religion, territory and government'.[31] He states that Israel is 'an all too obvious exemplar for Bible readers of what every other nation too might be, a mirror for national self-imaging'.[32] His central thesis is that Christianity, more than other religions, was responsible for nationalism and nation-formation because, in part, the political imagination of Christian people was influenced by the Old Testament example. He summarizes his thesis as follows:

> Nations developed, as I have suggested, out of a typical medieval and early modern experience of the multiplication of vernacular literatures and of state systems around them, a multiplication largely dependent upon the church, its scripture and its clergy. Nation-formation and nationalism have in themselves almost nothing to do with modernity. Only when modernization was itself already in the air did they almost accidentally become part of it, particularly from the eighteenth century when the political and economic success of England made it a model to imitate.[33]

Even Hastings seems to acknowledge that, even though national sentiment existed prior to modernity, it was during modernization that national sentiment became a political reality, whether accidentally or not. And the thesis that Israel was a nation (a nation-state to Hastings) is based on his assumption, rather than on the reality of Israel. What the Israelites wrote was not a narrative of a nation-state; one can call it a narrative of a kingdom or of a dynasty or of a people, but not of a nation. My point is not whether there existed national sentiments (a people/nation desiring their own land/state) prior to modernity, but that both nation-formation and narratives about national identity have occurred only in recent history.

The people of Josiah's kingdom were unfamiliar, therefore, with the modern understanding of the nation, and Josiah's kingdom never developed into one. One needs to be careful about using and appealing to the modern discourse of nationalism when discussing Josiah's kingdom, even if there seem to be similarities between that kingdom and modern nations. We need to keep in mind that Josiah's kingdom was a typical state in agrarian society, maintained through religion (the temple, the law, and Yahweh) and dynasty (the house of David seated in Jerusalem). Josiah's kingdom featured nothing extraordinary. Its features were common to agrarian society. Gellner lists some general features of agrarian society: 'The majority of the population is made up of agricultural producers, peasants. Only a minority of the society's population are specialists, whether military, political, religious or economic.

---

30. Hastings, *The Construction of Nationhood*, p. 4.
31. Hastings, *The Construction of Nationhood*, p. 18.
32. Hastings, *The Construction of Nationhood*, p. 18.
33. Hastings, *The Construction of Nationhood*, p. 205.

Most agrarian populations are also affected by the two other great innovations of the agrarian age: centralized government and the discovery of writing.'[34] The fact that Josiah's kingdom was a form of centralized government, namely a state, and that it had a clerisy, does not make Josiah's kingdom closer to being a nation than other agrarian states. Josiah's kingdom, even if Josiah had a program to form a nation, could not have been a nation. This is true since, as Gellner claims:

> in the agrarian order, to try to impose on all levels of society a universalized clerisy and a homogenized culture with centrally imposed norms, fortified by writing, would be an idle dream. Even if such a programme is contained in some theological doctrines, it cannot be, and is not, implemented. It simply cannot be done. The resources are lacking.[35]

To use the models and elements of nationalism to understand Josiah's kingdom is to put ourselves in danger of appealing to the identity discourse of the West. I am not saying that we can somehow completely avoid using or appealing to the discourse of nationalism, since it is inherent in the conditions of our time; however, we need to be wary of what we are doing and acknowledge the danger of framing one's discussion within the identity discourse of the West.

For example, when scholars use cultural artifacts to draw the boundaries of Josiah's kingdom, they are following nationalist logic. David's conquest of Palestine represents the moment of 'primary acquisition', conquering once and for all the land that would forever belong to David's progeny. Once the territory had been demarcated as Israel, cultural artifacts discovered within the geographical limits of Israel are deemed ethnically Israelite. Geary describes the practice of ethnoarchaeology: once the physical location of a 'people' is determined, 'then it was up to archaeologists to find the physical evidence of the cultural specificities of that people. Surely if language corresponded to a specific people who shared common customs and values, these same cultural differences would manifest in the physical artifacts recoverable by archaeologists.'[36] To complete this circular logic, biblical scholars use Judean 'ethnic' artifacts to draw the territorial limits of Josiah's kingdom, three hundred years after the house of David had ceased to be a power over greater Palestine. Not surprisingly, many scholars envision Josiah's kingdom to be similar in size and influence to that of David's kingdom. Thus, Josiah's supposed conquest of the northern kingdom is justified not as a *conquest* but as a *reunification*. This is a modern nationalist reading that needs to be questioned.

---

34. Gellner, *Nations and Nationalism*, p. 110.
35. Gellner, *Nations and Nationalism*, p. 17.
36. Patrick J. Geary, *The Myth of Nations: The Medieval Origins of Europe* (Princeton, NJ: Princeton University Press, 2002), p. 34.

1. *Introduction*

The Space of Liminality

In some ways, the Others are condemned to mimic the West. If postcolonial states model their development identically on that of the West, they are viewed as copies of the real things. If they imagine themselves differently, all the problems in those nations are attributed to under-development or to a failure to copy the West. It is ironic that nationalism as a form of narrative of identity of the West, in contrast to the narrative of the Other (Orientalism), was used by the colonized to resist colonialism and to form their own nations. The connection between nationalism in the West and its expansion and the eventual colonization of the rest of the world is undeniable. Brennan states: 'European nationalism was motivated by what Europe was doing in its far-flung dominions. The "national idea", in other words, flourished in the soil of foreign conquest.'[37] On the one hand, by using the concept of a shared community, an 'imagined community' as Anderson would say, the colonized states were able to invent an identity, a self-image of themselves, through which they could act to liberate themselves from the oppression of the West. On the other hand, the same movement is used in postcolonial states to maintain the hegemonic control of the imperial power over the masses by the ruling class. The nation is still the dominant form of socio-political formation in postcolonial states as well as in the West; nationalism will thus continue to privilege the West.

Then how can we imagine communities or groups of people outside of the discourse of nationalism, when this discourse is so fixed in our imagination? How do we talk about non-Western peoples without using the narration of nations, when any discourse or narrative of nations and nationalism is susceptible to being framed within the identity narrative of the West? How can we talk about the Other without always referring to the West? Homi Bhabha suggests that we need to move away from seeing the Western nation as the center of history and explore new places from which to write histories of peoples: 'It is when the western nation comes to be seen, in Conrad's famous phrase, as one of the dark corners of the earth, that we can begin to explore new places from which to write histories of peoples and construct theories of narration'.[38] He asks: 'When did we become "a people"? When did we stop being one? Or are we in the process of becoming one?'[39] The unstable nature of the nation and thus the failure to unify the people lies not in the failure of the postcolonial states to mimic the Western nation, but in the reality of living cultures at the level of locality. Bhabha notes that

---

37. T. Brennan, 'The National Longing for Form', in Bhabha (ed.), *Nation and Narration*, pp. 44-70 (59).
38. Bhabha, 'Introduction', in *idem* (ed.), *Nation and Narration*, pp. 1-7 (6).
39. Bhabha, 'Introduction', p. 7.

> It is an ambivalence that emerges from a growing awareness that, despite the certainty with which historians speak of the 'origins' of nation as a sign of the 'modernity' of society, the cultural temporality of the nation inscribes a much more transitional social reality.[40]

He argues that 'the "locality" of national culture is neither unified nor unitary in relation to itself, nor must it be seen simply as "other" in relation to what is outside or beyond it'.[41] He names 'a process of hybridity' in which new 'people' are incorporated 'in relation to the body politic, generating other sites of meaning and, inevitably, in the political process, producing unmanned sites of political antagonism and unpredictable forces for political representation'.[42] Bhabha reminds us that 'the "other" is never outside or beyond us; it emerges forcefully, within cultural discourse, when we *think* we speak most intimately and indigenously "between ourselves"'.[43]

Homi Bhabha suggests a new site of narration: the space of liminality. The nation is not a fixed social formation. Its instability to unite the people/culture and the state/land shows up as self-evident in 'a process of hybridity' and in the space of in-betweenness where people and culture do not simply comply with the script of the national discourse. Somehow the people have survived the homogenization of the nation. Bhabha argues that when we look at the nation from liminality, when we acknowledge that 'the nation is no longer the sign of modernity under which cultural differences are homogenized' and that the nation is an ambivalent and vacillating representation of the people, it 'opens up the possibility of other narratives of the people and their difference'.[44] Bhabha's purpose is to break away from the dualistic thinking that lies behind nationalism and Orientalism. This dualistic thinking is an 'us and them' thinking that sees the people and culture within the borders of the nation as 'us' and any people or culture outside of the imagined community as others. Bhabha argues that reality does not work according to such a scheme. Hybridity in culture and people is reality at the local level. Thus, Bhabha argues that once it is acknowledged that the nation is the space of liminality, then 'its "difference" is turned from the boundary "outside" to its finitude "within", and the threat of cultural difference is no longer a problem of "other" people. It becomes a question of the otherness of the people-as-one.'[45] It is in the space of liminality that different voices of the people emerge. It is in the space of liminality that 'the possibility of other contending

---

40. Bhabha, 'Introduction', p. 1.
41. Bhabha, 'Introduction', p. 4.
42. Bhabha, 'Introduction', p. 4.
43. Bhabha, 'Introduction', p. 4.
44. Bhabha, 'DissemiNation', in *idem* (ed.), *Nation and Narration*, pp. 291-322 (300).
45. Bhabha, 'DissemiNation', p. 301.

and liberating forms of cultural identification' can occur and where the differences between them can be translated into a kind of solidarity.[46]

Then how is it possible, given the all-encompassing sway of the colonialist reading of DH, to understand Josiah in other than colonialist terms? How does one draw attention to the connection between Western imperialism and the production of Western knowledge? How does one overcome the outrageous insularity of biblical studies—the separation of the world of biblical studies from the world at large, and particularly the failure of biblical studies to come to terms with its colonialist legacy? In short, one must do a postcolonial reading of Josiah from the space of liminality. In Chapter 2 I will describe postcolonial criticism in biblical studies and define the space of liminality. Postcolonial criticism, on the one hand, draws attention to the connection between Western imperialism and the production of Western knowledge. On the other hand, it works towards connecting biblical scholarship to the real social and political issues of the world in the hope of presenting an alternative arrangement. A postcolonial reading of Josiah must apply the historical imagination and make undiminished use of the tools of the critical historian. This reading must be informed by the experience, expressed with honesty and in all its complexity, of those who have lived as the 'other', as the colonized, as not at home in their own land, as interstitial beings—in my case, the experience of being Asian American. It is in conversation with Asian Americans' experience of liminality that I will read the story of Josiah. A critical and intellectual use of this experience in reading Josiah is a postcolonial reading.

In Chapter 3 I will explore how Martin Noth's and others' understanding of DH as history writing that appeals to Western metanarratives has affected the reading of the story of Josiah. I will argue that Josiah is framed within Western historiography, in which the experience, aspirations, destiny, and history of the West are inscribed at the expense of denying the subjectivity and history of non-Western peoples, including Josiah's own people.

I will briefly describe how postmodernism is challenging a deeply held belief that history writing (the discipline of history) is a type of science (epistemology) rather than a genre of literature (aesthetics). I will examine in particular Jacques Derrida, Hayden White, and Michel Foucault as representative figures who have critiqued the notion that history as narration can give an objective, scientific knowledge of the past. Then I will examine how biblical historians have responded to the postmodern challenge. In the 1970s, biblical historians went through an internal critique of their field and focused on methods and the question of the reliability of the Bible as a source for

---

46. Bhabha, 'DissemiNation', p. 311.

reconstructing the history of ancient Israel. In more recent years, biblical historians have been engaging more consciously with postmodernism.

However, I will argue that biblical scholars have responded to a lesser extent to postcolonial critique. I will explain why it is crucial to take into account the postcolonial critique of Western history, including that of Asian-America historians. The postcolonialists also critique Western history, but they are suspicious of postmodernism's attempt to undermine the whole project of writing history at the same time that they are trying to recover their subjectivity through writing 'a history of their own'. I am not saying that postcolonial critique has made no mark on biblical studies. Keith Whitelam and others have engaged with Edward Said and other postcolonialists' critique of Western epistemology, and they have attempted to draw attention to the connection between Orientalism and the production of knowledge in biblical studies.[47] However, the task of decolonizing Josiah seems to be very difficult because of the enduring mindset of Orientalism that seems to be entrenched in biblical studies.

In Chapter 4 I will explore a space that has been constructed, in part, by biblical scholars, in which Josiah acts out his reform. The land of the United Kingdom under the rule of David and Solomon is viewed as one indivisible whole belonging to the house of David. With this assumption, Josiah is viewed as a powerful king who expanded his kingdom to recover or to unify the Davidic empire; this thesis is driven not only by archaeological and textual evidence but more so by the discourse of nation-states that understands a space as 'empty' unless it is occupied by a centralized political entity like a nation-state. The Cross School in particular has advocated this thesis, exemplified recently by Gary N. Knoppers. However, this view of Josiah is not limited to the Cross School or to Western scholars.

Although the extent of Josiah's kingdom is debated in academia, some opting for an extensive expansion and some arguing for a much more limited expansion, most scholars advocate what I would like to call the 'expansion thesis'. This thesis assumes that the former kingdom of Israel belonged to the house of David. Therefore, Josiah has the right to recover the land; whether he did recover the north is a moot point. The problem I have with this thesis is not that there are no elements in DH that support this thesis; my problem is the fact that biblical scholars are siding with Josiah by appealing to the discourse of nation-states that believes that a land is 'empty' if there is no centralized political power.

Postcolonialism has critiqued the conception of space as a stage on which Western history is played out. Postmodern study of spatial history shows that the West was far more interested in searching for the 'roots' of Western

---

47. Keith Whitelam, *The Invention of Ancient Israel: The Silencing of Palestinian History* (New York: Routledge, 1996).

civilization than the 'routes' that can be traced in the land. I will examine how Asian Americans have been made 'unhomely' in a land they call home because the land is viewed as belonging to a particular people who followed the expansion thesis in America.

In light of the postcolonial critique on space and the experience of Asian Americans, I will examine whether the land north of Judah, commonly referred to as the former kingdom of Israel, but known during the time of Josiah as the province of Samerina, was 'empty' after the supposed retreat of the Assyrians. The question I want to articulate is whether, if there was no power vacuum in the north and if Josiah was unable to expand into it, Josiah was addressing the problem of the former inhabitants of the north who may have wanted to move back to the province of Samerina.

In Chapter 5 I will examine the *Realpolitik* of liminality in Josiah's kingdom and in Asian America. It seems reasonable to assume that Josiah and his court were responding to the pressure applied by the Neo-Assyrians and other imperial forces. I will emphasize that Judah was located in a political, ideological landscape shaped by the empire; that is, Josiah and his people were located in a place not of their own making. As a result, they experienced what I would like to call the '*Realpolitik* of liminality', the danger and promise of being situated in a location not of one's own making. Asian Americans know well the experience of *Realpolitik* of liminality due, in part, to the racialized landscape of North America. They have experienced it throughout their history. I will explore whether, perhaps, Judah also experienced this during the Assyrian domination. I will suggest that, perhaps more than any historical evidence, the fact that the story of Josiah is framed within two deaths, those of Amon and Josiah himself, best illustrates the *Realpolitik* of liminality.

Asian Americans, however, in spite of experiencing the *Realpolitik* of liminality throughout their history, are writing 'a history of their own' in order to help formulate their identity. They are doing this by recovering lost 'inscriptions' of the past, by going on pilgrimages to sites of injustice, and by inventing an Asian-American culture. Perhaps the story of Josiah was an attempt by some to write 'a history of their own'. I will examine the discovery of the book of the law, Josiah's campaign to the north, and the reinstitution of the Passover as part of an attempt by the Judeans to recover their identity and history after the overwriting of their history and identity during the Assyrian domination. By examining the *Realpolitik* of liminality in Asian America—Asian Americans' experience of living as interstitial beings and their struggle to recover and to reconstruct their history and identity in North America—and by reading the story of Josiah intercontextually with the story of Asian Americans, this book will make an attempt to decolonize the modernist reading of Josiah from the space of liminality; it will be a postcolonial reading of Josiah.

2

POSTCOLONIAL CRITICISM AND BIBLICAL STUDIES

In order to decolonize Josiah I will rely on postcolonial criticism. In general, postcolonial studies has emerged in our time as the most powerful critical theory in decolonizing Western epistemology. Many point to Edward Said's book *Orientalism* for paving the way for a new discipline now called postcolonial studies.[1] Said was able to expose the scandalous connection between the production of academic knowledge and imperialism in the West. Postcolonial studies is a critical theory that tries to draw attention to this connection and to critique knowledge as it is constructed by the West, and to retrieve and construct the knowledge of the Others which has been lost, neglected, or suppressed in Western scholarship. In relation to biblical studies, postcolonial studies offers a critical tool for analyzing the text and its interpreters. In some sense, it is more of an attitude and perspective than a theory or even a method. It is a way of reading or rereading that examines or investigates the link between colonialism and its cultural texts.[2] It is a way of reading that anyone can perform if he or she acknowledges the profound and inescapable effects of colonization on various types of literary production. Postcolonial criticism looks at the impact of colonialism on biblical studies and the Bible. It comes out of the commitment to the postcolonial project; it has a commitment to be on the side of the oppressed.

Said

The importance of taking into account the effects of colonialism in understanding and interpreting cultural and literary texts—that is, the connection between Western imperialism and the production of Western knowledge—

---

1. Edward Said, *Orientalism* (New York: Random House, 1978).
2. I suggest 'rereading' because the texts in question have already been 'read' by Western scholarship for hundreds of years, which is assumed to be the norm. To 'reread' is to take into account not only how it has been read, but how it could be read from postcolonial perspectives.

2. Postcolonial Criticism and Biblical Studies

has been brought to attention forcefully by Edward Said in his seminal work *Orientalism*. Said argued that one cannot avoid the connection between the production of knowledge about the Orient and the context of imperialism in the West because 'political imperialism governs an entire field of study, imagination, and scholarly institutions—in such a way as to make its avoidance an intellectual and historical impossibility'.[3] Thus, individual authors have been connected to the larger political concerns as shaped by Western imperialism, and their writings have therefore been produced within the intellectual and imaginative realms of Western imperialism.

Said traced the origins and development of Orientalism, demonstrating how the West's cultural representations of the Orient were implicated in the policy and mechanisms of European imperialism. He showed that the works of politicians, writers, historians, biblical scholars, and many others were connected to European colonialism.[4] In Said's own words:

> Taking the late eighteenth century as a very roughly defined starting point Orientalism can be discussed and analyzed as the corporate institution for dealing with the Orient—dealing with it by making statements about it, authorizing views of it, describing it, by teaching it, settling it, ruling over it: in short, Orientalism as a Western style for dominating, restructuring, and having authority over the Orient.[5]

Said argued that Orientalism was really about the West, rather than about the Orient. He systematically challenged the chronic tendency of the West to deny and distort the cultures and histories of the Orient as the Other in relation to the West. Thus the Orient was represented in the West as the inferior Other by a variety of institutions that had the means of producing cultural representations of the Orient. Both the Orient as a place and its inhabitants were represented as inferior, feminine, irrational, and weak, in comparison with the Occident and Westerners, who were superior, masculine, rational, and strong. Said demonstrated convincingly that the construction of the Orient in the image of the West, as an inferior Other, was simply part of colonization; in many ways, Said claimed, Orientalism was no more than a science of colonizing the Orient. Said exposed Orientalism for what it was: a discourse of imperialism. Orientalism was 'a cultural and a political fact'.[6] Orientalism made racism, the superiority of the West and the people of the West over and against the Others, legitimate.

---

3. Said, *Orientalism*, pp. 13-14.
4. The role of biblical scholars is elaborated especially in pp. 130-49. In fact, Said states, 'by and large, until the mid-eighteenth century Orientalists were Biblical scholars, students of the Semitic languages, Islamic specialists, or, because the Jesuits had opened up the new study of China, Sinologists' (*Orientalism*, p. 51).
5. Said, *Orientalism*, p. 3.
6. Said, *Orientalism*, p. 13.

However, the power of Orientalism, Said claimed, was based on something far greater than a mere collection of lies or fairy tales about the Orient; it was a discursive formation of knowledge constructed by the practices of networks of scholars and institutions that gave it the authority to speak about and for the Orient. Said employed Michel Foucault's notion of a discourse to contend that

> without examining Orientalism as a discourse one cannot possibly understand the enormously systematic discipline by which European culture was able to manage—and even produce—the Orient politically, sociologically, militarily, ideologically, scientifically, and imaginatively during the post-Enlightenment period.[7]

Said traced in his book how Orientalism became accepted as a discourse of knowledge that functioned to speak authoritatively on the subject of the Orient. Thus Orientalism was

> a created body of theory and practice in which, for many generations, there has been a considerable material investment. Continued investment made Orientalism, as a system of knowledge about the Orient, an accepted grid for filtering through the Orient into Western consciousness, just as that same investment multiplied...the statements proliferating from Orientalism into the general culture.[8]

In short, Orientalism became a discourse—a legitimate and scientific way of producing knowledge about the Orient. Said tried to show how the representation of the Orient became a discourse, a collection of 'scientific' knowledge about the Orient that was always involved in the question of the Orient, which supported the West's hegemony over the Orient. He argued that the knowledge of the Orient was viewed as a product of scientific, objective scholarship—as the knowledge of true reality—when in fact the construction of the Orient was shaped by the West's imagination, more so than by any reality.

Said then asked why the Oriental discourse has endured even today and is still powerful and prevalent in the imagination not only of the West but also among the colonized peoples. Said employed Antonio Gramsci's concept of hegemony in order to explain how Orientalism became a prevalent idea that was accepted in the West. Gramsci's concept of hegemony explains that certain ideas prevail over others by consent rather than by force and coercion. Said summarized this point:

> Culture, of course, is to be found operating within civil society, where the influences of ideas, of institutions, and of other persons works not through domination but by what Gramsci calls consent. In any society not totalitarian,

---

7. Said, *Orientalism*, p. 3.
8. Said, *Orientalism*, p. 6.

then, certain cultural forms predominate over others, just as certain ideas are more influential than others; the form of this cultural leadership is what Gramsci has identified as *hegemony*, an indispensable concept for any understanding of cultural life in the industrial West. It is hegemony, or rather the result of cultural hegemony at work, that gives Orientalism the durability and the strength I have been speaking about so far...and indeed it can be argued that the major component in European culture is precisely what made that culture hegemonic both in and outside Europe: the idea of European identity as a superior one in comparison with all the non-European peoples and cultures.[9]

Said claims that we are all implicated or have collaborated, either actively or passively, in this hegemony. Although many would argue that they have been involved in objective scholarship and have not collaborated in the hegemony of Western imperialism, Said would tell them that

> No one has ever devised a method for detaching the scholar from the circumstances of life, from the fact of his involvement (conscious or unconscious) with a class, a set of beliefs, a social position, or from the mere activity of being a member of a society... What I am interested in doing now is suggesting how the general liberal consensus that 'true' knowledge is fundamentally non-political (and conversely, that overtly political knowledge is not 'true' knowledge) obscures the highly if obscurely organized political circumstances obtaining when knowledge is produced.[10]

We biblical scholars must ourselves question whether we have participated, wittingly or unwittingly, in the consent to Orientalism in biblical studies that is still prevalent today, either by actively supporting Orientalism or by ignoring the connection between the knowledge that we produce and Western imperialism.

R.S. Sugirtharajah

R.S. Sugirtharajah, perhaps more than anyone, has been instrumental in introducing and disseminating the need to engage with postcolonialism in biblical studies.[11] Sugirtharajah maintains that biblical studies have been reluctant to

---

9. Said, *Orientalism*, pp. 6-7.
10. Said, *Orientalism*, p. 10.
11. R.S. Sugirtharajah's works include the following: (edited) *Voices from the Margin* (London: Orbis Books, 1991; new edn 1995); (edited) *The Postcolonial Bible* (The Bible and Postcolonialism, 1; Sheffield: Sheffield Academic Press, 1998); *Asian Biblical Hermeneutics and Postcolonialism: Contesting the Interpretations* (The Biblical Seminar, 64; Sheffield: Sheffield Academic Press, 1999); (edited) *Vernacular Hermeneutics* (The Bible and Postcolonialism, 2; Sheffield: Sheffield Academic Press, 1999); *The Bible and the Third World: Precolonial, Colonial and Postcolonial Encounters* (Cambridge: Cambridge University Press, 2001). His latest work, *Postcolonial Criticism and Biblical Interpretation* (Oxford: Oxford University Press, 2002), is in many ways a comprehensive summation of his work; in this book one can find most of his ideas from his previous

engage with postcolonialism. It has had little impact in the way biblical scholars go about their business. Sugirtharajah states that the problem is that biblical scholars over the last four hundred years have been obsessed with 'the impact of the Reformation or the Counter-reformation, or the effects of the Enlightenment'.[12] However, they have been reluctant to mention 'imperialism as shaping the contours of biblical scholarship'.[13] He remarks that 'there is a remarkable reluctance among biblical scholars to speak of imperialism as shaping the contours of biblical texts and their interpretation'.[14] In contrast to this reluctance, 'the singular aim of postcolonial biblical studies is to put colonialism at the centre of biblical scholarship', which 'needs to extend its scope to include issues of domination, Western expansion, and its ideological manifestations, as central forces in defining biblical scholarship'.[15] In short,

> Postcolonial criticism can do for biblical interpretation what the project initiated by Edward Said has been doing for the study of the literature, language, history, and documents which the West has produced and continues to produce about the Orient. His intervention has resulted in the introduction of a potent new critical marker—Orientalism.[16]

---

works. Sugirtharajah notes the difference between post-colonial and postcolonial: 'In its application, postcolonial criticism differs not only from location to location but also from discipline to discipline… In postcolonial discursive practice, several critics contend and recognize that, when it is used with a hyphen, "post-colonial", the term is seen as indicating the historical period aftermath of colonialism, and without the hyphen, "postcolonial", as signifying a reactive resistance discourse of the colonized who critically interrogate dominant knowledge systems in order to recover the past from the Western slander and misinformation of the colonial period, and who also continue to interrogate neo-colonizing tendencies after the declaration of independence' (*Postcolonial Criticism*, pp. 12-13). He uses the latter definition, that is, postcolonial without the hyphen. For a further discussion on the use of the hyphen in 'postcolonial', see Bill Ashcroft, 'On the Hyphen in Post-Colonial', *New Literatures Review* 32 (1996), pp. 23-32.

12. Sugirtharajah, *Postcolonial Criticism*, p. 25; that is, biblical scholarship has been preoccupied with inscribing the history, experience, and aspirations of the West.

13. Sugirtharajah, *Postcolonial Criticism*, p. 25.

14. Sugirtharajah, *Postcolonial Criticism*, p. 74.

15. Sugirtharajah, *Postcolonial Criticism*, p. 74. Fernando Segovia states this point emphatically: 'Postcolonial studies is a model that takes the reality of empire, of imperialism and colonialism, as an omnipresent, inescapable and overwhelming reality in the world: the world of antiquity, the world of the Near East or of the Mediterranean Basin; the world of modernity, the world of Western hegemony and expansionism; and the world of today, of postmodernity, the world of postcolonialism on the part of the Two-Thirds World and of neocolonialism on the part of the West' ('Biblical Criticism and Postcolonial Studies: Toward a Postcolonial Optic', in Sugirtharajah [ed.], *The Postcolonial Bible*, pp. 49-65 [56]).

16. Sugirtharajah, *Postcolonial Criticism*, p. 75.

2. Postcolonial Criticism and Biblical Studies

Sugirtharajah claims that postcolonial criticism shares with feminism and liberation hermeneutics the same frustration with mainstream biblical scholarship. He suggests that the reason for this frustration may have something to do with the 'what for' of biblical studies (for what purpose are we reading and interpreting the Bible?) and the sense of separation between the world of biblical studies and the world at large:

> The world of biblical interpretation is a calm and sedated world. To a great extent biblical interpretation is about taking refuge in the study of the biblical past, and occasionally it is about reassuring the faithful when their faith is rattled by new moral questions. Although there is a reluctance to admit it, the liberal interpretation is largely confessional and pastoral in its tone and direction.[17]

Sugirtharajah states that feminist and liberation hermeneutics 'have reacted with increasing impatience to the way mainstream biblical scholarship has detached itself from real social and political issues'.[18] It has not only been preoccupied with the past (Reformation, Counter-reformation, and the Enlightenment) and the text, but its professionalism and specialization have isolated itself from the wider world and life.[19] Postcolonial criticism is a different way of practicing biblical scholarship: 'The world of postcolonialism, by contrast, is about change and struggle. It is about being conjectural, hesitant, and interventionist.'[20] It tries 'to see links between life and work, and to facilitate a dialogue with the world whilst discouraging an insular and universalist mode of reading, writing, and theorizing'.[21]

---

17. Sugirtharajah, *Postcolonial Criticism*, p. 2. Sugirtharajah quotes José Cárdenas Pallares (*A Poor Man Called Jesus: Reflections on the Gospel of Mark* [trans. R.R. Barr; Maryknoll, NY: Orbis Books, 1986]) to describe the insular world in which biblical studies is located: 'Today, Sacred Scripture is studied with the benevolent approval of the *pax imperialis*; no exegetical activity disturbs the tranquility of the "empire" for a single moment' (quoted in Sugirtharajah, *Postcolonial Criticism*, p. 74); 'What biblical periodical has ever fallen under any suspicion of being subversive? Biblical specialists have curiously little to suffer from the Neros and Domitians of our time. But neither do their studies instill light and strength in Christians persecuted by the lords of this world'. (quoted in Sugirtharajah, *Postcolonial Criticism*, p. 202).

18. Sugirtharajah, *Postcolonial Criticism*, p. 26.

19. According to Laura E. Donaldson, 'the implications of postcolonialism for biblical studies are immense. Its broad parameters encompass the effects of the Anglo-European as well as Roman and Israelite imperial projects... And, although it lacks a unified field, postcolonial criticism powerfully enunciates the need for biblical critics to engage with colonialism as well as its "posts"—not just as official topics of inquiry, but also as present within their own practices of reading' ('Postcolonialism and Biblical Reading: An Introduction', *Semeia* 75 [1996], pp. 1-14 [10-11]).

20. Sugirtharajah, *Postcolonial Criticism*, p. 2.

21. Sugirtharajah, *Postcolonial Criticism*, p. 201.

Therefore, Sugirtharajah understands postcolonial criticism and liberation hermeneutics as partners, sharing similar goals and commitments: 'Liberation hermeneutics and postcolonialism share mutual agendas and goals, and hope for and work towards an alternative to the present arrangement'.[22] However, he argues that liberation hermeneutics need to 'eschew its homogenization of the poor, incessant biblicism, and hostility to religious pluralism that plague its interpretative focus' in order 'to join forces with postcolonial thinking to fathom and fashion a different world from the one we live in'.[23] Sugirtharajah points out that liberation theology has homogenized the poor, who are the focus of liberation theology, by narrowly defining them as the economically disadvantaged.[24] On the other hand, the application of theology for postcolonialists is not limited to the economically poor: 'Where postcolonialism differs is that it recognizes a plurality of oppressions... [and] acknowledges multiple identities based upon class, sex, ethnicity, and gender'.[25] He also notes that postcolonialism has a different understanding of the Bible than that of liberation hermeneutics:

> Postcolonialism...understands the Bible and biblical interpretation as a site of struggle over its efficacy and meanings. There is a danger in liberation hermeneutics of making the Bible the ultimate adjudicator in matters related to morals and theological disputes. Postcolonialism is much more guarded in its approach to the Bible's serviceability. It sees *the Bible as both safe and unsafe, and as a familiar and a distant text.*[26]

He continues that postcolonialism 'sees the Bible as both problem and solution, and its message of liberation is seen as far more indeterminate and complicated. It is seen as a text of both emancipation and enervation'.[27] Therefore, he cautions that

---

22. Sugirtharajah, *Postcolonial Criticism*, p. 122.
23. Sugirtharajah, *Postcolonial Criticism*, p. 122. He argues that liberation hermeneutics is still stuck in modernism. Although postcolonialism shares the critical stance on modernism with postmodernism, it has definite political and ideological commitments it shares with liberation hermeneutics.
24. In defense of liberation theologies in South America in particular and the Third World in general, the economically poor as the oppressed still make up the majority of the population. They have not wavered from this commitment and I applaud them for it. Furthermore, they have broadened their definition of the poor to include the oppressed of postcolonialism.
25. Sugirtharajah, *Postcolonial Criticism*, p. 120.
26. Sugirtharajah, *Postcolonial Criticism*, p. 117 (emphasis mine). Liberation theologians have in the past blamed the interpreters of the Bible, but not the Bible itself, for the problem of oppression. However, liberation theologians are now struggling not only with the interpretations but also with the Bible itself.
27. Sugirtharajah, *Postcolonial Criticism*, p. 117.

in our enthusiasm to expose colonial intentions in texts, we may end up restoring the text and making it safe. The purpose is not to recover in the biblical texts an alternative, or to search in its pages for a fresher way of coming to terms with the aftermath of colonial atrocity and trauma, and the current effects of globalization. The purpose is to interrupt the illusion of the Bible being the provider of all answers, and to propose new angles, alternative directions, and interjections which will always have victims and their plight as the foremost concern.[28]

Postcolonial criticism can be practiced by anyone and anywhere; it is not limited to certain territories or to the victims of colonialism or neo-colonialism. I believe that anyone can practice postcolonial criticism if he or she acknowledges that there is an intimate connection between colonialism and its cultural texts, and that this connection continues to exploit and oppress those who are considered the Other from the West's perspective.[29] Of course, we must acknowledge that postcolonial discourse emerged from the colonized, and we must not lose sight of the fact that the colonized are the primary subject of postcolonial discourse.[30] It is also important to understand Sugirthrajah's point that postcolonial criticism involves praxis as much as textual critique. It is not just about writing and thinking; it is also about doing and living. As Sugirtharajah puts it: 'Postcolonialism is essentially a style of enquiry, an insight or a perspective, a catalyst, a new way of life'.[31]

Sugirtharajah states that postcolonialism is 'a collection of critical and conceptual attitudes' that fits the term 'criticism' rather than a theory or a method.[32] As a criticism, Sugirtharajah explains, postcolonialism is 'not an exact science, but an undertaking of social and political commitment which would not be reduced to or solidified into a dogma'; therefore, postcolonial

---

28. Sugirtharajah, *Postcolonial Criticism*, pp. 101-102.
29. Sugirtharajah implies this later in the book: 'postcolonial criticism, like the hybridity it celebrates, is itself a product of hybridity. It is an inevitable growth of an interaction between colonizing powers and the colonized. It owes its origin neither to the First nor the Third World, but is a product of the contentious reciprocation between the two' (*Postcolonial Criticism*, p. 23).
30. As H. Bhabha, one of the foremost postcolonial critics, states: 'Postcolonial criticism bears witness to the unequal and uneven forces of cultural representation involved in the contest for political and social authority within the modern world order. Postcolonial perspectives emerge from the colonial testimony of the Third World countries, and the discourses of "minorities" within the geopolitical division of East and West, North and South. They intervene in those ideological discourses of modernity that attempt to give a hegemonic "normality" to the uneven development and the differential, often disadvantaged, histories of nations, races, communities, people' ('The Postcolonial and the Postmodern: The Question of Agency', in *idem*, *The Location of Culture* [London: Routledge, 1994], pp. 171-97 [171]).
31. Sugirtharajah, *Postcolonial Criticism*, p. 13.
32. Sugirtharajah, *Postcolonial Criticism*, p. 14.

criticism 'is always contextual; it is paradoxical, secular, and always open to its own contradictions and shortcomings'.[33] Postcolonial criticism is by its nature eclectic; it is a harvesting of insights, tools, and approaches, from all different fields of study and knowledge:

> One of the significant aspects of postcolonialism is its theoretical and intellectual catholicism. It thrives on inclusiveness and is attracted to all kinds of tools and disciplinary fields, as long as they probe injustice, reproduce new knowledge which problematizes well-entrenched positions, and enhances the lives of the marginalized. Any theoretical work that straddles and finds a hermeneutical home in different disciplines is bound to suffer from certain eclectic theoretical deficiencies and contradictions. Its selective bias, though unsafe, is sometimes necessary in order to press on for the sake of the task at hand.[34]

In biblical studies, postcolonial criticism does not possess its own tools. It uses all types of tools that are available to biblical scholars today. But the difference is how one uses those tools; it employs them as counter-tools and uses them to do 'oppositional' readings to expose the effects of colonialism on the text and on its interpreters. As Sugirtharajah puts it:

> Anyone who engages with texts knows that they are not innocent and that they reflect the cultural, religious, political, and ideological interests and contexts out of which they emerge. What postcolonialism does is to highlight and scrutinize the ideologies these texts embody and that are entrenched in them as they relate to the fact of colonialism.[35]

It is a way of reading using all available tools and methods, but with a postcolonial attitude and stance. It is a reading against the grain in the sense that it critiques and questions the reading of the Bible from the West's perspective; it is a disobedient reading or oppositional reading that refuses to accept the reading of the text by the West as the norm, as the only reading.[36] It is and must be confrontational at times. Such an attitude places postcolonial criticism together with other critical readings in our time; as Sugirtharajah puts it: 'Postcolonial criticism is at its best when it seeks to critique not only the interpretation of texts but also the texts themselves. In this, postcolonial criticism is allied with most oppositional practices of our time, especially feminist'.[37] However, it is not a one-dimensional reading; it is a contrapuntal reading, which is also complementary at times:

---

33. Sugirtharajah, *Postcolonial Criticism*, p. 14.
34. Sugirtharajah, *Postcolonial Criticism*, pp. 99-100.
35. Sugirtharajah, *Postcolonial Criticism*, p. 79.
36. I want to make clear that I am not limiting the reading from the West's perspective to Westerners only; non-Westerners read with the West's perspective as well.
37. Sugirtharajah, *Postcolonial Criticism*, p. 75.

contrapuntal reading paves the way for a situation which goes beyond reified binary characterizations of Eastern and Western writings. To read contrapuntal means to be aware simultaneously of mainstream scholarship and of other scholarship which the dominant discourse tries to domesticate and speaks and acts against.[38]

It is a way of reading two 'texts' (scholarship at the mainstreams and margins) horizontally (equally) rather than vertically (hierarchically). It is a cross-textual reading between the scholarship of the West and scholarship from a different 'location'. This way of reading, both confrontational and complementary, is a postcolonial reading. Ultimately, it seeks the Third reading—the First reading is the modernist reading and the Second reading is the postmodern and anti-colonialist reading that critiques the First reading—that is an alternative to the First and the Second reading. It is not simply a synthesis or a combination of the First and Second readings; it is another reading that is open to new possibilities.

Fernando Segovia

Fernando Segovia has been the most prolific biblical scholar in North America in articulating a reading strategy that advocates the postcolonial commitment to decolonize the reading of the Bible from the enduring legacy of colonialism.[39] He states that the goal of postcolonial reading is 'not merely one of analysis and description but rather one of transformation: the struggle for "liberation" and "decolonization" '.[40] In order to contribute to this struggle, biblical scholars need to move away from mainstream scholarship toward the margins, where voices that have been suppressed can be heard. He argues that a process of liberation and decolonization can occur when there is

---

38. Sugirtharajah, *Postcolonial Criticism*, p. 94.
39. Fernando Segovia's works include the following: Fernando Segovia and Mary Ann Tolbert (eds.), *Reading from this Place*. I. *Social Location and Biblical Interpretation in the United States* (Minneapolis: Fortress Press, 1994); *idem* (eds.), *Reading from this Place*. II. *Social Location and Biblical Interpretation in Global Perspective* (Minneapolis: Fortress Press, 1995); *idem* (eds.), *Teaching the Bible: The Discourse and Politics of Biblical Pedagogy* (Maryknoll, NY: Orbis Books, 1998); Fernando Segovia, 'Biblical Criticism and Postcolonial Studies: Toward a Postcolonial Optic', in Sugirtharajah (ed.), *The Postcolonial Bible*, pp. 49-65; *idem* (ed.), *Interpreting beyond Borders* (The Bible and Postcolonialism, 3; Sheffield: Sheffield Academic Press, 2000); *idem*, *Decolonizing Biblical Studies: A View from the Margins* (Maryknoll, NY: Orbis Books, 2000); Fernando Segovia and Eleazar S. Fernandez (eds.), *A Dream Unfinished: Theological Reflections on America from the Margins* (Maryknoll, NY: Orbis Books, 2001).
40. Segovia, 'Biblical Criticism and Postcolonial Studies', p. 64.

a movement away from the European and Euro-American voices and perspectives that had dominated biblical criticism for so long, toward a much more diversified and multicentered conception and exercise of the discipline...a movement away from the long-standing control of theological production by European and Euro-American voices and perspectives, toward the retrieval and revalorization of the full multiplicity of voices and perspectives in the margins.[41]

In order to accomplish this, he suggests a reading strategy that focuses on two factors: the importance of reading the Bible as a real, 'flesh-and-blood' reader, and describing the location of the reader. For Segovia, the first task in reading the Bible is to start with the point of view of the 'flesh-and-blood' reader, that is, the real reader 'not so much as a unique and independent individual but rather as a member of distinct and identifiable social configurations, as a reader from and within a social location'.[42] Segovia maintains that reading the Bible from the location of the flesh-and-blood reader will connect biblical scholarship with the specific struggles and issues of the real sociopolitical world. Thus, he states:

> I see this irruption of the flesh-and-blood reader into biblical criticism as a harbinger not of anarchy and tribalism, as many who insist on impartiality and objectivity often claim, but rather of continued decolonization and liberation, of resistance and struggle against a subtle authoritarianism and covert tribalism of its own, in a discipline that has been, from beginning to end and top to bottom, thoroughly Eurocentric despite its assumed scientific persona of neutrality and universality.[43]

---

41. Segovia, 'Biblical Criticism and Postcolonial Studies', pp. 53-54.
42. Segovia, 'Toward a Hermeneutics of the Diaspora: A Hermeneutics of Otherness and Engagement', in Segovia and Tolbert (eds.), *Reading from this Place*, I, pp. 57-73 (58). This is a critical difference between understanding the reader as an objective, impartial reader of historical criticism and the ideal or implied reader of literary criticism. Mary Ann Tolbert uses the metaphor of 'blood' and 'bread' to describe the factors involved in a 'politics of location' in order to articulate what is involved in describing one's location: 'The "facts of blood" connote the broad areas of physical and mental integrity, race, gender, ethnicity, sexual orientation, familial affiliation, etc. which individually have often formed the basis of definition of "essence" and the grounds for developing a politics of identity. But for each person, the "facts of blood" include all of these profoundly interrelated factors, a social and personal complexity that narrow descriptions of "essence" ignore or denigrate. The "facts of blood" constitute the shifting complexity of the one who speaks. The "facts of bread", on the other hand, situate where one speaks—the ground of authority, national and institutional context, economic and educational status that shape each utterance we make and often determine who will listen to what we say and who will not. The "facts of blood and bread" together locate each person politically in relation to access to power, freedom from oppression, and human dignity and integrity, and they indicate the possible options for political coalition of interest to each person' ('Afterwords: The Politics and Poetics of Location', in Segovia and Tolbert [eds.], *Reading from this Place*, I, pp. 305-17 [311-12]).
43. Segovia, 'Toward a Hermeneutics of the Diaspora', p. 57.

2. Postcolonial Criticism and Biblical Studies

Segovia's commitment to decolonizing the Bible is related to his experience as member of a minority living in a racialized landscape in the United States. He identifies himself as a Hispanic American in the United States, a son of the Third World living in the First World, who is characterized by living in multiple worlds and in-between worlds, and with multi-identities and hybrid identities.[44] In short, his identity and experience can be best explained if he is understood as a member of a diaspora community. He describes his location as a common one for many people 'from the world of the colonized who now have to live in the world of the colonizer'.[45] He continues that 'given the traditional relationship between colonizers and colonized—a relationship profoundly marked by a set of binary oppositions ultimately grounded in those of center/margins and civilization/primitivism—such a reality is global and comprehensive'.[46]

It is the experience of 'a web of diasporic experiences' as a member of that diaspora that frames Segovia's strategy of reading the Bible.[47] He calls this framework 'a hermeneutics of the diaspora'.[48] It is a hermeneutics that takes as central the context of varying imperial/colonial formations, which affects the reading of the biblical texts. Segovia argues that Westerners have imposed their readings of the Bible, determined, in part, by their specific location in the landscape constructed by imperial/colonial forces on non-Westerners, who are located at the margins of this landscape. However, this does not mean that a diaspora community should ignore the biblical texts, but approach them as if they would approach texts not of their own making. Therefore, a hermeneutics of diaspora views 'texts, readings of texts and readers of texts

---

44. Segovia describes his location in 'Toward a Hermeneutics of the Diaspora', pp. 60-65.

45. Segovia, 'Toward a Hermeneutics of the Diaspora', p. 60.

46. Segovia, 'Toward a Hermeneutics of the Diaspora', pp. 60-61. The view of the relationship between the colonizer and the colonized as binary opposites needs to be questioned. The relationship is characterized by hybridity, ambivalence, and mimicry that undermine the 'traditional' view (more below).

47. Segovia understands diasporic studies as a subdiscipline of postcolonial studies; thus, Segovia states that 'it should come as no surprise that the application of diasporic studies to biblical criticism should follow not long after that of postcolonial studies. Once the discourse of the postcolonial began to be deployed in biblical criticism, it was only a matter of time before the subdiscourse of the diasporic would be invoked as well, especially in the light of drastic changes at work within criticism itself' ('Interpreting beyond Borders: Postcolonial Studies and Diasporic Studies in Biblical Criticism', in *idem* [ed.], *Interpreting beyond Borders*, pp. 11-34 [14]).

48. Segovia elaborates on this idea in several articles: 'Interpreting beyond Borders'; 'Toward a Hermeneutics of the Diaspora'; 'Reading Across: Intercultural Criticism and Textual Posture', in *idem* (ed.), *Interpreting beyond Borders*, pp. 59-83. It is similar to Sugirtharajah's stance toward the Bible: the Bible as both safe and unsafe for liberative and decolonizing purposes.

as others—not to be bypassed, overwhelmed or manipulated but rather to be acknowledged, respected and engaged'.[49] Segovia concludes, a bit too optimistically, that

> I see this hermeneutics of the diaspora...as having *a manifest destiny* of liberation and decolonization... I believe that a hermeneutics of otherness must go hand in hand with a hermeneutics of engagement, and that I see as the very essence of the proposed hermeneutics of the diaspora.[50]

It is a hermeneutics of diaspora that gives rise to a specific reading strategy that sees three levels of 'texts' a reader must engage in: (1) the level of 'ancient texts', namely, the biblical texts, which were written in the context of varying imperial/colonial formations; (2) the level of 'modern texts', namely, the analysis of readings and interpretations of the Bible in modern, Western biblical studies, whose establishment and development parallel Western expansionism and diaspora from the early nineteenth century through the third quarter of the twentieth century; and (3) the level of 'postmodern' readers, namely, the influence on the discipline of biblical studies by the entry of non-Westerners, both outside the West and in a diaspora within the West, and the analysis of the real readers of the Bible, both inside and outside the West.[51] At all three levels, the reality of imperialism and colonialism is taken into account as fundamental in reading the three levels of texts. Segovia claims that such a stance and engagement with the texts will continue

> to break down the traditional and fundamental Eurocentric moorings and boundaries of the discipline in favor of a multidimensional and decentered mode of discourse, a global discourse in which all readers have a voice and engage one another out of their own respective social locations, out of their own otherness.[52]

---

49. Segovia, 'Reading Across', p. 60. Thus, Segovia also calls it 'a hermeneutics of otherness and engagement'.

50. Segovia, 'Toward a Hermeneutics of the Diaspora', pp. 72-73 (emphasis mine). Sugirtharajah remarks that 'though diasporic hermeneutics already has some profound things to say about hyphenated and hybridized forms of identity and how these operate within individuals and communities, it has yet to work out a hybridized form of textual interpretation as an interpretative strategy in biblical studies' (*The Postcolonial Criticism*, p. 191).

51. Segovia, 'Interpreting beyond Borders', p. 23; 'Reading Across', pp. 59-60; and 'Biblical Criticism and Postcolonial Studies', p. 54.

52. Segovia, 'Toward a Hermeneutics of the Diaspora', p. 59. Segovia maintains that this way of reading is not only oppositional but also complementary (or contrapuntal). Since the modern discipline of biblical studies produced the study of imperial and colonial formation in antiquity during the rise and development of imperialism and colonialism in the West, and thus discourses in biblical studies represent constructs of the West, which say as much about the West as about the Bible, and since postcolonial studies examine the effects of Western imperialism, Segovia states that 'in a very real sense, therefore, postcolonial studies and biblical studies constitute thoroughly interrelated and interdependent

Segovia wants to develop a reading strategy that helps to decolonize biblical studies by removing its Eurocentric leanings and making it a global discourse in which all readers (Westerners, non-Westerners, and various hybrids), as flesh-and-blood readers (both inside and outside the West) situated in their own social location, have an equal voice in interpreting the Bible while engaging with the three levels of the texts. Asian-American biblical scholars have much to gain by using Segovia's reading strategy. Moreover, for Asian-American biblical scholars, the dialogical partners include Asian biblical scholars in addition to other minority groups and those who are located in the West.

Kwok Pui-lan

Kwok Pui-lan is a leading voice in articulating Asian biblical hermeneutics. On the one hand, she follows the long tradition of Asian biblical interpretation: 'Since the early period of biblical interpretation, Asian scholars have interpreted the Bible in the context of their own cultures and native religious traditions'.[53] Asian biblical hermeneutics is often described as 'cross-textual' or 'dialogical' because it brings 'the realities of Asian cultures…into conversation with those of the biblical tradition'.[54] On the other hand, she goes beyond cross-cultural reading; she advocates a reading strategy that sees the Bible as a polyphonic text that needs to be read with dialogical imagination and from a multiaxial approach.[55] Such a reading allows multiple meaning and voices. There is no one voice that dominates the conversation about what the text means; it is a conversation in which every voice has an opportunity to be heard.

---

fields and discourse' ('Notes toward Refining the Postcolonial Optic', in *idem*, *Decolonizing Biblical Studies*, pp. 133-43 [140]). Sugirtharajah agrees with this view: 'To read contrapuntally means to be aware simultaneously of mainstream scholarship and of other scholarship which the dominant discourse tries to domesticate and speaks and acts against' ('A Postcolonial Exploration of Collusion and Construction in Biblical Interpretation', in Sugirtharajah [ed.], *The Postcolonial Bible*, pp. 91-116 [94]).

53. J. Kuan, 'Asian Biblical Interpretation', in J.H. Hayes (ed.), *Dictionary of Biblical Interpretation* (2 vols.; Nashville: Abingdon Press, 1999), I, pp. 70-77 (71).

54. Kuan, 'Asian Biblical Interpretation', p. 71.

55. She is in conversation with Mikhail Bakhtin. For an introduction to Bakhtin in relation to biblical studies, see Barbara Green, *Mikhail Bakhtin and Biblical Scholarship: An Introduction* (Atlanta: Society of Biblical Literature, 2000). For a general introduction on Bakhtin, see Katerina Clark and Michael Holquist, *Mikhail Bakhtin* (Cambridge, MA: Harvard University Press, 1984), and Sue Vice, *Introducing Bakhtin* (Manchester: Manchester University Press, 1997). For Bakhtin's work, see his *The Dialogic Imagination* (ed. Michael Holquist; Austin: University of Texas Press, 1981), and *Speech Genres and Other Late Essays* (ed. Caryl Emerson and Michael Holquist; Austin: University of Texas Press, 1986).

In *Discovering the Bible in the Non-Biblical World*, Kwok Pui-lan argues that the Bible has been both unsafe and safe, both oppressive and liberating, for the peoples of Asia.[56] She explains how this is so:

> During the nineteenth century the Bible was introduced to many parts of Asia as an integral part of the colonial discourse. It has been used to legitimate an ethnocentric belief in the inferiority of the Asian peoples and the deficiency of Asian cultures. But the same Bible has also been a resource for Christians struggling against oppression in Asia, especially in the Philippines and South Korea.[57]

However, in general, Asia has rejected or ignored the Bible and Christianity. Kwok Pui-lan notes two primary reasons for the rejection: the profound link between the Bible and colonialism and the vitality of Asian cultures and religions. In order for the Bible to be relevant or meaningful to the worlds and peoples of Asia, she argues that biblical scholars need to practice cross-cultural reading that allows Asian voices to be heard in a 'dialogue' between the Bible and Asian texts. The Bible must be read as one among many religious texts rather than as the normative text that judges other texts and traditions. She states that 'in the past the Bible has been used by Christians as the norm by which to judge other cultures. The time has come for us to listen to the questions and challenges posed by the people whose lives and cultures are not shaped by the biblical vision.'[58]

Kwok Pui-lan is very wary of the unequal power relations (in terms of gender, race, religion, class, culture, political organization, etc.) in the history of the interpretation of the Bible. She cautions Asian biblical scholars that 'since the Bible was used as an instrument of oppression in the colonial discourse, Asian theologians must be careful not to reinscribe the unequal power relations in the text'.[59] Instead, she suggests that Asian biblical scholars must practice a postcolonial interpretation that exposes and investigates 'the intersection of anti-Judaism, sexism, and cultural and religious imperialism in the history of the text's interpretation'.[60] A postcolonial interpretation must resist a single-axis approach that 'separates race, gender, class, and cultural from one another', and that is used to 'master' the others.[61] Thus, she suggests that Asian scholars adopt a multiaxial frame of reference that examines the Bible from a multidimensional perspective in order to neutralize the unequal power relations in the text and in the interpretations of the text.[62]

---

56. Kwok Pui-lan, *Discovering the Bible in the Non-Biblical World* (The Bible and Liberation Series; Maryknoll, NY: Orbis Books, 1995).
57. Kwok, *Discovering the Bible*, p. 1.
58. Kwok, *Discovering the Bible*, p. 2.
59. Kwok, *Discovering the Bible*, p. 5.
60. Kwok, *Discovering the Bible*, p. 79.
61. Kwok, *Discovering the Bible*, p. 79.
62. Kwok states that 'one of the most effective ways to debunk the authority of the "master's" framework is to see the Bible through multiple frameworks and lenses...

2. Postcolonial Criticism and Biblical Studies 33

Kwok Pui-lan is unapologetic in suggesting that Asian biblical scholars inscribe their history and experience in interpreting the Bible; she calls it 'interpretations rooted in Asian soil'. She is convinced, following the critique of Said, that Euro-American men inscribed their history and experience into the development of nineteenth-century historical criticism, which Asian scholars are expected to imitate. In the article 'Jesus/the Native', she investigates how the search for the historical Jesus is intrinsically linked to the empire-building ethos of the nineteenth century (and the most recent search for Jesus to the similar ethos of late twentieth-century America) and how the 'natives' are constructed as inferior others of white Euro-American men. She argues that European men were inscribing the search of their identity in relationship to the native into the scholarship behind the search for Jesus: 'It is within this larger framework of the search for European identity that the wider implications of the quest for the historical Jesus can be fully comprehended'.[63] She attributes the latest quest for Jesus that is taking place primarily in the US as an attempt to redefine white America's identity:

> The first quest [of Jesus] took place when Europe, flexing its colonial muscle, encountered the world (the 'natives') outside its borders; today, the United States, as the only superpower in the world, does not need to go out to seek the 'natives', because the 'natives' have come into its own borders. As middle-class, white America needs to redefine its identity and destiny, the search for the historical Jesus surfaces once again.[64]

Kwok Pui-lan refuses to be the 'native', which is the role she and other non-Westerners are assigned in the master–slave, white–native dialogue.[65] She argues that to be labeled the 'native' means that one will be forced to occupy, quoting Homi Bhabha, 'the space of the past of which the white

---

[which] serves to challenge the arbitrariness of assigning one interpretation as the normative one. People on the margins have shown that alternative readings are indeed possible and have offered such strategies as the following: materialist readings; postcolonial critiques; multifaith hermeneutics; and various shades of feminist and womanist criticism' ('Jesus/the Native: Biblical Studies from a Postcolonial Perspective', in Segovia and Tolbert [eds.], *Teaching the Bible*, pp. 69-85 [81]).

63. Kwok, 'Jesus/the Native', p. 79.
64. Kwok, 'Jesus/the Native', p. 81.
65. Kwok cautions that 'we should not assume that only the "common people", "the poor", or "the marginalized" are the authentic "natives" and that all others are inauthentic and thus unable to understand the Bible. There are many different kinds of "natives", some better educated than others; we have to avoid collapsing the "natives" into the "same"' ('Jesus/the Native', p. 82). We need to remember that she is critiquing the master–slave, West–Orient, Europeans–natives dichotomy. She cautions also that 'by claiming that Western societies are fundamentally different from "native" societies (past and present), we continue to set North Atlantic cultures apart from the rest of the world and, in so doing, unwittingly reinscribe the *we–they* dichotomy that has given such power to the white people' ('Jesus/the Native', p. 82).

[people] will be the future'[66] and the space of the present predetermined by the others.[67] She is not only suspicious of modernism that identifies Europe as the subject of the space of the past and that views the 'native' as the Other who is located in the present space not of his or her own making; she is also suspicious of postmodernism. She maintains that 'we will not endorse postmodern interpretations, which are getting momentum in biblical criticism, because they represent internal white critiques that fail to make connections with what is happening in the rest of the world'.[68] She continues that 'the postmodern emphasis on deconstructing the subject, indeterminacy of language, and excess of meaning will not be helpful at all if it does not come to grips with the colonial impulse and the sense of white supremacy that make "modernity" possible in the first place'.[69] She argues that we will have to enter a different space from that of modernity and postmodernity, namely, the interstitial space called postcolonialism.[70] In this cultural space and time, nobody is a 'native' (hence no 'masters') and yet we are all 'natives'.

Thus, Kwok Pui-lan is suspicious of historical critical methods; she cautions Asian scholars not to use historical criticism as the primary method in interpreting the Bible for the peoples of Asia. She maintains that the historical-critical method is basically a modernist project that 'was embedded in the episteme of the nineteenth century and decisively influenced by the colonial and empire-building impulses of Europe'.[71] But, she asks, 'given the fact that the historical method is still the reigning paradigm taught in most graduate schools in the United States and Europe, how can the "natives" use the "master's" tools without succumbing to their lure and power?'[72] It is the Asian scholars who must question the historical-critical method: 'since the "masters" would not go beyond their own episteme, we have to read their works within the larger framework of postcolonial criticism and other critical theories'.[73] Furthermore, she suggests that Asian scholars need to do 'a more

---

66. Bhabha, *The Location of Culture*, pp. 237-38. Kwok remarks that 'the natives are considered backward, underdeveloped, and without a future, whereas the white people are deemed as controlling the present and masterminding the future' ('Jesus/the Native', p. 85).

67. Kwok, 'Jesus/the Native', pp. 82-83.

68. Kwok, 'Jesus/the Native', pp. 82-83.

69. Kwok, 'Jesus/the Native', p. 83.

70. Kwok describes this space in terms of 'time-frame', adopting Homi Bhabha's description: 'To reconstitute the discourse of cultural difference demands not simply a change of cultural contents and symbols; a replacement within the same time-frame of representation is never adequate. It requires a radical revision of the social temporary in which emergent histories may be written' (*The Location of Culture*, p. 17).

71. Kwok, 'Jesus/the Native', p. 80.

72. Kwok, 'Jesus/the Native', p. 80.

73. Kwok, 'Jesus/the Native', p. 80.

in-depth digging of the historical and textual sites, the creation of more non-Eurocentric models for cross-cultural comparison, the collective critique of established biblical criticism, and the creative articulation of new hermeneutical paradigms'.[74] The effort to overcome the unequal power relations in interpreting the Bible, she suggests, 'requires sustained discussion within the Asian theological community and beyond'.[75]

The Space of Liminality

I find myself in the space shared by other Asian Americans in North America. Asian Americans know all too well what it is to live as interstitial beings, in the space of liminality, in the racialized landscape of North America. We all know the common experience of being asked by other Americans, 'Where are you from?' It is not about our hometowns that the inquirers are searching to know. If we respond by naming our hometowns in North America, they are not satisfied until they find out where we are from 'originally'. The inquirers may or may not be aware that their investigation is based on the premise that Asians or people of Asian descent are aliens in this nation. Their investigation follows the logic of identity politics and the contour of the racialized landscape of North America. Their investigation follows the script formulated by American Orientalism and nationalism that view people from Asia, no matter what their ethnicity may be, through racial categories—white, black, brown, Hispanic, and Asian.

I too have my story of following the contour of the racialized landscape of North America. My mother came to the United States in 1974 with my sister; I joined them in 1976. I often wondered why my mother left Korea.[76] It must have been difficult for her to leave a world that was so familiar and comfortable and to come to another world that was so foreign to her. Of course she was not alone. She was one of many thousands of Koreans who migrated to the United States after the 1965 Immigration Act, which abolished the immigration policy that was based on the national origins system.[77] My aunt was

---

74. Kwok, *Discovering the Bible*, p. 3.
75. Kwok, *Discovering the Bible*, p. 3.
76. H. Kane describes a global movement in which 100 million people left their country in an attempt to improve their standard of living after the official end of European colonialism in the 1950s ('Leaving Home', in Lester R. Brown *et al.* [eds.], *State of the World 1995* [New York: W.W. Norton, 1995], pp. 132-49 [134]); Kane notes that such a global migration was perhaps caused by the push of poverty and the pull of wealth (p. 143). Immigration of Koreans can be understood as part of this global movement.
77. According to the US Commission on Civil Rights, *Civil Rights Issues Facing Asian Americans in the 1990s* (Washington, DC: US Commission on Civil Rights, 1992), throughout American history, Asians have been victimized by discriminatory naturalization and immigration laws (p. 2). The Chinese Exclusion Act in 1882 excluded Chinese

the first one in our family to come to the United States. She came as a 'war bride' in 1964.[78] Then she invited the entire family, including my mother, because the 1965 Immigration Act also gave high priority to the reunification of families, which has largely become a chain migration.[79]

I had no idea at the time as to what kind of place I was thrown into, but I was clear as to who I was, at least for the first ten years. I thought I was a Korean living in America. My homeland was 'over there'; I had no idea at the time how far away Korea was, nor was I, as a boy, thinking of going back to my homeland.[80] I had a clear sense of who I was: a Korean living in America. So, it did not bother me too much that I was treated as a foreigner. I did not appreciate the kids who would call me a 'chink' or a 'Jap'; I would always make the point of correcting them that I was not Chinese or Japanese, but Korean. I thought defiantly that if they were going to make fun of me, at least they ought to get my nationality right. But it did not matter to them; they ignored my corrections; they were convinced that they knew me better than I did. They continued to label me with names they had learned from somewhere, from somebody.

When I became a US citizen in 1985, right after high school, I became unsure of who I was and where my home was—my sense of identity and

---

immigration for ten years, but eventually it was extended indefinitely (p. 3). In the Immigration Act of 1917, with a couple of modifications in subsequent years, immigration from all countries in the Asia–Pacific Triangle was banned (p. 4). The Quota Act of 1921 limited the annual number of arrivals from each admissible country to 3% of the foreign-born of that nationality as recorded in the Census of 1910; however, Western Europeans were allowed free immigration. The Immigration Act of 1942 barred the entry of aliens ineligible for citizenship (i.e. exclusion of Chinese and other Asians) and established a 'national origins' system that would replace the formal quota system in 1927 (this favored, once again, northern and western European groups). The total annual quota from all nations was now fixed at 150,000. Each country received the percentage of that figure equal to the percentage of people from that country, by birth or descent, in the Census of 1920. The intent was to prevent any further change in the ethnic-racial composition of US society. Northern and western Europe received 82% of the annual quota (150,000), southern and eastern Europe, 16%, and all others, 2%. The Immigration and Naturalization Act of 1965 overhauled the immigration policy dramatically. It eliminated both the national origins system of quotas and the designation of the Asia–Pacific Triangle. It increased the total annual immigration to 290,000: 120,000 in the Western hemisphere, without limit for any one country; 170,000 for the Eastern hemisphere, with no more than 20,000 for any one country. It also provided preferential treatment for certain quotas of immigrants (family members, special skills).

78. My aunt was able to come due to the 1945 War Brides Act, which permitted the immigration of spouses and children of American servicemen.

79. See H. Kitano and R. Daniels, *Asian Americans: Emerging Minorities* (Englewood Cliffs, NJ: Prentice–Hall, 2nd edn, 1995), p. 18.

80. I have not visited Korea since I moved to the US in 1976.

2. Postcolonial Criticism and Biblical Studies

home became a lot more complicated.[81] I became a Christian a year before I received my citizenship, that is, I applied for US citizenship the same year I became a Christian.[82] I was a Christian and a US citizen. I thought I had become an American. How naïve I was! I believed in the American dream that says that anyone can become an American if he or she believes in American values and ideals regardless of one's origin, nationality, gender, or ethnicity. Yet I was still being treated as a foreigner. It began to bother me. I was experiencing what Homi Bhabha refers to as the experience of being 'unhomely'.[83] But I could not go back to being a Korean living in America nor go back to Korea.[84] There were too many boundaries I had crossed in terms of language, culture, and experience.[85] I would have been a stranger in Korea as well. Thus, I found myself in a predicament in which other immigrants find themselves: we look like Koreans, but Korea is not our homeland anymore; we feel at home culturally and want to make our home here in

---

81. I wrote about the importance of my decision to become a US citizen in my article, 'Uriah the Hittite: A (Con)Text of Struggle for Identity', in Liew (ed.), *The Bible in Asian America*, pp. 69-85.

82. I believe that there is a direct connection between my conversion from being a self-proclaimed atheist to Christianity, which I believed was the religion of America at the time, and my decision to give up being a Korean and to become an American.

83. According to Homi Bhabha, 'unhomeliness' is 'the condition of extra-territorial and cross-cultural initiations' (*Location of Culture*, p. 9). It does not mean that to be 'unhomed' is to be homeless, 'nor can the "unhomely" be easily accommodated in that familiar division of social life into private and public spheres' (p. 9). Bhabha continues that 'in that displacement, the borders between home and world become confused; and, uncannily, the private and the public become part of each other, forcing upon us a vision that is as divided as it is disorienting' (p. 9). He states that the condition 'unhomely' is 'a paradigmatic colonial and post-colonial condition' (p. 9). In my case, since I am lumped into a group of people called Asians, who are perceived or constructed as a people living in a land that is not theirs, I am made 'unhomely' in a land I would like to call my 'home'. According to Bhabha, this is a dwelling in a state of 'incredulous terror'.

84. When the dominant group is angry at or dissatisfied with me, they say 'Go back to your country!' When they are genuinely concerned with my future, they ask 'When are you going back to your country?'

85. According to Sugirtharajah, the boundary crossing is a sign of postcoloniality: 'It is not always feasible to recover one's authentic "roots" or even to go back to the real "home" again. At a time when societies are becoming more multicultural, where traditions, histories, and texts commingle and interlace, a quest for unalloyed pure native roots could prove to be not only elusive but also dangerous. It could cause complications for the everyday business of living with neighbors of diverse cultures, religions, and languages. This means finding oneself subject to an ever wider and more complex web of cultural negotiation and interaction. What diasporic interpretation indicates is that we take for granted more-or-less fractured, hyphenated, double, or in some cases multiple identities' (*Postcolonial Criticism*, p. 197).

the United States, but we are treated as foreigners.[86] The term that seems to explain my predicament the best at the time was 'marginality'. Marginality is understood as a temporary condition that will eventually end when structural assimilation occurs, according to the assimilation theory that was based on the experience of European immigrants. But I suspected that the marginality that I and other Korean Americans were experiencing was a permanent one due to the non-acceptance by the host group that was grounded on race as the primary group boundary.[87] Marginality also described the state of 'in-between-ness' I was experiencing. I did not belong fully to any one world, though I could negotiate myself adequately in two worlds at the same time. So, I came to see myself as a hyphenated being, stuck at the margins of America.[88]

Although I was beginning to become more aware of my marginality as an individual and as a member of the Korean-American community, it was the LA Riots of 1992 that awakened me from my complacency—until then I was following the script I was expected to follow as a member of the 'model minority'—and that instilled in me the resolve to become *disobedient*.[89] For

---

86. Such experience is not limited to non-white immigrants. White immigrants also have experienced similar situations in US history.

87. See S.H. Lee, 'Pilgrimage and Home in the Wilderness of Marginality: Symbols and Context in Asian American Theology', *Princeton Seminary Bulletin* 16 (1995), pp. 49-64. Lee was one of the first, and perhaps the most influential, Korean-American theologians to articulate the experience of marginality among Korean Americans. See also Jung Young Lee, *Marginality: The Key to Multicultural Theology* (Minneapolis: Fortress Press, 1995).

88. The term 'marginality' is not adequate for me anymore. It situates me in relationship to the dominant group without taking into account other minority groups, except to note differences and similarities among minority groups in relationship to the dominant group. It does not force the dominant group to understand their own interstitiality. It always references itself to the center.

89. I will discuss the 'model minority' stereotype later in this study; at this point, it suffices to understand it as a 'mimicry' of the dominant group. Its thesis is that Asian Americans are successful because they have adapted the values and means of the dominant group. The ambivalence of this stereotype will also be noted in the present study: on the one hand, it flatters the dominant group; on the other hand, it punishes other minority groups that cannot duplicate the success of Asian Americans. Furthermore, Asian Americans as an imperfect 'copy' of the dominant group, for whom mimicry is not very far from mockery, can therefore appear to parody the dominant group. There is a sense of uneasiness on both sides, as well as among other minority groups. It was the LA Riots more than any other event that has affected and shaped the path and theology of my life. Although I was 3000 miles removed from LA and didn't know anyone personally who was involved directly, it had a direct impact on me. This is what I wrote right after the LA Riots: 'I was in the shower when the insuppressible emotions began to well up. It was the third day of the LA Riots. Before I knew what was happening, streams of hot tears were flowing down

Korean Americans, it was truly a jarring experience that awakened us to the inherent dangers of being situated in the racialized landscape of North America that views Asians as Others.[90] However, there was a pleasant surprise following the aftermath of the LA Riots for me. I found that other Asian-American communities were very interested in what had happened to the Korean Americans. Then it dawned on me that my wellbeing, my destiny and experience in America are inseparably tied to the situation of Asian-American communities.[91] I became aware of the shared history, experience, and destiny with other diaspora communities from Asia. I believe that my identity and destiny in North America are connected in particular with Asian Americans. We share common promises and predicaments. Simply, we share a diasporic condition that reflects 'something of a migratory world'.[92] My location is not at the margin of society, but at the interstitial space to which everyone can decide to migrate; I am migrating to that space where I can connect with a community of other Asian Americans without disconnecting myself from a community of Korean Americans, other minority groups, or the dominant group. I have become an Asian American.[93]

---

my face, and the water felt like bullets battering my body. Although I did not know anyone in Los Angeles at the time, I felt a profound empathy with the Korean-American community as news stations broadcasted the tragic aftermath of the Rodney King mis/verdict. There was no holding back the anguish I felt at being a member of a powerless minority; the water pounded relentlessly, wearing down my resistance. When the floodgates of emotion were finally thrown open, I wept bitterly and loudly.'

90. There are many examples from the experience of Asian Americans and other minority groups of the danger of being viewed as the Other in America. I will discuss other examples in what follows.

91. Of course my wellbeing will continue to be tied to the US's relationship to Korea (both North and South), my 'homeland' according to the discourse that has been shaped by the politics of identity and race in US history; Japanese Americans learned this painful lesson during World War II, and Arab Americans are beginning to experience this in recent days after September 11, 2001.

92. Sugirtharajah describes this shared condition in this way: 'Those who are on the margins have no option but to occupy in-between spaces as a survival strategy. From this interstitial space any claim to cultural purity, stability, or autonomy are less important than the hybridized diasporic conditions of perpetual intercultural exchange, juxtaposition, interrogation, and transgression' (*Postcolonial Criticism*, p. 196). He continues that this condition is 'about the ambiguity of being a wanderer and a transitional. It reflects something of a migratory world' (p. 196).

93. According to Rita Nakashima Brock, 'interstitial integrity' is to refuse to rest in one place, to reject a narrowing of who we are by either/or decisions, or to be placed always on the periphery ('Interstitial Integrity: Reflections Toward an Asian American Woman's Theology', in Roger A. Badham [ed.], *Introduction to Christian Theology: Contemporary North American Perspectives* [Louisville, KY: Westminster/John Knox Press, 1998], pp. 183-96). She argues that one can feel torn among several different

My experience of being 'unhomely' in the land I call my home may be seen as no more than the problem or the whining of an ill-adjusted minority living within the white majority society, as no more than an existential crisis on the individual level. But my experience is, as Henry Yu puts it, 'also the result of journeying through a certain kind of landscape'—a landscape shaped by American Orientalism.[94] Yu traces how American sociologists have studied Asian Americans in the framework of the 'Oriental Problem'—the question as to why Asians failed to assimilate into the mainstream and what to do with them in light of that fact—in the first half of the twentieth century, and how this legacy still shapes much of how Asian Americans are studied and viewed today. Asian Americans as 'Orientals' have been studied as objects. Orientals are viewed as problematic objects that need to be managed and controlled; they are advantageous and desirable if they would just stay in their place and play the subordinate role they are assigned in America; they are undesirable and dangerous if they refuse to stay in their place and play the role assigned to them and demand to be accepted as full Americans. The descendants of white Europeans are the rightful inhabitants of the land, but Asian Americans are lumped together as aliens in this land. The fact that Asian Americans are viewed as permanent strangers, foreigners, aliens in the US is due, in part, to the politics of race and identity in the US that is based on the nationalist principle of the congruence of the nation and the people.

How Asian Americans are viewed is related to the question of who are 'real' Americans—those who have the legitimate claim to the land in which they live. Asian Americans are caught in the middle of identity politics in North America. In the racialized landscape of America shaped by American Orientalism and nationalism, Asian Americans are racialized as yellow. The racial politics in America defines yellow in opposition to white but also as different from black. This sets up a peculiar problem for Asian Americans: is yellow white or black? Okihiro notes that this question is multilayered: 'Is yellow black or white? is a question of Asian-American identity. Is yellow black or white? is a question of Third World identity, or the relationships among people of color. Is yellow black or white? is a question of American

---

worlds that refuse to get along, yet, like a migrating bird, one can find nourishment along the way. It opens ways of speaking about the construction of complex cross-cultural identities, facing 'the monumental task of making meaning out of multiple worlds by refusing to disconnect from any one of them, while not pledging allegiance to a singular one. It allows space for the multiple social locations of identity in a multicultural context' ('Interstitial Integrity', p. 190). I believe it takes courage to stand in interstitial space; anyone could locate him/ herself in interstitial space, but not everyone wants to; we like to stay where we are most comfortable, whether at the center or at the margins.

94. Henry Yu, *Thinking Orientals: Migration, Contact, and Exoticism in Modern America* (New York: Oxford University Press, 2001), p. xi.

identity, or the nature of America's racial formation.'[95] Okihiro argues in his book that the position of Asian Americans caught in-between two racial poles (black and white) has caused unique disabilities as well as special opportunities: Asian Americans were often used by whites to punish blacks and other minorities and were also given opportunities to work because they were not black. Being yellow, being in the middle, produces a state of liminality, which is desirable at times, but can also be dangerous as well. Okihiro summarizes this problem of being colored as yellow: 'Asians have been marginalized to the periphery of race relations in America because of its conceptualization as a black and white issue—with Asians, Latinos, and American Indians falling between the cracks of that divide. Thus, to many, Asians are either "just like blacks" or "almost whites".'[96] Even the model minority stereotype, which credits the common elements between Asian culture and Anglo-American culture to have enabled Asian Americans, like all of America's white immigrants, to move from the margins to the mainstream, illustrates the ambivalent position of Asian Americans. The model minority stereotype 'instead of deconstructing the European identity... reifies and attests to its original'.[97] At the same time, it reflects the 'ambivalence' that the dominant group feels toward Asian Americans: it refers to a simultaneous attraction and repulsion from what the dominant group sees as Asian Americans' mimicry of the American identity. The model minority stereotype is used to uphold Asian Americans as 'near-whites' or 'whiter than whites' (as fully assimilated Americans) in bipolar racial politics, but it ignores the white racism that Asian Americans continue to face, and the stereotype is used to discipline African Americans and other minority groups, thereby, drawing suspicion and hatred from other minority groups.

Asian Americans are familiar with identity politics in which they are viewed as interstitial beings. They have experienced the *Realpolitik* of liminality, the danger of being in a political, ideological landscape not of one's own making, throughout their history in North America. They have been victims of violation and exploitation, collectively as well as individually, in their own home/land. Asians, understood as a race of aliens in opposition to whites, were victimized by institutionalized racial immigration policies. These moments in American history are reminders that Asian Americans are only a step away from experiencing the *Realpolitik* of liminality, from being viewed as aliens within their own land, which could result in discrimination and violence against them.

---

95. Gary Okihiro, *Margins and Mainstreams: Asians in American History and Culture* (Seattle: University of Washington Press, 1994), p. 33.
 96. Okihiro, *Margins and Mainstreams*, p. xi.
 97. Okihiro, *Margins and Mainstreams*, pp. 139-40.

An Asian-American Biblical Hermeneutics

To identify myself as an Asian American was a choice for me—a conscious choice to be in the interstitial space. I could have refused to identify myself as an Asian American. It signals my commitment to the struggle of the Asian-American community in North America.[98] So what? The question is whether my location as a member of the Asian-American community makes a difference in interpreting the Bible. Should it make a difference? Does it matter? As readers/interpreters of the Bible, we all inscribe our particular history and experience on the process. Answers one seeks to find from the Bible, issues and themes one brings up in conversation, the methods and approaches one uses, the attitude and stance one takes, and how one writes one's work are all influenced by one's location. So the question is: How does one's location in the Asian-American community affect the reading/interpreting of the Bible? The *Semeia* volume titled *The Bible in Asian America* tries to address this question.[99]

Jung Ha Kim, in response to the *Semeia* volume, compares the collection of articles as a two-course banquet that 'celebrates heterogeneity of social locations and voices that re-present struggles and issues pertaining to the survival of Asian North Americans'.[100] Although the contributors (or their foreparents) came from different parts of Asia through diverse routes, they seem to deal with a few common themes and issues that arise from the common experience and history of Asian Americans. The contributors, working independently, wrote articles that crisscrossed similar themes and issues. It displayed how the location of Asian Americans affects the interpretation of the Bible.

Liew, the editor of this volume, states that its purpose is not to define what Asian America is or what Asian-American biblical hermeneutics is. He fears that many will not find what they are looking for in this volume. He also lists the shortcomings of the volume: (1) the contributors focused on the intersection between race and religion, but did not focus enough on gender and class; (2) the contributions basically focused on cultural nationalism and spatial entitlement to the US as Asian Americans; (3) contributions were not multifocal enough; (4) by focusing too much on Asian-American experience in

---

98. The term 'Asian Americans' came out of a political movement in the 1960s. The Asian-American movement sought to 'liberate' Asian Americans from many forms of oppression in the US. It tried to recover the history and subjectivity of Asian Americans. One of the strategies was to consolidate various Asian groups into one pan-Asian group for political purposes, similar to the way Fernando Segovia, a Cuban American, identifies himself as a member of the Latino American community.

99. T.B. Liew (ed.), *The Bible in Asian America* (Semeia, 90–91; Atlanta: Society of Biblical Literature, 2002).

100. J.H. Kim, 'At the Tables of an Asian American Banquet', in Liew (ed.), *The Bible in Asian America*, pp. 325-37 (326).

relationship with the dominant group, with only a cursory acknowledgment of other minority groups, contributions failed to displace the White/Asian binarism.[101] However, Liew states that its readers will find 'the complexity, and the creativity of Asian America', and this was the purpose of the *Semeia* volume.[102]

Although the *Semeia* volume does not attempt to define what biblical hermeneutics by Asian Americans is, I believe it gives us a good idea of what it looks like. First, it is interdisciplinary, the primary partner being Asian-American studies. This needs to be so because Asian-American studies deals with the history and experience of Asian Americans. Second, Asian-American readers/interpreters of the Bible use 'different' sources, autobiography and novels in particular.[103] Because the official political history of the United States does not 'remember' minorities, it is often these sources that preserve and construct memories of Asian-American experience. Third, there were those who were not trained as biblical scholars. They were 'outsiders' to the guild of biblical studies. Asian-American biblical scholars need to keep in touch with the 'outsiders' so that we do not lose contact with what is going on in the community, and so that we do not become enclosed in the guild. The insights and questions the 'outsiders' bring are essential for Asian-American biblical scholars. The 'outsiders' are also Asian-American biblical readers/interpreters.

Jeffrey Kuan and Mary Foskett are the editors of the forthcoming volume *Ways of Being, Ways of Reading: Asian American Biblical Interpretation* (Chalice Press), which will be an important work that will try to formulate what Asian-American biblical hermeneutics is, and will give examples of how Asian-American biblical scholars are reading the Bible. Kuan, in particular, has written two articles that demonstrate what biblical hermeneutics by Asian-American scholars looks like.[104] He also thinks it is important to

---

101. T.B. Liew, 'Introduction: Whose Bible? Which (Asian) America?', *idem* (ed.), *The Bible in Asian America*, pp. 1-26.

102. Liew, 'Introduction', p. 19.

103. For examples of the use of autobiography, see Uriah Kim, 'Uriah the Hittite: A (Con)Text of Struggle for Identity'. See also the following articles in Liew (ed.), *The Bible in Asian America*: Mary F. Foskett, 'The Accident of Being and the Politics of Identity', pp. 135-44; Henry W. Rietz, 'My Father Has No Children: Reflections on a *Hapa* Identity toward a Hermeneutic of Particularity', pp. 145-57; and, for an example of the use of a novel, Jane Naomi Iwamura, 'The "Hidden Manna" That Sustains: Reading Revelation 2.17 in Joy Kogawa's *Obasan*', pp. 161-79.

104. J. Kuan, 'Diasporic Reading of a Diaspora Text: Identity Politics and Race Relations and the Book of Esther', in Segovia (ed.), *Interpreting beyond Borders*, pp. 161-73, and 'Reading Amy Tan Reading Job', in T. Sandoval and C. Madolfo (eds.), *Relating to the Text: Interdisciplinary and Form Critical Insights on the Bible* (JSOTSup, 384; London: T. & T. Clark International, 2003), pp. 266-79.

describe who we are (identity) and where we are located (location or positionality) as we engage with the texts. When he took his identity and location seriously, it led him into a new direction as a biblical scholar. His identity as a multi-hyphenated person (Chinese-Malaysian-American) located in the community of Asian Americans in North America affects his reading of the Bible.[105] He describes his transformation as follows:

> In my own journey to inscribe my own cultural identity, individually and collectively, I began to move in a new direction in my scholarly interests. Trained primarily as a biblical historian in my doctoral studies, I am no longer satisfied with the kind of disinterested inquiry traditional approaches to the interpretation and construction of ancient texts and society prescribe… Since the majority of the writings are late, exilic or post-exilic, I view these texts as the products of communities inscribing their religio-cultural identities in the midst of their existence under the empires. My scholarly interest is, therefore, informed by my social location as a diasporic person. It is through this lens that I am trying to make sense of the texts for my primary community of identification—Asian Americans in general and Chinese Americans from Southeast Asia in particular.[106]

There are important implications to this approach. For Kuan, agreeing with Sugirtharajah, the text is understood as both unpleasant (and unsafe) and pleasant (and safe) for the reader, depending on the reader's positionality in terms of identity and location. Kuan maintains that one does not sacrifice the reader's experience and life in order to 'save' the text: 'Biblical interpretation is not about saving the text or saving God, for that matter! It is coming to grips with the text, both its benefits and flaws, its blessings and curses.'[107] Kuan argues that there must a dialogical relationship between the readers and the text:

> Texts and community thus enter into a dialogical relationship, one impacting the other and vice versa. I am convinced that such a dialogical relationship holds true for many communities of readers, whereby the religio-cultural identity of the community impacts the way the community reads the text; in turn, its religio-cultural identity is impacted and inscribed by the reading.[108]

Finally, Kuan believes that 'when we begin to put the emphasis on readers rather than the text, we dislodge the center and create many new centers of biblical interpretation'.[109]

---

105. Kuan, 'My Journey into Diasporic Hermeneutics', *USQR* 56.1-2 (2002), pp. 50-54.
106. Kuan, 'My Journey', p. 53.
107. Kuan, 'Reading with New Eyes: Social Location and the Bible', *Pacific School of Religion Bulletin* 82.1 (2003), pp. 1-3 (3).
108. Kuan, 'Reading with New Eyes', p. 3.
109. Kuan, 'Reading with New Eyes', p. 3.

Kuan demonstrates what Asian-American biblical hermeneutics looks like in his article on the book of Esther.[110] Kuan looks at three texts in Esther through a diaspora lens to show that there are diasporic characteristics in the book. According to Kuan, ch. 2 highlights the Jewish diaspora community's hybridity: Mordecai as a 'Benjaminite-Judean/Jewish-Persian' and Esther (Hadassah) are multi-hyphenated characters that are able to negotiate their ways successfully into the mainstream of Persian society.[111] Chapter 3 highlights the Jewish diaspora community's liminality: 'If chapter 2 ends with a sense of "wantedness"…chapter 3 sees the situation quickly evaporating and turning into one of "unwantedness"… The diaspora community always sits on the edge of promise and pain.'[112] Kuan argues that the annihilation of their enemies by the Jews in ch. 9 can be understood as a way of formulating and maintaining cultural identity: 'Because diaspora communities live in a world of isolation and intimacy, alienation and embrace, it is only natural that such a story about eliminating the oppressors and alienators would be utilized to create community identity'.[113]

In 'Reading Amy Tan Reading Job', Kuan's reading of Job in conversation with Amy Tan's *The Kitchen God's Wife* is an innovative approach. It is a cross-textual reading between the Bible and an Asian-American novel. Whereas he had used his identity and location as a lens through which to read Esther, in this article he uses an Asian-American cultural product as a conversational partner with the Bible. Noting the reading strategy of Asian biblical interpreters as being cross-textual, using Asian textual and cultural traditions and the Bible, he states that Asian Americans also have two texts: the Bible and the cultural 'texts' produced by the Asian-American community. His experiment leads to a surprising and provocative insight on Job. In the final scene of *The Kitchen God's Wife*, Winnie the protagonist of the novel burns the picture of the Kitchen God, thereby rejecting the religious orientation that has tormented her life, and this leads to her new religious orientation through the symbolic creation of a goddess named 'Lady Sorrowfree'; this leads Kuan to argue that Job 'only by rejecting the God of his past that no longer makes sense is it possible for Job to enter into a new orientation of a

---

110. Kuan, 'Diasporic Reading of a Diaspora Text'.
111. Kuan, 'Diasporic Reading of a Diaspora Text', pp. 168-70. What is in a name? Asian Americans are very sensitive about names because we know that it is by our names that the dominant culture inscribes our place. Names often give away our 'otherness' from the perspective of the dominant group. Names indicate hybrid characters.
112. Kuan, 'Diasporic Reading of a Diaspora Text', pp. 170-71. Kuan does not treat Haman the Agagite. Haman is another hyphenated person who seeks to do harm to a different diaspora community. This makes it more complicated than seeing the Jewish diaspora community in relationship with the dominant group only.
113. Kuan, 'Diasporic Reading of a Diaspora Text', p. 172.

search, like Winnie, for a God that nobody knows'.[114] Kuan wants to encourage other Asian-American biblical scholars to use the cultural texts produced by the Asian-American community in dialogue with the texts of the Bible. This will also bring Asian-American cultural texts to the attention of other Americans.

I have described how I have come to see myself as a member of the Asian-American community in conversation with other Asian-American biblical scholars in developing strategies to read the Bible. What I want to practice is an Asian-American postcolonial hermeneutics. It has to start with the postcolonial attitude. We must have the courage to refuse to be the 'native' of the West's imagination. This means that we must be disobedient when the others want to impose their experience, history, and aspirations as the script for us to follow. Postcolonial studies have given us a critical tool we can use to identify Orientalism/colonial bias in the various levels of texts. Asian-American postcolonial hermeneutics takes into account the reality of the empire, as Segovia states, at all three levels of text: the level of the Bible, the level of the interpretation of the Bible in modern biblical studies, and the level of the readers in the post-colonial age. At the level of the Bible, it analyzes the unequal power relations in the Bible and in the world of the Bible and how this affects the reading of the Bible. It investigates the relationship between modern biblical scholarship and Orientalism and how this affects the reading of the Bible. At the level of the readers, it examines how the fact that Asian Americans are located in a racialized landscape of the American empire affects the reading of the Bible.

Asian-American postcolonial hermeneutics is committed: it takes sides with the oppressed in North America, especially with the struggle of Asian Americans, but it is not limited to them. It is not shy about advocating a modernist project of liberation, liberation not only for white European men, but also for all the oppressed. For Asian Americans are one community among many that are located in the racialized landscape of North America. This hermeneutics is committed to constructing identity as a means of inscribing agency and subjectivity to the Asian-American community. It cares about the history, experience, and aspirations of Asian Americans. It does not interpret the Bible for the sake of interpreting; it interprets the Bible for the liberation of the oppressed people in North America, while acknowledging that the Bible does not always lend itself to liberation.

Asian-American postcolonial hermeneutics uses a variety of postcolonial reading strategies. For the Asian-American community I suggest a combination of three approaches. We need to do a cross-cultural reading between the biblical traditions of Christianity and the various cultural traditions of Asia.

---

114. Kuan, 'Reading Amy Tan Reading Job', p. 18.

We need to do inter-textual reading between the Bible and Asian-American cultural texts. We also need to read from a multiaxial framework—reading with different perspectives and dimensions. We cannot read with only one frame of reference, no matter how important it may be (race, gender, class, etc.). We must read with several positional frameworks in mind. We must be both confrontational and complementary to Western scholarship in our approach to interpreting the Bible. We must continue to engage with the interpretation of the Bible by the West; but we must also interpret the Bible by inscribing our own history, experience, and aspirations, rather than just being anti-Western. We need to move away from setting up another dichotomy between the empire and the rest, between the West and the rest. Our reading refuses to reference itself always to the West, to the center. It sees itself as a center among many centers. Therefore, we need to seek a third way of reading that is not trapped in a colonialist and anti-colonialist dualism, or a modernist and postmodernist dualism, or any other dualism that limits a third option.

Finally, Asian-American postcolonial hermeneutics needs to be practiced at the space of liminality. It needs to move away from seeing the Asian-American community as situated in the margins in relationship to the center. In seeing ourselves through the diasporic lens, there are no centers or margins. We are all situated in the 'third' space, the interstitial space in which everyone is a native, where hybridity is the norm. There is a matrix of centers, rather than one center, and many margins. We must claim this space and invite others to join us in the interstitial space where we are always open to new possibilities and new relationships. Asian-American postcolonial hermeneutics is reading and interpreting from such space.

3

WHOSE HISTORY IS IT ANYWAY?

The disciplines of history in general and biblical history in particular need to be understood in the context of Oriental discourse. History in the West is intrinsically connected with Orientalism. The discipline of history emerged coterminously with modern colonialism: 'For the emergence of history in European thought is coterminous with the rise of modern colonialism, which in its radical othering and violent annexation of the non-European world, found in history a prominent, if not *the* prominent, instrument for the control of subject peoples'.[1] In fact, Europe created history:

> History as we know it was an invention of the nineteenth century, and of German scholars in particular. By *history* is meant a concern with verification of sources and evidence by a competent, trained community of scholars. Though different forms of historical writing had existed long before, the sort of history that emerged in the middle of the nineteenth century was a species apart.[2]

Other histories have been subsumed under a Eurocentric 'world' history. This is no accident. Said has pointed out that universalizing and self-validating has been endemic to the historicism that helped to create the discipline of studying the Orient as the Other.[3] To put it bluntly, Europe is the subject of history and Europe's identity, experience, aspirations, and destiny are narrated as the history of the world. Historical investigations in biblical studies are no exception; in searching for ancient Israel in the imagination of the West, biblical scholars inscribed the experience, aspirations, and destiny of the West. In relation to DH, biblical scholars imagined it in the likeness of Western modern historiography, due in part to the way Martin Noth framed DH and Dtr within the modernist understanding of history and the historian. Noth's view of DH contributed to the prevailing tendency in biblical studies to construe it as the wellspring and touchstone of Western civilization—imagining

---

1. B. Ashcroft, G. Griffiths and H. Tiffin (eds.), *The Post-colonial Studies Reader* (London: Routledge, 1995), p. 355.
2. J. Appleby *et al.* (eds.), *Knowledge and Postmodernism in Historical Perspective* (London: Routledge, 1996), p. 141.
3. Said, *Orientalism*, p. 22.

it as a narration of the original model of the nation which the West imitated and fulfilled—and, thereby, making the West the subject of DH. The story of the rise of the nation as the pinnacle of civilization is a success story written by the West. Appleby *et al*. comment that

> modern historians have recounted only those narratives which are a testimonial to the success of the Western world. In short, the historical profession has privileged the telling of a peculiarly Occidental success story. History has told only the 'right' stories in the past: if the central character of the Western story is the rational white male, the plot is this autonomous individual's correct preference for progress, its vindicatory rationale of utilitarianism, and its means, scientific technology.[4]

The West is the subject of DH, and Josiah is embedded in the history and imagination of the West with little chance of being placed within an alternative history and imagination.

Postmodernism, however, has been challenging and deconstructing modernist history for some time now. Robert Young summarizes the crisis of history that the West has had to face since World War II:

> What has been new in the years since the Second World War during which, for the most part, the decolonization of the European empires has taken place, has been the accompanying attempt to decolonize European thought and the forms of its history as well. It thus marks that fundamental shift and cultural crisis currently characterized as postmodernism.[5]

Europe has been questioning its form of history since it became obvious that its history was not absolute. Thus, Young defines postmodernism as European culture's self-consciousness about its own historical relativity 'which begins to explain why, as its critics complain, it also involves the loss of the sense of an absoluteness of any Western account of History'.[6] In light of such anxiety, postmodernism has challenged the discipline of history by questioning the philosophical foundation and practice of history. It has challenged the belief that history was epistemological—the belief that the discipline of history was the site of production of objective, scientific knowledge about the past. It has argued that all histories are akin to literature (aesthetics) rather than to science (epistemology).

In light of the postmodern challenge, biblical scholars have also undergone significant changes in writing and understanding the history of ancient Israel. They have responded to the postmodern challenge in writing the history of ancient Israel. In the 1970s some scholars challenged the so-called

---

4. Appleby *et al*. (eds.), *Knowledge and Postmodernism*, pp. 388-89.
5. R. Young, *White Mythologies: Writing History and the West* (London: Routledge, 1990), p. 119.
6. Young, *White Mythologies*, p. 19.

Albrightean Synthesis, a venerable modernist monument in biblical studies. When this modern monument in biblical history began to fragment, the world of biblical historians divided into two camps: the maximalists and the minimalists. The debates in biblical history moved from questions about methods and the Bible as a source for reconstructing the history of ancient Israel to questions about ideology and the discourse of scholars and the discipline of biblical studies. In recent years biblical historians have become increasingly engaged with postmodernism. There are still many who dismiss postmodernism as no more than an academic 'fad' or a spiteful attempt to undermine the project of writing the history of ancient Israel, but it seems postmodernism is more than an academic concept, method, or critique. Postmodernism is here to stay, some would argue, because it is a condition of the contemporary world.

However, criticisms against postmodernism come not only from the West, but also from non-Westerners, particularly from the postcolonialists. There is a sense of dissatisfaction among postcolonial historians with postmodernism because it deconstructs not only modernist history, but it also undermines the project of writing history altogether, thereby undermining the attempt by non-Western peoples to write 'a history of their own'. It has been noted by many that the form of history developed by Europe has the tendency to incorporate other histories into its own history; in the process, it distorts the histories of others and imposes the values and ideas of European civilization on others as universal. As a result, other peoples and histories are judged to be 'unhistorical'—to fall short of the West's universal standards, and to be viewed as inferior and 'primitive'. Postmodernists do not seem to be too concerned about the problem faced by non-Western peoples in writing a history of their own, dismissing their efforts as merely 'catching up' with the West or simply applying Western methods. But postcolonialist historians critique modernist history, which is intertwined with Orientalism, without abandoning the project of writing about the past altogether. They advocate a different way of writing history that attempts to represent the Other as the subject.

In spite of the accusation that they are continuing the modernist project and the fact that their project has theoretical and practical problems, postcolonial historians are committed to writing the history of those whose voices have been marginalized, subjugated, neglected, or lost. Asian-American historians, in particular, are trying to write 'a history of their own' in North America. We will see that for Asian-American historians the issue is not necessarily whether history can be written outside the framework of the West, the US in particular, but to express authentically the subjectivity of a marginalized group within the United States.

Unfortunately, the response to postcolonial critique within biblical studies has not been very enthusiastic. Keith Whitelam is one of the first scholars consciously to investigate the connection between Orientalism and biblical scholarship about ancient Israel. Whitelam, following the critique of Said and other postcolonialists, examines the limitations that are in place in the discipline of biblical studies due to the enduring legacies of Orientalism. The legacies of Orientalism are still operative today in the understanding of DH. DH is still framed within Western history, which is implicated in Orientalism. More than anything, it is the peculiar mindset that is deeply ingrained in biblical studies that limits the understanding of DH as 'our history' rather than as 'a history of their own'. Therefore, Josiah in DH is still colonized by Eurocentric history, and there seems to be no urgency to decolonize DH from the discourse of nationalism; DH is framed within the Western mindset that discourages the consideration of other forms of telling about the past.

Understanding of the Deuteronomistic History as Modern Historiography

We need to examine Noth's understanding of DH in order to get a better sense of the extent of the problem. Noth understood Dtr as a historian and the genre of DH as history writing. He imagined Dtr as an honest (objective) historian with a genuine antiquarian interest, who had an access to an archive of official documents and who discovered a narrative embedded in the source and constructed a logical reconstruction of the past according to the narrative. I would like to quote the first paragraph of Chapter 12 of *The Deuteronomistic History* in its entirety, because here we can see clearly Noth's understanding of what made Dtr a historian and DH history writing:

> Dtr. has no intention of fabricating the history of the Israelite people. He wished to present it objectively and base it upon the material to which he had access. Like an honest broker he began by taking, in principle, a favourable view of the material in the traditions. In describing the various historical events he spoke in his own person only at certain exceptional points, letting the old traditions speak for themselves instead. He did so even when these old traditions told of events which did not fit in with his central ideas. We owe the preservation of valuable old material wholly and solely to this respect for the value of old narratives and historical accounts which reported matters of which Dtr. could have no first-hand knowledge, to the considerable importance he placed in the traditional material and, following from it, to his reverent attitude towards historical fact. Dtr. was not a redactor trying to make corrections, but a compiler of historical traditions and a narrator of the history of his people. When we have learned to regard his work as a self-contained whole, we shall find that he has crafted a work of art which merits our respect.[7]

Dtr was a historian because, first, he was objective and disinterested: 'He wished to present it objectively', Noth claims. Dtr is disinterested and has no

---

7. Noth, *Deuteronomistic History*, p. 84.

bias or invested interests: 'Dtr. has no intention of fabricating the history of the Israelite people' and he is 'like an honest broker'. Dtr is not subjective but relies on his sources: 'He wished to…base it upon the material to which he had access' and 'he spoke in his own person only at certain exceptional points, letting the old traditions speak for themselves instead'. To Noth, these are characteristics that make Dtr a good historian, a person who writes about the past 'objectively' and without 'bias', not speaking in one's own person but letting the source do the talking 'even when these old traditions told of events which did not fit in with his central ideas'. Therefore 'Dtr. was not a redactor trying to make corrections, but a compiler of historical traditions and a narrator of the history of his people'.

Secondly, it is the type of sources Dtr used and Dtr's attitude toward these sources that make Dtr a historian. Noth maintains that Dtr used reliable, official sources that 'reported matters of which Dtr. could have no first-hand knowledge'. Noth expresses his gratitude to Dtr for preserving historical facts for us. He says that it is due to 'the considerable importance he placed in the traditional material' and to Dtr's 'reverent attitude towards historical fact' that 'we owe the preservation of valuable old material wholly and solely to this respect for the value of old narratives and historical accounts'. Dtr had access to the reliable sources he used to write 'the history of his people'. Once again, his intention was not to correct the sources but to let the sources speak for themselves. To summarize, Noth believed that Dtr was a historian because he believed that the sources Dtr used were an archive of 'historical facts', and that Dtr used them with utmost respect when incorporating them into his work—that is, without imposing corrections.

Noth had no problem noting the creative input of Dtr as a narrator: 'When we have learned to regard his work as a self-contained whole, we shall find that he has crafted a work of art which merits our respect'. It is to Dtr's credit that the narrative is compelling and well told. Dtr used these sources to create a narrative, but it is important to note that Dtr finds the storyline in the past; he does not impose a narrative.[8] Dtr used several schemes and central theological ideas to bring out the story. But it is important to understand that Noth understood a historian as someone who finds a historical narrative embedded in the past, namely in the sources from the past. Noth claimed:

> [Dtr] was motivated by the universal inclination to see the historical process, as relatively clear and simple in its movement, and so he endeavoured to find in the various separate traditions, large and small, to which he had access a simple historical process, and to depict it in the sections of his work, which was meant to be as self-contained and homogeneous as possible.[9]

---

8. Noth, *Deuteronomistic History*, p. 99.
9. Noth, *Deuteronomistic History*, pp. 86-87.

Noth maintained that Dtr found a simple historical process (a coherent historical narrative) embedded in his sources/traditions; thus, Noth comments that 'in general, then, Dtr. gave his narrative very markedly the character of a traditional work[;] the intention was to be a compilation and explanation of the extant traditions concerning the history of his people'.[10]

Noth framed the story of Josiah in particular within DH as a historical account of theodicy, and in the process we could see how he imagined Dtr in the likeness of a modern historian. Noth saw the account of Josiah as being written by Dtr using official sources, so Noth believed that Dtr presented the account of Josiah as a historical fact without adding much to it. Noth took for granted that the account of Josiah is historical because he attributes most of it to the 'Books of the Chronicles', one of the sources Dtr purported to have used in writing DH.[11] Noth suggested that this source has a message that supports the theme of the inevitable march to judgment. Thus, Noth writes,

> Dtr.'s history of the temple in the period of the monarchy, drawn from the 'Books of the Chronicles' of the kings of Judah, is primarily of how the temple was stripped of its wealth by its own king; and he must have seen this as a sure sign of progressive decay.[12]

The source itself is about the progressive decay of the monarchy. Josiah's reform is passed over in order to move the story along the line of inevitable judgment:

> In this context, it is particularly significant that he says nothing of Josiah's far-reaching attempt to restore the empire of David which all kinds of casual references in the tradition indicate; even though Josiah is one of the few figures in the Israelite and Judaean monarchical period whom Dtr. counts as outstanding and worthy of unqualified praise. He has made a point, therefore, of passing over the king's political and military achievements—any casual reference to them certainly has a very specific reason.[13]

Josiah, even with all his efforts to reform and to live according to the law, functioned only to delay the on-going march to the end: ' It is true that before the fate of the Judaean state is accomplished, the reign of Josiah ([2 Kgs] 22.1–23.30) supplies an element of retardation'.[14] But Josiah and his reformation cannot stop the relentless march of history. So, Noth suggests that 'this section characterizes Josiah's reign in the light of the subsequent process of history, as an episode which does no more than show how things should

---

10. Noth, *Deuteronomistic History*, p. 88.
11. Noth, *Deuteronomistic History*, p. 66.
12. Noth, *Deuteronomistic History*, p. 66.
13. Noth, *Deuteronomistic History*, p. 140 n. 3. Noth assumes that Josiah tried to restore the empire of David, but provides little evidence to support his assumption.
14. Noth, *Deuteronomistic History*, p. 73.

have been done all along; and it is followed at once by the conclusion to the account of Josiah (23.28-30)'.[15] After a reminder of what could have been, the account of Josiah abruptly ends in tragedy, thus partaking in the overall narrative of, as Frank Cross puts it, 'irrevocable doom'.

To Noth, Josiah plays an important part in DH, not for what he did or who he was, but because of what happened during his reign, namely, the discovery of the book of the law. Noth states that Dtr's account of the discovery of the law is 'probably based on *an official record* of this important event'.[16] To Noth this is the crucial event that has influenced Dtr; Josiah's reign and what he did were subordinate to the discovery of the law. Josiah's reign was important to Dtr 'because in it that law which he has placed at the beginning of his history as the authentic exposition of the Sinai decalogue was found in the temple and put into practice by the king'.[17] Dtr assigned to the law 'a crucial role, regarding it as a norm for the relationship between God and people and as a yardstick by which to judge human conduct'.[18] Dtr also used Josiah as a yardstick to judge other kings, but in terms of upholding the law, 'Dtr elevates the event of Josiah's time to a general norm and makes it the main function of the monarchy as such to uphold the religious prescriptions in the Deuteronomic law'.[19] Noth assigns upholding the Deuteronomic law as the main function of the monarchy, and Josiah was the example *par excellence* of this principle. Nevertheless, it is the discovery of the law that is central to the overall framework of DH. It is according to the law that Israel and Judah were judged. It is in the law that Dtr finds justification for the punishment that Yahweh handed down to the exiles. There is no sense of hope in Josiah. Josiah played a minor role in the overall storyline of DH. Josiah showed what could have been, but he would not have changed the inevitable march of history toward judgment. Noth 'discovers' the history of theodicy in DH and frames Josiah within it.

Thus, Noth has portrayed Dtr as a modern historian who had access to the state archives, the discipline to remain objective, and the integrity to tell the story as he found it in the sources. This image of Dtr is none other than that of a modern day historian working carefully with various sources.[20] Thus, Whitelam notes:

---

15. Noth, *Deuteronomistic History*, pp. 73-74.
16. Noth, *Deuteronomistic History*, p. 73 (emphasis mine).
17. Noth, *Deuteronomistic History*, p. 73.
18. Noth, *Deuteronomistic History*, p. 81.
19. Noth, *Deuteronomistic History*, p. 82.
20. Whitelam, in discussing Baruch Halpern's *The First Historians* (San Francisco: Harper & Row, 1988), notes the similarity between Noth's Dtr whom Baruch Halpern wants to defend and the modern historian: 'It is this objective historian which Halpern is determined to defend against all detractors: a scribe painstakingly comparing and arrang-

Noth's Deuteronomistic Historian is conceived in terms of the state archivist sorting, arranging, and interpreting extant written material, which he used with the greatest of care... For Noth, the Deuteronomistic History is no fabrication but is an objective presentation of Israel's history based upon authentic sources.[21]

Dtr is imagined as a historian with similar interests, concerns, and methods to those of modern historians.[22] As a result, Dtr and modern historians are looking to write the same history—the history of the West.

Even after more than a half century since Noth's book, biblical scholars continue to view DH as the first and archetypical Western history. In fact, in their search for the roots of Western civilization, biblical scholars follow a contour formed by Western imperialism; their discourses are still framed by Orientalism and nationalism. There are constraints in place in biblical studies that limit the imagination of biblical scholars to the history and experience of the West. I would like to look at John Van Seters' work in order to examine the modernist landscape shaped by Orientalism and nationalism.[23]

Van Seters, in his important work on historiography in general, and his understanding of Dtr as a historian in particular, follows Noth in viewing DH as a unified work from the Exile, but he differs from Noth in that he contends that Noth 'still attributed too little of the work to the author himself and too much to his sources and traditions'.[24] He claims that Dtr 'completely reshaped traditions to conform to his thematic concerns and perspectives' and this fact—the creative activity of Dtr rather than the preservation of the historically reliable and recoverable sources—leads him to conclude that Dtr was a historian.[25]

---

ing source material while his modern counterparts work equally carefully to expose these same sources so that they might form the basis of a modern objective history of Israel' (*Invention*, p. 32).

21. Whitelam, *Invention*, p. 32.
22. We must note in fairness that Baruch Halpern does defend Noth's Dtr as an honest historian with antiquarian interests who did his best to write the past, but with given limitations of sources and methods. Halpern describes the different limitations Dtr had to deal with that the modern historian does not have.
23. Van Seters, *In Search of History*.
24. Van Seters, *In Search of History*, p. 359.
25. Baruch Halpern claims that John Van Seters has imagined Dtr as 'a rogue and a fraud, a distributor of taffy' (*The First Historians*, p. 31). Halpern's book attempts to defend Noth's characterization of Dtr as an honest historian who had a genuine antiquarian interest. According to Halpern, Dtr did his best to produce a logical reconstruction of past events. It is ironic that both Van Seters and Halpern attempt to defend Noth as a historian, but each takes a very different approach. Halpern defends Noth's thesis that Dtr used sources honestly to render the past of Dtr's people, but Halpern maintains that Dtr first wrote during Josiah's reign rather than in the Exile. Van Seters maintains Noth's thesis that Dtr wrote in the Exile, but argues that it is the imagination and creativity of Dtr

However, the main point of his book is that 'the first Israelite historian, and *the first known historian in Western civilization* truly to deserve this designation, was the Deuteronomistic historian'.[26] He asserts that Dtr is the first historian in Western civilization by virtue of being the first historian of the Bible without any further qualification or explanation.[27] He assumes that this is a given, a common understanding that needs no further explanation. Van Seters arrives at his conclusion that Dtr is the first historian in Western civilization by disqualifying other history writings from Israel's neighbors because the other 'nations' did not produce a genre of history comparable to Herodotus and Dtr, whose works Van Seters deem to belong to the genre of history. This conclusion is based on Van Seters's understanding of a three-stage evolutionary paradigm in the development of history writing, comprising (1) mythology, (2) historiography, and (3) history. The history writings of Israel's neighbors do not move to the final step of this evolutionary paradigm; they remain stuck in stage two. It is Israel (with Greece) that develops the genre of history (the final step in this evolutionary paradigm).

Van Seters uses a modern definition of history as the standard to judge ancient history writings. It is not that the other 'nations' (Egypt, the Hittites, Mesopotamia, Syria-Palestine) did not have historiographical works (writings that refer to the past), but they were not 'history writing', which, he argues, was a new genre inaugurated by Dtr and Herodotus. Van Seters uses the definition of Johan Huizinga—'History is the intellectual form in which a civilization renders account to itself of its past'—to evaluate history writings from the ancient Near East.[28] He interprets Huizinga's definition to mean that 'only when the history itself took precedence over the king, as happened in Israel, could history writing be achieved', which is none other than the history of the nations.[29] He uses this definition to reject all historical writings from the ancient world from the genre of history writing; they are defined as 'historiographical' but not as 'history writing'.[30]

---

to render an account of the past rather than the honest use of the sources that makes Dtr a historian. Halpern's Dtr is a modernist historian and Van Seters' Dtr is a postmodern historian (more on this point below).

26. Van Seters, *In Search of History*, p. 362 (emphasis mine).

27. B. Halpern also does not explain the title of his book *The First Historians*. Why do Halpern and Van Seters believe that Dtr is the first historian? The first historian of whose world, whose civilization? It is simply assumed this is the case.

28. J. Huizinga, 'A Definition of the Concept of History', in R. Klibansky and H.J. Paton (eds.), *Philosophy and History: Essays Presented to Ernst Cassirer* (Cambridge: Cambridge University Press, 1963), pp. 1-10 (9).

29. Van Seters, *In Search of History*, p. 355.

30. K.L. Younger argues that Van Seters has misunderstood Huizinga's definition (*Ancient Conquest Accounts: A Study in Ancient Near Eastern and Biblical History Writing* [JSOTSup, 98; Sheffield: JSOT Press, 1990]). See also Younger's Review of John

We need to point out that the discourse of nationalism is at the heart of Johan Huizinga's famous definition of the concept of history. Its Eurocentrism becomes clear when we examine what he means by 'civilization'. He believes that 'every civilization creates its own form of history, and must do so. The character of the civilization determines what history shall mean to it, and of what kind it shall be. If a civilization coincides with a people, a state, a tribe, its history will be correspondingly simple.'[31] A 'primitive' civilization will have a simple form, but a well-developed civilization like Europe will have a more complex form. He understood the ancient and the more recent East as 'the primitive civilization of the whole world'; it and classical antiquity together 'have become constituent parts of *our own* civilization',[32] that is, Western civilization. He concludes that 'our civilization is the first to have for its past the past of the world, our history is the first to be world-history'.[33] Somehow Western civilization was able to swallow up the whole world, ancient and modern. Just as the Western powers colonized non-Westerners and incorporated them into their epistemological framework, the histories of non-European peoples became part of 'our' history, which Huizinga calls 'world-history'.

Van Seters argues that DH is unique in the ancient Near East because Dtr was the first historian to use a new genre of history writing, a genre of writing very similar to the modern history of nations.[34] DH is unique because it was the first to render 'an account of the past' in order to articulate 'the people's identity'.[35] This attempt to give primacy or the status of uniqueness to biblical historiography is nothing new in biblical studies. According to Thomas Bolin, the previous generations of scholars, especially those who were part of the so-called Biblical Theology Movement that blossomed in the 1950s, also believed that biblical historiography was unique:

Van Seters, *In Search of History*, *JSOT* 40 (1988), pp. 110-17. Younger argues that Van Seters has equated history writing with national identity, which is inadequate for an investigation of ancient Near Eastern or biblical history writing. Furthermore, Van Seters has deemed a particular genre of history writing as the only valid genre. Finally, Van Seters eliminates the Court History and other passages from DH in order to establish a single continuous narrative history comparable to the national history of Herodotus.

31. Huizinga, 'A Definition of the Concept of History', p. 7.
32. Huizinga, 'A Definition of the Concept of History', p. 8 (emphasis mine).
33. Huizinga, 'A Definition of the Concept of History', p. 8.
34. Van Seters's argument is indeed circular. David Petersen, Review of John Van Seter, *In Search of History*, *CBQ* 47 (1985), pp. 336-40, remarks that Van Seters's argument is 'definitionist' in that 'in adopting a specialized definition of history writing, he is able to exclude material which, if a less refined definition were used, might fall under the rubric of history writing' (p. 339).
35. Van Seters, *In Search of History*, p. 320.

> Since the rise of modern scholarship, the Israelites have been designated the inventors of history writing by scholars both of the Bible and of history in general, some of whom contrast biblical historiography with the 'poor and thin records of the great empires of the East', or emphasize its 'distinctive and superior character'. This stress on difference in quality is also expressed as a difference in kind, which anoints biblical historiography with uniqueness born from its alleged moral and theological superiority to the other cultures of antiquity.[36]

Bolin does not mention that this tendency to view biblical historiography as unique and superior to other writings of the past in the ancient Near East is connected to the Orientalist mindset of biblical scholars. In fact, the scholars themselves believed that other cultures were inferior to their own Western culture. They saw biblical historiography as their own; they saw ancient Israel as the model of the nation the West imitated and fulfilled. These scholars saw the Israelites as the spiritual ancestors of the West and assumed that the historiographical writings of Israel were morally and theologically superior to those of its neighbors. Van Seters's claim is the same: he maintains the primacy and superiority of biblical historiography.[37]

Biblical scholars tend to focus on differences rather than similarities when making comparisons between Israel and its neighbors, thereby reconfirming the uniqueness of ancient Israel, which, once again, is seen as a taproot of Western civilization (which in turn is seen as a unique and superior civilization). The belief that the history and ideas of the Bible are unique limits any kind of comparison: 'the claim of uniqueness renders impossible both comparison and, ultimately, any knowledge at all about the thing in question… and the act of comparison is perceived as both an impossibility and an impiety'.[38] It is this tendency in biblical studies that draws its participants to the center where a discourse that has been shaped in the context of Western imperialism continues to be operative.

DH is still being framed within the context of Western history without any alternative in sight. It is the long-practiced habit of biblical scholars to see biblical historiography, DH in particular, as Western history. We must open

---

36. T. Bolin, 'History, Historiography, and the Use of the Past in the Hebrew Bible', in Christina S. Kraus (ed.), *The Limits of Historiography* (Mnemosyne, 191; Leiden: E.J. Brill, 1999), pp. 113-40 (113).

37. Van Seters's understanding of the three-step evolutionary paradigm parallels an evolutionary paradigm of the development of the nations. How convenient that, just as other peoples fail to develop into nation-states (except Israel), the genre of history develops only in Israel. What is not surprising is that in my reading of several reviews of Van Seters's book I find a lack of criticism of Van Seters's claim that Dtr is the first historian. The reviewers criticize Van Seters's book for all sorts of things, but there is a lack of critique of how he connects Dtr as the first historian of Western civilization (read 'the world').

38. Bolin, 'History, Historiography', p. 115.

up the possibility that DH is 'a history of their own' outside of the framework of modernist history of the West. Western history has framed Josiah as part of the history of the West according to the discourse of nationalism. It has understood the West as the subject of history. In search of continuities and the roots of its civilization, it has imposed its own development as nations as the norm; in the process, it has viewed other histories and civilizations as inferior, including those of the non-Israelite peoples of the ancient Near East, but it has viewed the culture and history of ancient Israel as their own because ancient Israel is seen as the taproot of Western civilization. As Whitelam puts it: 'This is history...in which Europe or the West is the real subject... It is ultimately a pursuit of the roots of Western "civilization".'[39]

The Postmodern Challenge

We will now take a closer look at the landscape that the discipline of modern history has shaped in order to understand better what type of landscape biblical scholars travel when they claim that DH is a history. Noth's understanding of DH as history writing is clearly in the tradition of the modern discipline of history, which emerged as a professional discipline in the nineteenth century with Leopold von Ranke (1795–1886) as its most influential champion. Ranke's famous declaration that he wanted not to pass judgment on the past but simply to report *wie es eigentlich gewesen ist* ('as it actually happened') has been used both as a symbolic description of his achievement and as the principle of the modern discipline of history.[40] Ranke combined 'the methodological achievements of philologists, erudites, and legal historians with substantial interpretation and traditional narrative history', which was based primarily on a central principle of philology—'check the source for trustworthiness and against its own context'—in order to establish objective facts.[41] But Ranke also maintained that 'God with his plan and his will' stood behind history, and that states functioned as God's agents with 'the purpose of civilizing mankind'; therefore, the affairs of states 'must be the central concern of the historian'.[42] With Ranke's understanding of the coexistence of states for a civilized human life and 'with most students making pilgrimages to state archives in search of state documents, Rankean history became primarily

39. Whitelam, *Invention*, p. 50.
40. E. Breisach, *Historiography: Ancient, Medieval, and Modern* (Chicago: University of Chicago Press, 2nd edn, 1994), p. 233.
41. Breisach, *Historiography*, p. 233.
42. Breisach, *Historiography*, pp. 233-34. Breisach observes that the struggle for national identity in the German area was acute during Ranke's time. Breisach also notes that 'Ranke...was confident that the European state system and its overseas dependencies were part of God's plan guaranteeing meaning, order, and continuity' (p. 319).

political history'.[43] The discipline of history was born as a science that wished to narrate the development of nations by means of rigorous study of the sources.

History as an academic discipline sought to recount the past *wie es eigentlich gewesen ist* by applying rigorous 'scientific' methods to evaluate written sources (usually official documents) 'objectively' and by recounting the findings (facts) in the form of a coherent, continuous, chronologically ordered narrative around a central theme or *Zeitgeist*.[44] In its practice, it took the form of a narrative of political events, the great deeds of great men (statesmen, generals, kings, etc.), on the national and international level. It believed that the great men were agents of historical change. It had a particular explanation for historical events that was rooted in the Enlightenment—the belief that reason and science ensure progress and freedom for humankind—namely, the metanarratives of the West. The philosophical foundation of traditional history was the idea of scientific objectivity—the belief that historians are able to know the past 'as it actually happened' by using scientific methods. This form of history dominated the discipline of history in the West without a serious challenge until the 1960s.

The rise of postmodernism in the 1960s challenged the basic foundations of the modern discipline of history. In general, postmodernism is an umbrella term used to describe various critiques of the Enlightenment and its cultural and historical product: modernism. It is in some sense an assault on or a challenge to reason and the notion of objectivity on which the knowledge and culture of the West is supposedly based. Postmodernism is more than a 'fad' in academia; it is a state of the contemporary world that is, according to Jean-Francois Lyotard, characterized by 'incredulity towards metanarratives' of the *modern*. Lyotard describes the *modern* as follows:

---

43. Breisach, *Historiography*, p. 234. Breisach also notes that 'most of Ranke's own words contain primarily narratives of war, diplomacy, and the deeds of statesmen' (p. 234).

44. Modern historiography is in a way a synthesis of the Enlightenment's emphasis on reason (verification of sources through rigorous scientific methods) and Romanticism's emphasis on aesthetics (each period must be understood according to its own *Zeitgeist*, and thus a discontinuity between various periods was argued). Appleby *et al.* summarize: 'Faith in history as an objective process allowed scholars to claim the ground for reason for their interpretations, and claim that reason enabled them to decipher otherwise incomprehensible cultures and time periods. The German historian Leopold von Ranke…in his efforts to increase the rigor of history through meticulous attention to detail and his belief that the acts of people in all periods may be understood only through comprehension of the single great idea of the time, exemplifies this sort of practice. He, like other historians of his time, felt that earlier historical writings had neither been 'objective' nor 'scientific', nor had they attempted to tell a full story on the basis of their evidence. Ranke led the German 'Historical School', which greatly influenced later generations of historians worldwide' (*Knowledge and Postmodernism*, pp. 141-42).

> I will use the term *modern* to designate any science that legitimates itself with reference to a metadiscourse of the kind making an explicit appeal to some grand narrative, such as the dialectics of Spirit, the hermeneutics of meaning, the emancipation of the rational or working subject, or the creation of wealth.[45]

Postmodernism challenged the metanarratives that have been generated by the West in order to understand itself as the subject of history, epistemology, and ontology. It is not that the Enlightenment project was not challenged or questioned prior to the emergence of postmodernism in the 1960s; for many had challenged

> the modern supposition that the accumulation of knowledge through scientific practice necessarily bettered the human condition... The imperialist projects undertaken by both Europeans and Americans during the late nineteenth and early twentieth centuries exemplifies [*sic*] some of the inconsistencies inherent to modern thought and practice...[46]

However, many more believed that the imperial projects were successful, and they supported the claims of the West's grand narratives. For example, they were able to justify colonialism as an Enlightenment project that was improving the lives of the colonized:

> To many observers, Western imperial expansion represented the triumph of Enlightenment values. Imperial domination of subjected peoples was legitimated by the notion that Westerners were serving the interests of the 'less civilized' by wiping out superstition, magic, and false religion and substituting in their place justice, reason, and truth. This sense of responsibility for bringing civilization to 'savages' was called the 'White Man's Burden'.[47]

History is one of the disciplines of knowledge that has appealed to some grand narratives of the West, especially the discourse of nationalism, in order to legitimize itself as a producer of objective, scientific knowledge about the past. Postmodernism challenged the discipline of history by questioning the very notions and practices of history. It challenged the premise that historical narratives (text) represented the past as it was (reality); it challenged the view of the historian as a disinterested 'scientist' searching for truth and nothing but the truth; and it challenged the type of source the historians were using to write history. It challenged the discipline of history as the producer of objective, scientific knowledge about the past.

45. Jean-Francois Lyotard, quoted in Keith Jenkins (ed.), *The Postmodern History Reader* (London: Routledge, 1997), p. 36. Lyotard is referring to grand narratives by Hegel (the dialectics of Spirit), Marx (the emancipation of the rational or working subject), and historians who believe capitalism will bring the Enlightenment project to success (the creation of wealth).
46. Appleby *et al.* (eds.), *Knowledge and Postmodernism*, p. 259. They note that this general recognition came about as social scientists lost confidence in the modernist projects when they failed to materialize in the colonized places.
47. Appleby *et al.* (eds.), *Knowledge and Postmodernism*, p. 259.

The Social Turn

In contrast to a modernist belief that a proper historian is someone whose location in which he or she is situated plays no part (who has no vested interests, who is able to write an objective, detached account of the past), the social changes since the 1960s have shown clearly that the historian's context does matter. The historian has a vested interest in his or her topic and location does influence what the historian looks for.

Many point to the 1960s as one of the more important turning points in the twentieth century, and this applies also to the discipline of history. Georg Iggers remarked that 'in many ways the 1960s were a turning point at which the consciousness of a crisis of modern society and culture, long in preparation, came to a head'.[48] One of the consequences was that it marked the end of a 'grand narrative' for many—the narrative that Western civilization offered liberty and progress to all humans. The feminist movement and the Civil Rights movement in the 1960s challenged such grand narratives and created an environment in which to write different narratives. The 1965 Immigration Act shifted the demography of immigrants to the United States from Europe to the so-called Third World, and this has contributed to an environment that made writing different narratives possible. Multiculturalism in the United States expanded beyond black and white; the feminist movement went beyond white as well. Iggers summarized a result of such social changes in the 1960s as follows:

> the claims of segments of the population previously excluded from historical narratives, foremost among them women and ethnic minorities, led to the creation of new histories sometimes integrated into a larger narrative, but often apart from it.[49]

As a result of many movements and changes in the 1960s, there was a significant increase in the number of women and ethnic and racial minorities attending colleges and graduate schools. In particular the demography of graduate students in the discipline of history changed, which may have resulted in social history becoming more common than ever. Appleby, Hunt and Jacob state that

> The effect of the influx of new graduate students could be seen almost immediately in the topics of their doctoral dissertations. Between 1958 and 1978, the proportion writing on subjects in social history quadrupled, overtaking political history as the principal area of graduate research.[50]

---

48. G.G. Iggers, *Historiography in the Twentieth Century: From Scientific Objectivity to the Postmodern Challenge* (Hanover: Wesleyan University Press, 1997), p. 6.

49. Iggers, *Historiography*, p. 7.

50. J. Appleby, L. Hunt and M. Jacob, *Telling the Truth about History* (New York: W.W. Norton, 1994), pp. 147-48. The authors had in mind the ethnic minority groups from Europe and Africa.

These young social historians brought new perspectives with them. The social historians' perspectives were different from those of the political historians'. The political historians wrote from the perspective of the elite, from 'above', focusing on major events pertaining to national interests. The social historians wrote from 'below', focusing on social groups and their lives in the United States. Many, including Asian Americans, were searching for their group histories.[51] Thus Appleby, Hunt, and Jacob trumpeted that 'the social history research of the past twenty years has lifted from obscurity the lives of those who had been swept to the sidelines in the metahistory of progress'.[52] Those who have been ignored by traditional history have become the subjects of their own histories.

The social historians made significant differences in writing history by searching different types of sources; they searched different archives. The sources these social historians researched were different from those used by traditional (national) historians. Instead of looking at the official documents of the nation by going through official archives, they were looking at sources that were deemed irrelevant or trivial by traditional national historians. For example, social historians closely examined 'long-ignored records of births, marriages, death, probate inventories, land titles, slave purchases, city plans, and tax assessments'.[53] They also began to use oral testimonies of ordinary people as another source. What they found was not only difficult to assimilate to the American dream narrative, but often contradicted and challenged the American success narrative espoused by traditional American history.

Asian Americans were one of the groups that challenged the standard American history that either ignored them or stereotyped them as aliens. In the 1960s they started the so-called Asian-American movement that gave rise to Asian-American studies in academia. This movement was part of a larger movement that gave rise to ethnic studies in the 1960s. Gary Okihiro summarizes the manifesto of ethnic studies:

> Ethnic studies began with an alternative vision of American history and culture that was broadly inclusive. It started with the idea that American society consisted not only of Europeans but also of American Indians, Africans, Latinos, and Asians. It went on to propose that the histories of all of America's people were so intertwined that to leave out any group would result in sizable silences within the overall narrative. It noted a global dimension to the American experience, both in the imperial expansion of European peoples and in the incorporation of America's ethnic minorities... Ethnic studies fundamentally sought to move the pivot, by fracturing the universalism of white men and by repositioning gender, class, race, and sexuality from the periphery to the core, decentering and recentering the colors and patterns of the old fabric.[54]

51. More below on Asian Americans' attempt to write their own histories.
52. Appleby, Hunt and Jacob, *Telling the Truth*, p. 154.
53. Appleby, Hunt and Jacob, *Telling the Truth*, p. 148.
54. Okihiro, *Margins and Mainstreams*, pp. 150-51.

In this manifesto, writing a different history of America became part of envisioning an alternate America, which challenged the *status quo* of America in the 1960s.

Many point to the 1968 student strike at San Francisco State College as the birth of the Asian-American movement, which was part of larger movements for liberation from many forms of oppression during the 1960s.[55] In Glenn Omatsu's important article on the significance of the Student Strike and the Asian-American movement, he states that 'the movements that occurred in the United States in the sixties were also part of a worldwide trend, a trend Latin American theologians call the era of the '"eruption of the poor" into history'.[56] Asian Americans struggled with similar 'prisons' of oppression—'the historical forces of racism, poverty, war, and exploitation'—as other 'politically submerged' and 'economically marginalized' peoples 'that redefined human values' and 'that transformed the lives of "ordinary" people as they confronted the prisons around them'.[57] Omatsu contends that Asian Americans, through these struggles, redefined their experience in North America and, most importantly, transformed their consciousness.

For our discussion, the struggles enabled Asian Americans to recover 'a buried cultural tradition' as part of seeing Asian Americans as the subject of their own history.[58] Omatsu describes this period as a 'decisive moment' for Asian Americans—'a time for reclaiming the past and changing the future'.[59] There were important ideas that emerged during this period that helped to alter Asian Americans' understanding of history and their place in it:

> (1) Asian Americans became active participants in the making of history, reversing the standard accounts that had treated Asian Americans as marginal objects; (2) history was viewed as created by large numbers of people acting

---

55. At San Francisco State College, members of the Third World Liberation Front (TWLF), a coalition of African Americans, Latino Americans/Chicanos, Native Americans, and Asian Americans, launched a student strike in November 1968 demanding the following: (a) changes in curriculum to include the experience, history, culture, and issues that are related to minority groups; (b) a better representation of minority in the administration and the student body; and (c) the creation of an ethnic studies department. For a detailed summary of the role of Asian-American students in the San Francisco State College Strike, see K. Umemoto, '"On Strike" San Francisco State College Strike, 1968–1969: The Role of Asian American Students', in M. Zhou and J.V. Gatewood (eds.), *Contemporary Asian America: A Multidisciplinary Reader* (New York: New York University Press, 2000), pp. 49-79.

56. G. Omatsu, 'The "Four Prisons" and the Movements of Liberation: Asian American Activism from the 1960s to the 1990s', in Zhou and Gatewood (eds.), *Contemporary Asian America*, pp. 80-112 (83).

57. Omatsu, 'The "Four Prisons"', p. 80.

58. Omatsu, 'The "Four Prisons"', p. 80.

59. Omatsu, 'The "Four Prisons"', p. 86.

together, not by elites; (3) ordinary people became aware that they could make their own history by learning how historical forces operated and by transforming this knowledge into a material force to change their lives.[60]

It was during this period that the redefinition of the Asian-American experience occurred that continues to shape the agenda of Asian-American communities:

> The redefinition of the Asian American experience stands as the most important legacy from this period... This legacy represents far more than an ethnic awakening. The redefinition began with an analysis of power and domination in American society. It provided a way for understanding the historical forces surrounding us. And, most importantly, it presented a strategy and challenge for changing our future. This challenge...still confronts us today.[61]

The coalition of minority students at the San Francisco State College Strike was able to win one concession: the establishment of an institutional site for ethnic studies.[62] This was perhaps the most important factor in the establishment and legitimation of Asian-American studies in general and of Asian-American historiography in particular. For without an institutional site, the production of knowledge about Asian Americans 'independently' would have been impossible. Although Henry Yu shows that there are still legacies of American Orientalism from the past that continue to limit the study of Asians in America within the framework of the 'Oriental Problem', there is no doubt that the institutional site made it possible to attempt to produce knowledge about Asian Americans differently from the framework constructed by American Orientalism.[63] Yu states the significance of having an institutional site for the production of knowledge for Asian Americans:

---

60. Omatsu, 'The "Four Prisons"', p. 88. Omatsu lists six changes in all. I have listed three that are related to the understanding of history.

61. Omatsu, 'The "Four Prisons"', p. 88.

62. Omatsu states that 'although their five-month strike was brutally repressed and resulted in only partial victories, students won the nation's first School of Ethnic Studies' ('The "Four Prisons"', p. 84). Zhou and Gatewood state that 'shortly after the founding of the first ethnic studies program at San Francisco State College in 1968...[by 1978] at least fourteen universities established Asian American studies programs...[by 1999] an estimated forty-one departments, centers, or programs' ('Introduction', in Zhou and Gatewood [eds.], *Contemporary Asian America*, pp. 3-4).

63. Yu, *Thinking Orientals*. Yu argues that the earlier generations of Asian scholars were constrained by their teachers and the institutions that were interested in investigating Asians in America in terms of the Oriental Problem. Asian scholars were valuable as 'informants' of the exotic culture and had to perform the part of Oriental in front of non-Asian audience. Yu says that he wants 'to emphasize the constraints that limited possibilities' for these earlier generations of Asian scholars. But he argues that some of these legacies still operate today.

> In many ways the rise of Asian American studies was predicated on the need for a separate institutional existence in which Asian Americans as a self-identified group could define the validity of their ideas. On academic campuses at San Francisco State, at the University of California, Berkeley, and at UCLA, Americans who had long been identified as Orientals came to define themselves as Asian Americans.[64]

Yu credits the establishment of the institutional site of production of knowledge as the biggest difference in the ability of Asian Americans to produce knowledge about themselves in comparison with that of the earlier generations of Asian scholars:

> Asian American studies and ethnic studies were attempts to control the site of production of knowledge about Asians in America. In the transition from sociology's Oriental Problem to Asian American studies, the biggest difference has been the creation of a separate institutional network where research can be produced and validated.[65]

The Linguistic Turn

The social turn was one of the major turning points that challenged traditional historiography. But postmodernism was about more than changes in what archives the historians were using or who the historians were. Postmodernism proper is the questioning of the modern production of knowledge itself, challenging history's claim to be epistemological. Thus, Appleby *et al.* formulate the challenge as follows:

> If the Enlightenment thinkers first queried, 'what is knowledge?', nineteenth-century social theorists added, 'what is knowledge *good* for?' Poststructuralists such as Foucault reformulated such generic questions, asking 'how does knowledge work?' Derrida goes one step further, searching for what is beyond knowledge and meaning. He asks the radical question 'do knowledge and its supposed corollary, meaning, truly exist?'[66]

Many view the so-called linguistic turn as the critical change that has prompted a challenge to traditional historiography. Among the most important elements in the linguistic turn was the questioning of referentiality or correspondence between language and the reality it is supposed to represent. In relation to history, it was believed that a historical account functioned as a 'window' through which the past can be observed, but the questioning of referentiality of language also questioned the supposed transparency of language. This represents a significant shift in the understanding of the

---

64. Yu, *Thinking Orientals*, p. 196.
65. Yu, *Thinking Orientals*, p. 196.
66. Appleby *et al.* (eds.), *Knowledge and Postmodernism*, pp. 389-90.

3. Whose History is it Anyway?

nature of language. There had been a general belief in the ability of the word (linguistic expression; signifier) to represent the world (reality; signified) in some form of direct or transparent correspondence. Postmodernism challenged this understanding and supported the view that a word's meaning was determined by its reference to other words rather than to the world/reality. A signifier gets its specific meaning in relation to other signifiers, not the world/reality (signified). In fact, Derrida argues that a signified is not of the world but a construction of words (signifiers).[67] Therefore, Derrida's well-known statement summarizes this view: 'Il n'y a pas de hors-texte' ('There is nothing beyond the text').

Jacques Derrida often receives the lion's share of credit for the idea of the instability of meaning in the text in addition to the argument that there is no meaning outside of the text. Derrida's well-known neologism, *la différance*, explains the instability of the text well: 'All texts can be read in different ways (*la différence*) and exhaustive interpretation is forever deferred (*la différance*)'.[68] In relation to history, we cannot draw one meaning or story of the past from a text that purports to tell it. The linguistic turn truly undermined the whole project of the traditional historians—to come to know about and to write about what happened (truth) in the past by writing a coherent narrative. It views a text as a linguistic construction that has no direct, one-to-one correspondence with reality. Thus, Keith Jenkins summarizes the ramification of this view on history: 'what we want our inheritance/history "to be" is always waiting to be "read" and written in the future like any other texts: the past as history lies before us, not behind us'.[69]

For historians, Hayden White is considered the foremost critic of modernist history. White argued that history is closer to a literary artifact (aesthetic) than an objective, 'scientific' narrative (epistemological). It was not that modernist historians did not recognize the literary aspects of narrative form in which history was written; however, they still claimed that history was not a class of literature. That is, historical narratives are epistemological and, therefore, they produce 'scientific' knowledge about the past. White challenged this distinction between history and literature by arguing that history is in fact a class of literature and thus should be analyzed as such. He demanded 'that his colleagues question the formulaic structures with which they represent the past'.[70]

---

67. According to K. Jenkins, 'a signifier always needs what Derrida calls supplementing by another signifier or set of signifiers to become a concept—what Derrida calls a signified' (*Refiguring History* [London: Routledge, 2003], p. 20).
68. Quoted in N.J. Wilson, *History in Crisis? Recent Directions in Historiography* (Upper Saddle River, NJ: Prentice–Hall, 1999), p. 115.
69. Jenkins, *Refiguring History*, p. 30.
70. Appleby *et al.* (eds.), *Knowledge and Postmodernism*, p. 386.

According to Alan Munslow, for historians, White's 'analysis of how historians, as they describe and evaluate past events, effectively invent the past is probably the most radical development in historical methodology in the last thirty years'.[71] Historians use narratives as the form in which to reconstruct or represent the past with the assumption that the past indeed contained a storyline, a narrative for the historians to discover. However, White argued against such an assumption; he claimed that historians employ literary devices to impose meaning on the data; a historical account is an invention rather than a discovery, a creation rather than a revelation. History is a form of representation influenced as much by the imagination of historians as by the data.[72]

Thus, White argued that '*the* narrative does not pre-exist but *a* narrative is invented and provided by the historian'.[73] White collapsed the distinction between the facts (data or information) and the interpretation (explanation or story told about the facts):

> It is not the case that a fact is one thing and its interpretation another. The fact is presented where and how it is in the discourse in order to sanction the interpretation to which it is meant to contribute. And the interpretation derives its force of plausibility from the order and manner in which the facts are presented in the discourse. The discourse itself is the actual combination of facts and meaning which gives to it the aspect of a *specific* structure of meaning that permits us to identify it as a product of one kind of historical consciousness rather than another.[74]

Furthermore, White claimed that not only the form but to a certain extent the content of historians' accounts were predetermined by literary tropes: 'historical narratives are verbal fictions, the contents of which are as much invented as found and the forms of which have more in common with their counterparts in literature than they have with those in the sciences'.[75] White argued that historians employ the four master tropes (metaphor, metonymy, synecdoche, and irony) to translate the data into a meaningful story:

---

71. A. Munslow, *Deconstructing History* (London: Routledge, 1998), p. 140.

72. Munslow states that White's view of history 'is more like a painting than a forensic reconstruction—an aesthetic appreciation of a past world rather than the recovery of its lost reality from the sources composed of individual statements about past reality' (p. 148). However, some biblical historians turn this argument on its head and argue that the 'representation' by the Bible is trustworthy, therefore, it is believable as a valid 'representation' of the past (more below). See also V.P. Long, *The Art of Biblical History* (Grand Rapids: Zondervan, 1994), for a detailed discussion on this point.

73. H. White, 'The Historical Text as Literary Artifact', in *idem*, *Tropics of Discourse* (Baltimore: The Johns Hopkins University Press, 1978), pp. 81-100 (82).

74. H. White, 'Historicism, History, and the Figurative Imagination', in *idem*, *Tropics of Discourse*, pp. 101-20 (107).

75. White, 'Historical Text', p. 82.

> Historical situations are not *inherently* tragic, comic, or romantic. They may all be inherently ironic, but they need not be emplotted that way. All the historian needs to do to transform a tragic into a comic situation is to shift his point of view or change the scope of his perceptions. Anyway, we only think of situations as tragic or comic because these concepts are part of our generally cultural and specifically literary heritage. *How* a given historical situation is to be configured depends on the historian's subtlety in matching up a specific plot structure with the set of historical events that he wishes to endow with a meaning of a particular kind.[76]

Therefore, White argued that history should be subject to rhetorical analysis like other literary works. To modernist historians, to equate history (epistemology) with literature (aesthetic) is anathema. That is exactly, however, what White did by showing that it is the prefigurative tropes that predetermine the narrative forms in which the content is accounted; the content itself is inherently influenced by the imagination of the historian.

The Site of Knowledge

Foucault challenged modernist history by locating the historian's production of knowledge in the matrix of power relations. He was able to advocate and practice plural histories rather than a singular history. He showed that truth statements were part of discourse that was embedded in the whole body of practices and institutions related to that area of knowledge (a network of power relations). He demonstrated that the discourse of history creates its own object from the present rather than finding it from the past; the discourse functions to legitimate the subject of history, namely, the West. He exposed the claim that the production of knowledge was objective and scientific as no more than a discursive formation that is conditioned historically and culturally within a network of scholars and institutions that produce and legitimate certain knowledge. Foucault effectively displaced the historian working alone in a vacuum into the matrix of power relations.

Foucault was against a single, unified, continuous, universal, totalizing history produced by the modernist historian. Jürgen Habermas, in critique of Foucault, notes:

> Foucault wants above all…*to put an end to global historiography* that covertly conceives of history as a macroconsciousness. History in the singular has to be dissolved, not indeed into a manifold of narrative histories, but into a plurality of irregularly emerging and disappearing islands of discourse.[77]

76. White, 'Historical Text', p. 85.
77. Jürgen Habermas, 'The Critique of Reason as an Unmasking of the Human Science: Michele Foucault', in idem, *The Philosophical Discourse of Modernity* (trans. Frederick G. Lawrence; Cambridge, MA: MIT Press, 1990), pp. 238-65 (251).

In reaction to generalization and centralization in history, Foucault's work was characterized most prominently by 'its specificity and its marginality'.[78] Foucault was against modernist national history's tendency to search for continuities with the past, which was a way of smoothing over discontinuities, conflicts, and ruptures in history in order to explain and justify the road taken to the present. As a result, modernist history portrayed present conditions as inevitable outcomes of the events of the past. But Foucault investigated in his histories 'the contingency—and hence surpassability—of what history has given us'.[79] Thus, we can not only construct or imagine different images of the past, but also change present conditions. Foucault showed that everything that a society takes for granted, as a given fact of reality, as common sense, has its own history of conflicts before being subsumed under the great narrative of the West. Everything had its own chronology, discrete temporalities opposed to a universal chronology, before it was incorporated into the totalizing chronology of the West.[80]

Foucault is famous for excavating the subjugated knowledge of history, which was laid aside by the desire and will to pave a straight, continuous history to the present. He argued that, underneath the stable layer of discourses of truth, there exists an insurrection of subjugated knowledges. He saw two types of subjugated knowledge:

> On the one hand, I am referring to the historical contents that have been buried and disguised in a functionalist coherence or formal systemisation... Subjugated knowledges are thus those blocs of historical knowledge which were present but disguised within the body of functionalist and systematising theory... On the other hand, I believe that by subjugated knowledges one should understand something else, something which in a sense is altogether different, namely, a whole set of knowledges that have been disqualified as inadequate to their task or insufficiently elaborated: naïve knowledges, located low down on the hierarchy, beneath the required level of cognition of scientificity.[81]

Foucault sought to recover the subjugated knowledges that have been either co-opted or dismissed by standard history in order to justify the status quo and to legitimate the order of things. Thus, Foucault remarked that 'our task...will be to expose and specify the issue at stake in this opposition, this struggle, this insurrection of knowledges against the institutions and against effects of the knowledge and power that invest scientific discourse'.[82] It was

---

78. G. Gattung, *The Cambridge Companion to Foucault* (Cambridge: Cambridge University Press, 1994), p. 3.

79. Gattung, *Cambridge Companion*, p. 10.

80. M. Foucault, *The Archaeology of Knowledge* (New York: Pantheon Books, 1972), pp. 3-20.

81. M. Foucault, *Power/Knowledge* (New York: Pantheon Books, 1980), pp. 81-82.

82. Foucault, *Power/Knowledge*, p. 87.

through the method of 'archaeologies' that he was able to reveal or dig up the subjugated knowledges that had been incorporated, ignored, silenced, or disqualified in the effort to form a stable, unified, universal discourse of the present.

To Foucault, discourses were more than just texts that made some truth statements about certain objects. Discourses were contextualized texts that were embedded in a whole body of practices and institutions, in networks of power relations. Foucault's analysis of discourse effectively changed from questions about the meaning of texts and questions about the methods of scholars, which modern historians were accustomed to asking, to the description of the function of discourse. Discourses are generated by a given field of knowledge through 'discursive formations'. Discursive formations are a process by which certain rules and practices around a field of knowledge give rise to a discipline in a specific historical context that include certain knowledge because of its 'scientificity', but exclude other knowledge because it is not deemed worthy of the title 'scientific' knowledge. It is worth emphasizing that the very object under investigation and scholarship of a given field of knowledge come 'into existence only contemporaneously with the discursive formations that made it possible' for the discipline to talk about them.[83] In other words, networks of scholars and institutions within a discipline form discourses as systems of knowledge that 'establish statements as events (with their own conditions and domain of appearance) and as things (with their own possibility and field of use)'.[84] Thus, the object of modern history's investigation and scholarship functions to legitimate the very field of knowledge it helped to form. The object of Western history is none other than Europe's subjectivity (self-realization). Modern history legitimates the West but not the rest.[85] In the production of its object it has subjugated other histories and incorporated them as part of its own history. Therefore, it is impossible to talk about knowledge ('meaning' of discourses) without talking about power (functions of discourses).

Foucault does not understand power as a discrete entity one can point to; it is something that exists within a network of scholars and institutions that produce discourses:

> Power must be analysed as something which circulates, or rather as something which only functions in the form of a chain. It is never localised here or there, never in anybody's hands, never appropriated as a commodity or piece of wealth. Power is employed and exercised through a net-like organisation… In other words, individuals are the vehicles of power, not its points of application.[86]

83. Gattung, *Cambridge Companion*, p. 93.
84. Foucault, *Archaeology*, p. 128.
85. M. Foucault, *The Order of Things* (New York: Pantheon Books, 1970), pp. 219-20.
86. Foucault, *Power/Knowledge*, p. 98.

Foucault could not think of talking about knowledge or truth outside of networks of power relations.[87] To Foucault, knowledge and power cannot be separated. However, it is important to keep in mind that Foucault's understanding of power is not one-dimensional. Power is not simply a negative, repressive force:

> If power were never anything but repressive, if it never did anything but to say no, do you really think one would be brought to obey it? What makes power hold good, what makes it accepted, is simply the fact that it doesn't only weigh on us as a force that says no, but that it traverses and produces things, it induces pleasure, forms knowledge, produces discourses. It needs to be considered as a productive network which runs through the whole social body, much more than as a negative instance whose function is repression.[88]

Therefore, to Foucault, power cannot operate 'without a certain economy of discourses of truth' which operates through and on the basis of the intimate connection between power and knowledge.[89] Foucault concludes that 'we are subjected to the production of truth through power and we cannot exercise power except through the production of truth'.[90] Networks of power/knowledge relations attempt to produce hegemony through the production of discourses that benefit 'us' more than others, that legitimate 'us' rather than others.

Foucault's understanding of history can be summarized in his understanding of how historians have turned *documents* into *monuments*. According to Foucault, it was around the questioning of the *document* of the past that the discipline of history was established:

> It is obvious enough that ever since a discipline such as history has existed, documents have been used, questioned, and have given rise to questions; scholars have asked not only what these documents meant, but also whether they were telling the truth, and by what right they could claim to be doing so, whether they were sincere or deliberately misleading, well informed or ignorant, authentic or tampered with. But each of these questions, and all this critical concern, pointed to one and the same end: the reconstitution, on the basis of what the documents say, and sometimes merely hint at, of the past from which they emanate and which has now disappeared far behind them; the document was always treated as the language of a voice since reduced to silence, its fragile, but possibly decipherable trace.[91]

In order to reconstitute the past the historians had to decipher the silent voice of the *document*. The historians developed methods and practices to

---

87. Gattung, *Cambridge Companion*, p. 99.
88. Foucault, *Power/Knowledge*, p. 119.
89. Foucault, *Power/Knowledge*, p. 93.
90. Foucault, *Power/Knowledge*, p. 93.
91. Foucault, *Archaeology*, p. 6.

3. Whose History is it Anyway? 73

hear the silent voice from the past through documents: 'history now organizes the document, divides it up, distributes it, orders it, arranges it in levels, establishes series, distinguishes between what is relevant and what is not, discovers elements, defines unities, describes relations'.[92] In their effort to decipher the document scientifically, they no longer view the document as 'an inert material' through which they are trying to reconstitute the past, instead they are substituting the 'past' they have organized in the documentary material itself as the reconstitution of the past.[93] The historians, according to Foucault, have turned the document, a silent voice from the past, into the monument that can be studied as an object:

> To be brief, then, let us say that history, in its traditional form, undertook to 'memorize' the *monuments* of the past, transform them into *documents*, and lend speech to those traces which, in themselves, are often not verbal, or which say in silence something other than what they actually say; in our time, history is that which transform *documents* into *monuments*.[94]

Thus, Foucault claimed that historians were more like archaeologists, deciphering the monuments they created:

> There was a time when archaeology, as a discipline devoted to silent monuments, inert traces, objects without context, and things left by the past, aspired to the condition of history, and attained meaning only through the restitution of a historical discourse; it might be said, to play on words a little, that in our time history aspires to the condition of archaeology, to the intrinsic description of monument.[95]

Foucault argued that the *monuments* produced by historians should be studied for themselves, their function in the present society, rather than as *documents* having a valid reference to the historical reality of the past. To study the *monuments* constructed by the historians as documents from the past would be an attempt to reconstitute the 'truth' of history, which does not exist.

Postmodernism has effectively deconstructed modernist history. Hayden White argued that modernist historical narratives were no different from other types of literary artifacts. Modernist historical narratives do not reveal the content of the past, according to White; rather, the content is prefigured and emplotted by the imagination of the historian. Historical narratives do not give access to the past; they give access to the rhetoric of the historian. In addition, according to Derrida, there is not one meaning or closure to the text; the text is open indefinitely to more meanings; the text is unstable and unpredictable. The existence of knowledge itself is in doubt; at least, the

92. Foucault, *Archaeology*, pp. 6-7.
93. Foucault, *Archaeology*, pp. 6-7.
94. Foucault, *Archaeology*, p. 7.
95. Foucault, *Archaeology*, p. 7.

ability to represent the past *via* text is in doubt. Historical narratives do not represent the past (reality), they represent a concept (another signifier). Foucault has problematized the objects of historical inquiry; they are determined by the discursive formation in the discipline of history, the objects that served the interests of the West. The historians are describing *monuments* they constructed through scientific investigation and the organization of *documents* as the reconstitution of the past. Their narratives should be studied for what they are: discourses produced by networks of power/knowledge relations that function to legitimate the objects of their inquiry; namely, the identity, destiny, aspirations, and experience of the West. Keith Jenkins summarizes the critique of the postmodernists with a swan song to modernist history:

> All histories always have been and always will be aesthetic, figurative discourses; all histories are thus of the aesthetic type postmodernists raise to consciousness. Which is another way of saying that postmodernism is 'the only game in town'. So that in coming to the end of epistemological histories we have as it were come home to ourselves. And so let us accept this homecoming; this happiest of thoughts which can at this point be thrown into the wake: epistemological histories just ought never to have existed; histories ought never to have been modern.[96]

Biblical Historians Respond to Postmodernism

Biblical scholars responded slowly to the postmodern challenge of the 1970s. Then, in the 1980s, they became more conscious of the postmodern challenge, leading up to the 1990s, since which time many biblical scholars became actively engaged with postmodernism. Biblical historians' response in the 1970s began as more of an internal critique rather than as a response to the postmodern challenge taking place outside of the discipline. It began as a challenge to or an assault against the Albrightean synthesis that was forged by Albright and many of his students and followers throughout most of the

---

96. Jenkins, *Refiguring History*, p. 70. However, modernists who believe that the past can be represented *via* historical narratives and do not want to abandon the Enlightenment projects respond strongly against postmodernism. We will see that postcolonial historians also object to postmodernism's deconstruction of history, but for different reasons (more below). Many historians ignore critiques made by Foucault and White and continue to write history as they have been practicing it. A. Munslow suggests three reasons for the limited use of White as well as Foucault: 'First, there is a general suspicion of both Foucault and White because their work questions history as a distinctively empiricist epistemology; second, and flowing from this, we have the professional investment in the existence of history as a distinct profession; and finally...there is a deep antipathy to any model of historical change predicated upon the existence of dominant (and subordinate) tropic prefigurative bases to knowledge—a reconstructionist suspicion of constructionism welded to the irrational fear that somehow literature will steal the soul of history' (Munslow, *Deconstructing History*, p. 150).

twentieth century. Albright marshaled archaeological evidence and extrabiblical written materials to support the biblical claims of the patriarchs and the exodus–conquest account. This secured the base from which to correlate archaeological evidence to support the rest of the biblical claims. There was a broad consensus among biblical scholars on the validity of Albrightean synthesis and methods, especially among English-speaking scholars. Albright's synthesis correlated text and archaeology, but was inclined to disregard problems raised by critical analysis of biblical texts when it appeared that reasonable correlations could be made between the biblical claims and archaeological evidence.[97] It was an event-oriented history that closely followed the claims made in the Bible. The Albrightean synthesis was firmly rooted in modernism; it was a modern *monument* to be viewed and studied within the discipline of biblical studies. In the 1970s, however, the consensus in biblical studies for the Albrightean synthesis began to fragment. During this time, methods and the use of the Bible as a source for reconstructing the history of ancient Israel were examined and questioned. But it was in the late 1980s, I believe, that biblical scholars began to respond more deliberately to the postmodern challenge and to engage more actively with postmodernism.

When John Hayes wrote the article 'The History of the Study of Israelite and Judean History' in 1977, there was no sense of crisis or an awareness of the postmodern challenge to talk about.[98] Hayes mentioned four current approaches employed in reconstructing Israelite history at the time, of which only one was relatively new, namely the 'social-economical' approach, practiced most noticeably by Mendenhall and Gottwald.[99] Hayes did not mention John Van Seters's *Abraham in History and Tradition* and Thomas Thompson's *The Historicity of the Patriarchal Narratives* in his essay.[100] Many

97. This is a major difference from the Alt–Noth School, which insisted on a thoroughgoing critical analysis of the biblical texts as the proper starting point for reconstructing the history of ancient Israel.

98. J.H. Hayes, 'The History of the Study of Israelite and Judean History', in J.H. Hayes and J.M. Miller (eds.), *Israelite and Judaean History* (Philadelphia: Westminster Press, 1977), pp. 1-69.

99. The four 'current approaches' are: (1) the 'orthodox or traditional' approach (this position operates on the assumption that the Bible is of supernatural origin and in its autograph form was totally free of any error; this approach works primarily from the evidence of the biblical text, supplying this with illustrative and supportive material drawn from extrabiblical texts and archaeological data); (2) the 'archaeological approach', represented by Albright and John Bright, which seeks to substantiate much of the biblical data by appealing to external evidence, but which is supportive of the biblical text; (3) the 'traditio-historical' approach, represented by Albrecht Alt and Martin Noth, which seeks to extract 'history' from biblical texts that were formed through long oral and written stages; and (4) the 'social-economical' approach represented by Mendenhall and Gottwald.

100. John Van Seters, *Abraham in History and Tradition* (New Haven: Yale University Press, 1975). Van Seters refuted the position that the social customs depicted in the

biblical scholars now point to these two works as the catalyst that broke the Albrightean consensus, which was firmly rooted in modernism. This started a crisis in the field of the reconstruction of ancient Israel. In the mid-1980s, when John Hayes and J. Maxwell Miller co-wrote *A History of Ancient Israel and Judah*, there was a sort of 'riot' in the field of Old Testament history.[101] On the one hand, Miller and Hayes were accused of being 'biblicists' or 'maximalists' for using the Bible as their primary source in their reconstruction of ancient Israel, and, on the other hand, they were accused of being 'skeptics' or 'minimalists' for questioning the reliability of the Bible as a source for reconstructing ancient Israel. They found themselves caught between two camps of scholars, sometimes called 'maximalists' and 'minimalists', who were sharply divided on the question of how much history the Bible contains and how to go about writing the history of ancient Israel.[102] What is more important about Miller and Hayes's book for the present discussion is that it started a self-examination of methods among biblical scholars. This opened the gate for biblical historians to critique their methods, and in turn to examine every historian's methods of writing history.[103] They began to discuss their approaches to writing history and, as a result, they revealed their methodological assumptions.

The debate between the maximalists and the minimalists hinges on the reliability of the Bible as a source for reconstructing the history of ancient Israel. Moreover, they both believe that it is the other camp that is ideologically motivated and not practicing objective scholarship. In many ways, they are both positivists; each camp claims to be more positivistic than the other. Both camps want to get at the past as it really was. But they differ as to how much

---

patriarchal narratives pointed to the early second millennium and showed that Albright and others read too much into the Nuzi texts to make them compatible with the patriarchal narratives. He concluded that the patriarchal narratives were produced by and for the social and religious community of the period of the Exile and later. Thomas L. Thompson, in his *The Historicity of the Patriarchal Narratives: The Quest for the Historical Abraham* (Berlin: W. de Gruyter, 1974), also challenged the Albrightean consensus and argued that Abraham was a fabrication *ex nihilo* of the early monarchy. He claimed that it was the faith community that created Abraham.

101. J.M. Miller and J.H. Hayes, *A History of Ancient Israel and Judah* (Philadelphia: Westminster Press, 1986).

102. Of course, not all scholars belonged to these two camps, and many scholars do not belong to any camp. It is better to think of the picture as a maximalist–minimalist continuum—with someone like Edwin Yamauchi at the maximalist end and someone like Thomas Thompson at the minimalist end.

103. Marc Brettler, *The Creation of History in Ancient Israel* (London: Routledge, 1995), believes that the focus of biblical historians has shifted from history (what happened in the past) to historiography (how one writes history) in recent debates. Brettler suggests that this shift started with Miller and Hayes's *History*.

history the Bible contains and how to use it or, for some, not to use it, to reconstruct the history of ancient Israel.

How reliable is the Bible as a source for reconstructing Israel's past? The Bible is the primary written source, often the only source, for most of ancient Israel's history. Until the rise of historical criticism in the nineteenth century, most people did not question the reliability of the Bible as a source for reconstructing the past of ancient Israel, accepting the Bible at face value. Most scholars are now involved in critically evaluating the Bible before using it as a source. The 'maximalists' point to all the instances where the Bible got it right and the 'minimalists' point to all the details that the Bible got wrong.[104] The maximalists want to give the Bible the benefit of the doubt if there is no 'hard' evidence to refute its 'facts'. They understand the biblical accounts as sincere attempts to tell the truth about the past. The minimalists, on the other hand, do not want to give the benefit of the doubt to the Bible when there is no 'hard' evidence to support its claims. They understand the biblical accounts as ideologically motivated writings that cannot be relied upon to tell the truth about the past. J. Maxwell Miller maintains a difficult position: 'Of course it is not a reliable source, taken at face value. But neither should it be dismissed as totally irrelevant... The appropriate question is not whether we should use the Hebrew Bible in historical research, but how we should use it.'[105] Miller is a minimalist to the maximalists and a maximalist to the minimalists. There are many other scholars who fall into the 'middle of the road' category.[106]

There is an assumption that the closer the writing is to the actual event, the more reliable is the account of the actual event in the text. The conflict in this

---

104. E. Yamauchi uses the terms 'maximalists' and 'minimalists' extensively in his article, 'The Current State of Old Testament Historiography', in A.R. Millard, J. Hoffmeier, and D.W. Baker (eds.), *Faith, Tradition, and History: Old Testament Historiography in its Near Eastern Context* (Winona Lake, IN: Eisenbrauns, 1994), pp. 1-36. Yamauchi's article is a tour de force against the minimalists, refuting and contesting every point the minimalists use to question the reliability of the Bible. He also makes fourteen general observations about the minimalists' recent attempts to write history. The contributors to this book argue vigorously for the reliability of the Bible as a historical source. On the other hand, the minimalists do not think there is any point in using the Bible as a historical source for the periods prior to the divided kingdoms or even later.

105. J.M. Miller, 'Is it Possible to Write a History of Israel without Relying on the Hebrew Bible?', in D.V. Edelman (ed.), *The Fabric of History: Text, Artifacts and Israel's Past* (JSOTSup, 127; Sheffield: JSOT Press, 1991), pp. 93-102 (100).

106. I believe that there are more scholars in this category than there are die-hard maximalists and minimalists. B. Halpern's assessment 'The State of Israelite History', in Knoppers and McConville (eds.), *Reconsidering Israel and Judah*, pp. 540-65, is more judicial than E. Yamauchi's assessment. Although he is arguing against the minimalists, he would be considered a minimalist sympathizer by the maximalists for making too many 'compromises'.

case is between the maximalists, who want to date the texts earlier (i.e. closer to the actual event the text is relating), and the minimalists, who want to date the texts later (i.e. closer to the time of the actual writing of the text).[107] The maximalists do not contend that the writing process took place after the actual events by many years. But they argue that the final redactors had access to older documents or oral traditions that date back to the actual events. The minimalists argue that the biblical accounts were created by authors using their imagination as much as older documents. This debate affects the question of the reliability of the Bible if we hold to the assumption that the closer the text is to the actual event, the more reliable it is. The minimalists, by assigning late dates to the composition of the historical writings, believe that one cannot rely on the Bible for knowledge of the past prior to the time of writing.[108] Some argue that most of Israel's history is a fictitious invention of an author far removed from the time during which the events were supposed to have taken place. The maximalists, by dating closer to the events, often using source, form, and tradition-history criticisms to isolate the sources and the traditions used by the author, believe that one can rely on the Bible for a knowledge of the past prior to the final form of the writing.

The question of the reliability of the Bible as a source for reconstructing the history of ancient Israel also depends on the question of the genre of writings in the Bible that appear to be historical. Are they history, based on epistemology, or fiction, based on aesthetics? Is DH, which gives a continuous narrative of past events written in chronological order, a fictionalized history or a historicized fiction? If one understands it as a historical work, it is assumed that it contains much history that is useful in reconstructing ancient Israel's past. If one understands it as fiction, an invention of an author, it is assumed that it contains no reliable history that can be used for writing a history of ancient Israel. Therefore, the question of genre was an important one for some time.

Previous generations of scholars, trained in historical criticism, understood DH as a historical work containing facts and details of Israel's past. It is not that they did not recognize the literary aspects of the biblical historical accounts, but they did believe that there were historical facts embedded in the telling of stories/narratives or that the narrative built its stories around factual events. Understanding the Bible as a historical work, the maximalists continued to search for historical facts and to understand the biblical narratives as an accurate representation of ancient Israel. They did not question the

---

107. One of Yamauchi's fourteen observations is that 'the Hebrew Scriptures have been rejected as historical sources because their composition is later than the events they purport to describe' ('The Current State', p. 25).

108. Some, among them Thomas Thompson, date them to as late as the Hellenistic period.

referentiality of historical writing to reality (the past). Thus, they believed that, to use the often-used metaphor, the Bible was a window to ancient Israel; there was a world (Israel) 'behind' the text (the Bible) that scholars can discover. However, some scholars, using theories and techniques borrowed from the discipline of literature, began to analyze and to interpret even historical works as literature, as a story. The referentiality of the historical works to the reality 'behind' the text was questioned. The literary critics argued that the text constructs its own world, the world 'within' the text, which does not necessarily correspond to reality. In addition, the minimalists argue that even the historical narratives are basically ideologically driven. Therefore, they argued that it was not appropriate to search for historical facts in fictitious accounts. However, the sharp division between historical writings and literary writings that was maintained for generations of scholars has been blurred in recent years.[109] The dichotomy between history and story has been questioned for some time now. A narrative that has been highly stylized or that uses narrative techniques is not disqualified from being a historical source. Historical reliability and creative representation are not mutually exclusive.[110]

If the Bible is used as the primary source for reconstructing the history of ancient Israel, then it limits what methods biblical scholars can use for reconstructing Israel's past. It subordinates other evidence to the biblical witness. The Albrightean methodology, which reconstructs Israel's history based on the correlation of archaeological evidence with the Bible, has been thoroughly criticized by many, including Albright's students.[111] Now almost all agree

109. One should not assume that the maximalists use historical criticism and the minimalists use literary criticism exclusively. They use both criticisms to some extent. The issue is not whether one is using one method or the other, but to which genre one believes DH belongs.

110. See Long, *The Art of Biblical History*, for a helpful discussion on literary aspects of historical writings. Long uses Hayden White's insight that historical narratives are literary artifacts to argue that biblical narratives 'represent' the past, and are thus deserving our trust. They present the reliability of the Bible as a case of trust, whether or not the Bible as a witness is trustworthy. The question posed is a matter of faith. Philip R. Davies, *In Search of 'Ancient Israel'* (JSOTSup, 148; Sheffield: JSOT Press, 1992), understands Hayden White's critique in a very different way. Davies argues that if all stories, including historiography, are fiction, then they are all ideological since literature is a form of persuasive communication (rhetoric, as White has argued). 'If so, historiography, as a genre of literature, is also ideology' (p. 13). Then 'texts cannot reproduce reality except as a textual artifact, crafted by rhetoric and limited by the boundaries of language' (p. 15). In other words, biblical literature 'represents' biblical Israel (a literary construct), not the Israel of history.

111. See J.M. Miller, 'W.F. Albright and Historical Reconstruction', *BA* 42 (1979), pp. 37-47; W. Dever, 'Syro-Palestinian and Biblical Archaeology', in G.M. Tucker (ed.), *The Hebrew Bible and its Modern Interpreters* (Philadelphia: Fortress Press, 1985), pp. 31-74.

that one cannot use archaeological evidence simply to verify and corroborate the Bible.[112] This is not what the Albrightean method was supposed to be, but in some cases it turned out that way. However, the method of evaluating the Bible first and using it to shed light on other available sources (external textual materials as well as nonwritten artifacts) is still valid for many biblical scholars. Miller defends this position by answering the question 'Is it possible to write a history of Israel without relying on the Hebrew Bible?' with an emphatic no. 'While the nonwritten artifacts provide information about general socioeconomic conditions, settlement patterns, life styles and the like, they are silent regarding specific people and events.'[113] Miller continues, 'The artifacts are still silent unless interpreted in the light of written documents. And the interpreting document in this case is the Bible.'[114] Miller is convinced that any reconstruction of Israel's history must begin with the literary text, albeit only after a systematic literary-critical analysis of the biblical material (following Alt and Noth). This approach is clearly demonstrated in Miller and Hayes's *A History of Ancient Israel and Judah*.

Miller and Hayes's work is in many ways a crowning achievement of the historical-critical approach. Their approach to writing a history of Israel is evident in their sources. Miller and Hayes used four types of sources in their reconstruction of ancient Israel: biblical texts, nonbiblical texts, nonwritten archaeological remains, and analogical data (contemporary social-scientific models). Miller and Hayes extracted as much historical information as is judiciously possible from the biblical texts. Most of the nonbiblical texts Miller and Hayes used were official inscriptions from the great powers of the ancient Near East: Assyria, Babylon, and Egypt. Archaeological evidence was used to shed more light on the background of biblical accounts and to modify and supplement or to reject the textual accounts. But they used sociological models minimally. Many reviewers of their book criticized them for the limited use or neglect of other sources and methods: for example, the *Annales* School's three-level structural analysis of history and specific social-scientific models such as the ancients' folk model and kinship model.[115] The overall weakness the reviewers were pointing out was that Miller and Hayes were too narrow in their approach; they were in fact continuing traditional

---

112. But see W.C. Kaiser's recently published *A History of Israel: From the Bronze Age to the Jewish Wars* (Nashville: Broadman & Holman, 1998), as an example of this approach.

113. Miller, 'Is it Possible?', p. 97.

114. Miller, 'Is it Possible?', p. 97.

115. The political history or the event-oriented layer of history is seen in the context of more slowly changing socio-economical and cultural structures, and both layers must be grounded in the 'long duration' of a very slowly changing environment (climate, geography, demographics).

historiography—a narrative of political events of a nation or people told through the great deeds of great men, using official documents.

However, there were a number of scholars who argued that Israel's history should begin with the archaeological evidence. There were basically two reasons for this shift—the question of the reliability of the Bible and the question of ideology. These scholars believed that the Bible was too unreliable as a basis for the history of ancient Israel. They also believed that the Bible had been so thoroughly tainted with the ideologies of the ancient writers and modern scholars that it needed to be set aside.[116] They argued that the archaeological evidence should be interpreted independently of the Bible because it was more reliable and not tainted with ideologies. They pointed out that archaeology in Syria-Palestine in previous generations, so-called Biblical Archaeology, had functioned as a handmaid of biblical study—excavating possible biblical sites and limited to the centers of habitations, always looking for possible connections with the Bible.[117] Therefore, scholars called for a new archaeology that was independent of biblical studies, that was far broader in many aspects—excavating in a number of sites not related to the Bible, investigating the peripherals instead of being limited to the centers, and looking more for social data than event-oriented data. They used more inclusive terms like 'Palestinian', 'Syro-Palestinian' or 'Near Eastern archaeology' to describe this 'new' archaeology. They believed that this method would give a more accurate picture of ancient Palestine (Israel and its neighbors). This approach was demonstrated in Ahlström's *The History of Ancient Palestine*.[118]

In effect, it came down to the issue of which evidence, the textual or the nonwritten evidence, should come first in reconstructing Israel's past. This

---

116. K.W. Whitelam, 'Recreating the History of Israel', *JSOT* 35 (1986), pp. 45-70 (52). Giovanni Garbini argues in *History and Ideology in Ancient Israel* (New York: Crossroad, 1988), that histories of ancient Israel written in the 1970s and 1980s are written by theologians rather than historians, thereby continuing the theological assertions made by previous generation of theologians who wrote histories of ancient Israel. Garbini argues that in addition to the theological reflections offered by the 'historians' of ancient Israel, the Old Testament itself is a series of theological reflections by Israel on its history rather than the actual history of Israel: 'it must be stressed that these are not so much historical reflections (though sometimes these are there, too) as theological reflections. That means that the value of the Old Testament as a historical source is very relative and that a particular piece of information cannot be considered reliable until it has been confirmed from elsewhere' (p. 16).

117. This was expressed even in the 1970s. See R.J. Coggins, 'History and Story in Old Testament Study', *JSOT* 11 (1979), pp. 36-46.

118. G. Ahlström, *The History of Ancient Palestine: From the Palaeolithic Period to Alexander's Conquest* (Minneapolis: Fortress Press, 1993). The manuscript was completed in the same year as the publication of Miller and Hayes's *History*.

made an enormous difference in the kind of history a scholar wrote. If one chose to go with the Bible first, the kind of history one wrote was framed by the biblical narrative, especially the chronological scheme, and the archaeological data were used to correct or to supplement the biblical account. If one chose to go with the archaeological evidence first, the kind of history one wrote was not an event-oriented history and the Bible was used to fill in some details, but no more than that. Ahlström's work demonstrated this approach well. His sources were literary remains (including the Bible), archaeological remains, geography, and climate. He was closer to Robert Coote and Keith Whitelam and other scholars who use the methodologies developed by the *Annales* School. Coote and Whitelam also argued for the priority of the interpretation of archaeological data over the interpretation of biblical texts as a starting point.[119] They related settlement patterns (part of the first-level structure) with the middle-level structures (interregional trade, economic and social relations) and concluded that the emergence of Israel was a continuum, rather than a distinctive stage. Coote and Whitelam limited their study to the emergence of Israel, but Ahlström wanted to rely on archaeological evidence as the main source for his reconstruction of Palestinian history from the Paleolithic period to Alexander the Great.

Ahlström's book had a mixed reception. He relied heavily on the biblical texts in reconstructing periods that lacked archaeological evidence, thus proving Miller right in the sense that biblical historians cannot help but use the Bible as a hermeneutical key for interpreting archaeological evidence. Another criticism was that Ahlström's history was still a traditional history, not very different from Miller and Hayes's history. John Bartlett's review of Ahlström's book was telling: 'his own resultant "history" is still very much based on kings and battles and near eastern politics, and shows much less concern with the recently more fashionable matters of ancient society, anthropology, and ecology'.[120] However, Ahlström was a pioneer in writing the history of Palestine as a regional history rather than as a history of a particular people (Israel).

This stage was more of an internal correction and modification of the practice of writing history that had been going on for two centuries; the maximalists and the minimalists debated the reliability of the Bible as a source for reconstructing the history of ancient Israel. A significant challenge to writing history came from those who advocated writing history by using nonbiblical evidence as a starting point; they in fact changed biblical archaeology to a more inclusive Syro-Palestinian or Near Eastern archaeology. They were still in the vein of positivism, trying to improve their way toward the truth. It was

---

119. R.B. Coote and K.W. Whitelam, *The Emergence of Early Israel in Historical Perspective* (The Social World of Biblical Antiquity, 5; Sheffield: Almond Press, 1987).

120. J. Bartlett, Review of G.W. Ahlström, *PEQ* 127 (1995), pp. 70-71.

when biblical historians began to question the function of the history of ancient Israel, rather than to question how to reconstruct ancient Israel most accurately, that biblical scholars began to engage with postmodernism more consciously.

We are now at another stage in terms of biblical historians' engagement with the postmodern challenge. In this stage of the response to postmodernism, the question is not 'what kind of history?' or 'how much of the Bible should be used?', but rather whether it is even possible to write a history of ancient Israel.[121] Some are wondering whether the discipline of biblical history will survive the crisis.[122] But some still maintain that postmodernism is no more than an academic 'fad' and not a condition of the contemporary world.[123]

Recently there has been a conscious effort among biblical historians to engage with postmodernism. David Clines believes that it is detrimental to biblical scholars if they do not engage with postmodernism:

> In my view, it will be the end of biblical studies as an intellectual discipline if we do not interact with the intellectual currents of thought of our time, and if we pretend that doing the same things as we have for a century or more, with refinements and improvements, is addressing our contemporary cultural and intellectual situation in the slightest. If we dismiss postmodernism as a fashion, a fetish, an aberration, we doom our own subject to extinction.[124]

Clines defines postmodernism as 'the modern conscious of itself' and argues that to engage with postmodernism is to examine the very act of writing the history of ancient Israel by biblical historians, that is, to look at the

---

121. For example, L. Grabbe (ed.), *Can a 'History of Israel' Be Written?* (JSOTSup, 245; Sheffield: Sheffield Academic Press, 1997). An ASOR plenary session was titled 'Can a History of Ancient Israel Be Written?' at Denver in 2001.

122. For example, Philip R. Davies predicts a grim future for biblical history if it neglects to deal with postmodernism in 'The Future of "Biblical History"', in David J.A. Clines and Stephen D. Moore (eds.), *Auguries: The Jubilee Volume of the Sheffield Department of Biblical Studies* (JSOTSup, 269; Sheffield: Sheffield Academic Press, 1998), pp. 126-41.

123. Frank M. Cross and others characterize the 'minimalist' movement as a postmodern 'fad' and are surprised that it has lasted this long, predicting that it will last no more than five to ten years in Hershel Shanks's article, 'The Age of BAR: Scholars Talk about how the Field has Changed', *BARev* 27/2 (2001), pp. 21-35. However, Philip R. Davies in his article, 'Biblical Studies in a Postmodern Age', *Jian Dao* 7 (1997), pp. 37-55, remarks that some areas of biblical studies are not yet consciously affected by the age of postmodernism and 'many biblical scholars, mostly of the older generation, will remain modernists until they die' (p. 42). Davies maintains that 'the discipline will not remain in a time-capsule insulated from developments in other humanities. It will become, and indeed is becoming, postmodern' (p. 42).

124. D.J.A. Clines, 'The Postmodern Adventure in Biblical Studies', in Clines and Moore (eds.), *Auguries*, pp. 276-91 (290).

'buried' assumptions that are shared by biblical historians.[125] It is more than a conscious effort to discuss one's methods; it is a conscious effort to understand why biblical historians do what they do and for what purpose.

David Clines describes an important development in the study of biblical history as a collapse of the distinction between history and historiography:

> Instead of a body of indisputable, retrievable facts, history becomes textualized; that is, it becomes a group of linguistic traces that can be recalled, but which are always mediated through the historian/interpreter. There is no history or at least no history accessible to us, that is not already history-writing. And every attempt at a history of Israel, for example, is the creation of a literary text. The history of Israel is not the background to the literature of the Old Testament, but the name for a type of literature of our own time.[126]

We can see that Clines has been informed by Hayden White, but less by Michel Foucault. Clines sees the history of Israel as a type of literature of our own time, but he does not deal with the power aspect or the function of historiography.

Biblical scholars do more than textualize history; that is, they create history as a literary imagination. According to Foucault, it is discourse as knowledge/power that is embedded in networks of practices and institutions and that functions to legitimate the knowledge it produces and the network of powers in which it is formed. The role of the intellectual in society is critical in legitimizing the validity of a text (knowledge) and its function (power).

It was Keith W. Whitelam's book, *The Invention of Ancient Israel*, which consciously examined the discipline of writing the history of ancient Israel in terms of discourses as functions of power/knowledge produced by networks of power relations. Whitelam argues:

> There exists, then, what we might term a discourse of biblical studies which is a powerful, interlocking network of ideas and assertions believed by its practitioners to be the reasonable results of objective scholarship while masking the realities of an exercise of power.[127]

Whitelam spells out what other scholars have implied before his work. He openly discusses the political contexts of biblical scholars and 'buried' assumptions in a discourse of biblical studies. Whitelam's book, in my opinion, marks a conscious turning away from asking questions about the meaning of the text and methods of scholars to asking questions about the function of the discourse. He turns away from asking questions about the reliability of the Bible as a source for reconstructing a history of ancient Israel toward asking questions of the function of the history of ancient Israel as constructed

---

125. Clines, 'Postmodern Adventure', p. 277.
126. Clines, 'Postmodern Adventure', p. 284.
127. Whitelam, *Invention*, p. 4.

by biblical scholars.[128] He argues that the history of ancient Israel is a discourse produced by scholars and institutions embedded within networks of assumptions and power relations. In some ways the debate between the maximalists and the minimalists, which has not abated but rather intensified in recent years, testifies to the importance of this 'turn' that biblical studies seems to be making.[129] Whitelam believes that 'the heated reaction to the revisionism of the late 1980s and early 1990s signals that the consensus is beginning to fracture, that the master narrative is becoming increasingly difficult to maintain and defend'.[130] Whitelam attributes the intensity of the debate between scholars to 'the political, cultural and religious implications of the constructions of ancient Israel'.[131] It is the matrix of implications in which the scholars are situated that Whitelam wants to investigate.

Whitelam claims that biblical scholars have been shielded by a belief in objective scholarship from examining the role they play in their own political contexts. What Whitelam questions in his book is that the ancient Israel that biblical studies have constructed owes as much to the political context of the scholars as to the empirical data. Thus, he argues that the history writing of ancient Israel is a political act. After giving examples of the connection

128. Whitelam owes much to Philip R. Davies's *In Search of 'Ancient Israel'*. Davies differentiates three 'Israels': (1) biblical Israel is a literary construction of biblical literature, and as a literary artifact, it is an ideological construct; (2) historical Israel consists of the inhabitants of the northern Palestinian highlands who formed a political entity commonly called the northern kingdom and left their traces in the soil of Palestine over a couple of centuries; and (3) 'ancient Israel' is what scholars have constructed out of an amalgamation of the two others. Davies argues that 'this "ancient Israel"…is both literary, in that it takes its point of departure from biblical Israel, and historical, in that scholars treat of its interaction with other states, its political evolution, and so on. But it is a mixture of two different sorts of entities, and as such is something *sui generis*; neither biblical nor historical. It is the result, to be precise, of taking a literary construct and making it the object of historical investigation' (p. 17). To make the situation more complicated, or to complete the circularity of biblical scholarship, scholars assume that 'ancient Israel' (their own literary-historical hybrid construct) is the producer of the biblical literature—'in other words as the creator of the biblical Israel' (p. 17). Davies claims: '"Ancient Israel" was never a *hypothesis*, a possibility to be reconstructed. It was always taken for granted. And the onus of proof has always been on those who doubted the validity of this procedure, who questioned the hypothesis, who were accused of scepticism and hypercriticism, negativism, minimalism, cynicism' (pp. 24-25). The maximalists would argue that 'ancient Israel' is, if not an accurate representation of the historical Israel, then at least the best representation of the historical Israel we have.

129. A heated dialogue between Philip R. Davies and W. Dever exemplifies this situation; see Philip R. Davies, 'What Separates a Minimalist from a Maximalist? Not Much', *BARev* 26 (2000), pp. 24-27, 72-73, and W. Dever, 'Save Us from Postmodern Malarkey', *BARev* 26 (2000), pp. 28-35, 68-69.

130. Whitelam, *Invention*, p. 227.

131. Whitelam, *Invention*, p. 11.

between politics and scholarship (construction of the past as a political act), Whitelam claims that 'the construction of Israel's past in particular carries important political consequences which cannot be ignored'.[132] Whitelam's goal is for biblical scholars to acknowledge and accept the fact that they do not practice scholarship as disinterested historians. He wants to expose the disguise of objective scholarship that separates scholars from their works and knowledge from its context. 'The discourse of biblical studies cloaks the cultural and political factors which shape it by divorcing the production of knowledge from the context in which it is produced.'[133] Whitelam utilizes Foucault's understanding of discourse to summarize this dynamic: 'It is only slowly and begrudgingly recognized that the "virtual self-evidence"…of the network of ideas and assumptions that have sustained the discourse of biblical studies is the product of self-interest and subjectivity'.[134]

Furthermore, Whitelam contends that the discourse of biblical studies has ignored, negated, and silenced the history of ancient 'Palestine' and legitimized the study of ancient Israel, a particular people, as the only scholarly way to study Palestine and its peoples.[135] By such scholarship, biblical historians have participated in supporting, wittingly or unwittingly, the Western narratives of nationhood and later the formation of modern Israel. He implicates just about every scholar, including himself, as a participant in the discourse of legitimizing ancient Israel and a Western metanarrative (modern Israel) at the expense of excluding the histories of other Palestinian peoples. After unmasking the realities of the close relationship between scholarship and politics, Whitelam calls for a different 'location' for the history of Palestine: 'If Palestinian history is to be freed from the tyranny of the discourse of biblical studies, it must be freed from the theological constraints which have governed the history of the region'.[136]

However, Philip Davies does not think this is possible. He believes that it is time to abandon the idea that there is a history of ancient Palestine. He

---

132. Whitelam, *Invention*, p. 23.
133. Whitelam, *Invention*, p. 26.
134. Whitelam, *Invention*, p. 227.
135. This is a problematic term in today's political context. Whitelam's 'Palestine' is a term for the land-area in which the present Israel and Palestinians are situated, that is, the land of the ancient Israelites, Philistines, Ammonites, Moabites, Canaanites, and other indigenous populations in that area. However, it cannot be a neutral term under present circumstances.
136. Whitelam, *Invention*, p. 235. I will continue to discuss Whitelam's call for a history of ancient Palestine when I examine how biblical scholars are responding to the postcolonial critique. At this point, it suffices to note that Whitelam is part of a shift in biblical studies that is characterized by a conscious engagement with postmodernism, which includes investigating the matrix of power relations in biblical studies that produces discourses on the history of ancient Israel.

argues that 'because history is narrative it cannot be "history". It will always be *someone's* history'.[137] He argues that histories do not exist independently: 'they are stories, and all stories have tellers. Histories do not converge, they diverge. There is no master-narrative that represents *the* history of ancient Palestine; there are more inclusive narratives and less inclusive ones, but that is all.'[138] Davies reminds us that it would be a mistake to believe that biblical historians are doing 'any kind of objective history merely on the basis of modifying or even rejecting the biblical story'.[139] Therefore, Davies suggests that what we can hope for in a postmodern age is to understand the Old Testament for what it is: 'the Old Testament does not and cannot give us any kind of authorized account of history. Its detailed and factual accuracy is less of an issue than its ideological character. And that it shares with all histories.'[140] And biblical scholarship needs to recognize that 'the history told by scholarship is important when it recognizes no privilege, when it refuses to sanction any particular story but balances agreed data and the diverging stories that exploit these data'.[141] Finally, Davies hopes that in a postmodern world both the great Western myths and the biblical narrative from which they grow, which have enjoyed privilege and power over other stories, 'will be relativized to the status of powerful and important stories, but no more'.[142]

The Postcolonial Critique of Western History

We have seen that biblical historians have been actively engaged with postmodernism in recent years; however, in my opinion, they have so far resisted engaging with postcolonialism. Postcolonial historians use the thoughts and critiques of postmodernism, especially Foucault, in their effort to write 'a history of their own'.[143] There is, however, a sense of dissatisfaction with

---

137. Davies, 'Biblical Studies', p. 48. In other words, history in narrative form is a literary artifact (story). As a story, it is couched in a rhetorical situation: there is the speaker/writer who wants to communicate a certain message. It is always someone's story. Davies states that there is a Christian history of Israel and a Zionist history of Israel, and even a space for a history the modern Palestinians can tell, but, he asks, who will tell the history of other peoples of Palestine—the Phoenicians, Hurrians, Philistines?

138. Davies, 'Biblical Studies', p. 49.

139. Davies, 'Biblical Studies', p. 48.

140. Davies, 'Biblical Studies', p. 49.

141. Davies, 'Biblical Studies', p. 49. Davies notes that this will be a very difficult thing to do because 'for Western culture, the history in the Bible has become part of our own history; we are children of the new Israel, and our God started out by creating the world and then calling Abraham. We can perhaps escape bondage to the literal but the mythical is harder' (p. 49).

142. Davies, 'Biblical Studies', pp. 49-50.

143. I am by no means saying that there is no reaction against postmodernism in biblical studies; there does continue to be a strong reaction and resistance against it. However,

postmodernism because it is in essence the West's self-critique, a self-examination of modernist history that deconstructs not only Europe (more specifically, the White Man) as the subject of history but also the possibility of subjectivity in the process.[144] They are suspicious of postmodernism's deconstruction of history at a time when they are trying authentically to represent themselves as agents of history by articulating their own history, experience, and aspirations. For them, postmodernism is a double-edged sword.[145] Postcolonial historians advocate a different way of writing history that challenges modernist history, without abandoning the project of writing about the past altogether.[146] In spite of the accusation that they are continuing the modernist project, postcolonial historians are committed to writing the history of those whose voices have been marginalized, subjugated, neglected, or lost. They are committed to writing 'a history of their own', knowing that such a project is filled with theoretical and practical problems.

The question the postcolonial historians are struggling with is: How can we write a new history when the only history is that of the West? How can we represent the Other when it has been imagined and constructed as opposite to the Occident? Although Edward Said's analyses in *Orientalism* were instrumental in questioning the assumptions of Western knowledge and exposing its connection to the institution of power, he did not provide an alternative to Orientalism. Young points out that 'an objection to *Orientalism* has always been that it provides no alternative to the phenomenon which it criticizes'.[147] Said has refused to provide an alternative to Orientalism because that would be tantamount to accepting the truth of 'Orient' as the object of knowledge. Said is similar to other postmodernists in that he is able to deconstruct Orientalism, a product of modernism, without providing an alternate form of constructing the Other. Said hopes to eliminate the structure of cultural dominance imposed by the duality of 'the Occident' and 'the Orient'

in my opinion, postmodernism is accepted as part of the legitimate discourse in biblical studies.

144. The Enlightenment challenged the authority of Christianity by offering reason as its god; postmodernism seeks to challenge modernity by deconstructing reason without offering a constructive goal of its own. It wants to discontinue the Enlightenment projects without redressing the damages done by them, thereby leaving the world as it is in its state of inequality. It undermines non-Western peoples' attempt to undo the damages done to them by modernity and their efforts to write their own histories.

145. For example, Appleby *et al.* note that Hayden White's critique that history is a literary artifact 'lends support to those critical of traditional histories which write minorities and women out of the historical record' but also undermines the claims of revisionist historians, including postcolonial historians, that 'their work has substantive validity' (*Knowledge and Postmodernism*, pp. 491-92).

146. Foucault has been very helpful in retrieving subjugated histories for postcolonial historians. But see Spivak's criticism of Foucault below.

147. Young, *White Mythologies*, p. 127.

by showing that the duality is an ideological construct, an illusion (albeit a powerful one), rather than a construct based on epistemology. But denying the existence of this duality (Occident/Orient) does not eliminate it; it needs to be undone.[148] Bart Moore-Gilbert notes that 'Said's text focuses almost exclusively on the discourse and agency of the colonizer' while paying no attention to the agency of the subject peoples 'who were rendered almost entirely passive and silent by conquest'.[149] Other postcolonialists have responded to this lack of attention to the agency of subjugated peoples, and have attempted to represent the Others by writing a different, non-Western history.[150]

The Subaltern Studies scholars have been pioneers in trying to write a different history that represents the 'subaltern'.[151] Dipesh Chakrabarty gives a short history of this group and its project.[152] A group of Indian scholars formed around Ranajit Guha was dissatisfied with the history of nationalism (how India became a nation-state) written from the institutional perspective of the elite classes, whether British or Indian. They decided to write a history of the 'people' by taking into account the contributions of the subaltern, independent of the elite classes. Thus the goal of the project, *Subaltern Studies*,

148. This argument is similar to the argument made by those who believe that race is an ideological construct: since race is an ideological construct, an illusion, therefore fighting against racism perpetuates the illusion rather than eliminating it. The problem is that the concept of race has a long and powerful effect in the West, in particular in American society, and by ignoring its historical and structural legacies that are interwoven into the very fabric of American society, we are in danger of not addressing these effects and legacies adequately and of freezing racial inequities for the future. See Michael Omi and Howard Winant, 'On the Theoretical Status of the Concept of Race', in J.Y.S. Wu and M. Song (eds.), *Asian American Studies: A Reader* (New York: Rutgers University, 2000), pp. 201-207, for a concise discussion of this issue by two leading scholars on racial formation in the United States.

149. B. Moore-Gilbert, 'Spivak and Bhabha', in Henry Schwartz and Sangeeta Ray (eds.), *A Companion to Postcolonial Studies* (Oxford: Basil Blackwell, 2000), pp. 451-66 (452).

150. Giyatri Spivak and Homi Bhabha represent the second generation of postcolonial scholars who are focusing more on the subjectivity of the colonized rather than on what has been done to the colonized by the colonizer. Robert Young, *Colonial Desire* (London: Routledge, 1995), referred to Spivak, Bhabha, and Said as 'the Holy Trinity' of postcolonial theory.

151. According to B. Ashcroft, G. Griffiths and H. Tiffin, 'Subaltern…is a term adopted by Antonio Gramsci to refer to those groups in society who are subject to the hegemony of the ruling classes… The term has been adapted to post-colonial studies from the work of the Subaltern Studies group of historians, who aimed to promote a systematic discussion of subaltern themes in South Asian Studies' (*Post-Colonial Studies: The Key Concepts* [London: Routledge, 2000], pp. 215-16).

152. D. Chakrabarty, 'A Small History of Subaltern Studies', in Schwartz and Ray (eds.), *A Companion to Postcolonial Studies*, pp. 467-85.

90   *Decolonizing Josiah*

is 'to make the subaltern the maker of his own destiny'.[153] It was 'to produce historical analyses in which the subaltern groups were viewed as the subjects of their own history'.[154] Its rejection of the nation-form of history, which favored the elite classes as the subject, was one difference that lay at the beginnings of 'a new way of theorizing the intellectual agenda for postcolonial histories'.[155] Furthermore, Guha's rejection of all stagist theories of history, especially the view that the non-Western worlds were in a 'primitive' stage (pre-political, pre-capitalistic, pre-nation, etc.; that is, at least one step behind the West) and that the capitalist nations of the West represent the apex of civilization, led to a critical stance toward official nationalism and its historiography as 'narratives of nationalist histories which portrayed nationalist leaders as ushering India and her people out of some kind of "pre-capitalist" stage into a world-historical phase of "bourgeois modernity" replete with the artifacts of democracy, citizenry rights, market economy, and the rule of law'.[156] Instead, Guha favored a postnationalist form of historiography, which is an important characteristic of postcolonial history, one which envisioned the subaltern as the subject of their own history outside of the framework of the nation-state. It was history writing on the side of the subaltern. It was a history of the 'people' rather than that of the nation-state of India.

Chakrabarty also points out that in order to write 'a history of their own', they had to rely on a different archive of 'documents' and a different hermeneutics toward the 'documents'. It is a well-known fact that historical archives are collections of written documents (texts) produced by the ruling classes; therefore, in order to construct an archive of documents of the subaltern, they had to search for other 'archives', relying on other disciplines, such as anthropology, to recover the 'experience' (often nonwritten evidence) of the subaltern. But official documents are also useful in recovering the history of the subaltern if one 'reads' (a metaphor reflecting an active stance) the documents rather than 'listens' (a metaphor reflecting the passive stance of the modernist historian) to them. Chakrabarty summarizes Guha's hermeneutics:

> Guha describes his hermeneutic strategy through the metaphor of 'reading'. The available archives on peasant insurgencies are produced by the counter-insurgency measures of the ruling classes and their armies and police forces. Guha…emphasizes the need for the historian to develop a conscious strategy for 'reading' the archives, not simply for the biases of the elite but for the textual properties of these documents in order to get at the various ways in which elite modes of thought represented the refractory figure of the subaltern

---

153. We will see below when we discuss Gayatri Spivak that there are complex problems and objections to the straightforward project of 'letting the subaltern speak'.
154. Chakrabarty, 'A Small History', p. 472.
155. Chakrabarty, 'A Small History', p. 472.
156. Chakrabarty, 'A Small History', p. 477.

and their practices. Without such a scanning device, Guha argued, historians tended to reproduce the same logic of representation as that used by the elite classes in dominating the subaltern.[157]

Thus, postcolonial history takes seriously the question of archives: What are the archives, who produces them, and how are they used? It pays close attention to the question of the relationship between text and institution, knowledge and power.

In another article, Dipesh Chakrabarty articulates a strategy of writing a new or different history, but he also notes the complications in writing 'a history of their own' different from that of the West.[158] Chakrabarty states that it is more than calling history 'Indian', 'Cambodian', 'Korean', and so on, as if simply replacing the Others of the West as the subject of their own history will produce a different history. He first notes that history is 'a discourse product at the institutional site of the university', and although there are any number of non-Western histories, 'there is a peculiar way in which all these other histories tend to become variations on a master narrative that could be called "the history of Europe"'.[159] Thus, 'Indian' history, or for that matter any other non-Western history, remains in a subordinate position to the history of Europe. The idea of the subaltern representing their own history is problematized by this reality—the place of writing history remains within the academic institutions of the West. The form of history and the object of inquiry are predetermined by the history of the West that understands the nation-state, in particular, as the highest development of civilization; all history is embedded in the matrix of this discourse of the nation-state. He notes this predicament as follows:

> 'History' as a knowledge system is firmly embedded in institutional practices that invoke the nation state at every step—witness the organization and politics of teaching, recruitment, promotions, and publication in history departments, politics that survive the occasional brave and heroic attempts by individual historians to liberate 'history' from the meta-narrative of the nation-state. One only has to ask, for instance: Why is history a compulsory part of education of the modern person in all countries today including those that did quite comfortably without it until as late as the eighteenth century? Why should children all over the world today have to come to terms with a subject called 'history' when we know that this compulsion is neither natural nor ancient? It does not take much imagination to see that the reason for this lies in what European imperialism and third-world nationalism have achieved together: the universalization of the nation-state as the most desirable form of political community.

---

157. Chakrabarty, 'A Small History', p. 479.
158. D. Chakrabarty, 'Postcoloniality and the Artifice of History', in Ashcroft, Griffiths and Tiffin (eds.), *The Post-Colonial Studies Reader*, pp. 383-88.
159. Chakrabarty, 'Postcoloniality', p. 383.

> Nation-states have the capacity to enforce their truth games, and universities, their critical distance notwithstanding, are part of the battery of institutions complicit in the process.[160]

Chakrabarty concludes that even with the best intention of putting the subaltern as the subject of their history, that history 'speaks from within a metanarrative that celebrates the nation-state; and of this metanarrative the theoretical subject can only be a hyperreal "Europe", a "Europe" constructed by the tales that both imperialism and nationalism have told the colonized'.[161] Therefore, 'Indian' history, or any other non-Western history, remains a mimicry of the master discourse of the nation-state.

In order to break out of this predicament, Chakrabarty suggests 'the project of provincializing Europe' as a strategy to write a new or different history.[162] Provincializing of Europe does not mean 'a simplistic, out-of-hand rejection of modernity' as a culture-specific product of Europe that belongs only to European cultures.[163] This project recognizes that European imperialism and third-world nationalisms have been equal partners in the construction of modern 'Europe'. Chakrabarty notes that it is not fair that 'a third-world historian is condemned to knowing "Europe" as the original home of the "modern", whereas the "European" historian does not share a comparable predicament with regard to the pasts of the majority of humankind', but he recognizes that 'Europe' is a piece of global history that all need to acknowledge.[164] Therefore, the project of provincializing Europe is doing '"European" history with our different and often non-European archives' which 'opens up the possibility of a politics and project of alliance between the dominant metropolitan histories and the subaltern peripheral pasts'.[165] It is a hybrid history of postnationality rather than a mimicry of the history of the nation-state.

However, Chakrabarty notes the difficulty of this project. He claims that there are no institutional/structural sites to write over the history of the nation-state 'where collectivities are defined neither by the rituals of citizenship nor by the nightmare of "tradition" that "modernity" creates'.[166] The project of provincializing Europe is restrained by the site of doing history—the institutional site of the university where Europe is the subject of history and the development of the nation-state is the main discourse.[167] Thus, the strategy is

160. Chakrabarty, 'Postcoloniality', pp. 384-85.
161. Chakrabarty, 'Postcoloniality', p. 384.
162. One could call this 'decolonizing' Europe as well.
163. Chakrabarty, 'Postcoloniality', pp. 385-86.
164. Chakrabarty, 'Postcoloniality', p. 385.
165. Chakrabarty, 'Postcoloniality', p. 385.
166. Chakrabarty, 'Postcoloniality', p. 388.
167. One also needs to note that in many places in the subaltern, 'modern' universities were established by the colonial powers.

3. Whose History is it Anyway?   93

to write 'a history that deliberately makes visible, within the very structure of its narrative forms, its own repressive strategies and practices' and to lay bare to its readers 'the reasons why such a predicament is necessarily inescapable' so that 'the world may once again be imagined as radically heterogeneous'.[168] A new form of history reveals what the discourse of the nation-state represses or subjugates in order for the West to be 'modern'.

Gayatri Spivak also problematizes the notion that in order to write 'a history of their own' one simply has to make subalterns the subjects of their own histories, that is, to make the subalterns speak for themselves. She argues that the subalterns cannot speak for themselves, and that they are situated in a position where they can only be known, represented, and spoken for by others.[169] She states that 'in the context of colonial production, the subaltern has no history and cannot speak'.[170] Spivak conceives of the subaltern as the 'silent interlocutor' and suggests that this is 'an inevitable consequence of the fact that in colonial discourse the subjectivity of the subaltern is necessarily constructed according to the terms and norms of the dominant culture which produces the archive in which the historical subaltern exists'.[171] She critiques the assumption held by both the subaltern historians and some postmodernists that the subaltern or the oppressed can speak for themselves. For example, she critiques Foucault for asserting that 'the oppressed, if given the chance… and on the way to solidarity through alliance politics…*can speak and know their conditions*'.[172] Spivak, however, argues that by ascribing a voice to the subaltern, the scholars are in actuality speaking for the subaltern; as a result, they have placed, once again, themselves as the centered subject/agent in respect to marginalized groups.[173] Spivak also sees the same tendency among

---

168. Chakrabarty, 'Postcoloniality', p. 388.

169. Gayatri Spivak, 'Can the Subaltern Speak?', in Patrick Williams and Laura Chrisman (eds.), *Colonial Discourse and Post-colonial Theory* (New York: Columbia University Press, 1994), pp. 66-111. Spivak is concerned especially with Third World women and is influenced most by Derrida. Her argument is not that the women cannot speak, but that 'there is no space from where the subaltern (sexed) subject can speak' (p. 103). Young in his critique of Spivak states that the argument 'that "the subaltern cannot speak" is in many ways Spivak's most far-reaching argument of all, posing radical questions to all orthodox and even subaltern forms of historicization' (*White Mythologies*, p. 164).

170. Spivak, 'Can the Subaltern Speak?', pp. 82-83.

171. Moore-Gilbert, 'Spivak and Bhabha', p. 454.

172. Spivak, 'Can the Subaltern Speak?', p. 78 (italics original).

173. Moore-Gilbert, 'Spivak and Bhabha', p. 453. The postmodernists announced the death of the (white male) subject, but they retained themselves as the center in relationship to the peoples in the margin. By the virtue of their position, they become the subjects again. Spivak also critiques the First World feminists for exploiting 'the Third World woman for the purposes of *self*-constitution, a process which she sees as entirely consistent with the West's long history of appropriations of Oriental cultures' (Moore-Gilbert, 'Spivak and Bhabha', p. 455).

the counter-history of the subaltern historians when they homogenize the oppressed, the poor, or the subaltern as the subject; they are also speaking for the constructed, monolithic, singular subject. Spivak asks whether the subalterns can speak for themselves when it is the historians situated in the First World institution speaking for them.[174] The dilemma is deepened by the fact that the historians construct the subject simply as opposites to the West.[175] Spivak, however, suggests that the possibility of speaking for the subaltern exists not in terms of retrieving a lost historical voice but as an effect of being constructed as a representative of the Other.[176]

Asian-American Historiography

Asian-American historians in particular have been writing 'a history of their own' in North America. Their effort started with the attempt to articulate authentically the subjectivity of a marginalized group in North America by moving away from self-referencing always to the West or being framed within the discourse of Western history. Ronald Takaki's *Strangers from a Different Shore* represents the first comprehensive history of Asian Americans written from the perspective of Asian Americans rather than from the perspective of the dominant group.[177] Takaki attempted to tell 'a history of

---

174. Spivak asks, 'Can the subalten speak? What must the elite do to watch out for the continuing construction of the subaltern?' ('Can the Subaltern Speak?', p. 90).

175. Robert Young explains the dilemma as follows: 'If the man/woman duality as it is currently constituted is simply inverted, then, as many feminists have pointed out, the constitution of "woman" is still determined according to the terms of the original opposition. In a similar way, those who evoke the "nativist" position through a nostalgia for a lost or repressed culture idealize the possibility of that lost origin being recoverable in all its former plentitude without allowing for the fact that the figure of the lost origin, the "other" that the colonizer has repressed, has itself been constructed in terms of the colonizer's own self-image' (*White Mythologies*, p. 168).

176. Spivak's suggestion is similar to Chakrabarty's suggestion above.

177. R. Takaki, *Strangers from a Different Shore: A History of Asian Americans* (New York: Penguin Books, 1989). We need to note that, unfortunately, Asian-American studies, due perhaps to its roots in Marxism and thus a suspicion of religion, has ignored the way Asian Americans have been portrayed in American religious history. If Asian-American historians had examined how they have been portrayed in American religious history, they would have found similar problems to those they had encountered in writing of American (social and political) history. Timothy Tseng, 'Beyond Orientalism and Assimilation: The Asian American as Historical Subject', in Fumitaka Matsuoka and E.S. Fernanez (eds.), *Realizing the America of Our Hearts: Theological Voices of Asian Americans* (St Louis, MO: Chalice Press, 2003), pp. 55-72, argues that Asian Americans have been portrayed in American religious history through the lens of Orientalism. He states that religious studies in general is framed within a Western understanding of 'religion', which developed universal categories that were imposed upon non-Western cultures; as a result, 'much of Euro-American based religious studies have interpreted Asians and Asian Americans through

their own' by looking into 'archives' that held stories and voices of Asian Americans themselves:

> By 'voices' we mean their own words and stories as told in their oral histories, conversations, speeches, soliloquies, and songs, as well as in their own writings—diaries, letters, newspapers, magazines, pamphlets, placards, posters, flyers, court petitions, autobiographies, short stories, novels, and poems.[178]

Takaki wanted to change the perception of Asian Americans as objects that needed to be analyzed in terms of statistics and in terms of what was done to them; he wanted to tell a history in which Asian Americans were viewed as subjects, 'as men and women with minds, wills, and voices'.[179] He wanted to write a history that was full of stories of Asian Americans in their own voices to fill the large void that was left unfilled by the standard history books of America that often overlooked them all together or were filled with stereotypes and myths of Asians as aliens and foreigners.[180] He claims that 'their

---

the lens of Orientalism' (p. 60). For example, although many Asian Americans are Christians, a comparative religious studies approach tends to identify Asian Americans exclusively with Eastern religions. Tseng critiques this approach as follows: 'Their tendency to exclude Asian American Christian narratives, however, reveals an excessive dependency on phenomenology or comparative studies of religion to interpret "Eastern" religions. Consequently, even though they question the dominance of Christianity in "Western" societies, they reproduce the Orientalist tendency to reify difference between East and West... Religious Asians, therefore, are required to be viewed through the lenses of "Eastern" religions' (p. 59). Although the topic of Asian Americans in American religious history is beyond the scope of this work, we need to acknowledge that similar problems exist in how Asian Americans are viewed in American religious history as in American history in general. It would do much good if Asian-American studies scholars paid more attention to American religious history as well.

178. Takaki, *Strangers*, p. 7.
179. Takaki, *Strangers*, pp. 7-8.
180. Timothy Tseng argues that one could see similar problems in American religious historiography. Tseng states that 'to assert that American religious historiography has viewed Asian Americans through Orientalist lenses is to suggest that Asian Americans have been perceived as innately foreign or completely assimilated. This is no less true for American historiography in general and popular perceptions as well' ('Beyond Orientalism and Assimilation', p. 58). It is easy to understand how the Orientalist construct of Asian Americans as the Other (people of Eastern religions) has negated the subjectivity of Asian Americans from American religious history. But it is more difficult to see how the assimilationist construct of Asian Americans as 'model minority' Christians who were able to assimilate completely into the mainstream negates the subjectivity of Asian Americans. Tseng argues that the assimilationist approach is another reason for Asian-American invisibility in recent American religious historiography (p. 61). He continues that 'though the "traditional" Protestant-centered narratives have broadened in recent years, its disciplinary assumptions remain rooted in an assimilationist or "color-blind" framework. This framework prevents American historians of religion from seeing the Asian American religious people as historical subjects' (p. 61). That is, Asian-American cultural differences

stories can enable us to understand Asians as actors in the making of history and can give us a view from below—the subjective world of the immigrant experience'.[181] Takaki told a history of Asian Americans not as objects for study but as agents of their own destinies. This was perhaps the most important contribution of Takaki's seminal work.

Another objective of Takaki's work was to show the major distinction between the experience of Asian Americans and of Europeans in America. Asian Americans were viewed as 'sojourners', as permanent 'strangers', whereas European immigrants were accepted by American society as 'one of their own'. The experience of Euro-Americans in the United States was shaped by their acceptance by American society, following the assimilation model, but the experience of Asian Americans was shaped by their lack of acceptance by American society, and they were seen as a problem.[182] 'Their experiences here, as they turned out in historical reality, were profoundly different from the experience of European immigrants.'[183] Takaki argued that the permanent marginality of Asian Americans was due to identity politics based on race, which was not good for America as a whole:

> Eurocentric history serves no one. It only shrouds the pluralism that is America and that makes our nation so unique, and thus the possibility of appreciating our rich racial and cultural diversity remains a dream deferred. Actually, as Americans, we come originally from many different shores—Europe, the Americas, Africa, and also Asia.[184]

---

and their religious experience are erased beneath the canopy of white Christianity. Tseng argues that unless enough attention is given to the social and historical experiences of religious Asian Americans, American religious historians risk 'essentializing Asian American subjects or rendering them invisible' (p. 69).

181. Takaki, *Strangers*, p. 8. Takaki's work was an attempt to write a history from 'below'. Takaki was similar to other social historians who argued that so much of history has been written from 'above' (from the perspective of kings and elites) that it had rendered invisible and silent the people 'below'; therefore, they argued for the need to write history from 'below'.

182. Takaki argued that the reason for lack of acceptance was due not only to cultural prejudice, or ethnocentrism, but also to racism. Asian Americans wore a 'racial uniform' that marked them as different from European Americans. We need to acknowledge that Italians, Irish, Jews and many others were victims of prejudice on the part of Anglo-Americans; however, those who had immigrated from Europe were eventually accepted by American society as 'one of their own'.

183. Takaki, *Strangers*, p. 12.

184. Takaki, *Strangers*, p. 7. The experiences of various immigrant groups were different. Even among Asian Americans, Takaki saw different experiences among various groups, depending on when and where each group entered the United States. He covered the Chinese, Japanese, Koreans, Asian Indians, and Filipinos in his book. See Takaki's attempt to write a history of multicultural America that takes into account the differences

He argued that we need to re-vision Asian Americans into the history of multicultural America: 'Their stories belong to our country's history and need to be recorded in our history books, for they reflect the making of America as a nation of immigrants, as a place where men and women came to find a new beginning'.[185]

Takaki's work represents a break from the approaches of history writing in which Asians in America were not viewed as subjects but as objects of study. Sucheng Chan states that scholars have studied Asian Americans and other minority groups in the United States from at least four different perspectives:

> the oldest approach... implies that members of minority groups are deviant or deficient. To become 'normal', they must shed their 'dysfunctional' cultures in order to assimilate into the majority Anglo-American one;[186] the second stance is celebratory and emphasizes the colorful cultural contributions that various immigrant groups or the indigenous peoples of the America have made;[187] the third viewpoint depicts minority groups as victims, exploited in myriad ways

and similarities among various immigrant groups in *A Different Mirror: A History of Multicultural America* (New York: Little, Brown & Company, 1993).

185. Takaki, *Strangers*, p. 10. Takaki's understanding of America as a multicultural society and the place of Asian Americans in it have been criticized. G. Okihiro in particular notes 'liberalism' in Takaki's understanding. Okihiro comments that liberals saw the United States as 'a nation of immigrants, that its political and economic institutions allow for boundless opportunities and freedom among its citizens, and that US history, like the careers of individual immigrants, moves progressively from repression to liberation and from poverty to plenty' (*The Columbia Guide to Asian American History* [New York: Columbia University Press, 2001], p. 203). Okihiro critiques Takaki for following this 'liberal' paradigm. More on this point below.

186. Sucheng Chan, *Asian Americans: An Interpretive History* (Boston: Twayne, 1991), p. xiii. Yu in *Thinking Orientals* characterizes this approach as framing the study of Asians in America as scholars attempt to understand what they perceive as the 'Oriental Problem' in America. Okihiro identifies three interpretive strands in the scholarly literature on Asian Americans (anti-Asianists, liberals, and Asian Americanists). According to Okihiro, it was the anti-Asianists who defined the question and the object of study: 'Anti-Asianists... are those who maintain that Asia and Asian migrants pose threats to the interests of the United States and therefore advocate separation, exclusion, and expulsion. Anti-Asianists direct their writings to white Americans and commonly position themselves as defenders of the American self in opposition to the Asian other' (*Columbia Guide*, p. 194).

187. Chan, *Asian Americans*, p. xiii. Chan remarks that this approach, although heartwarming, does not deal with why 'the different components of America's multiethnic mosaic have not been treated equally' (p. xiii). Okihiro would understand this approach to be similar to that of liberals. Liberals, in response to anti-Asianists' view of Asians as problems, have faith that the assimilation paradigm will also work for Asians as well. They frequently speak for Asians mainly to the white audience as helpless or voiceless victims of anti-Asianists, but they 'rarely concerned themselves with the perspectives and voices' of Asian Americans (*Columbia Guide*, p. 219).

as a result of their low placement within the institutional structure of the United States;[188] the fourth angle of vision sees members of minority groups as agents of history in spite of the many limitations beyond their control.[189]

Takaki's work rejects the first approach and attempts to write according to the fourth approach, but there are traces of the second and third approaches. Chan's work resists writing a history of Asian Americans as 'victims' and attempts to recount 'the history of struggle' in order 'to tell the story from an Asian American point of view'.[190] Chan focuses on 'how Asian immigrants themselves have fought against the discrimination they faced, as they tried to claim a rightful place for themselves in American society'.[191]

Okihiro goes one step further in his attempt to write 'a history of their own'. He breaks away from the standard periodization and other formulaic frameworks in which histories of Asian Americans are narrated.[192] The standard periodization perceives Asian Americans as foreigners who first came to the West in search of gold in 1848. But Okihiro, by starting Asian-American history from the point at which Asians first entered the mindset of Europeans and by placing American history and identity within the global arena, shows that, in fact, it is the West that came to the East, not the other way around. It is the Orientalist constructions that have viewed Asians as permanent 'sojourners' rather than as 'settlers' in the United States. Okihiro also moves away from writing the history of Asian Americans from the perspective of

---

188. Chan, *Asian Americans*, p. xiii. Chan attempts to move away from this approach in her work.

189. Chan, *Asian Americans*, p. xiii. Chan suggests biographies as the most effective way of demonstrating 'agency' on the part of Asian Americans. Thus biographies play an important role in writing Asian-American histories. Okihiro characterizes Asian Americanists as those who are concerned with 'the experience of Asians in America as a legitimate subject quite apart from the problems Asians presumably posed for white Americans' (*Columbia Guide*, p. 219). Okihiro maintains that what distinguishes Asian Americanists from the anti-Asianists and liberals is 'the centrality of Asian Americans as their subject matter, authors, and principal readers' (*Columbia Guide*, p. 219). But Okihiro cautions that the three interpretive strands on Asian Americans are 'neither completely distinctive one from the other nor confined to particular historical periods. Anti-Asianists held liberal ideas about American democracy, liberals sought to recover Asian American voices, and Asian Americanists claimed to speak for their subjects as much as the anti-Asianists and liberals' (*Columbia Guide*, p. 225).

190. Chan, *Asian Americans*, p. xiv.

191. Chan, *Asian Americans*, p. xiv.

192. The standard periodization has three periods, starting with the Chinese coming to the West looking for gold: the Period of Immigration (1848–82), which begins Asian-American history with the founding of gold at Sutter's Mill in 1848 that brought Chinese immigrants; the Period of Exclusion (1882–1965), which begins with the passing of the Chinese Exclusion Act; the Post-Exclusion Period (1965 to the present), which begins with the Immigration Act of 1965.

'Asians as victims' and the approach of writing about Asian 'contributions' to American history and culture.[193] Instead, he argues that the true significance of Asians in American history and culture is that through their struggles for equal rights they have helped build America as a more democratic and just society.[194] Therefore, Okihiro concludes that Asian Americans at the margin of American society were actually at the mainstream of American democracy:

> Although situating itself at the core, the mainstream is not the center that embraces and draws the diverse nation together. Although attributing to itself a singleness of purpose and resolve, the mainstream is neither uniform nor all powerful in its imperialism and hegemony. Although casting the periphery beyond the bounds of civility and religion, the mainstream derives its identity, its integrity, from its representation of its Other. And despite its authorship of the central tenets of democracy, the mainstream has been silent on the publication of its creed. In fact, the margin has held the nation together with its expansive reach; the margin has tested and ensured the guarantees of citizenship; and the margin has been the true defender of American democracy, equality, and liberty. From that vantage, we can see the margin as mainstream.[195]

Asian Americans' writing 'a history of their own' for Asian Americans is not an easy task. They have to retrieve 'archives' that articulate 'voices' of Asian Americans.[196] They need institutional sites to produce knowledge about

193. Okihiro notes that the 'Asians as victims' approach has celebrated what injustice has happened to them, especially 'as objects of exclusion in the nineteenth-century anti-Chinese movement and as "Americans betrayed" in the twentieth-century concentration camps' (*Margins and Mainstreams*, p. 152). The 'contributions' approach highlights Asian labor in the building of America, but 'when compared with the centrality of the founding fathers, the framers of the Constitution, the shapers of American letters and culture, the movers and shakers in the worlds of industry and government, Asian contributions seem trivial, and rightfully so' (*Margins and Mainstreams*, p. 154).

194. R. Lee agrees with this point: 'The historical struggle of Asian Americans to achieve full citizenship in the United States has challenged and revivified every aspect of citizenship in a liberal democracy, including the right of entry and naturalization, equal protection and economic rights, and the right to participate fully in the public culture' (*Orientals: Asian Americans in Popular Culture* [Philadelphia: Temple University Press, 1999], p. 13).

195. Okihiro, *Margins and Mainstreams*, p. 175.

196. Tseng states the difficulty in retrieving religious 'voices' from Asian-American religious history as well: 'The hermeneutical labor of the historian of Asian American religion is a daunting challenge because of the pervasive presence of orientalist and assimilationist assumptions in American society today and the paucity of Asian American religious historians' ('Beyond Orientalism and Assimilation', p. 70). Tseng concludes that the historian of Asian-American history needs to go beyond orientalism and assimilation in order to retrieve the social and historical experiences of religious Asian Americans. He suggests three directions that will more effectively include the Asian-American subject in American religious history: (a) 'the retrieval of religious Asian American subject will

Asian Americans that is different from the standard history of America in which Asian Americans are overlooked or misrepresented, or framed within the discourse of the nation-state of the US. They need to construct different periodizations and frameworks in which the agency of Asian Americans can be expressed. Asian-American historians are writing 'a history of their own' in North America in order authentically to articulate the subjectivity of a marginalized group in the United States by moving away from always self-referencing the West or being framed within the discourse of modernist national history. They are ascribing the experience, history, aspirations, and destinies of Asian Americans in 'a history of their own'. But this is not done only to change Asian Americans; it is to change America as a whole, to envision an alternate America:

> Asian American culture is the site of more than critical negation of the US nation: It is a site that shifts and marks alternatives to the national terrain by occupying other spaces, imagining different narratives and critical historiographies, and enacting practices that give rise to new forms of subjectivity and new ways of questioning the government of human life by the national state.[197]

The Response to the Postcolonial Critique

Postcolonial historians, including Asian-American historians, have criticized not only modernist history that subjugates the experience and history of non-Western peoples, but also the postmodernist deconstruction of writing history altogether. Postcolonial historians want to write 'a history of their own' that authentically expresses the experience and history of non-Western peoples, knowing that there are theoretical and practical problems in doing so. We have seen above that in order to produce history as knowledge there needs to exist institutional sites, archives, scholars, and the object of study. The Western historians had all these elements in place for two centuries to write 'a history of their own'. I am not criticizing this point. However, they have universalized 'a history of their own' as the history of the world, and have incorporated or subjugated histories of others into their own history. Biblical historians have also had all these elements in place for two centuries to construct the history of ancient Israel. Although they are engaging more actively in recent years with postmodernism, which shows the ideological and aesthetic nature of writing the history of ancient Israel, they are slow in

---

require engagement with current Asian American and racialization theorists' (p. 69), (b) an approach that views 'Asian American religious communities and individuals as creative sites and agents of cultural synthesis' (p. 69), and (c) 'American religious historians need to incorporate themes of transnationalism and diaspora in their study of Asian American religious communities' (p. 70).

197. L. Lowe, *Immigrant Acts: On Asian American Cultural Politics* (Durham, NC: Duke University Press, 1996), p. 29.

responding to the postcolonial critique: the West has subjugated histories of non-Western peoples, and as a result, the subject of history is the West and the narrative is inscribed with the experience, history, aspirations, and destiny of the West. Biblical historians have also incorporated the history of Israel as their own. As a result, the subject of ancient Israel is the modern West and the narrative of ancient Israel follows closely the discourse of the history of the West—perhaps, as Keith Whitelam maintains, at the expense of the histories of other peoples of ancient and modern Palestine. The question is: Is it possible to imagine the history of ancient Israel in general and DH in particular outside of the framework of Eurocentric history? Is it possible to envision Josiah within 'a history of their own' away from the discourse of nation-states, away from always referencing the West? Is it possible to envision Josiah within 'a history of their own' similar to the way postcolonial historians, Asian Americans in particular, are writing 'a history of their own'?

It is a common assumption that the history of ancient Israel is an integral part of a history of 'our own', that is, part of Western civilization. The West has incorporated the history of ancient Israel into its own history; in the process, its own experience, history, aspirations, and destiny (in short, their subjectivity) are inscribed in it. Giovanni Garbini, although he critiques the 'historians' of ancient Israel for their theological biases, seems to agree without much reflection with the discourse that links ancient Israel with the history of Europe. He summarizes a 'buried' assumption that Israel is not only part of 'our' history but also plays a critical role in bridging the West (Europe) and the East (Asia):

> The ancient Near East, with its civilization and its history, has been rescued from the oblivion of time by just over a century of European science. With it have appeared the remotest roots of Western civilization: before Paris, Rome, Athens and Jerusalem there were Babylon and Uruk... Historical knowledge of this now long past of ours, i.e. the capacity to recover it, grows progressively less the further back we go in time; the record becomes increasingly more faded the further back we trace the route from West to East, from Europe to Asia. Perhaps it is not just chance that the clearest break between what is well known and what is little known comes half way, around the sixth century BC, when the creative force of this civilization was passing from Asia to Europe. In the trajectory so far followed by our civilization, Israel is the central point, the link between Asia and Europe... This was the historical function of Israel.[198]

Garbini acknowledges that the preservation of the writings by the 'Hebrews' is an exception in an area in which not much evidence exists; the Syro-Palestine area was culturally a much poorer area in comparison to Mesopotamia and Egypt. His critique is on the way modern historians have

---

198. Garbini, *History and Ideology*, p. 1.

(mis)used the biblical writings rather than a critique of the 'buried' assumption:

> this tradition has been handed over to modern historians who have considered it *de facto* complete, because it has all the essentials: events, historiographical reflection and theological, i.e. philosophical, reflection. For these historians all that needed to be done was to make this history writing their own, and this is what they had done; often to the point of neglecting even the few pieces of information that epigraphy and the Akkadian sources have put at their disposal, so as not to interrupt the smoothness of the historical picture presented by the Bible.[199]

The West embraces the historical picture of the Bible that supports the West's tendency to universalize its claims, values, and views. Daniel Boyarin summarizes this tendency in connection with universalism in Christianity via Paul: given the emphasis of Christianity *via* Paul on universality, the 'genius' of Christianity lies in its concern for all peoples; such concern, however, can easily turn into coercion, and when combined with power, universalism tends toward imperialism, cultural annihilation, even genocide.[200] It is important to emphasize that 'universalism' is not the only historical picture or tendency supported by the Bible. Judaism *via* the rabbis, according to Boyarin, is characterized by particularism: given its emphasis on particularities, the 'genius' of Judaism lies in its ability to leave other people alone; such ability, however, can easily turn into neglect of the other and, when combined with power, particularism tends toward tribal warfare or fascism.[201] The point is that what the West saw in the Bible is not the only picture the Bible portrays and what the West sees in the Bible is influenced by its development as an imperial power. Under the influence of modernist history, the history of ancient Israel constructed by biblical scholars has universalized its claims, values, and visions in conjunction with power in order to enforce its views on others. Davies critiques the tendency to universalize in modernist history:

> Modernist history is...universal; the one story we all share in. All histories intersect, and Western rational civilization, of course, represents the most advanced stage of historical progress and understanding. Thanks to colonialism, the rest of the world can catch up, if it has the innate ability to do so, and if not, could enjoy the benefits of true human civilization in return for some kind of servitude.[202]

What Davies is alluding to is the connection between the discipline of history and Orientalism in biblical studies.

199. Garbini, *History and Ideology*, p. 2.
200. D. Boyarin, *A Radical Jew: Paul and the Politics of Identity* (Berkeley: University of California Press, 1994), pp. 232-36.
201. Boyarin, *A Radical Jew*, pp. 232-36.
202. Davies, 'Biblical Studies', p. 47.

Whitelam consciously examines the connection between the scholarly construct of the history of ancient Israel and Orientalism in the discipline of biblical history. His work makes a deliberate turn away from asking questions about the meaning of the text and the methods of the scholars to questions about the function of the discourse. Whitelam was one of the first openly to discuss the political contexts of biblical scholarship and the 'buried' assumptions in the discourse of biblical studies. It was his work that deliberately engaged with postcolonialism, including Edward Said's critique of Orientalism. Whitelam states: 'Said…has exposed the interconnection between culture and imperialism in the West. What he has to say about great literatures is equally applicable to the role and position of historical narrative.'[203] Whitelam challenges fellow scholars to recognize the context in which biblical studies emerged and was sustained—that it emerged coterminously with Western colonialism. Therefore, he calls on biblical scholars to see 'the need for self-reflection of its practitioners on the development of biblical studies in the context of the colonial enterprise'.[204]

Whitelam argues in Chapter 2 of *The Invention of Ancient Israel* that the culture and history of ancient Palestine have been denied space and time because biblical scholarship has pursued ancient Israel as the only entity within that space–time matrix. Other inhabitants were viewed as 'non-existent' or 'anonymous', thus making the land effectively 'empty' for the Israelites to occupy. The inhabitants were inferior or unruly and did not deserve the right to the land. By contrast, the Israelites were seen as a people with a superior religion and morality and having the ability for self-governance; thus, they were fit to occupy the land. Whitelam argues that this is no more than a retrojection of the modern situation. Whitelam argues that there is a connection between the Zionist movement that saw the land as 'empty' and the inhabitants as 'non-existent' and biblical scholarship's portrayal of the land and its inhabitants prior to the emergence of the Israelites.

> What we have in biblical scholarship from its inception to the present day is the presentation of a land, 'Palestine', without inhabitants, or at the most simply temporary, ephemeral inhabitants, awaiting a people without a land… The foundation of the modern state has dominated scholarship to such an extent that the retrojection of the nation-state into antiquity has provided the vital continuity which helps to justify and legitimize both.[205]

An alternative perspective on the history of the whole region was also denied in regard to time because the time was framed by the chronology of ancient Israel. What came before the emergence of Israel was labeled as the pre-Israelite period, effectively framing all history in the land within the

---

203. Whitelam, *Invention*, p. 22.
204. Whitelam, *Invention*, p. 236.
205. Whitelam, *Invention*, p. 58.

chronology of Israel. Whitelam argues that this practice is rooted in Western metanarrative:

> The discovery of 'deep time' has been at the heart of Western historiographical perception of the evolutionary development of culture and history… The evolutionary scheme which links Babylon, Egypt, and Greece through Israel culminating in the triumph of Western civilization is so deeply ingrained that it pervades such a radical critique of recent histories of ancient Israel in biblical studies… Europe is the subject of this history and it is Europe's conception of time which determined its course.[206]

In Chapter 3 of his book, Whitelam critiques three models of the origin or emergence of Israel that have been standard explanations in biblical studies: the infiltration model (Alt), the conquest model (Albright), and the revolution model (Mendenhall and Gottwald). They all tell how Palestine has been occupied by a distinctive group called Israelites. He argues that all three models were in effect attempts to justify the claim of Palestine for the modern state of Israel. Whitelam wants to show 'various models or theories to be inventions of an imagined past'—an image of ancient Israel that is a retrojection of the Western concept of the nation-state, an image constructed more by Western imagination than empirical data, as biblical scholarship has insisted.[207] He maintains that 'the driving force of biblical studies has been the need to search for ancient Israel as the taproot of Western civilization, a need that has been reinforced by the demands of Christian theology in search of the roots of its own uniqueness in the society which produced the Hebrew Bible'.[208]

In Chapter 5, Whitelam continues his investigation into the reasons behind biblical studies' obsession in searching for ancient Israel: to seek continuities between the West through the modern state of Israel and the ancient Israel of the past. He looks at newer archaeological and historical approaches from the mid-1980s to the early 1990s and reprimands these attempts as being under the sway of the dominant paradigm of the scholars he criticized in Chapter 3, the paradigm that views the whole history of Palestine through the imagined entity of ancient Israel, as constructed by scholars searching for a connection between the Western metanarrative and the past. He believes that the problem lies in focusing on the cross-examination of ancient sources while ignoring 'the political, economic, and theological factors which have shaped contemporary scholarship'.[209] Whitelam believes that the more recent attempts, including his own, to re-evaluate the origin or emergence of Israel have failed

---

206. Whitelam, *Invention*, p. 59.
207. Whitelam, *Invention*, p. 119.
208. Whitelam, *Invention*, p. 119.
209. Whitelam, *Invention*, p. 221.

to develop an alternative construction of ancient Palestine because they are still rooted in an Orientalism that practices 'retrojective' imperialism:

> The enterprise which has begun in the last few years to revise understandings of the history of ancient Israel and to develop Palestinian history as a subject in its own right freed from biblical studies will not be achieved unless this crucial issue of the political nature of the past and the Orientalist nature of the discourse of biblical studies is addressed explicitly... If what I am saying is right, biblical scholarship is guilty of retrojective imperialism, which displaces an otherwise unknown and uncared-for-population in the interests of an ideological construct... Biblical scholarship is not just involved in 'retrojective imperialism', it has collaborated in an act of dispossession, or at the very least, to use Said's phrase, 'passive collaboration' in the act of dispossession.[210]

Therefore, Whitelam calls for a different 'location' for the history of Palestine: 'If Palestinian history is to be freed from the tyranny of the discourse of biblical studies, it must be freed from the theological constraints which have governed the history of the region'.[211]

Whitelam's book was controversial, to say the least, from the moment it was published. Steven W. Holloway remarks that Whitelam's book 'is a timely pioneering study in a minefield that will evoke applause from some quarters and, perhaps, obloquy and death-threats from others'.[212] Sure enough, it created a riot among biblical scholars. There were those who were sympathetic to Whitelam; for example, Graeme Auld notes in his review that Whitelam's book 'could not have been other than controversial' and 'the furore that has immediately followed its publication, and its political rather than academic motivation, nicely confirm' Whitelam's point that there is a close correlation between biblical scholarship and the politics of the biblical scholars.[213] In contrast, William Dever in his very emotional review of

---

210. Whitelam, *Invention*, pp. 221-22. I will look at the importance of placing a discourse of biblical studies within the wider context of Oriental discourse below.

211. Whitelam, *Invention*, p. 235. Whitelam's call for a history of Palestine independent of biblical studies is based upon his argument that as long as the history of Palestine is researched and represented under the auspices of biblical studies, it will continue to be the history of a 'singular people' (Israel) rather than a more broad, inclusive regional history (Palestine) because of the network of buried assumptions that are deeply rooted in biblical studies, which serves as the infrastructure of the discipline of biblical history. I agree with Whitelam that there is a need for a different institutional site for producing knowledge about the history of ancient Palestine. Who knows when this will happen? What I suggest in addition to a different location for a history of ancient Palestine is that biblical scholars need to view the history of ancient Israel from a different historical framework, as 'a history of their own' informed by postcolonial historians.

212. S.W. Holloway, 'Review of Keith Whitelam, *The Invention of Ancient Israel*', *JBL* 117 (1998), pp. 117-19.

213. G. Auld, 'Review of Keith Whitelam, *The Invention of Ancient Israel*', *Expository Times* 108 (1996), pp. 25-26.

Whitelam's book, makes an unfortunate suggestion: 'Personally, I think that it borders on anti-Semitism, as other reviewers have implied'.[214] Dever counters that it is not the biblical scholars' 'ancient Israel' that is an invention, but rather Whitelam's 'Palestinian population in the Iron Age'.[215] He objects strongly to the idea that ideologies and politics had anything to do with the biblical scholars' reconstruction of 'ancient Israel': 'There is indeed a deception going on here; but it is Whitelam's, not that of American and Israeli archaeologists. It is *his* "Israel" that has been "invented", not ours.'[216] He accuses Whitelam of writing a pro-Palestinian political manifesto: 'Let us examine this work as a political manifesto, for that is what it is'.[217] Baruch Levine and Abraham Malamat make a similar conclusion:

> His book comes close to being a political manifesto. If Whitelam is to be regarded as an ideologue, he qualifies as a skilled spokesman. If, however, he is to be evaluated as a scholar, he must be considered to be at least once removed, in his present work, from the realities of the ancient Near East.[218]

In spite of these objections, Whitelam has, overall, provided a valuable service to biblical studies. Just as Miller and Hayes's discussion of their assumptions about methods started self-examination of other scholars' methods in reconstructing ancient Israel, Whitelam's book has opened the door for other scholars to examine and be candid about their own political and ideological assumptions in their work as biblical historians. We need to address the network of buried assumptions that are in operation in contemporary biblical scholarship.

In the midst of name-calling and fury, there are valid objections to Whitelam's book that we need to consider. There are four objections that the reviewers seem to bring up most often. (1) They argue that Whitelam's description of the recent state of the discipline of archaeology is no more than a caricature, and that his critique is obsolete in light of the changes that have occurred in archaeology in recent years. (2) They object to Whitelam's wholesale dismissal of the Bible as a source for reconstructing the history of ancient Israel and his claim that the Bible is implicated in negating the history of ancient Palestine. (3) They object to Whitelam's portrayal of biblical studies as a discipline driven more by ideology and the politics of the practitioners than by the empirical data; they claim that he has misrepresented the well-intended scholars and the works of some of the most significant scholars

---

214. W. Dever, 'Histories and Nonhistories of Ancient Israel', *BASOR* 316 (1999), pp. 89-105 (100).
215. Dever, 'Histories and Nonhistories', p. 94.
216. Dever, 'Histories and Nonhistories', p. 99.
217. Dever, 'Histories and Nonhistories', p. 96.
218. B. Levine and A. Malamat, 'Review of Keith W. Whitelam, *The Invention of Ancient Israel*', *IEJ* 46 (1996), pp. 284-88 (288).

of modern biblical scholarship by portraying their works as politically motivated, ideologically laden, and implicated in Orientalism. (4) Some scholars object to Whitelam's pro-Palestinian bias and imply anti-Semitism in Whitelam's rhetoric. I will summarize below three reviews of Whitelam's book that will better inform what these objections are.

William G. Dever argues that Whitelam's description of archaeology is obsolete. He argues that 'Whitelam's general discussion of archaeology throughout his book is based on "beating the dead horse of biblical archaeology"'.[219] He points out that Whitelam has failed to mention to the readers that the dominant figures of the past who receive the bulk of Whitelam's criticism have long passed away and that their students 'without exception have openly repudiated the "positivist" presuppositions of their mentors, not to mention their somewhat naïve advocacy of "biblical archaeology"'.[220] Then Dever lists 'facts' about the present situation of archaeology that contradict and undermine Whitelam's description of the way archaeology is carried out in biblical studies.[221] Dever is confident that 'fair-minded readers can now readily see how baseless Whitelam's charges of bias are'.[222] He maintains that 'all periods, from the Chalcolithic to the Islamic and Ottoman, were treated with precisely the same objectivity, indeed, with the same methods that would be used in archaeological surveys anywhere in the world'.[223]

Baruch A. Levine and Abraham Malamat object to Whitelam's claim that the Bible has negated the histories of other peoples who inhabited Palestine. They argue that the Bible has provided much information about other peoples in ancient Palestine:

> The Hebrew Bible does not deny the existence or identities of those other people, and is, in fact, a major source of information about where they lived, when they came if they were not indigenous, and which gods they worshiped. Such information pertains to Philistines and Egyptians; to various Canaanites, even Amalekites and Midianites and other little-known peoples; to Ammonites, Edomites and Moabites, not to mention Phoenicians, so called Amorites and Hittites..., Arameans and others.[224]

---

219. Dever, 'Histories and Nonhistories', p. 97.
220. Dever, 'Histories and Nonhistories', p. 97.
221. Dever cites non-Israelite sites that have been excavated in recent years, and states that 'more American archaeological work has been carried out in the last 20 years in Jordan than in Israel' ('Histories and Nonhistories', p. 98); so he questions Whitelam: 'Here we come to the major problem I have with Whitelam's broadside on Syro-Palestinian archaeology. He claims that in their quest for biblical Israel, scholars have neglected the "history of Palestine". Where has he been? We archaeologists, of all persuasions, have been engaged in writing that history for more than 100 years now' ('Histories and Nonhistories', p. 98).
222. Dever, 'Histories and Nonhistories', p. 99.
223. Dever, 'Histories and Nonhistories', p. 99.
224. Levine and Malamat, 'Review', p. 286.

They also object to Whitelam's judgment that as 'a result of the intellectual tendencies that have informed the field', scholars have corroborated in negating or denying the histories of ancient peoples other than the Israelites.[225] They argue that it is the very establishment, which Whitelam criticizes, that 'pioneered regional studies and exhibited a high degree of interest in peoples other than the Israelites'.[226] They also question the connection Whitelam implies between ancient inhabitants of Palestine and the modern Palestinians:

> One is left wondering whom Whitelam has in mind when referring to ignored, ancient 'Palestinians'... All Whitelam does, however, is to suggest a bond between the non-Israelite groups of ancient Palestine *per se* and the modern Palestinians, without adducing a shred of evidence to this effect.[227]

In the end, they dismiss Whitelam's argument as obsolete and his book as a political manifesto.

Iain Provan argues that Whitelam paints 'a portrait of the discipline of biblical studies which is at variance with reality'.[228] He argues that it is not the will to believe (religion) and the will to power (politics), as Whitelam argues, that has directed the discipline, but, rather, it is based on carefully evaluating evidence (detached, objective scholarship). Although Provan believes that Whitelam makes many important points that biblical scholars need to listen to carefully, he finds many of Whitelam's individual arguments unpersuasive. Provan notes that Whitelam, like other minimalists, has dismissed the Bible as a viable source for reconstructing ancient Israel and has brought scholars' ideology and motivations into scholarly discussion. Whitelam has effectively portrayed the discipline as driven more by political ideology than by the evidence. Provan objects to such a portrayal: 'To portray that scholarship as not dealing seriously with evidence because of ideological commitments of one kind or another ("imagining the past"), when in fact the real issue is *which* evidence is to be taken seriously, is very much to misrepresent reality'.[229] Provan maintains that in the past scholars were driven by evidence rather than ideology. Provan wants to stay with the question of what counts as evidence, including the Bible, in reconstructing ancient Israel, rather than focusing on the politics of the scholars. He questions Whitelam

---

225. Levine and Malamat, 'Review', p. 286.
226. Levine and Malamat, 'Review', p. 287.
227. Levine and Malamat, 'Review', p. 286.
228. I.W. Provan, 'The End of (Israel's) History? K.W. Whitelam's *The Invention of Ancient Israel*. A Review Article', *JSS* 42 (1997), pp. 283-300 (287).
229. Provan, 'K.W. Whitelam', p. 296. Provan suggests that Whitelam's description of the biblical discipline is 'closer to the recent political situation in Eastern Europe than of the current situation in Western universities' (p. 293).

and other minimalists for dismissing the Bible as an essential source by deciding in advance that the Bible cannot inform us about ancient Israel:

> *Why*, exactly, does the fact that Hebrew narrative is artistically constructed and ideologically shaped mean that it is somehow less worthy of consideration as source material for modern historiographers than other sorts of data from the past? *Why*, exactly, does the fact that the biblical traditions about the premonarchic period in their current forms are late (if it is conceded for the sake of argument that this is the case) mean that these are not useful for understanding the emergence or origins of Israel? The points need to be argued. I am all for caution in the use of *all* evidence, including biblical texts, in the construction of Israelite history. It is not particularly cautious, however, to decide in advance what these texts can and cannot inform us about.[230]

Provan objects to Whitelam's ambivalent stance on archaeology as well. He notes that Whitelam, like other minimalists, has used a considerable amount of archaeological evidence over against the evidence of text (the Bible), but is not clear on his use of archaeology in his argument:

> It does not seem to me, however, that Whitelam can have it both ways. Either archaeological data in fact do, or they do not, give us the kind of relatively objective picture of the Palestinian past which can be held up beside our ideologically compromised texts and be said to 'show' that the ancient Israel of Bible and scholars is an imagined entity. If he wishes to say that they do not, that 'the historian' is faced with partial texts in every sense of the term, and archaeological data must be understood in the context of the ideologically-loaded narrative in which they are interpreted, then he must explain why archaeology is in a better position than texts to inform us about a 'real' past over against an imagined past—why these particular 'partial texts' are to be preferred to others.[231]

Provan calls for the biblical discipline to move 'the focus away from ideology and back to evidence'.[232] He is not convinced that it is ideology that drives the discipline. Therefore, he maintains that the discussion should return to questions of the evidence (what counts as evidence, how to use it to reconstruct the past). In the end, Provan questions Whitelam's motivation in writing his book: 'So here is a question: is this book really a plea for a more objective picture of Palestinian history, or is it rather a very committed and partisan treatise in favour of the Palestinian cause?'[233]

I agree with the critics that biblical scholarship has changed a great deal since the days of the Albrightean consensus. The critics acknowledged that the old scholarship did focus too much on the Bible and on Israel, but that

---

230. Provan, 'K.W. Whitelam', p. 289.
231. Provan, 'K.W. Whitelam', p. 291.
232. Provan, 'K.W. Whitelam', p. 293.
233. Provan, 'K.W. Whitelam', p. 299.

has changed today. Biblical Archaeology has become Near Eastern Archaeology.[234] The discipline has become far more interdisciplinary than before; thus the history of ancient Israel is not solely in the hands of biblical scholars at all. However, I believe that Whitelam's main point is still correct to a certain extent: the intimate connection between Western imperialism and the production of knowledge in biblical studies needs to be accepted. There are 'buried' assumptions and recurrent themes that continue to shape how the biblical historians' practice of writing history needs to be critiqued. The old concepts and schemes have not ceased to operate. The scholars may not express them, but they operate within the same discourse of biblical studies in which scholars of the past have operated.

Although the notion of absolute objectivity and the notion of completely detached scholarship cannot be defended, I believe that 'relative' objectivity and detached scholarship that are driven by evidence can be defended. Any reconstruction of the past is a combination of evidence and a scholar's hermeneutics that are informed by his/her imaginative faculty and his/her contexts. Any reconstruction of ancient Israel needs to take into account all the evidence that is available to the scholars; any reconstruction should be evaluated on what it uses as evidence and how it uses this evidence in its reconstruction. It is possible to detect a reconstruction that is more a result of a scholar's imagination without considering the evidence than it is an imagination that has been informed by the evidence; we could point to evidence that has not been incorporated or misused. The discipline of biblical studies will be the arbiter in most instances. This institution, like other institutions, will sometimes misuse its power in legitimating certain ideas at the expense of other ideas that do not seem to fit into the overall scheme of things. Nevertheless, it is a place in which scholars can dialogue. I agree with the critics of Whitelam's work that we need to continue to discuss what counts as evidence and how to use it to reconstruct the history of ancient Israel; we should also, however, continue to discuss our political and ideological stances that inform our practises.

I think it is almost impossible to avoid or to silence the Bible when it comes to reconstructing the history of the Palestine region. Of course, we need to recognize the ideological nature of the Bible, but that is no reason to dismiss completely the Bible as a source. I believe that the Bible is an essential source for reconstructing the history of ancient Israel and the whole region of Palestine. The Bible is a rich source of historical facts, but often the facts cannot be extracted from the ideological mine in which they are embedded. If the archaeological evidence is available, it should be taken into account first, although this evidence is also always subject to interpretation. If there

---

234. A telling sign of this shift is the change in name of *Biblical Archaeologist* to *Near Eastern Archaeology* in the year 2000.

is a discrepancy between the archaeological evidence and the biblical text, the scholars should opt for the archaeological evidence over and against the text.

I would also suggest that we need to view the scholars' ideology as part of the evidence. I do not think we should ignore the scholars' ideology and only stick with the evidence. We need to consider the social-political matrix in which the scholars operate in order to detect 'obvious' political and religious *Tendenz* that have affected their reconstructions. There is a discourse within biblical studies that needs to be taken into account. Any reconstruction is based partially on evidence and driven partially by ideology. We need to accept this reality; this is how knowledge is produced. As of now, the history of the region and peoples of Palestine is couched in the history of one particular people and political entity. The fact that institutional networks of power relations that produce knowledge about ancient Israel are implicated in Orientalism needs to be acknowledged as well. This is not to judge the scholars involved in the history of ancient Israel as 'bad' people who conspire to do harm to non-Western peoples, but it is to point out that there are limitations put on these scholars by the institutional networks of power relations within the discipline of biblical studies that determine what sort of knowledge they are expected to produce.

Summary

The story of Josiah is embedded in DH, which is viewed as history in the likeness of Western history. It was Martin Noth who characterized Dtr in the likeness of the modern historian as an honest, objective historian with genuine antiquarian interests, who had access to the state archives that enabled him to write DH as a history of his people. In effect, Noth has placed DH in the tradition of the modern discipline of history, which developed coterminously with Orientalism and nationalism. As a result, DH is viewed as the first and archetypical Western history that describes the creation of an all-Israel state in Palestine as a nation, imagining it as a narration of the original model of the nation which the West imitated and fulfilled. This makes biblical scholars susceptible to making appeals to the discourse of nationalism. It is not that inscribing the experience, aspirations, and destiny (in short, their subjectivity or identity) in their history is wrong. But we must acknowledge that, in general, there are unequal power relations between the West and the rest. This gives clear advantages to the West in establishing legitimate discourses on DH and Josiah. Therefore, we must question the West's tendency to impose their history, including the discourse on DH and Josiah, on others as objective, scientific knowledge of the past that other peoples must adhere to.

However, much has changed in biblical studies since Noth. Biblical historians have undergone an internal critique of the discipline in order to write a more objective, 'scientific' history of ancient Israel. The maximalists and the minimalists have debated the reliability of the Bible as a source for reconstructing the history of ancient Israel; they have discussed the methods biblical historians were using to reconstruct this history. In more recent years, they are engaging more actively and consciously with postmodernism, which has undermined the philosophical foundations and practices of writing history altogether. Some biblical historians are questioning whether it is even possible to write a history of Israel at all. Some are questioning the history of ancient Israel as a scholarly construct that has little relationship with the real Israel of the past. Some are questioning the 'buried' assumptions in biblical studies that are driving the scholarship on ancient Israel.

Postmodernism has challenged the epistemological claim of the modern discipline of history in general and biblical history in particular, but, nevertheless, postcolonial historians are committed to writing 'a history of their own' without appealing to the Western metanarratives. Some biblical scholars are using insights and issues from postcolonialists to critique the practice of writing the history of ancient Israel. But the extent of engagement with postcolonialism among biblical scholars is minimal in comparison to postmodernism. In general, it is business as usual in the scholarship on DH. Even after more than a half century since Noth's book, there are constraints in biblical studies that limit the imagination of biblical scholars to the modernist view of DH. Biblical historians are still practicing history as an epistemological enterprise that seeks to give an accurate, 'scientific' picture of ancient Israel, but they seldom question the link between their production of knowledge and Western imperialism. Biblical historians are not actively engaging with the critique raised by postcolonial historians. History as we know it and practice it in the West is intimately related to Western imperialism and its cultural product, Orientalism. The postcolonial historians, in particular Asian-American historians, are actively involved in writing 'a history of their own' that is independent of the discourse of nationalism. Biblical scholars need to pay attention to postcolonial historians, who are offering a third way of writing history that is different from both the modernists' and the postmodernists'.

The attitude toward DH has not changed: it is part of 'our' history of the West. The first step to decolonize Josiah is to view the history of Josiah as 'their history', not ours. If we are going to inscribe our subjectivity in other people's history, we must acknowledge that this is what we are doing. But the question is: Is it possible to understand DH as a history that is different from the Western modernist history when the Western modernist history is the only form of history biblical studies knows? I believe that postcolonial historians have shown us a way to read Josiah within DH not as part of the history of the West, but as 'a history of their own'. We need to see Josiah as an 'other' and his story as part of an attempt to write a history that is different from that of the history of the nation. We need to attempt to understand Josiah in DH as an attempt authentically to articulate the subjectivity of Josiah's kingdom without appealing to the discourse of nationalism. Josiah's people need to be envisioned in 'a history of their own' that does not inscribe only the history, experience, aspirations, and destiny of the West, but also the history and experience of the Others.

4

Whose Space is it Anyway?

Foucault reminds us that that there is a bias against space in Western thought and experience: 'Space was treated as the dead, the fixed, the undialectical, the immobile. Time, on the contrary, was richness, fecundity, life, dialectic.'[1] Human experience unfolds in time, and history narrates this unfolding. Foucault states that 'the great obsession of the nineteenth century was, as we know, history: with its themes of development and of suspension, of crisis and cycle, themes of the ever-accumulating past, with its great preponderance of dead men and the menacing glaciation of the world'.[2] But in our present epoch the attention has shifted from time to space:

> The present epoch will perhaps be above all the epoch of space. We are in the epoch of simultaneity: we are in the epoch of juxtaposition, the epoch of the near and far, of the side-by-side, of the dispersed. We are at a moment, I believe, when our experience of the world is less that of a long life developing through time than that of a network that connects points and intersects with its own skein.[3]

Foucault does not deny that there is an intimate connection between time and space—space has a history or that history has spatiality—but he believes that 'the anxiety of our era has to do fundamentally with space, no doubt a great deal more than with time. Time probably appears to us only as one of the various distributive operations that are possible for the elements that are spread out in space.'[4] This shift in attention to space is sometimes called a spatial turn, which parallels other 'turns' of postmodernism.

Space has a history or, as Foucault would say, a genealogy. It is something we construct, imagine, and shape; therefore, it can be contested, changed, transformed, and reimagined. Edward Soja, employing Henri Lefebvre's work, advocates a way of thinking about spatiality that moves beyond

---

1. Foucault, *Power/Knowledge*, p. 70.
2. Michel Foucault, 'Of Other Spaces', *Diacritics* 16 (1986), pp. 22-27 (22).
3. Foucault, 'Of Other Spaces', p. 22.
4. Foucault, 'Of Other Spaces', p. 23.

4. *Whose Space is it Anyway?*

modernist, mechanistic understanding of space.[5] In the past, Soja argues, the geographical imagination was limited by what he calls the Firstspace Secondspace dualism: Firstspace refers to the 'real' empirical space ('perceived space' in Lefebvre's term) that is directly sensible and open to accurate measurement and description, and Secondspace refers to 'imagined' representations of space ('conceived space' in Lefebvre's term) that are based on the 'real' empirical space but are derived more from discourses. Soja argues that this dualism has relegated space 'into the background as reflection, container, stage, environment, or external constraint upon human behavior and social action'.[6] He suggests that one must also understand the existence of Thirdspace ('lived space' in Lefebvre's term) where space is experienced by people as lived realities. Thirdspace is where the Firstspace–Secondspace construction is contested since people, who are situated especially at the margin, experience the lived space differently from the constructed space that gives advantages to the people at the center. He does not deny the importance of understanding space in terms of physical space (Firstspace) and mental space (Secondspace), but he argues that those in power who produce the imagination of Secondspace control the spatial relationship between center and periphery resulting in maintaining and controlling the power differential between those at the center and those at the margin:

> 'We' and 'they' are dichotomously spatialized and enclosed in an imposed territoriality of apartheids, ghettos, barrios, reservations, colonies, fortresses, metropoles, citadels, and other trappings that emanate from the center–periphery relation. In this sense, hegemonic power universalizes and *contains* difference in real and imagined spaces and places.[7]

He maintains that no one mode of thinking in a 'trialectics of spatiality' (Firstspace, Secondspace, and Thirdspace) is '"better" than the others as long as each remains open to the re-combinations and simultaneities of the "real-and-imagined"'.[8]

But it is precisely Thirdspace that has been neglected in biblical studies. It has studied Josiah's kingdom as a Firstspace–Secondspace construct in which spaces are measured and plotted in political boundary maps. More specifically, it has relied on the discourse of nationalism to plot 'real-and-imagined' places onto the political boundary map of ancient Israel. Berquist points out biblical scholars' tendency to use these two categories of space and confuse their construction for the reality:

---

5. Edward W. Soja, *Thirdspace: Journeys to Los Angeles and Other Real-and-Imagined Places* (Cambridge, MA: Blackwell, 1996).
6. Soja, *Thirdspace*, p. 71.
7. Soja, *Thirdspace*, p. 87.
8. Soja, *Thirdspace*, p. 65.

Scholarship's traditional use of maps has confused representations and reality. Two-dimensional maps are not real, since reality is (at least) three-dimensional. Representations that exist in only one or two dimensions are imaginary. Maps participate in a Firstplace project of perceiving and measuring space, but maps are always Secondspace products that structure conception of space and reinforce certain ideas and the hierarchies that undergird those ideas.[9]

Therefore, Berquist concludes, 'understanding space as a constructed reality is vital to understanding the societies that inhabited those spaces, as we continue to realize the constructedness of our own images of the past and of our own scholarly practice as well'.[10] If we want to understand the lived space of biblical times and how the constructed space of biblical studies functioned to maintain the power differentials of the lived space of our time, biblical scholars need to acknowledge the limitation of this type of geographical imagination and be open to seeing Thirdspace through experiences of those who are contesting the Firstspace–Secondspace construct that is in place today.

If biblical scholars are reluctant to listen to the experience of those who inhabit the Thirdspace, they will continue to be susceptible to appealing to the discourse of nationalism, which gives the authority and identity of space/land to a particular people with a centralized government, especially in the form of a nation-state. This is a driving force behind many assumptions that biblical scholars make in understanding the account of Josiah's reign in 2 Kings 22–23. A particular slant in modernist history understands space/land as empty until a centralized power occupies it. It is then that an 'empty' space/land becomes a 'historical' place. This gives a history of a land to a particular people who were successful in founding a nation-state. The understanding of the kingdom of David and Solomon as a full-blown state that ruled over all of Palestine, effectively turning a space into a historical place, needs to be put into critique because this assumption has functioned to construct the stage on which the story of Josiah unfolds. Some biblical scholars, particularly the Cross School, argue that Josiah's reforms were, in part, an attempt to recover the empire of David and Solomon; that is, to reunify the two 'nations' into one 'nation'. As a result, Josiah is a hero playing his part on a stage constructed by biblical scholars following the script written by the discourse of nationalism.

It is fascinating that just as there are 'battles' over the text, there are 'battles' over the land. When it comes to the history of composition of the

---

9. J.L. Berquist, 'Critical Spatiality and the Construction of the Ancient World', in D.M. Gunn and P.M. McNutt (eds.), *'Imagining' Biblical Worlds: Studies in Spatial, Social and Historical Constructs in Honor of James W. Flanagan* (JSOTSup, 359; London: Sheffield Academic Press, 2002), pp. 14-29 (22).

10. Berquist, 'Critical Spatiality', p. 29.

DH, several camps are in competition to draw different 'boundaries' in the text—sometimes contesting every word in a verse—but most still maintain that DH is one unified text. The Deuteronomistic History Hypothesis offers the stage on which different textual 'boundaries' are drawn. Similarly, the one indivisible land of the empire of David is the stage on which scholars draw boundaries. They base their decisions on their understanding of the historical context of Josiah and the principle of equating the authority of the land with the identity of ethnic artifacts. Different camps draw different 'boundaries' in the land—every town is contested—but they all assume that the land is one unified land belonging to the heirs of David.[11] They differ on the extent of Josiah's kingdom, but they agree on the unity, indivisibility, or ownership of the land itself. In the end the extent of Josiah's kingdom does not matter; what matters is that Josiah is on the stage constructed in part by biblical scholarship that follows the discourse of nationalism that supports the aspirations, experience, and 'roots' of the West.

In the process of searching for the 'roots' of the West in the territories the nations control, inscriptions and routes of the people were often overwritten and erased, leaving only traces of their existence and history on the palimpsest of Western historical narratives. Postcolonialists are looking for 'routes' in the land the people had taken, rather than 'roots' of the present world order. Postcolonialists are trying to recover 'inscriptions' left by those whose histories have been erased or overwritten. Spurred by their experience of being 'unhomely' in the space in which they live, the postcolonialists have been questioning the discourse of nationalism, which gives the identity and authority of the space to a particular group of people who founded the nation in the land. Asian Americans, in particular, are caught in a place that views them as foreigners. They were limited to their own ethnic space in North America, pressured to play the part of the Other on the stage called America where the whites are the heroes of the great American narrative. They continue to live in a historicized, racialized place that hinders them from being 'homely' in the land in which they live.

Using a critique exemplified by Asian Americans, I will examine the assumption that the province of Samerina, the land north of Josiah's kingdom, was 'empty' of power and people as soon as Assyria supposedly withdrew from that part of Palestine, clearing the stage for the history of ancient Israel

---

11. Every site and every archaeological artifact are contested because they are used to draw the boundaries of Josiah's kingdom. S.V. Gallagher, in referring to the contentious nature of drawing maps as between Russians and Americans, states that 'as discursive symbols, maps both represent and embody power... Getting the contributors to discuss disagreements civily in the text was one thing...rhetoric can always be toned down. But when it came to drawing the maps, we had some major battles' ('Mapping the Hybrid World: Three Postcolonial Motifs', *Semeia* 75 [1996], pp. 225-40 [235]).

to unfold. There is an assumption in biblical studies that there was a power vacuum as soon as the central power/government of Assyria supposedly lost its hegemony over that part of the region. This assumption is similar to the way the West colonized the Others. The West equated the lack of perceived central power with the land being 'empty'. It determined the natives to be unequipped to rule for themselves and without the authority to own the land on which they lived for generations. The assumption that there was a power vacuum during the latter part of Josiah's reign, when Josiah supposedly reunified or attempted to reunify the divided kingdoms, needs to be questioned in light of the political context of the time. I want to show what is obvious: Josiah did not act on an empty stage. There were powers and peoples in the province of Samerina competing and coexisting with Josiah's kingdom.

I am not denying that the picture of Josiah's kingdom portrayed by DH and understood by the West as the model of nations can support the aspirations, experience, and destiny of the West. But, it is not the only way to understand Josiah's kingdom. However, the question remains: Is it possible to imagine Josiah on a different stage from that constructed by the West? Is it possible to understand space without applying the discourse of nationalism that equates identity and authority of the land with the centralized power? Is it possible to imagine Josiah in an alternative space from the one constructed by the West?

Looking for Other Spaces

Paul Carter argues in *The Road to Botany Bay* that it is imperial history that reduces space to a stage that 'pays attention to events unfolding in time alone'.[12] Carter examines how the histories of Australia have been written as a history of 'settlement', as a history of 'foundation' of a country, rather than as a history of traveling. There lies the prejudice against space (land) in favor of time (past) that resulted in an ethnocentric, exclusivistic, nation-oriented history. Although the object of Carter's study is Australia, his work may be applied to all histories that explain European colonialism as a history of 'settlement' and 'foundation' of a nation. Carter argues that historians continue to confuse 'routes' with 'roots'. In their efforts to find 'roots' (in the past) of their nations, they have incorporated all data, including facts and artifacts prior to the settlement of Europeans in a foreign land, in the framework of European chronology. This contributes 'to the emergence of historical order and narrative clarity' and legitimates the 'settlement' and 'foundation' of their civilization.[13] They continue to ignore the 'routes' (in the land) that

12. Paul Carter, *The Road to Botany Bay: An Essay in Spatial History* (London: Faber & Faber, 1987), p. xvi.
13. Carter, *The Road to Botany Bay*, p. xix.

have been taken by all inhabitants (settlers as well as natives) of the land. Carter wants to trace the 'routes' (criss-crossing of the land) taken by the inhabitants of the land: 'It is a prehistory of places, a history of roads, footprints, tails of dust and foaming wakes' that attempts to recover 'a world of experience' that has been dismissed by imperial history that has sought legitimacy.[14]

Carter advocates a different type of history: a spatial history.[15] He argues that historians overlook the space (the land) where history occurred as an empty stage waiting for actors (heroes) to act out the script. They understand history as a theatrical performance:

> It is not the historian who stages events, weaving them together to form a plot, but History itself. History is the playwright, coordinating facts into a coherent sequence: the historian narrating what happened is merely a copyist or amanuensis. He is a spectator like anybody else and, whatever he may think of the performance, he does not question the stage conventions.[16]

To this kind of history, namely, modernist imperial history, 'the primary object is not to understand or to interpret: it is to legitimate'.[17] It sets the stage for the hero (the West) to perform according to the Western metanarrative of how the West has brought order (power) out of chaos (absence of power) and civilization/settled (identity) into the uncivilized/wild (lack of identity). The West gives the land another name, and thereby the space is 'transformed symbolically into a place, that is, a space with a history'.[18] This kind of history does not care for the land or the people. The inhabitants are removed or erased from the land/space, or renamed as 'foreigners' or 'immigrants' or 'natives', who do not belong in the land they have lived in for generations, in order to legitimate the West and its people as the rightful 'owners' of the land. It is a way of constructing the stage on which the theatre of history with a new script, the discourse of nationalism, can be performed.

Carter calls for a spatial history in which the experience of Australian Aborigines is included, without appropriating it to white ends. Carter argues that the Aborigines remain outside white history and white space in their own

---

14. Carter, *The Road to Botany Bay*, p. xxi.
15. This term 'spatial history' may sound like an oxymoron because we are so used to understanding history in terms of time, as Foucault reminds us: 'For all those who confuse history with the old schemas of evolution, living continuity, organic development, the progress of consciousness or the project of existence, the use of spatial terms seems to have the air of an anti-history. If one started to talk in terms of space that meant one was hostile to time. It meant, as the fools say, that one "denied history", that one was a "technocrat"' (*Power/Knowledge*, p. 70).
16. Carter, *The Road to Botany Bay*, p. xiv.
17. Carter, *The Road to Botany Bay*, p. xvi.
18. Carter, *The Road to Botany Bay*, p. xxiv.

land. Imperial history is 'essentially a legitimation of selected earlier documents' that gave no credence to 'a world of experience' in the spatial history of the Aborigines.[19] Carter claims that Whites made no effort to learn aboriginal languages; instead, the Aborigines were made to speak a language that was not theirs. The Aborigines' inability to communicate in a language that was not their own was 'the main epistemological reason for the exclusion of the Aborigines, from both white space and white history'.[20] The Aborigines were given names: 'Names, in short, made them white history'.[21] The Whites also treated the Aborigines' spatial history like their language:

> Pools, pastures and tracks were taken out of context and used, like quotations, to symbolize their own historical presence. They were punning authorities which made cultivation look natural. Here was a country *waiting* to be occupied. All too quickly the brittle criss-cross of the newcomers' gaze sliced up and fenced off what had formerly been imagined. The result was the collapse of aboriginal space, its flight inwards into isolated objects, and its fragmentation into farms.[22]

The settlers herded the natives into centers believing that the Aborigines did not have a social and political organization because they were always wandering from place to place. But Carter states:

> It was not that the Aborigines were unorganized, only that their power was distributed horizontally, dynamically. Their wandering did indeed constitute a 'state'—a form of social and political organization. But this was expressed, not as a power over past and future—the pet obsession of the usurping historical culture—but as a power over space.[23]

Carter continues that 'for theirs was a world of travelling, where succession, rather than stasis, was the natural order of things: succession as a spatial, rather than temporal phenomenon… If the white historian feels the need to validate his present by reliving the past, the Aborigine travelled in order to stay where he was.'[24] Carter argues throughout the book that the Aborigines were always there, informing and conversing with the whites at every turn along the 'routes' that have been taken in the land. 'And it is this fact which enables us to get beyond the solipsism of a history merely reflecting on itself.'[25] But, Carter asks:

---

19. Carter, *The Road to Botany Bay*, p. 324.
20. Carter, *The Road to Botany Bay*, p. 327.
21. Carter, *The Road to Botany Bay*, p. 332.
22. Carter, *The Road to Botany Bay*, pp. 344-45.
23. Carter, *The Road to Botany Bay*, p. 336.
24. Carter, *The Road to Botany Bay*, p. 336.
25. Carter, *The Road to Botany Bay*, p. 337.

4. *Whose Space is it Anyway?*

> Short of abandoning linear writing, short of writing no more books, how, then, is a history of aboriginal space to be written? What kind of representation could make present to us the historical space which has been so effectively excluded from our own historical narratives?[26]

He does not think that deconstructing the devices of imperial history is enough: 'But, after the critical dismantling, there has to be something more: a restoration of meaning, a process which cannot avoid being interpretative and imaginative'.[27] He suggests 'recollection' of overwritten inscriptions as a key strategy to writing an aboriginal history of space, which is a symbolic history rather than an 'empirical' history:

> It would not be an anthropologist's account of the Aborigines' beliefs. Nor would it be a history of frontiers and massacres. Rather than seek by a newly ingenious means to translate the otherness of their experience into empirical terms, it might take the form of a meditation on the absent other of our own history. It might begin in the recognition of the suppressed spatiality of our own historical consciousness. It would not be a question of comparing and contrasting the *content* of our spatial experience, but of recognizing its form and its historically constitutive role. A history of space which revealed the everyday world in which we live as the continuous intentional re-enactment of our spatial history might say not a word about 'The Aborigines'. But, by recovering the intentional nature of our grasp on the world, it might evoke their historical experience without appropriating it to white ends.[28]

Carter's strategy of understanding the space as a palimpsest 'written and overwritten by successive (historical) inscriptions is one way of circumventing history as the "scientific narrative" of events'.[29] This type of history examines space/land not as a stage on which a modernist imperial history—which narrates how the nation has brought order and civilization to an empty land—is enacted, but as a palimpsest on which 'the traces of successive inscriptions form the complex experiences of place, which is itself historical'.[30] Modernist imperial history cannot overwrite the people and the land permanently; there are traces of other histories and memories in the land. 'Colonial discourse erased prior construction of the land, allowing it to be seen as an empty space, ready to receive their own inscriptions.'[31] But post-colonialists believe that there are always traces of previous inscriptions that can be recovered.

---

26. Carter, *The Road to Botany Bay*, p. 347.
27. Carter, *The Road to Botany Bay*, p. 349.
28. Carter, *The Road to Botany Bay*, p. 350.
29. Ashcroft, Griffiths and Tiffin (eds.), *The Post-colonial Studies Reader*, p. 356.
30. Ashcroft, Griffiths and Tiffin, *Post-Colonial Studies: The Key Concepts*, p. 182.
31. Ashcroft, Griffiths and Tiffin, *Post-Colonial Studies: The Key Concepts*, p. 175.

Asian Americans are trying to recover previous inscriptions overwritten by the standard history of America that views Asians in America as permanent aliens. They are trying to move away from playing the part of the exotic Other on the stage called America. They are trying to make a home in the land in which the deed (identity and authority) of the land is held by the white Americans.

The standard American history is similar to other foundational histories of the West. Ernst Breisach explains that American historiography was shaped by 'the momentous creation of a new nation through a revolution, [and] told the story of the grand adventure of stretching a small nation across a vast continent'.[32] This story joined hands with the assertion of Divine Providence and progress to form the most powerful historical imagination in America: the frontier thesis. The frontier thesis was proposed by Frederick Jackson Turner in 1893 in a brief essay, 'The Significance of the Frontier in American History', that has shaped American historiography for generations of America which historians and continues to dominate public memory.[33] Klein states: 'For decades Turnerian history dominated the profession as no other field ever has. And Turner's "frontier thesis" became a testing ground for attempts to formalize historical discourse.'[34] Klein notes that the frontier thesis is identified most often in the following sentence: 'The existence of an area of free land, its continuous recession, and the advance of American settlement westward explain American development'.[35] The frontier thesis states that the development of the particular American democracy (the identity and destiny of the American people) can be explained primarily by one factor: its conquest and settlement of the west. Breisach explains that Turner's thesis was quickly accepted because it 'allowed for a great deal of optimism because of what it said about the American character and the origin of American democracy'.[36] Breisach states:

---

32. Breisach, *Historiography*, p. 228.

33. Kerwin Lee Klein, *Frontiers of Historical Imagination: Narrating the European Conquest of Native America, 1890–1990* (Berkeley: University of California Press, 1997).

34. Klein, *Frontiers of Historical Imagination*, p. 13. Klein examines Turner's thesis extensively in his book in order not only to understand the thesis but also to trace the development of American historiography by putting subsequent generations of historians in conversation with Turner.

35. From Turner's essay quoted in Klein, *Frontiers of Historical Imagination*, p. 14. Klein remarks that 'the sentence contains neither "frontier" nor "hypothesis", but many historians liked the label' (p. 14).

36. Breisach, *Historiography*, p. 314. Klein quotes Fredric Paxson's objection in 1933 to show how the thesis dominated the understanding of America's past without much critical thinking: 'As rapidly as the frontier hypothesis was recognized it was accepted. Its author was acclaimed as prophet and lawgiver… It is almost without precedent that a fundamental new philosophy should be substituted for an old one, or for none at all,

4. Whose Space is it Anyway?

> The thesis spoke of an American nation that was unique in character and development because it had been shaped less by cross-Atlantic links than the dramatic conquest of a vast continent... The frontier thesis became America's declaration of historiographical independence from Europe.[37]

Turner believed that it was the vast, empty continent that offered free land that was the key to shaping a particular American character, identity, and destiny, and a decisive factor in severing America's ties to Europe.[38] That democracy 'was born of no theorist's dream' but was 'shaped in ceaseless struggle with the environment'.[39] This historical imagination is captured well by Theodore Roosevelt:

> The Americans began their work of western conquest as separate and individual people, at the moment when they sprang into national life. It has been their great work ever since. All other questions save those of the preservation of the Union itself and the emancipation of the blacks have been of subordinate importance when compared with the great questions of how...they [the people] were to subjugate that part of their continent lying between the eastern mountains and the Pacific.[40]

Asian Americans have no roles except to play the exotic Other in the historical imagination of America, which views the land as an empty stage on which the European settlers played out their destiny. Okihiro remarks, 'In truth, America's manifest destiny was "an additional chapter" in the Orientalist text of Europe's "dominating, restructuring, and having authority over" Asia... The filling of those "red wastes", those empty spaces, was, of course, the white man's burden.'[41] In the framework of the frontier thesis, the Indians stood in the way of American democracy and represented the past: to kill the Indians was 'to kill the past. History would thus be the key to the moral worth of cultures; the history of American civilization would thus be conceived of as three-dimensional, progressing from past to present, from east to west, from lower to higher.'[42] The fact that Indians were widely viewed as descendants of Asians facilitated in relating the frontier thesis directly to the confrontation between whites and Asians as 'America's westward march

---

without resistance' (quoted in Klein, *Frontiers of Historical Imagination*, p. 21). Klein states that 'the profession had adopted Turner's claim with a good deal of haste and almost no critical testing of the notion. Turnerians had adopted the hypothesis as gospel without putting it to the empirical test' (p. 21).

37. Breisach, *Historiography*, p. 314.
38. It is ironic that white Americans were trying to write 'a history of their own' independent of Europe, or, at least, not always referring to Europe.
39. Breisach, *Historiography*, p. 314.
40. Quoted in Breisach, *Historiography*, p. 310.
41. Okihiro, *Margins and Mainstreams*, p. 27.
42. Roy Harvey Pearce, quoted in Okihiro, *Margins and Mainstreams*, p. 123.

continued into the Pacific, extending to Asia, where the "Far East" became the nation's "Far West"'.[43] Asian Americans were viewed also as those who stood in the way of American development.

Asian Americans are viewed as foreigners and/or immigrants because the assumption is that they do not belong in the land; they came from somewhere else. Of course, every American, including Native Americans, came from somewhere else from the perspective of spatial history; the difference is a matter of time. However, the land is viewed as an 'empty' land that the Euro-Americans, particularly Anglo-Americans, 'discovered' and transformed into a stage on which History's great narrative of how white people brought order and civilization to the primitives was acted out. Although Asian Americans as an ethnic group have been living in the land for over 150 years, they are still viewed as foreigners. There is an assumption that history on the land began with the founding of the nation-state (United States): 'the nation-state exists with its citizens and its institutions' so that 'Asians derive from over there, away from the United States, and come here to the United States as immigrants, as strangers to our shores'.[44] It is a nationalist history. The land is viewed as being 'owned' by the United States (as a nation-state) and its citizens as the lawful inhabitants (the white people as the heirs of this land), so that even the native Americans are viewed as 'foreigners' displaced (and enclosed and preserved in the so-called 'Indian reservations' like a living museum artifact) in their own land.

Henry Yu states what is common knowledge among Asian Americans: the unsuccessful attempt by Asian Americans to be viewed as Americans has been hindered by the racialized landscape constructed by Euro-Americans.[45] Yu notes that in an effort to define white people as Americans (identity and authority to live on the land), Asians were constructed as the exotic other 'representative of a faraway place that was defined as being un-American, and how this helped to define what was America'.[46] Asians were called upon to play out their parts as exotic foreigners on the stage of American history for the white audience. 'The exoticization of Orientals belies an obsession with America, not Asia. Thinking about Orientals has always been thinking about what it means to be American.'[47] Yu traces how the theories of Chicago sociology that connected space and race (place and identity) still influence our thoughts today. The Chicago sociologists saw Chinatowns as the 'great walls' that separated and isolated the Chinese from America proper; thereby the Chinese were separated from America:

43. Okihiro, *Margins and Mainstreams*, p. 123.
44. Okihiro, *Columbia Guide*, p. 34.
45. Yu, *Thinking Orientals*.
46. Yu, *Thinking Orientals*, p. vii.
47. Yu, *Thinking Orientals*, p. 190.

> The boundaries, of course, were never hermetically sealed... But because the sociologists had such a definite awareness of the spatial dimensions of the Chinese in America, they began to see this geographic distinctiveness as equivalent to the cultural difference of the Chinese. The fact that the Chinese were so effortlessly distinguishable by physical traits made connections to other physical substantiation in the landscape all the more easy. The spatial boundary surrounding a Chinatown was equivalent to the social barrier that isolated the Chinese within the assimilation cycle.[48]

This view in some ways has limited Asian Americans to tracing the history and memory of Asian Americans to urban settings, neglecting to search for erased inscriptions outside of the 'great walls' of ethnic towns. Okihiro maintains that Asian-American scholars continue to construct Asian-American space in this way. According to Okihiro, 'The main spatial binary in the extant literature is between the urban and rural. Urban Asian America is assumed to be typical of the Asian American experience.'[49] Okihiro notes that the studies in rural space in recent years have been 'more effective in critiquing the urban paradigm and underscoring that space is both social and historical'.[50] In an effort to recover inscriptions left behind by Chinese miners who lived and worked throughout the west in the mid-1850s, Randall Rohe suggests that scholars need to look at archaeological evidence to trace their history and memory in the mining camps.[51] Archaeology, in many ways, is reading or recovering inscriptions left behind by those who had lived on the land. Rohe shows that there were Chinese miners working and living outside of Chinatowns, which were viewed as strict demarcated boundaries within which Chinese lived. This assumption is based on spatial identity—each ethnic group belongs to a certain location. 'Discursive analyses reveal Chinatown to be a constructed space initiated by whites and abetted by certain classes of Chinese, a place of racialization for white and Chinese alike.'[52] This was a way of limiting the access and mobility of the Other in the land. This was a form of erasing or limiting inscriptions that can be recovered; it is like saying, yes, it is true that Asians were here for a long time, but they are not 'really' Americans because they stayed in their own spaces apart from America proper. Asian Americans, for the most part, are pressured to play the part of the Other on the stage called America, where it is the white people who

---

48. Yu, *Thinking Orientals*, p. 175. Okihiro also remarks that 'As a spatial and social entity, Chinatown has been stereotyped as rigidly insular and separate from American society' (*Columbia Guide*, p. 136).

49. Okihiro, *Columbia Guide*, p. 135.

50. Okihiro, *Columbia Guide*, p. 136.

51. Randall Rohe, 'Chinese Camps and Chinatowns: Chinese Mining Settlements in the North American West', in J. Lee, I.L. Kim and Y. Matsukawa (eds.), *Re-Collecting Early Asian America: Essays in Cultural History* (Philadelphia: Temple University Press, 2002), pp. 31-51.

52. Okihiro, *Columbia Guide*, p. 135.

are heroes of the great American narrative. Asian Americans lived and, in many ways, continue to live without the (right to) land—living with the sense of 'unhomely' in their own place.

In light of discussion above on spatiality, we need to question the understanding of David's kingdom as a stage on which history unfolds and as a constructed space where Josiah represents the only legitimate power. We also need to examine the efforts to draw the boundaries of Josiah's kingdom. The idea of one culture per territory is fictional. Boundaries do not enclose a fixed culture or people. By closing the borders, by fixing the borders, we are creating an artificial view of the reality. Then, we will examine the notion that there was a power vacuum in the province of Samerina (the former northern kingdom of Israel).

The Stage David Built with Some Help from Biblical Scholars

Josiah's reform has been understood within the domain assumption of the existence of the Davidic empire ('Greater' Israel); consequently, his actions, in part, have been interpreted, especially by the Cross School, as an attempt to reunite 'Greater' Israel. Whitelam argues that the creation of an Israelite state has been interpreted as the climax of the development of civilization in the region—a radical break from the inferior indigenous political structures—by creating the nation-state that is understood as the height of civilization in the West.[53] The concept of 'Greater' Israel founded by David, Whitelam argues, is a construction of biblical scholars participating, wittingly or unwittingly, in Orientalism, which perpetuates the hegemony of the West (through the modern state of Israel) over the non-Western peoples (the present day Palestinians) and has effectively excluded alternative representations of the past:

> Biblical specialists and archaeologists have searched for and constructed a large, powerful, sovereign and autonomous Iron Age state attributed to its founder David. It is this 'fact' which has dominated the discourse of biblical studies throughout this century, providing a location for the development of many of the biblical traditions at the royal court—'a fact', more than any other, which has silenced Palestinian history and obstructed alternatives to the past.[54]

Whitelam argues that the evidence for such a large and powerful empire is scarce to non-existent, and claims that its basis is the scholars' imagination based on their political and cultural contexts, rather than empirical data.[55] The on-going hold on the imagination of biblical scholars has to do with the discourse of biblical studies:

53. Whitelam, *Invention*, Chapter 4.
54. Whitelam, *Invention*, p. 124.
55. See also Garbini, *History and Ideology*.

What is striking are the recurrent themes, images, and phrases which appear throughout this discourse from the 1920s onwards to the present day: the Davidic monarchy as the defining moment in the history of the region, the existence of a Davidic empire to rival other imperial powers in the ancient world, the defensive nature of David's state, the paradox of the alien nature of the monarchy to Israel, and Israel as a nation set apart from surrounding nations.[56]

Whitelam claims that even the more recent reconstructions of the Davidic Empire are under the sway of the dominant paradigm. More recent scholars like Miller and Hayes, Ahlström, and those who use social-scientific data and theories have not been freed 'from Alt's domain assumption that Israel's political development represents a radical break with and replacement of (inferior) indigenous political structures'.[57]

Biblical scholarship constructed a model of ancient Israel based on the blueprint found in the Bible with additional props from archaeological findings, and claimed that this was a model for historical Israel. John Bright's model of the Davidic Empire is considered the example *par excellence* of this strategy.[58] His reconstruction follows the 'facts' in the biblical texts.

56. Whitelam, *Invention*, p. 129.
57. Whitelam, *Invention*, p. 156.
58. I engage with John Bright throughout my work. Some will wonder why I chose to engage with a scholar whose methods and theological biases in his work, *A History of Israel*, have been thoroughly criticized and this textbook, in many ways, is outdated and no longer useful for the present discussion on writing history of ancient Israel except to show how much biblical scholarship has changed. But we cannot underestimate the power such a theologically motivated book has on the imagination of today's students and professional readers and how it continues to influence the present generation of students and professional interpreters of the Hebrew Bible. In the introduction to the fourth edition of *A History of Israel* (Louisville, KY: Westminster/John Knox Press, 4th edn, 2000), William Brown argues the case in point. Brown states the profound influence of Bright's textbook with these facts: 'For at least twenty-seven years, *A History of Israel* was a standard text among mainline theological schools and seminaries across the country. Its influence on previous and present generation of theology students is inestimable. Translated into German, Spanish, Korean, and Indonesian, Bright's magisterial work continues to be widely used, having achieved a total sale of over 100,000 copies since the publication of its first edition in 1959' (p. 1). He acknowledges that the textbook has its problems but it remains a standard textbook because 'the strength of Bright's textbook lies in its power to provoke theological reflection *from within* the field of historical inquiry' (p. 1). It is the theological vision the textbook offers that is so appealing to so many interpreters of the history of Israel and the Hebrew Bible. Bright's book is 'a robustly theological investigation' (p. 20). Brown states Bright's core belief that is behind his work: 'There is no authentic understanding of God without Israel's history, and there is no true understanding of Israel's history without God' (p. 21). Brown reveals his own theological bias when he gives an example of Bright's belief: 'In the end, it matters not whether Abraham's journeys took place in the Middle Bronze, Late Bronze, or early Iron Age. What matters is that the patriarch's sojourn was an act of faith, something that archaeology will never be able to

According to Bright, after defeating the Philistines, the entire land of the Canaanites became 'Israel':

> This meant a great rounding out of Israel's territory. It was, indeed, the completion of the conquest of Canaan. The name 'Israel', properly the designation of a tribal confederacy whose members occupied but a part of the area of Palestine, now denoted a geographical entity embracing virtually the whole of the land.[59]

David did not stop there, according to Bright, but continued his military campaigns against his neighboring states. David was victorious against the Ammonites; he conquered Southern Transjordan; he even conquered all of Syria. It is worth quoting Bright again because he clearly appeals to the metanarrative of the West:

> His own house in order, David was free to launch aggressive action against his neighbors. Whether he embarked upon his victorious career at the beck of some '*manifest destiny*', or stumbled into it a step at a time, we do not know… But in the end David was master of a considerable empire.[60]

Bright's assessment of David's 'empire' lifts it to another level never reached before or after until the birth of the modern state of Israel: 'With dramatic suddenness David's conquests had transformed Israel into the foremost power of Palestine and Syria. In fact, she was for the moment probably as strong as any power in the contemporary world. With it all, she was committed irrevocably to the new order.'[61]

There are also those who are willing to equate biblical Israel with historical Israel without much critical analysis of the biblical narratives and by

---

verify or falsify' (p. 22). Brown does not include the possibility that Abraham's journey might have never taken place or that Abraham might be a fictional character. Theology matters in interpreting the history of Israel! Although it is beyond the scope of this work to examine how theology continues to influence how we interpret the Hebrew Bible and the history of ancient Israel, it is important to note that it does. Therefore, I chose to engage with John Bright because of the continuing legacy of his textbook in spite of it being outdated and fraught with methodological problems, and because it makes no secret about it being theologically biased.

59. Bright, *A History of Israel* (Philadelphia: Westminster Press, 2nd edn, 1972), p. 197. Bright does not necessarily follow the chronological order presented in the biblical texts.

60. Bright, *A History of Israel* (2nd edn), p. 197 (emphasis mine). Bright's description (and his whole narrative) is deeply embedded in the Western metanarrative. This may not trouble some but to those who have suffered from the West's 'manifest destiny', it can have a chilling effect.

61. Bright, *A History of Israel* (2nd edn), p. 200. In criticizing Bright's reconstruction, Whitelam points out: 'What Bright has constructed is a biblically inspired view of "Greater Israel" which coincides with and helps to enhance the vision and aspiration of many of Israel's modern leaders' (*Invention*, p. 126).

appealing to the ancient Israel of biblical scholarship.⁶² Such a model is no more than a mirror image of Biblical Israel. In such a model, the Davidic Empire will remain far more considerable in size and power than what the evidence allows. Such a view of the Davidic Empire is still common even to this day. A case in point is W. Kaiser's reconstruction, which is no more than a paraphrasing of biblical texts, without much of a critical literary analysis.⁶³ Kaiser does not include any archaeological evidence, perhaps acknowledging that there is none, in his discussion of the extent of David's empire. He uses the account of David's census in 2 Samuel 24 and 1 Chron. 21.1-27 to describe the territories ruled by David without any qualifications; he presents it simply as a matter of fact:

> The geographical extent of the kingdom is described as beginning at the Arnon River in Transjordania, proceeding to a point near Dan at the foot of Mt. Hermon in the north, then crossing Upper Galilee westward almost to the cities of Sidon and Tyre. Another survey covered the Negev of Judah to Beersheba. Accordingly, the entire western side of the Jordan except for the Gaza strip, or Philistia, and all of Transjordania possibly including most of Moab and Edom. It also became clear that the territory of Aram was also included in the realm over which David exercised authority, meaning that David's control reached up to Damascus and in to the Lebanon and Anti-Lebanon ranges.⁶⁴

A more critical view of David's kingdom of the Bible is that of Miller and Hayes. Their reconstruction turns a massive empire of the Bible into a small but still considerable kingdom. Miller and Hayes also use biblical texts to draw the extent of David's kingdom, but they use them after a critical literary analysis.⁶⁵ They acknowledge that David probably was more successful than Saul was 'in consolidating and extending the frontiers of his domain', but they doubt whether David was able to conquer or rule over all of Palestine.⁶⁶ They certainly do not think that David conquered all of Syria. They believe David was involved in frontier wars with the surrounding kingdoms and may have yielded some influence on surrounding kingdoms, but he did not rule over them.

But whatever the size of David's domain, it represents for many scholars the first 'full-blown' state born in Palestine.⁶⁷ In addition to the questioning

62. See Davies, *In Search of 'Ancient Israel'*.
63. Kaiser, *A History of Israel*.
64. Kaiser, *A History of Israel*, p. 255.
65. Miller and Hayes, *A History of Ancient Israel and Judah*. There are three important texts they use to reconstruct the boundaries of David's kingdom: the account of David's census in 2 Sam. 24 (= 1 Chron. 21.1-27), the list of Levitical cities in Josh. 21.1-42 (= 1 Chron. 6.54-81), and the list of 'unconquered cities' in Judg. 1.27-33.
66. Miller and Hayes, *A History of Ancient Israel and Judah*, p. 179.
67. We need to keep in mind that this is a separate question from the question of whether David's kingdom became a nation-state. The answer to the latter question is negative (see Chapter 1).

of the extent of David's domain, biblical studies have been debating about the formation of the state during David's reign.[68] Israel Finkelstein's article in 1999 represents one of the latest developments (some would say a radical break) in this debate.[69] In his article Finkelstein wants to re-examine some assumptions he once advocated:

> I believe that it is time for a fresh look at a central paradigm in the Bible: that which describes the days of the United Monarchy as the Golden Age of Early Israel, views its breakdown into the northern and southern kingdoms as a temporary calamity that diverged from the evolutionary history of Israel, and argues that Israel and Judah were sister states that emerged from one ethnic, cultural body.[70]

Finkelstein argues that contrasting circumstances between Israel and Judah contributed to different lines of development into 'full-blown' states. Israel was located on the crossroads of international politics and its location encouraged openness to trade and foreign contacts, but 'Judah was isolated, rustic, and closed, with a large pastoral component until the eighth century BCE'.[71] He maintains that 'the openness of Israel and the isolation and conservatism of Judah are reflected in almost every aspect of their material culture'.[72] Finkelstein claims that it was the northern kingdom of Israel that first became a full-blown state in the first half of the ninth century BCE. He cites two pieces of evidence for this conclusion: Israel was a major regional power in the coalition that confronted Shalmaneser III at the battle of Qarqar (853), and the Omrides established elaborate cities in Samaria and Jezreel.[73] It was

---

68. For a concise guide to the discussion, see J.J. McDermott, *What are they Saying about the Formation of Israel* (New York: Paulist Press, 1998). For a more comprehensive introduction to the emergence and development of Israel as a society, see P.M. McNutt, *Reconstructing the Society of Ancient Israel* (Louisville, KY: Westminster/John Knox Press, 1999). McNutt examines biblical and extrabiblical literary sources only when they reflect the 'reality' of the reconstructed society of ancient Israel; thus they only play a minor role in her synthesis. However, surprisingly, she still uses the 'historical' scheme outlined in the Hebrew Bible to organize her book: the conquest and settlement in Joshua (Chapter 2: 'Iron Age I: The Origin of Ancient "Israel"'); the period of the judges in Judges (Chapter 3: 'Iron Age IA and B: The "Tribal" Period'); the triumph of the Davidic monarchy in the books of Samuel (Chapter 4: 'Iron Age IC: The Rise of Monarchy'); the rule of Davidic dynasty in the books of Kings (Chapter 5: 'Iron Age II: The Period of the Monarchy'); the exile and the Persian dominance in Chronicles–Ezra–Nehemiah (Chapter 6: 'The Babylonian and Persian Periods'). She does not explore other possible schemes (periodizations) that might fit the ancient information better.

69. Israel Finkelstein, 'State Formation in Israel and Judah', *NEA* 62/1 (1999), pp. 35-52.

70. Finkelstein, 'State Formation', p. 36.

71. Finkelstein, 'State Formation', p. 43.

72. Finkelstein, 'State Formation', p. 43.

73. Finkelstein, 'State Formation', p. 40.

4. *Whose Space is it Anyway?* 131

only 150 years after the formation of a state in the northern kingdom of Israel that Judah became a fully developed state in the second half of the eighth century BCE, after Assyrian domination of the entire region of Palestine. Although he maintains the possibility that David's kingdom could have been an expanding 'early state' rather than a full-blown state, it would have been an exception to the history of the highlands. Finkelstein summarizes his argument:

> The Bible draws a picture of two sister states, Israel and Judah, which emerged from one demographic and cultural body. At first glance this description seems justified... But from other angles, the biblical portrayal, which serves late-monarchic ideological and theological goals, does not fit the picture painted by the archaeological data... Assuming that a United Monarchy did exist (that is, regardless of its exact territorial-political status, it was not a fictitious, later invention), the unification of the central hill country in the 10th century BCE was a short-lived exception in the history of the highlands, while the contrasting circumstances and political systems of the two kingdoms, Israel and Judah, better reflect the deeper, pervasive, and long-term structures of Levantine regional history... Israel emerged as a full-blown state in the early 9th century BCE, together with Moab, Ammon and Aram Damascus, while Judah (and Edom) emerged about a century and a half later, in the second half of the 8th century... Judah opened to international trade and to neighboring civilizations only with the Assyrian takeover of the entire region in the late 8th century BCE. The Assyrian conquest brought about the collapse of the cultural barriers between the inland national states of the Levant.[74]

In response to Finkelstein's article, Anson F. Rainey argues that Finkelstein's interpretation of the archaeological data is 'subjective'.[75] But Rainey's argument is more 'territorial' than anything else. He advocates that history should be written by historians using source criticism as developed by Ranke rather than by archaeologists. He asks the readers:

> The fundamental issue that must be dealt with here is whether an archaeologist, untrained in detailed historical linguistics and philology, can use his subjectively interpreted archaeological data to create a history that is in contradiction to the written sources. Must the properly trained historian be forced to adjust his interpretations to the dictates of the archaeologist?... Will you ignore the original texts in favor of the 'latest trends' or will you get serious about the 'Ranke Game'?[76]

74. Finkelstein, 'State Formation', p. 48.
75. Anson F. Rainey, 'Stones for Bread: Archaeology Versus History', *NEA* 64/3 (2001), pp. 140-49. Rainey accuses Finkelstein of being subjective: 'Finkelstein's archaeological arguments are based largely on his personal interpretation of the data and involve a great deal of subjective selectivity' (p. 148).
76. Rainey, 'Stones for Bread', p. 148. Rainey thinks that essentially both minimalists and fundamentalists 'are all commentators on the Bible who do not employ Ranke's methodology of source research in ancient documents' (p. 145).

Thus the title of his article is 'Archaeology versus History'. He maintains that the original text (the Bible) indicates that 'the population in the plains and valleys was Canaanite and only now begins to be incorporated into "greater Israel"' during the United Monarchy.[77] His evidence for this view is the Tel Dan inscription which mentions the 'house of David'.[78] He argues that the Tel Dan inscription is indisputable evidence for the existence of the house of David. But was the house of David a 'full-blown' state? He seems to believe that with the Tel Dan inscription he has the foundation on which to build the house of David as a 'full-blown' state.

The debate on the size of David's domain and the time of the birth of a state in Palestine will go on, but biblical scholarship on Josiah uses the existence of the state/nation/empire of David as the stage on which Josiah's reform took place. There is an assumption that the land of Palestine belonged to the heirs of David because his kingdom—but actually understood as a nation—once ruled over this land. There is an assumption that a nation determines the identity (name) of a land and the authority (ownership) to live in it. Whitelam argues that there is a connection between a discourse in biblical studies that gives identity and authority of the land (Palestine) to David and his heirs and the political context surrounding the present situation of the modern state of Israel, thereby denying competing identities which might lay claim to the same land:

> Israel is conceived…in terms of the nation state, which is inextricably linked to nation territory by right of 'occupation'… The appeal to the boundaries of the Davidic–Solomonic kingdom, 'from Dan to Beersheba', as a definition of the geographical extent of Eretz Israel…betrays that it is the biblical perception of the past which is dominant.[79]

He continues that it is the discourse of nationalism that influences the understanding of space/land as a property belonging to a nation:

---

77. Rainey, 'Stones for Bread', p. 144.

78. The Tel Dan inscription is a fragmentary text written in Aramaic and inscribed on a stele of basalt stone that was found in 1993. A translation of *bytdwd* in line 9 in the inscription has stirred much excitement. A. Biran and J. Naveh, 'An Aramaic Stele Fragment from Tel Dan', *IEJ* 43 (1993), pp. 81-98, and 'The Tel Dan Inscription: A New Fragment', *IEJ* 45 (1995), pp. 1-18, translated the word in question as the 'house of David'. This would make the inscription the first known reference outside of the Bible to David and the ruling dynasty he founded. However, there are scholars who question the translation as well as the circumstances in which the fragment was found. See Z. Radovan, '"David" Found at Dan', *BARev* 20/2 (1994), pp. 26-39, for an enthusiastic acceptance of the discovery, and Frederick H. Cryer, 'On the Recently Discovered "House of David" Inscription', *SJOT* 8 (1994), pp. 1-19, for a cautious, skeptical view.

79. Whitelam, *Invention*, pp. 53-54.

> The essence to the claim on the land and therefore the right to name it, which is to possess it, is made on the basis of nationhood and statehood... Once again the controlling factor is the nation state since it is the 'local national entity' which defines the space... Nation and land become synonymous in this analysis since the territory belongs to and is identified with the nation. Here it should be noted that once again it is the nation state, Israel, which has replaced Canaanite culture characterized as merely a loose conglomeration of city-states. Israel represents the ultimate in political evolution, the European nation state, and the pinnacle of civilization which surpasses and replaces that which is primitive and incapable of transformation.[80]

The land, whether perceived as the 'promised' land or as the once occupied land of the state of David, is understood as a whole, unfragmentable, indivisible piece belonging to the Israelites (ancient and modern). Although the view that the theme of the promised land provides the title deed of the land to the Israelites (ancient and modern) is more common among lay believers (Christian and Jewish), biblical scholars involved in 'serious' scholarship do not assent to such an argument. They are, however, open to a more 'scientific' argument: the title deed of the land belongs forever to David's' progeny because the 'conquest' of Palestine by David's kingdom, understood as a model of a nation-state, represents the moment of primary acquisition. Thus this land is recoverable, reunifiable, even after the collapse of Israel (the northern kingdom) over 100 years prior to Josiah's reformation, even after being repopulated by Assyria with peoples from its vast empire.

Josiah is interpreted within the fixed and indivisible land of David, constructed in part by the discourse of biblical studies and in part by the picture presented by DH. The view of Josiah's reform as an attempt to recover or reunite this empire has been especially advocated by the Cross School. Cross claimed that Dtr portrayed Josiah as a new David who attempted to restore the empire of David through his reformation and imperialistic program. The Josianic edition of DH was a great sermon or propaganda work to rally Israel to the new possibility in King Josiah, a new David. Cross also suggested that DH was written primarily as propaganda for Josiah's reform.

To Cross, Josiah was the bedrock of his theory. The account of Josiah was the climax of the second and main theme in DH: God's promise of salvation in the faithfulness of David culminated in the reform of Josiah, which superseded the first theme of God's judgment on the northern kingdom (Israel) on account of Jeroboam's sin. Cross made it clear, in contrast to Noth, that 'it is not enough that the faithfulness of God to David and Jerusalem merely delay the end, postpone disaster'.[81] Cross argued that the theme of hope in God's

---

80. Whitelam, *Invention*, pp. 55-56.
81. Cross, *Canaanite Myth and Hebrew Epic*, p. 285.

faithfulness to David and Jerusalem was realized in Josiah. He made it clear that it was important to understand that 'the juxtaposition of the two themes, of threat and promise, provide the platform of the Josianic reform'.[82] It was toward the Josianic reform that the two themes had been moving. Cross emphasized this point that 'the second theme reaches its climax in the reform of Josiah'.[83]

The faithfulness of Josiah is overemphasized in 2 Kings 22–23, to a point where one has to suspect that something more is going on than what Noth had to say about the importance of Josiah. Cross argued that the faithfulness of Josiah was highlighted or overemphasized because the account was written during Josiah's reign, not during the Exile. Cross noted that 'Josiah alone escaped all criticism' when 'even King David and Hezekiah had peccadilloes'.[84] The author/editor during Josiah's reign portrayed Josiah in such a way as to present Josiah as the king in whom was 'centered the hope of a new Israel and the renewing of the "sure mercies" shown to David' and 'in David and in his son Josiah is salvation'.[85] The book of the law was important to Cross, but it did not overshadow the importance of Josiah. Josiah was more important to Cross than the book of the law, contrary to Noth. Josiah used the book to implement his reform rather than the book serving as the catalyst for his reform.[86] Cross summarized his view of Dtr's purpose in writing DH as follows: 'He has written a great sermon to rally Israel to the new possibility of salvation, through obedience to the ancient covenant of Yahweh, and hope in the new David, King Josiah'.[87]

Cross reinterpreted the function of 1 Kings 13, the prophecy of the coming destruction of the sanctuary in Bethel by King Josiah, as more than a mere reworking of Dtr who wanted to make a connection with the well-known prophecy with Josiah because Josiah happened to have destroyed the sanctuary. It was a deliberate attempt to prepare the reader's mind for the coming climax in Josiah's reform.[88] Josiah as the reformer was anticipated in 1 Kings 13 when the prophet had named Josiah as the one who would destroy the sanctuary in Bethel: 'The prophet is made to give utterance to one of the most astonishing as well as rare instances of a *vaticinium post eventum* found

---

82. Cross, *Canaanite Myth and Hebrew Epic*, p. 284.
83. Cross, *Canaanite Myth and Hebrew Epic*, p. 283.
84. Cross, *Canaanite Myth and Hebrew Epic*, p. 283.
85. Cross, *Canaanite Myth and Hebrew Epic*, p. 284.
86. Cross favors the account of Chronicles as more historical, which describes the reform as beginning prior to the discovery of the book; see F.M. Cross and David Noel Freedman, 'Josiah's Revolt Against Assyria', *JNES* 12 (1953), pp. 56-58. So the discovery of the book in 2 Kings is used by Josiah to support his reform, not the other way around.
87. Cross, *Canaanite Myth and Hebrew Epic*, p. 285.
88. Cross, *Canaanite Myth and Hebrew Epic*, p. 280.

in the Bible, obviously shaped by an overenthusiastic editor's hand'.[89] Cross himself was a bit 'overenthusiastic' about Josiah's reform: 'He attempted to restore the kingdom or empire of David in all detail'.[90] Therefore, Cross concluded that DH was 'a propaganda work of the Josianic reformation and imperial program'.[91]

Gary N. Knoppers is a leading scholar on DH and one of many who support Cross's interpretation.[92] His two-volume work *Two Nations under God* essentially elaborates upon and reinforces the dual redaction theory of Cross.[93] It is an important contribution, perhaps the most extensive apologia yet for the pre-exilic Josianic redactor. He argues that Josiah's reforms are an attempt to reverse 'the unrequited transgressions committed by Solomon, by Jeroboam, and by his other southern and northern predecessors' and to restore 'the orthopraxis that should have been the legacy of the united kingdom'.[94] His main contribution lies in his argument that Dtr depicts Solomon's reign as two different models of rule: the first half represents an ideal realization of the divine promise to David and the second half represents the antithesis of the first embedded in Solomon's apostasy. Knoppers suggests that 1 Kings 11–14 (Solomon's apostasy; the founding of the northern kingdom by Jeroboam and the prophecy against the Bethel cultus) sets up the problem for Josiah to resolve. It is Solomon's apostasy that causes the division of his kingdom. But the northern kingdom is valid as well because it was founded on God's promise to Jeroboam; thus two nations under one god. Jeroboam, however, goes astray by setting up rival cults—'the sin of Jeroboam'. Other kings follow this path, until Josiah tries to go back to the thesis represented in the first part of Solomon's reign. Therefore, the return to Solomon's ideal period coincides with the recovery of the northern kingdom—the reunification of two kingdoms—to exist once more as one nation under one god.

Knoppers clearly states his understanding of the purpose of Josiah's reforms in DH:

> The choice of one king as the peerless reformer does not strike me as arbitrary. I will argue that the depiction of Josiah's reforms is best understood as the work of a preexilic Deuteronomist (Dtr1) who promotes Josianic ambitions to enhancing Jerusalem's influence in Judah and the former northern kingdom.[95]

---

89. Cross, *Canaanite Myth and Hebrew Epic*, p. 279.
90. Cross, *Canaanite Myth and Hebrew Epic*, p. 283.
91. Cross, *Canaanite Myth and Hebrew Epic*, p. 284.
92. He is a co-editor with J.G. McConville of *Reconsidering Israel and Judah* and the chair of the Deuteronomistic History Group of the SBL (2002).
93. Knoppers, *Two Nations under God*, I and II (see p. 4 n. 7, above, for details).
94. Knoppers, *Two Nations*, I, p. 12.
95. Knoppers, *Two Nations*, II, p. 175.

Josiah's reforms are understood as a resolution to the problem of two 'nations' gone astray from the way of YHWH: the northern kingdom following the way of Jeroboam and the southern kingdom following the way of Solomon's apostasy—but they are part of the same solution, namely, Josiah's reforms. Knoppers argues that 'the northern kingdom's problems were longstanding and endemic' (they began at the inception of the northern kingdom) and 'the ill effects of Jeroboam's Bethel cultus upon the course of Israelite history absolve the Jerusalem cultus Jeroboam abandoned'.[96] Therefore, the solution lies in the destruction of the Bethel cultus and the cleansing of the Jerusalem cultus.

Knoppers depicts Josiah's reforms in the north as a 'crusade': 'Josiah's *northern crusade* represents the resolution to the bane of northern existence... The deuteronomistic description of Josiah's reforms...announces the long-awaited solution'.[97] In the second half of his second volume Knoppers argues that the literary strategy in depicting Josiah's northern reforms against the background of one event—Jeroboam's sin—in Israelite history is similar to the depiction of Josiah's southern reform, even though 'the Deuteronomist presents Josiah's southern reforms against the sweep of Solomonic and Judahite history'.[98] Knoppers summarizes his argument as follows:

> The author's [Deuteronomist's] self-conscious and coherent approach to disunion serves long-range designs. Because Judah and Israel comprise two nations under one God, united by cult, but disunited by YHWH's promises to David and Jeroboam, the Deuteronomist recounts and synchronizes the histories of both kingdoms... The Deuteronomist's very configuration of two nations under God is geared toward a positive evaluation of Josiah's southern and northern campaigns.[99]

Book reviews of Knoppers's books have been generally positive.[100] They praise Knoppers for his contribution to the on-going dialogue on the scholarship of DH. Surprisingly, no one questioned the title of his book: *Two Nations under God*. Knoppers has placed his understanding of Josiah's reforms

---

96. Knoppers, *Two Nations*, II, p. 71.
97. Knoppers, *Two Nations*, II, p. 71 (emphasis mine).
98. Knoppers, *Two Nations*, II, p. 196.
99. Knoppers, *Two Nations*, II, p. 237.
100. Reviews generally in favor of the work include: S.J. DeVries, *Int* 50 (1996), pp. 293-95; R.W. Klein, *JBL* 114 (1995), pp. 302-304, and *JBL* 115 (1996), p. 732-34; J.S. Rogers, *CBQ* 57 (1995), pp. 351-52, and *CBQ* 58 (1996), pp. 117-18; C.T. Begg, *RSRev* 20 (1994), pp. 328-29; D.M. Howard, *JETS* 39 (1996), pp. 471-73; R.P. Gordon, *JTS* 47 (1996), pp. 569-72; M. Köckert, *ZAW* 108 (1996), p. 473. One exception is T.L. Thompson's review, *JNES* 57 (1998), pp. 141-43, which sees Knoppers's work as an example of poor methodology in biblical studies (mixing biblical Israel and historical Israel). Thompson also sees Knoppers as Americocentric (being ignorant of works outside of the Harvard square, especially current scholarship in Europe).

within the discourse of nationalism just by the title of his book alone. There was no mention, never mind a critique, of Knoppers's understanding of 'nation', 'people', 'land', and other ideological terms. To be fair, Knoppers did not attempt to write an ideological reading of DH; he was reading and interpreting the text the only way he knows—from the center of biblical scholarship, which views itself as being 'objective' without vested interests or ideology. Nevertheless, it surprised me that no one questioned some of Knoppers's assumptions. Ralph Klein's review is a case in point.[101] Klein's review is detailed and meticulous. There is no doubt that Klein has done a close reading of Knoppers's work. Klein points out 'a number of stylistic infelicities', including typos, choice of words, 'incorrect use of the definite article', misquotation, and so on. He is a close reader when it comes to reading the text, but he, like other reviewers, is silent when it comes to reading Knoppers's assumptions.

Knoppers assumes that DH is a national history, without any qualification or explanation—note again the title of his work: *Two Nations under God*. He states plainly that 'the Deuteronomist composes *a national history* with the thesis that royal (and popular) fate is cultically derivative'.[102] The Josianic edition of DH is a national history that climaxes in the celebration of 'a national Passover'.[103] In Knoppers's own words:

> Like the *national* ratification of covenant, the *national* observance of the Paschal sacrifice is an ideal scene attended by 'all the people' (2 Kgs 23.21)... The discovery of 'the book of the Torah' leads Josiah to seek prophetic counsel and to ratify a *national* covenant based on this book. The *national* covenant signals renewed popular commitment to the terms of the book (2 Kgs 23.3).[104]

Since when did a kingdom of Judah become a 'nation' (that is, a nation-state)? Knoppers continues, 'The very possibility of holding a national Passover in Jerusalem assumes centralization. Moreover, this Passover, like the ratification of covenant, is mandated by royalty... He enlists and transforms the past to commend the present.'[105] I believe that is exactly what Knoppers is doing as well: It is Knoppers who is enlisting and transforming the past (DH) to commend the present (Euro-American understanding of the nation as the pinnacle of civilization). Furthermore, his depiction of Josiah's reforms is, once again, that of an internal religious dialogue. Assyria and other foreign powers and peoples play little part in Josiah's reforms historically and analogically. Knoppers maintains that Josiah's reforms are unique in the ancient Near East: 'The authority the Deuteronomist imputes to kings in overseeing

---

101. Klein, review of Gary N. Knoppers.
102. Knoppers, *Two Nations*, II, p. 70 (emphasis mine).
103. Knoppers, *Two Nations*, II, p. 175.
104. Knoppers, *Two Nations*, II, p. 222 (emphasis mine).
105. Knoppers, *Two Nations*, II, p. 224.

the practice of religion within their territories is, to my knowledge, unrivalled in the ancient Near East' because 'as a rule kings of the Levant do not destroy sanctuaries within their own states'.[106] Thus, he suggests, 'One must therefore go beyond seeking ancient Near Eastern analogies to Josiah's reforms to consider developments within Israel and Judah as comprising the context for the Deuteronomist's commendation of intrusive royal reforms'.[107] Not only is DH a national history, it narrates a unique development in world history, incomparable to anything that happened in the ancient Near East. Then where is he to go to seek a comparison? Is he not going beyond the ancient Near East toward modernist Euro-American understanding of the nation as an analogy?

Knoppers uses most often the term 'the former northern kingdom' to refer to the province of Samerina, the region north of Jerusalem, which tells much about his understanding of Josiah's reforms. He argues that the purpose of Josiah's northern campaign is to reunify the empire of David and Solomon, which was divided into two kingdoms about 300 years prior to Josiah's reign, the collapse of the northern kingdom having occurred about one hundred years prior to Josiah's reforms. He maintains that Dtr, in depicting the northern campaign in 2 Kgs 23.15-20, 'legitimates Josiah's incursion into northern Israel, because these incursions represent a resolution to a great impediment hindering a return to Israel's ancient grandeur'.[108] He reports, 'The Deuteronomist promotes Josiah's systematic campaigns as the severe, but necessary, means to revitalize his society and recover past glory'.[109] But we have to keep in mind that these assertions are not Dtr's, but Knoppers's interpretation of what Dtr is saying. Knoppers does not characterize the supposed northern campaign as an invasion or a conquest. Josiah's reforms were for the good of the region north of Jerusalem: 'Josiah *liberates* the former northern kingdom from its own past'.[110] Knoppers's suggestion that Josiah's reforms were mandated by God echoes the 'Manifest Destiny' or 'Divine Providence': 'Josiah's success *manifests* the deity's reassertion of sovereignty over land, history, and people'.[111] Ultimately it is Knoppers's understanding of the region north of Jerusalem as part of the bygone empire of David and Solomon that he uses for the argument for reunification. He reiterates this point over and over in his book.[112]

    106. Knoppers, *Two Nations*, II, p. 251.
    107. Knoppers, *Two Nations*, II, p. 251.
    108. Knoppers, *Two Nations*, II, p. 214. Have we not heard this rhetoric before? The West 'liberate' the people of the Third World for their own good because they do not know better.
    109. Knoppers, *Two Nations*, II, p. 215.
    110. Knoppers, *Two Nations*, II, p. 214 (emphasis mine).
    111. Knoppers, *Two Nations*, II, p. 209 (emphasis mine).
    112. A couple more examples will suffice: 'Josiah's return to Jerusalem (2 Kgs 23.20) marks his success in reunifying Judah and Samaria under the aegis of the Davidides' royal

4. Whose Space is it Anyway?

We also need to look at Knoppers's understanding of the peoples in the region north of Jerusalem. He summarizes Josiah's effort to 'reunification' as follows:

> The Deuteronomist justifies Josiah's intervention into northern affairs and at the same time appeals to both Judahites and the inhabitants of the former northern kingdom to rally behind this David *redivivus*... The future holds considerable promise, because for the first time the deuteronomistic ideals of one cult, one sanctuary, and one king—all devoted to one deity—have been realized.[113]

What he does not spell out, but assumes, is the idea of one people in addition to one cult, one sanctuary, one king, and one god. He understands the 'inhabitants' of the province of Samerina (the former northern kingdom) to be made up of 'Israelites' and 'foreigners'. Knoppers states this assumption when he acknowledges that there may have been opposition to Josiah's reforms in Jerusalem and the northern region:

> Josiah's imperialism may even have been questioned by the elite within his own capital. If Josiah's reforms were controversial in Judah, his forays into northern territory could scarcely have been more popular. Josiah's attempts to extirpate northern cults must have been viewed by many residents of the former northern kingdom, especially those who were *descendants of foreign immigrants*, as an unsolicited and merciless intrusion into their affairs.[114]

It is fascinating that Knoppers uses the phrase 'those who were descendants of foreign immigrants' to describe some inhabitants in the northern region. These were the descendants of those who were transplanted into Samaria during Assyrian hegemony, who have followed the script of the land:

> In spite of Assyrian hegemony over Samerina, YHWH continues to be active. The Assyrians conquer Samaria, deport Hoshea and the Israelites, and import foreign settlers into the former northern kingdom (2 Kgs 17.5-6, 24). Yet the Deuteronomist maintains the historical and prophetic ties that bind the fate of North and South... The nation of Israel is finished, but its people, land, and cult are not. The very trouble foreign settlers experience in worshiping their own gods, courtesy of marauding lions, implies that YHWH has not rescinded his claim to the land of Israel (2 Kgs 17.25). These *émigrés* only find peace when they are instructed on how to obey YHWH, 'the god of the land'.[115]

Why does Knoppers call them 'foreigners' or 'immigrants'? Why not call them the 'people of Samerina' for example? After all, they have been living

---

shrine' (Knoppers, *Two Nations*, II, p. 215); 'If purifying both the South and the North is essential to recovering the glory of the united kingdom, covenant renewal and Passover observance recall a time before the advent of the united kingdom itself' (pp. 223-24).
113. Knoppers, *Two Nations*, II, pp. 245-46.
114. Knoppers, *Two Nations*, II, p. 226 (emphasis mine).
115. Knoppers, *Two Nations*, II, p. 240 (emphasis mine).

in the province of Samerina for a hundred years or more. By referring to them as non-Israelites, he is implying that the land belongs to the 'Israelites' of the two kingdoms. By referring to the land as the former kingdom of Israel, he is assuming the view that the 'people' of Samerina have no right to feel at home in their own land.

The point of looking at Knoppers closely is not to show that he is being deliberately 'imperialistic' but to show that Knoppers, a first-rate scholar, is referring to Western metanarratives and is making assumptions, perhaps unwittingly, that often facilitate the inscribing of the aspirations, experience, and destiny of Western civilization. This tendency, however, is not limited to the Cross School. Although Antti Laato is not so much interested in Josiah in DH, his understanding of Josiah's reforms is similar to that of the Cross School. Laato is interested in how Josiah was regarded as a type of the coming ideal king in the imagination of the messianic expectations of exilic and postexilic times.[116] He also assumes that 'the political programme of Josiah was closely connected with *the restoration of the empire of David*'.[117] He believes that the biblical account in 2 Kgs 23.15-20 and the archaeological excavation at Mesad Hashavyahu (more below) support the view that 'Josiah also wanted to establish his kingdom in the territory of the northern kingdom (*and so restore the great empire of David's time*)'.[118] Laato also refers to the region north of Jerusalem as 'the former northern kingdom'. Once again, it is not the text that refers to the land north of Jerusalem as 'the former northern kingdom'. It is the modern interpreters who are using the term, and with this usage there is an assumption that Palestine is an indivisible land belonging to Israel because it was once occupied by the kingdom of David. Other peoples in the land are not mentioned in the discussion of Josiah's attempt to re-establish the Davidic Empire. Laato asks whether 'Judah and Egypt had drawn up a treaty concerning the division of Palestine?'[119] Egypt is clearly understood as a power and people from outside of the region. But how is it that other peoples in the region are not taken into account? The land is negotiable between the outside power, in this case Egypt, and Judah, the legitimate 'owner' of the region. Once again, Laato follows the view that sees the land as an empty stage on which Josiah's reform takes place.

I do not wish to give the impression that it is only Western scholars who are making the assumption that Josiah's reform takes place on the stage built by David. Eun Suk Cho, a Korean scholar living in the US, and Kong-hi Lo,

---

116. Antti Laato, *Josiah and David Redivivus: The Historical Josiah and the Messianic Expectations of Exilic and Postexilic Times* (Stockholm: Almqvist & Wiksell, 1992)

   117. Laato, *Josiah and David Redivivus*, p. 58 (emphasis mine).

   118. Laato, *Josiah and David Redivivus*, p. 58 (emphasis mine).

   119. Laato, *Josiah and David Redivivus*, p. 79.

a Taiwanese scholar who did his study in the US, are two non-Western scholars who also make this assumption.[120]

Cho's dissertation supports Cross's suggestion that the Josianic edition was written as propaganda or apology for Josiah's reform. His dissertation accepts almost *in toto* basic arguments of the Cross School while developing the idea of DH as a royal apology further perhaps than anyone else.[121] Cho argues that Josiah's reform—the centralization of the cult—was motivated not only by the desire to free Judah from imperial powers, but by the desire to reunite the two divided political entities, the former northern kingdom and Judah, into one United Kingdom. He accepts as a matter of fact that Josiah extended his territory to the former northern kingdom of Israel.[122] He assumes that after a lapse of one hundred years since the fall of Samaria to Assyria, the political entity north of Judah still saw itself as part of the unified kingdom of David and Solomon (three hundred years after the division). One must wonder about this assumption. It is one thing to assert that the court of Josiah saw itself as the legitimate inheritor of the province of Samerina, but it is hard to believe that the province of Samerina saw itself as part of the bygone kingdom of David and Solomon. Cho asks that very question but does not give a direct answer. Instead, he tries to answer how the two sides came to the agreement to reunify the two kingdoms. He suggests that although the North (the term Cho uses to refer to the province of Samerina) was not a politically independent entity at the time of Josiah, nevertheless, the 'reunification' ideology existed within the northern political entity that helped to bring Josiah's reform to a success.[123] He argues that it was not just by means of military conquest that Josiah was able to bring the North into his kingdom, but also by consolidating marginalized factions in the North and in the South (the term Cho uses to refer to Judah) that wanted to reunify the once united Israel. Thus Josiah's reformation is an actual, historical account of the reunification of the North and the South.[124] He accepts the assumption

---

120. Eun Suk Cho, 'Josianic Reform in the Deuteronomistic History Reconstructed in the Light of Factionalism and Use of Royal Apology' (PhD dissertation, The Graduate Theological Union, 2002); Kong-hi Lo, 'Cultic Centralization in the Deuteronomistic History: A Strategy of Dominance and Resistance' (PhD dissertation, Chicago Theological Seminary, 2003).

121. Cho's dissertation (which is close to 700 pages in length) is perhaps the most extensive defense of the Josianic edition as a royal apology.

122. Unfortunately, Cho does not question what I call the 'expansion' thesis in reading Josiah.

123. Cho, 'Josianic Reform', p. 84.

124. In my opinion Cho is thinking more of the current situation in Korea (North and South) and the yearning among many Koreans in both the North and the South for reunification of the two Koreas. His use of 'the North' and 'the South' seem to suggest this connection—the division of ancient Israel and the modern Korea.

of the existence of 'Greater' Israel as an empty stage on which Josiah's reform unfolds without much critical reflection.[125]

Kong-hi Lo's dissertation argues that Dtr wrote a 'nationalist' narrative that tries to consolidate different groups in Judah and in the province of Samerina into one people through the cultic centralization in order to achieve dominance over 'Greater' Israel and to resist Egyptian imperialism. Lo's analysis of the cultic centralization, using postcolonial theory, suggests that the idea of cultic centralization contains 'the elements necessary to the construction of a nation—people, organization, land, capital, religion/culture, way of communication and practice'.[126] Lo claims that Josiah's attempt to re-establish the Davidic kingdom narrated by Dtr1 is 'very nationalistic in tone'.[127] He argues that there is a strong anti-Egyptian motif in Deuteronomy and the Passover implemented by Josiah is viewed as an anti-Egyptian strategy. This leads to Lo's conclusion that Josiah was preparing his people to resist the Egyptians who were trying to fill the 'power vacuum' left by the supposed retreat of the Assyrians from the region. Josiah's cultic centralization was an attempt to unify his people around the Davidic dynasty and Yahwism, but it alienated 'the people of Samaria' from their own land. This made 'the people of Samaria' feel 'unhomely' in their own land.[128] By the term 'the people of Samaria' Lo is referring to groups of peoples that were brought to Samaria from various parts of the Assyrian empire (2 Kgs 17.24).[129] The identity and the place of the people of Samaria became ambiguous within the narration of DH: 'Were they foreigners, or were they

---

125. Cho's dissertation is intriguing to me because he is from a formerly colonized country, now living in the United States, who has accepted the discourse of nation-states because, in many ways, it helps him to understand the current situation in the divided Koreas. Once again, I do not fault him at all on this point. He is inscribing his experience and aspirations just as Knoppers and others have inscribed their experience, history, and aspirations in interpreting the DH. But I suspect that his 'inscribing' will seem more obvious than that of Knoppers and other Western scholars to a Western audience.

126. Lo, 'Cultic Centralization in the Deuteronomistic History', p. 278. Lo qualifies Josiah's kingdom as a 'nation' (as a 'nation-kingdom') that bears similarities with the modern nation-state in terms of basic elements—namely, people, power, territory—that make up a 'nation' but differs in terms of social structures and practices of power. Although 'nation-states tend to be organized and controlled by citizens, nation-kingdoms are dominated by kings or royal courts', Lo suggests that if we keep the difference in mind 'then we can consider Josiah's kingdom as a "nation"' (p. 55).

127. Lo, 'Cultic Centralization in the Deuteronomistic History', p. 41.

128. Lo argues that the people of Samaria were not 'selected' in the narration (DH) that justifies the possession of the land; therefore, the people of Samaria were constructed as the unhomely in their own land ('Cultic Centralization in the Deuteronomistic History', p. 75).

129. Lo, 'Cultic Centralization in the Deuteronomistic History', pp. 52-53, claims that the people of Samaria were exiles who were dominated politically by the Assyrians and religiously by the Israelites (the native inhabitants of Samaria).

part of Israel?'[130] Lo examines the narration of DH from the point of view of the people of Samaria, whom he calls the subaltern of DH. From the perspective of the people of Samaria, Josiah's policy is a strategy of 'dominance or even colonialism' rather than a strategy of resistance to foreign powers.[131]

Lo's suggestion that the people of Samaria are the subalterns of DH has merits. From the point of view of the people of Samaria, Josiah's policy is no more than a strategy of domination by another power that deprives the people of Samaria of their religious and political subjectivity and their land rights of.[132] Lo takes into account the subjectivity of the subaltern, which has been neglected or ignored in the discourse of DH and in biblical scholarship. However, he makes the same basic assumptions to clear the stage for the narration of Josiah to unfold: (1) the complete withdrawal of the Assyrians from Palestine that gave Judah an opportunity for independence; (2) Josiah wanted to recover the province of Samerina, the former kingdom of Israel, in order to re-establish the kingdom of David; (3) Josiah annexed Samaria; and (4) the existence of a power vacuum in the north.[133] Lo gives the people of Samaria subjectivity without power; Egypt has the power but has not yet come in contact with Josiah's kingdom. Lo summarizes that Josiah's effort to consolidate his people in order to resist imperialism is liberatory (or postcolonial), but, from the perspective of the people of Samaria, Josiah's policy is oppressive (or colonialistic). However, once again, the story unfolds on the stage of the indivisible, fixed land of the kingdom of David.[134]

Expanding Josiah's Kingdom for All it's Worth

Biblical scholars in general, and the Cross School in particular, have constructed a stage on which Josiah's story has been played out. But who wrote

---

130. Lo, 'Cultic Centralization in the Deuteronomistic History', p. 52. Lo asks: 'How did the land of Samaria, outside of Josiah's kingdom, become "inside" of Israel in hi/storical past and in Yahwistic tradition, but the people of Samaria themselves still remained the people without the rights on the land?' (p. 76).

131. Lo, 'Cultic Centralization in the Deuteronomistic History', p. 53.

132. Lo reflects this point by referring to the modern context in which China is trying to dominate Taiwan, his point being that colonialism is practiced 'not only by the westerners, but also by non-westerners, then and now' ('Cultic Centralization in the Deuteronomistic History', p. 49).

133. The people of Samaria do not have the power to resist; they are victims of Josiah's policy. Egypt has not entered the province of Samerina; thus Lo argues that Josiah was preparing for the coming confrontation with Egypt.

134. Lo does not wish that we repeat what Josiah did, especially the violence that is associated with Josiah's reform, nor condone the justification narrated by Dtr. Lo points out that China's claim to the right to possess Taiwan 'based on a historical period when Communist China did not even exist should not be justified' ('Cultic Centralization in the Deuteronomistic History', p. 281).

the script? In part Dtr wrote the script. But I contend that biblical scholars situated in Western institutions who continue to refer to the discourse of nationalism are the ones who continue to edit, modify, change, and rewrite the basic script of imperial history. The Cross School has viewed the authority and identity of the land north of Jerusalem as belonging to David and his heirs because the house of David once ruled that part of the land. The land, even though it was divided into two kingdoms three hundred years prior to Josiah's reign and even though the northern kingdom of Israel collapsed about a hundred years prior to Josiah's reforms, is viewed as one unified stage for Josiah's reforms. The Cross School, when interpreting Josiah's reform, refers to the discourse of nationalism, which claims that the authority and identity of a land that belongs to a centralized power. As Foucault reminds us, the modernist understanding of 'territory' is 'first of all a juridico-political one: the area controlled by a certain kind of power'.[135] The nation occupies or draws boundaries around the 'empty' land even though there are inhabitants living on it—the imperial doctrine of *terra nullius*. The indigenous peoples become foreigners in the land in which they have lived for generations; and the inhabitants who are different from the people of the nation are considered immigrants and foreigners. The discourse considers a land empty when there is no central power, the nation. Biblical scholars have viewed the inhabitants —who were not of Israelite descent—of the land north of Jerusalem during Josiah's reign as foreigners and immigrants. Even though they acknowledge that the northern kingdom collapsed a hundred years prior to Josiah and the land was renamed by Assyria as the province of Samerina, they assume that as soon as Assyria supposedly pulled out of the region, the land became empty—empty of people and power—and therefore ready to be occupied by Josiah, the legitimate ruler of the land.

There is what can be called the 'expansion thesis' that is associated with the assumption of the indivisible, unified land of Davidic Empire in operation in biblical studies. The expansion thesis envisions (1) Josiah as having achieved independence soon after so-called 'retreat' of Assyria from the region and (2) Josiah attempts to expand his kingdom in order to recover the lost empire of David. Josiah's activities described in 2 Kings 22–23 and the archaeological evidence are used as proof of this thesis. Even those who do not believe that Josiah expanded his kingdom beyond what is considered Judah proper believe that Josiah attempted to legitimize his claim to the land that once belonged to the house of David.

There are many scholars who argue that Josiah expanded his kingdom and dominated Palestine.[136] There are three general reasons for this sug-

---

135. Foucault, 'Questions on Geography', in *idem, Power/Knowledge*, pp. 63-77 (68).

136. Among many scholars, perhaps Abraham Malamat has been the most influential proponent of this thesis in recent years. His works include: 'The Last Wars of the Kingdom

gestion: (1) Josiah's 'campaigns' in 2 Kgs 23.15-20 (and its parallel in Chronicles) can be understood as a 'conquest' of the north; (2) Josiah's death at Megiddo (2 Kgs 23.28-30) is seen as a result of a battle between two rival powers, Judah and Egypt; and (3) there are several sites, including Mesad Hashavyahu, a small fortress not far north of Ashdod, and Megiddo in the north that can be viewed as belonging to Judah. These factors are used to envision a great expansion during Josiah's time. The vast kingdom of Josiah envisioned by Bright and others that rivaled the size of David's empire was based on the Chronicler's report. The Chronicler reports that Josiah's reform reached 'the towns of Manasseh, Ephraim, and Simeon, and as far as Naphtali' (2 Chron. 34.6).[137] These scholars believe that the Chronicler gives more accurate information on Josiah's expansion than what is given in 2 Kgs 23.8, which states that Josiah's reform was limited to the area 'from Geba to Beersheba'. Geba usually refers to a site in Benjaminite territory, but there are those who argue that Geba refers to a site much farther north, thus matching the claim of the Chronicler.

Bright's reconstruction of Josiah's political geography is a good example of those who believe in the expansion thesis. Bright believed that as Assyria lost its grip on Palestine, Judah gained its independence under Josiah's reign.[138] He correlated the chronological outline of Josiah's reign given in 2 Chronicles with political events in the Near East.[139] According to this reconstruction, Judah gained its independence gradually. Bright proposed that in Josiah's eighth year (633/32 BCE) Judah had changed the national policy from pro-Assyria to anti-Assyria.[140] In the twelfth year (629/28), Assyria was

of Judah', *JNES* 9 (1950), pp. 218-27; 'The Historical Background of the Assassination of Amon, King of Judah', *IEJ* 3 (1953), pp. 26-29; 'The Twilight of Judah: In the Egyptian–Babylonian Maelstrom', *SVT* 28 (1955), pp. 123-45; 'Josiah's Bid for Armageddon: The Background of the Judean–Egyptian Encounter in 609 B.C.', *JANES* 5 (1973), pp. 268-79; 'The Kingdom of Judah between Egypt and Babylon: A Small State within a Great Power Confrontation', in W. Claassen (ed.), *Text and Context* (JSOTSup, 48; Sheffield: JSOT Press, 1988), pp. 117-29.

137. It is interesting that the same scholars who believe in the expansion thesis opt to follow the Chronicler's version rather than the account in 2 Kings even though many view the Chronicler's work as less reliable. Nadav Na'aman states that 'many scholars have used the text of 2 Chr. 34.6-7, 33 as a basis for arguing that Josiah's expansion extended into Galilee, and that that area was even included in his cultic reform. This is the origin of the radical view which holds that Josiah had concrete claim to the entire territory of the kingdom of Israel, and that he attempted to reinstate the kingdom of David, in theory and practice, throughout the territory of Israel, up to its remotest borders' ('The Kingdom of Judah under Josiah', *Tel Aviv* 18 [1991], pp. 3-71 [43]).

138. My summary of Bright's reconstruction is based on *A History of Israel* (2nd edn), pp. 315-23.

139. Similar to Cross and Freedman, 'Josiah's Revolt Against Assyria'.

140. Bright, *A History of Israel* (2nd edn), p. 316.

no longer in a position to interfere with Josiah's ambition because of its internal troubles.[141] Then Josiah began his reform by destroying the temples outside of Jerusalem including the one at Arad where there were Greek mercenaries in Josiah's payroll. Josiah then took possession of the provinces of Samaria, Megiddo, and Gilead.[142] Josiah also extended his control as far as the sea, based on the understanding that Mesad Hashavyahu was controlled by Josiah.[143] In the eighteenth year (622), Josiah's reformation reached the climax when the 'book of the law' was discovered and Judah became truly a free country. Bright viewed Assyria and Egypt as rivals at the beginning of Josiah's reign, but, near the end of his reign, they became allies. When the Medes and the Babylonians took Nineveh in 612 and Haran in 610 from Assyria, Egypt was already an ally of Assyria. In 609, Necho II, son of Psammetichus, with a large force, was marching toward Carchemish to assist Asshur-uballit, the last ruler of Assyria, to retake Haran from the Babylonians. According to Bright, Josiah tried to stop Necho at Megiddo, which was a part of the territory of reunited Israel, but died in the process.[144]

The days when scholars described the extent of Josiah's kingdom based solely on biblical accounts or based on correlating archaeological evidence to biblical accounts have, for the most part, passed. John Bright's *History* represents the time when the expansion thesis was taken for granted and it was enough to show that some archaeological evidence corroborated biblical accounts in order to reconstruct Josiah's kingdom. Thus, Bright assumed the following while acknowledging that there was no extrabiblical evidence to support all his claims:

> It is reasonable to suppose that at this time (when Ashurbanipal was old, around 629—Josiah's twelfth year) Josiah both launched a sweeping reform and moved to take possession of the provinces of Samaria and Megiddo (and probably Gilead as well), into which the Assyrians had divided the territory of northern Israel. He also, at least for a time, extended his control as far as the Mediterranean Sea, as a fortress of his on the coast south of Joppa indicates. Whether Josiah annexed these areas all at once, or over a period of time, is unknown; *but since there could have been few, if any, Assyrian troops left to oppose him, and since most northern Israelites probably welcomed the change, it is unlikely that he encountered much resistance.*[145]

Bright maintained that Josiah expanded his kingdom greatly, including a successful campaign to annex the northern kingdom, 'though we have no

---

141. Bright, *A History of Israel* (2nd edn), p. 316.
142. This assertion is based on 2 Chron. 34.6. Bright assumes without any evidence that there were no Assyrian governors in these provinces.
143. Based on the fact that a letter in Hebrew was discovered at the site (more below).
144. Bright, *A History of Israel* (2nd edn), p. 321.
145. Bright, *A History of Israel* (4th edn), p. 316 (emphasis mine).

direct evidence of this, it seems *a priori* likely'.[146] Bright's (and many other scholars') 'a priori' was the belief in the expansion thesis and the understanding of the historical context based primarily, often solely, on the biblical accounts.

The death of Josiah is a key factor in reconstructing the political context of his reign. This affects the extent of the size of Josiah's kingdom (Josiah's death will be dealt in greater detail in Chapter 5).[147] Those who favor the expansion thesis argue that Josiah was killed in a battle against Necho II of Egypt at Megiddo.[148] Although the extent of expansion varies, they believe that Josiah was trying to maintain his newly acquired independence and to protect his expanded kingdom by attacking Necho because Necho had entered Josiah's territory.

There are several sites in question that have been used to argue that Josiah indeed expanded his kingdom greatly: Megiddo in the north, Mesad Hashavyahu in the west, and Beer-sheba and Arad in the south. The earlier excavators at Megiddo, as Finkelstein and Silberman summarize, attributed Stratum II, which is characterized by the abandonment of the Assyrian buildings of Stratum III and the building of a fortress dated toward the end of the seventh

---

146. Bright, *A History of Israel* (2nd edn), p. 321 (emphasis mine).

147. Na'aman states that 'the scarcity of Biblical data invited a wide variety of opinions concerning the extent of the kingdom, its internal structure, economy, etc. Some scholars have concluded that Josiah's kingdom consisted mainly of the area between the Beer-sheba Valley and Bethel; others, by contrast, have suggested that Josiah attempted to restore the kingdom of David in all its glory, and that he controlled much of the Cisjordanian areas' ('The Kingdom of Judah', p. 4).

148. B. Alfrink, 'Die Schlacht bei Megiddo und der Tod des Josias (609)', *Bib* 15 (1934), pp. 173-84; Christopher Begg, 'The Death of Josiah in Chronicles', *VT* 37 (1987), pp. 1-8, *idem*, 'The Death of Josiah: Josephus and the Bible', *ETL* 64 (1988), pp. 157-63; Julius Boehmer, 'Konig Josias Tod', *ARW* 30 (1933), pp. 199-203; Bright, *A History of Israel* (2nd edn), pp. 323-24; Cross and Freedman, 'Josiah's Revolt Against Assyria', p. 58; Stanley Brice Frost, 'The Death of Josiah: A Conspiracy of Silence', *JBL* 87 (1968), pp. 369-82; A. Malamat, 'Josiah's Bid for Armageddon', pp. 268-79; T.C. Mitchell, 'Judah until the Fall of Jerusalem (c. 700–586 B.C.)', in John Boardman *et al.* (eds.), *The Assyrian and Babylonian Empires and Other States of the Near East, from the Eighth to the Sixth Centuries B.C.* (The Cambridge Ancient History, Vol. III, Part 2; Cambridge: Cambridge University Press, 1991), pp. 371-409; Donald Redford, *Egypt, Canaan, and Israel in Ancient Times* (Princeton, NJ: Princeton University Press, 1992); M.B. Rowton, 'Jeremiah and the Death of Josiah', *JNES* 10 (1951), pp. 128-30; Anthony Spalinger, The Concept of the Monarchy', *Or* 47 (1978), pp. 12-36; Ephraim Stern, *Archaeology of the Land of the Bible. II. The Assyrian, Babylonian, and Persian Periods (732–332 B.C.E.)* (The Anchor Bible Reference Library; New York: Doubleday, 2001), p. 131; H.G.M. Williamson, 'The Death of Josiah and the Continuing Development of the Deuteronomic History', *VT* 32 (1982), pp. 242-48, and *idem*, 'Reliving the Death of Josiah', *VT* 37 (1987), pp. 9-15; Yigael Yadin, *The Art of Warfare in Biblical Lands in the Light of Archaeological Study*, II (New York: McGraw–Hill, 1963).

century, to Josiah 'in his efforts to reunite the two kingdoms' and 'its partial destruction was attributed to the encounter that would ultimately end Josiah's life'.[149] These scholars argued that 'the Megiddo fort, therefore, presumably provided the missing link to explain the showdown with Necho'.[150] But not a single *lmlk* stamp, which was used as a proof of the expansion of Josiah's kingdom, had been found at Megiddo.[151] Lance pointed out that the extent of Josiah's kingdom described as 'Geba to Beer-sheba' in 2 Kings fits closely with the northern and southern limits of the distribution of the *lmlk* stamps.[152] The use of the *lmlk* stamps to draw the boundaries of Josiah's kingdom has been rejected by many, and now there seems to be a consensus that the *lmlk* stamps were used by Hezekiah in his efforts to defend against the Assyrian invasion. Na'aman summarizes this change in understanding the *lmlk* stamps:

> For many years it was widely accepted to date these impressions to the seventh century, and specifically to Josiah's day. For that reason, archaeologists tended to date the layers of settlement in which such impressions were unearthed to the seventh century, and to use their distribution as a basis for determining the extent of Josiah's kingdom. However, recent studies have indicated that the jars bearing the *lmlk* seal impressions were manufactured in the late eighth century BCE, and that their production and distribution are apparently related to the preparations for Sennacherib's campaign against Judah. These conclusions led to the redating of levels in many sites in Judah, and eliminated the basis for the assumption that any direct connection might have existed between the *lmlk* jars and Josiah's kingdom.[153]

---

149. Israel Finkelstein and Neil Asher Silberman, *The Bible Unearthed: Archaeology's New Vision of Ancient Israel and the Origin of its Sacred Texts* (New York: Free Press, 2001), p. 348. Malamat, 'Josiah's Bid for Armageddon', stated that there was a general consensus that Stratum III represents the seat of the Assyrian province after the annexation of northern Israel towards the end of the eighth century and Stratum II is dated toward the end of the seventh century (p. 268). The question is who controlled Megiddo after Assyria retreated. Malamat thinks it is either Egypt or Judah, but he does not think there is conclusive evidence to support either. Graham Davies, *Megiddo* (Cambridge: Lutterworth Press, 1986), also concludes that it is difficult to determine who controlled Megiddo after Assyria. G.D. Ogden, 'The Northern Extent of Josiah's Reforms', *ABR* 26 (1978), pp. 26-34, argued that Megiddo did not belong to Josiah and the extensive reform program in the northern kingdom ascribed to Josiah represents the elaboration of a memory of the king's removal of foreign cultic paraphernalia in a program of religious reform in Jerusalem.

150. Finkelstein and Silberman, *The Bible Unearthed*, p. 348.

151. H. Darrell Lance, 'The Royal Stamps and the Kingdom of Josiah', *HTR* 64 (1971), pp. 315-32 (332).

152. Lance, 'The Royal Stamps', p. 332. See also, A.D. Tushigham, 'A Royal Israelite Seal (?) and the Royal Jar Handle Stamps (Part One)', *BASOR* 200 (1970), pp. 71-78, and 'A Royal Israelite Seal (?) and the Royal Jar Handle Stamps (Part Two)', *BASOR* 201 (1971), pp. 23-35.

153. Na'aman, 'The Kingdom of Judah', p. 4.

4. *Whose Space is it Anyway?*

Israel Finkelstein, who is the director of the present excavation at Megiddo, concludes unequivocally, 'There is no evidence whatsoever to attribute the fort of stratum II to Josiah'.[154] Now the question seems to be: If Josiah did not expand as far as Megiddo, how far north did he expand?

In the western borders, some biblical scholars have used the finds at the fortress of Mesad Hashavyahu, which is on the coast not far north from Ashdod, to support their claim that Josiah expanded his kingdom all the way to the coast, giving him an access to the sea. This fortress proved, according to these scholars, that Josiah had an access to the sea because a few Hebrew ostraca were discovered there.[155] The answer may depend on how one interprets three Hebrew ostraca found there. One of the ostraca (two are too short and difficult to translate) is a plea entered by an unnamed plaintiff with an authority in Mesad Hashavyahu.[156] A number of Yahwistic names appear in the letter. Naveh assigned the letter to the reign of Josiah and assumed that Hebrew was a 'national language' used exclusively by the 'Hebrews', which proved to him that this fortress was under Josiah's control.[157] Naveh proposed the following historical scenario based on his conclusion:

> Although there is no such indication in the Old Testament or other sources, it may reasonably be assumed that Josiah did not rule only over 'the cities of Manasseh, and Ephraim, and Simeon, even unto Naphtali' (2 Chron. xxxiv, 6), but extended his kingdom also to the west. Perhaps this expansion should be regarded as part of his attempt to bar the way to the Egyptian forces, comparable to his leading his army against Pharaoh Necho at Megiddo.[158]

Once again, Naveh was persuaded by the biblical accounts. He did not entertain the possibility that Mesad Hashavyahu belonged to the Egyptians. In addition to the Hebrew ostraca, the typical Eastern Greek pottery was discovered on the site in large quantities; this suggests, according to Nadav Na'aman, 'the presence of mercenaries of western origin'.[159]

Na'aman proposes that the fort belonged to the Egyptians who were known to have used Greek mercenaries. Even though there is no indication that Judah ever used them, there are many who claim that Josiah did use Greek mercenaries. Ephraim Stern supports this view by rejecting Na'aman's suggestion:

---

154. Finkelstein and Silberman, *The Bible Unearthed*, p. 350.
155. Finkelstein and Silberman note that 'the prize find for the maximalists was Mesad Hashavyahu' (p. 348).
156. Shemaryahu Talmon, 'The New Hebrew Letter from the Seventh Century B.C. in Historical Perspective', *BASOR* 176 (1964), pp. 29-38 (29).
157. J. Naveh, 'A Hebrew Letter from the Seventh Century B.C.', *IEJ* 10 (1960), pp. 129-39.
158. Naveh, 'A Hebrew Letter', p. 139.
159. Na'aman, 'The Kingdom of Judah', p. 45.

Around 609 BCE, the fort was destroyed, probably by the invading Egyptians, and for a short time the entire coastal region fell into their hands. A recent proposal that the fort was Egyptian with East Greek and Judaean soldiers serving under the Egyptian regime appears to be unacceptable. This totally contradicts both the evidence of the Hebrew ostraca and the absolute lack of Egyptian remains of any kind. It is impossible that an Egyptian fort of any period would be totally void of Egyptian remains.[160]

Finkelstein and Silberman disagree with Stern and accept the idea that 'Mesad Hashavyahu was an Egyptian coastal outpost staffed by, among others, Greek mercenaries'.[161] The 'ownership' of the fort at Mesad Hashavyahu will continue to be contested, depending on one's understanding of the political context at the time (more below).

On the southern borders, Beer-sheba and Arad are important sites of contention. The previous generation of scholars was divided between attributing the two sites to either Hezekiah or Josiah. Yigael Yadin argued that Stratum II of Beer-sheba with its system of fortifications did not belong to the end of the eighth century (Hezekiah), but to the end of the seventh century (Josiah).[162] He also attributed the destruction of the altar (Building 430) in Beer-sheba to Josiah based on the account in 2 Kgs 23.8 rather than to Sennacherib's invasion during Hezekiah's reign.[163] Thus, Yadin maintained that the archaeological ruin in Beer-sheba supported the description of Josiah's reform described in 2 Kings. On the contrary, Anson Rainey argued that the system of fortifications did not belong to Josiah's time, but to Hezekiah's time.[164] Thus Rainey argued against Yadin's theory and concluded that the altar in Beer-sheba was destroyed during the reign of Hezekiah.[165]

In Arad, a series of ostraca ordering the Arad fortress commander Elyashib to transfer large quantities of supplies to members of a group referred to as Kittim (probably Greek mercenaries) were found.[166] One of Yadin's suggestions was that this letter referred to Josiah's attempt to move his troops in Arad to a particular rallying-point in order to resist Necho's march through his territory.[167] Yadin assumed that Arad was Josiah's fortress. However, the

---

160. Stern, *Archaeology of the Land of the Bible*, p. 142.
161. Finkelstein and Silberman, *The Bible Unearthed*, p. 351.
162. Yigael Yadin, 'Beer-sheba: The High Place Destroyed by King Josiah', *BASOR* 222 (1976), pp. 5-17.
163. Yadin, 'Beer-sheba', p. 14.
164. Anson Rainey, 'Hezekiah's Reform and the Altars at Beer-sheba and Arad', in Michael Coogan, J.C. Exum and L.E. Stager (eds.), *Scripture and Other Artifacts: Essays on the Bible and Archaeology in Honor of Philip J. King* (Louisville, KY: Westminster/ John Knox Press, 1994), pp. 333-54.
165. Rainey, 'Hezekiah's Reform', pp. 338-49.
166. Na'aman, 'The Kingdom of Judah', p. 47.
167. Yigael Yadin, 'The Historical Significance of Inscription 88 from Arad: A Suggestion', *IEJ* 26 (1976), pp. 9-14.

question remains whether the Kittim were hired by Josiah, indicating that Josiah used Arad as a fortress, or if they were serving the Egyptians. Na'aman thinks it is the latter case: 'It is…more likely that these mercenaries were in the Egyptian army, and that the king of Judah, then subordinate to Egypt, was obligated to transfer supplies to these units'.[168] Beer-sheba and Arad, and another site in the south, Kadesh-barnea, remain controversial in the drawing of boundaries of Josiah's kingdom. I will discuss these sites again within the discussion of two comprehensive reconstructions of Josiah's kingdom in more recent years.

In one of the most recent reconstructions of the extent of Josiah's kingdom, Ephraim Stern argues that in the days of Josiah Judah's borders expanded in all directions.[169] Stern's reconstruction of Josiah's kingdom, however, is more limited than that of Bright', especially when it comes to the northern borders. Stern, in contrast to Bright, relies first and foremost on archaeological evidence rather than on biblical accounts. Stern's reconstruction has Josiah essentially recovering the Judah of Hezekiah's reign. There seems to be a consensus among biblical scholars that Josiah's expansion to the north was very limited.

Stern uses two assumptions to draw the boundaries of Josiah's kingdom. First, we will see that his understanding of Josiah's political situation influences many of his decisions in determining the extent of Josiah's kingdom. He believes in the following historical scenario: Josiah was an ally of Egypt against Assyria in the beginning of his reign, but after the complete withdrawal of Assyria around 630 BCE, if not earlier, Josiah was at war against Egypt, competing with Egypt for hegemony over the region; then, Josiah was killed in a battle at Megiddo by Necho II. Secondly, he applies the principle that equates the identity of land with cultural artifacts. Any site that has Judean 'ethnic' artifacts belongs to Josiah's kingdom. Stern uses all the available archaeological evidence to draw the boundaries of Josiah's kingdom. He uses the following evidence to designate a town as belonging to Judah during the days of Josiah: (1) the ethnic artifacts—the 'four-room' type structures, the Judean clay figurines, pottery vessels, weights; (2) the rosette seal impressions, and to a lesser extent, *lmlk* seal impressions produced by the royal court of Josiah; and (3) epigraphical material written in Hebrew. Stern seems to argue that if any site (town or fort) has any item designated as Judean, then it belongs to Judah.

There seems to be little discussion on the eastern border of Josiah's kingdom. The eastern border does not seem as crucial as the western and the southern borders for many scholars. Stern argued in an earlier article that

---

168. Na'aman, 'The Kingdom of Judah', pp. 47-48.
169. Stern, *Archaeology of the Land of the Bible*.

Josiah added the southern part of the former Assyrian province Jericho to the eastern border.[170] Stern claimed that 'Josiah's accomplishments along his eastern border, in the region extending from Jericho down to En-gedi' are even more impressive than the other fronts.[171] He updates his conclusion:

> The results of three major excavations permit us to conclude with certainty that the town was settled and flourishing during the Late Iron Age and that the finds from this period are *typically Judaean*. This means that during the 7th century BCE Jericho passed from Assyrian rule (for it previously belonged to the Israelite monarchy) to Judaean.[172]

He concludes that the eastern settlements were 'part of a greater plan intended to defend the entire kingdom'.[173]

In the northern border, Judaean artifacts are used to draw the northern boundaries: Bethel to Mizpah to Gezer to Mesad Hashavyahu. For example, Bethel, according to Stern, was annexed by Josiah shortly after the withdrawal of Assyria:

> Its sanctuary is mentioned in 2 Kings 23, which states that it was destroyed by King Josiah in about 622 BCE. This information alone is enough to include the city in Judah, but in the excavations of the site, some *Judaean* finds were reported, including a *sheqel* weight and *Judaean* figurines.[174]

In the city of Mizpah were found 'many *Judaean* weights, rosette impressions, clay figurines; and a large assemblage of 7th century BCE *Judaean* ceramics'.[175] Therefore, Stern concludes, 'There can be no doubt, therefore, that this town in Benjamin was, in the late 7th century BCE, within the borders of Judah'.[176] Stern also concludes that Gezer belonged to Judah, although he acknowledges that there is no conclusive evidence for it:

> It again became Judaean after the collapse of Assyrian control and the destruction, perhaps by Josiah, of the large Assyrian center there. The latest excavation at the site, conducted by W. Dever, strengthened this possibility, for the 7th century BCE stratum uncovered here certainly had a *Judaean* character.[177]

Stern's understanding of Mesad Hashavyahu as a Judaean fortress, rejecting Na'aman's view, is based ultimately on his understanding of the political context:

---

170. Ephraim Stern, 'The Eastern Border of the Kingdom of Judah in its Last Days', in Coogan, Exum and Stager (eds.), *Scripture and Other Artifacts*, pp. 399-409.
171. Stern, 'The Eastern Border', p. 399.
172. Stern, *Archaeology of the Land of the Bible*, p. 134 (emphasis mine).
173. Stern, *Archaeology of the Land of the Bible*, p. 137.
174. Stern, *Archaeology of the Land of the Bible*, p. 139 (emphasis mine).
175. Stern, *Archaeology of the Land of the Bible*, p. 139 (emphasis mine).
176. Stern, *Archaeology of the Land of the Bible*, p. 139.
177. Stern, *Archaeology of the Land of the Bible*, p. 140 (emphasis mine).

4. *Whose Space is it Anyway?* 153

Josiah gained access to the sea. This was probably the northwestern corner of the kingdom. One may assume that the coastal region captured by Judah in those days was even larger and that it encompassed the entire area between Mesad Hashavyahu and Tell Qasile, which means that the northern boundary of Judah was on the bank of the Yarkon River in the north, and nearly reached Ashdod in the south. Ashdod may have been an ally of Josiah in his wars against the Egyptians... It is interpreted as a Judaean fortress under a Judaean officer, in which soldiers originating in various East Greek islands were garrisoned. According to the accepted view, this fortress was established and existed for only one generation or less: between 630 and 609 BCE, from the time of the Assyrian retreat from the Palestinian coast to the battle between Josiah and the Egyptians at Megiddo, where he was killed trying to stop the Egyptians from aiding the Assyrians.[178]

Although the evidence is not conclusive, the evidence available is enough to confirm his understanding of the political context of Josiah; therefore, he concludes that Mesad Hashavyahu belonged to Josiah. The northern border of Josiah's kingdom stretched from Jericho all the way to the fortress of Mesad Hashavyahu on the coast. This conclusion is based on a reconstruction informed by interpretation of the archaeological data, which is in turn based on his understanding of the political context of Josiah and the belief in the equation of the identity of the place and of ethnic artifacts.

It is in the western and southern border that Stern sees a great expansion by Josiah. This conclusion is based on his theory that there existed a sophisticated two-line defense system that was closely controlled by the central administration in Jerusalem to curtail the Egyptian advancement. The two-line defense system in the west consists of 'an external line that bordered the Philistine territories in the Shephela, and an internal line that constituted the real line of defense, and not a mere boundary'.[179] Although the outer line was sparsely built and lacked the clear evidence of Judaean character, nevertheless, it 'served as outposts or guardposts and warning stations' for Josiah's kingdom, effectively expanding Josiah's kingdom to the outermost boundaries.[180] Stern explains this very sophisticated defense system in this way:

> There can be no doubt that these two defensive lines were connected with each other in many ways and that all were efficiently connected with the headquarters in Jerusalem, as we have already noted in the case of the other boundaries on the north, east, and west. This system made Judah's defenses look like one huge fortress... From his capital, the king could, in times of necessity, support any portion of the border or even a single site by sending soldiers, whether mercenaries or his own troops, when called upon... It should therefore be recognized that the overall number of Judaean fortresses in Judah's southern defensive line was certainly much larger.[181]

178. Stern, *Archaeology of the Land of the Bible*, p. 140.
179. Stern, *Archaeology of the Land of the Bible*, p. 143.
180. Stern, *Archaeology of the Land of the Bible*, p. 143.
181. Stern, *Archaeology of the Land of the Bible*, p. 162.

Stern asks, rightly so, where all the people who inhabited these desert settlements came from. He answers his own question by suggesting four different sources: (a) the Judean refugees after Sennacherib; (b) the Israelite refugees after the collapse of the kingdom of Israel; (c) internal immigration; (d) those who were sent for short periods of service as garrison soldiers.[182] All the forts were well manned by Josiah's subjects. In the end, Stern is convinced that the archaeological evidence clearly attests to the sophisticated defense system that had been established to defend the kingdom of Josiah. To Stern, Josiah had outmaneuvered and defeated Egypt in controlling most of southern Palestine.

In order to come to his conclusions, Stern rejects several accepted views. He rejects the accepted view that after Sennacherib's devastating campaign in the Shephelah only 39 out of 354 Judaean settlements were re-established during the seventh century BCE. He claims that 'as more sites are excavated, the more evidence there is for the existence of 7th century BCE settlements'.[183] Some sites already 'produced rosette seal impressions and a few *Judaean* clay figurines, which are the best chronological evidence for the existence of a 7th century BCE site'.[184] He argues that Tel Batash belongs to Judah, although there seem to be good reasons to attribute it to Ekron. He states, 'The similarity between the finds there and those from Ekron led the excavator to suggest it belonged to its Philistine neighbor at that time. This suggestion appears to be unnecessary in view of the many official *Judaean* remains here.'[185]

At the southwest corner is a fort at Kadesh-barnea. Stern claims that it belonged to Judah, even though a few Egyptian hieratic documents were found at the site. Furthermore, the fort was in existence from the mid-eighth to the early sixth centuries BCE without a disruption, which suggests that Kadesh-barnea was transferred from Assyria to Egypt peacefully. But Stern rejects the view that the fort belongs to Egypt. He argues that the discovery of a few Egyptian hieratic documents at the site as an indication of the site belonging to Egypt is not necessary; instead, he notes that 'similar documents appear to have been found at other Judaean forts, such as Arad'.[186] He prefers the view that 'the Egyptian script and especially its numbers were deeply rooted and widely used in Judaean administrative tradition'.[187] Once again,

---

182. Stern, *Archaeology of the Land of the Bible*, p. 162. We must ask: Where have all the non-Israelites gone? Once again, the theme of an empty land for the Israelites to settle is repeated.

183. Stern, *Archaeology of the Land of the Bible*, p. 142.

184. Stern, *Archaeology of the Land of the Bible*, p. 142 (emphasis mine).

185. Stern, *Archaeology of the Land of the Bible*, p. 144 (emphasis mine).

186. Stern, *Archaeology of the Land of the Bible*, p. 158. He does not entertain the thought that perhaps this fact shows that Arad also belonged to Egypt.

187. Stern, *Archaeology of the Land of the Bible*, p. 158.

his reconstruction fits his understanding of the political context of Josiah. He maintains that Josiah's policy toward Egypt changed after the supposed withdrawal of Assyria. Judah and Egypt competed over Palestine, with Judah having the upper hand until Josiah was killed by Necho II in the battle at Megiddo.

Israel Finkelstein and Neil Asher Silberman also use two assumptions to interpret the archaeological data in drawing the boundaries of Josiah's kingdom in their reconstruction of the extent of Josiah's kingdom: the political context of Josiah and the principle of the congruence between the land and the ethnic artifacts. Their borders are more limited than those of Stern. Once again, the death of Josiah is a key factor in reconstructing the political context of Josiah, which affects the size of the extent of Josiah's kingdom. In contrast to the scholars who understand Josiah to have been killed in a battle, Finkelstein and Silberman follow the scholars who believe that Josiah did not die in a battle.[188] This view argues that Josiah's kingdom was not fully independent and did not expand greatly, if at all, after Assyria's supposed retreat from the region because Egypt had stepped in to control the region.[189] Ahlström describes the political context which supports the view Josiah was not killed in a battle:

> 1) When Assyria pulled out of southern Syria and Palestine, Egypt moved in as the new master of that region. 2) Egypt and Assyria were not enemies; it was more of a cooperative transference of power. 3) Judah was probably the

---

188. The following scholars believe that Josiah was killed not as a result of a battle but as a result of court-martial or treachery or execution: Ahlström, *The History of Ancient Palestine*; Robert Althann, 'Josiah', in *ABD*, III, pp. 1015-18; Miller and Hayes, *A History of Ancient Israel and Judah*; Na'aman, 'The Kingdom of Judah'; Richard Nelson, 'Realpolitik in Judah (687–609 B.C.E.)', in William W. Hallo, James C. Moyer and Leo G. Perdue (eds.), *Scripture in Context. II. More Essays on the Comparative Method* (Winona Lake, IN: Eisenbrauns, 1983), pp. 177-89; Zipora Talshir, 'Three Deaths of Josiah and the Strata of Biblical Historiography', *VT* 46 (1996), pp. 213-36; A.C. Welch, 'The Death of Josiah', *ZAW* 43 (1925), pp. 255-60.

189. The logic is circular in some sense: the political context of Josiah's death informs the extent of Josiah's kingdom and the extent of Josiah's kingdom explains Josiah's death. That is, the question of Josiah's death depends largely on the extent of Josiah's kingdom and the historicity of his reforms. If we knew the extent of Josiah's kingdom then we would have a better idea as to why Josiah was killed. If Josiah's kingdom included the former Israel, then it may explain why Josiah confronted Necho when Necho tried to pass his army through Megiddo. If Josiah's kingdom included no more than the Benjaminite territory in the north, then it would be difficult to believe that Josiah intended to fight Necho. In that case, it would be better to assume that Josiah was summoned by Necho. If we can confirm the historicity of Josiah's reforms, then that may perhaps explain the reason for Necho's suspicion of Josiah's allegiance. Consequently, Necho may have called Josiah to explain himself and when he was not satisfied with Josiah's explanation, he killed him. If archaeological data cannot confirm the historicity of Josiah's reforms, then it will be of no help in understanding why Josiah was killed.

largest nation in western Palestine but its territory did not extend beyond Geba to the north and Beer-sheba to the south. 4) Josiah could not have expanded his territory to the north (Samaria, Megiddo, and Galilee) because Egypt controlled the territory of Palestine and the roads leading to the north. 5) Megiddo was an Egyptian garrison just as Arad and Mesad Hashavyahu were. 6) Judah probably was a vassal or a junior ally of Egypt. 7) It may have been that Josiah was playing a double game after Nineveh's fall, which could explain his death at Megiddo in 609.[190]

Finkelstein and Silberman believe that Judah was in no position to expand. Their reconstruction differs from Stern's in the following details: (1) Mesad Hashavyahu belongs to Egypt, following the argument of Na'aman; (2) Arad and Kadesh-barnea also belong to Egypt; and (3) the western borders were more limited to the upper Shephelah, due in part to the strength of Ekron, a Philistine city.

Finkelstein and Silberman believe that there was a peaceful transfer of power between Assyria and Egypt. Thus, in commenting on Megiddo they state: 'we can safely accept the alternative view, that stratum II at Megiddo represents a peaceful takeover by the Egyptians'.[191] They, following Na'aman, maintain that the fort at Mesad Hashavyahu belonged to Egypt and not to Judah. It is acknowledged that the relatively high ratio of eastern Greek pottery at Mesad Hashavyahu indicates the presence of Greeks. But the question as to which army the Greeks served is very much contested. They conclude, 'Mesad Hashvyahu was an Egyptian coastal outpost staffed by, among others, Greek mercenaries'.[192] In addition to the archaeological evidence, their conclusion is also based on their understanding of the political context in the day

---

190. A summary from Ahlström, *The History of Ancient Palestine*, pp. 763-69.

191. Finkelstein and Silberman, *The Bible Unearthed*, p. 350.

192. Finkelstein and Silberman, *The Bible Unearthed*, p. 350. Redford, *Egypt, Canaan, and Israel*, gives a similar argument as Na'aman: 'In the context of Psammetichos' reassertion of control over the Levantine coast, the mercenary troops he had acquired were also used to garrison the strongpoints. One such post has come to light through excavations at Mesad Hashavyahu on the coast not far from Ashdod' (p. 444). Redford examines the southeast region and concludes that 'similar pottery has come to light at Tel Melah in the Negeb. In the same area, at the Judaean frontier fortress of Arad, the archives that have been unearthed in the excavations of Aharoni mention contingents of *Kittiyim*, the word used in the Bible for "Greeks", to whom the Judaean authorities issue rations. Rather than to assert that inland Judah independently employed Greek soldiers from across the sea, it seems wiser to construe their presence in the area as the result of Egyptian imperial encroachment. Whether Judah, already under Josiah, had signed a treaty with Psammetichos, whereby it suffered reduction to vassal status, is a moot point: the Bible does not mention such a treaty, but an understanding of some sort might well explain the exchange of Judaeans for military service in Egypt in return for horses and Greek garrison troops' (p. 444). However, Redford believes that Josiah annexed the province of Samaria around 623 shortly after the revolt by the Babylonians (p. 445).

of Josiah: 'In any event, regarding Mesad Hashavyahu, there can be little doubt that Egypt, which expanded in the late seventh century along the coast of the Levant, was strong enough to prevent Josiah from building an isolated fort in the middle of an area in which Egypt had strong strategic interests'.[193] As for the presence of Judahites in Mesad Hashavyahu, they suggest that the Judahites were perhaps there as 'corvée workers who were sent there as part of Judah's obligation as a subordinate of Egypt'.[194] Therefore, they conclude, 'There is thus no reason to stretch the territory of Josiah as far west as the coast'.[195]

Finkelstein and Silberman claim that Kadesh-barnea was identified as belonging to Judah primarily because of 'the idea of the great expansion of Judah in the time of Josiah'.[196] Although there are some types of Judaean pottery and a few Hebrew ostraca, there is also evidence of the Egyptian presence.[197] They conclude that Kadesh-barnea was built under Assyrian auspices with the assistance of the local vassal states. Then, in the late seventh century it was passed on to the Egyptians; this view is supported by the lack of disruption and the discovery of a few Egyptian hieratic documents. They follow the hypothesis that Egypt and Assyria had an alliance that left the hegemony uninterrupted in Palestine. Therefore, they do not identify a site as belonging to Josiah's kingdom just because Judaean artifacts are found there. If there is evidence of Egyptian presence in a site, they attribute the site to Egypt rather than to Judah, contrary to Stern.

Finkelstein and Silberman support their view of Josiah's kingdom as more limited than that envisioned by Stern on the same archaeological evidence. They work with a premise similar to Stern's: 'we may speculate that if Josiah extended the borders of Judah, the typical Judahite finds must also have gradually expanded to the new territories'.[198] What they found was that the typical Judahite finds were limited to what is considered Judah proper. One of the more important artifacts of the late seventh century are small inscribed weights made of limestone: 'They appear mainly in the heartland of Judah,

193. Finkelstein and Silberman, *The Bible Unearthed*, p. 351.
194. Finkelstein and Silberman, *The Bible Unearthed*, p. 351. Na'aman states that: 'The exact date of the Mesad Hashavyahu ostraca is unknown, nor can we determine whether they belong to Josiah's day (and thus indicate his subordination to Psammetichus I), or to those of his sons Jehoahaz or Jehoiakim, both of whom were vassals to Necho II. The destruction of the fortress may be dated to 604 BCE... The subordination of Judah to Egypt is also indicated by the findings at Arad' (p. 47).
195. Finkelstein and Silberman, *The Bible Unearthed*, p. 351.
196. Finkelstein and Silberman, *The Bible Unearthed*, p. 352.
197. Na'aman suggests that 'the findings from the fortress at Kadesh-barnea may also indicate the service of Judeans in a local garrison' belonging to Egypt ('The Kingdom of Judah', p. 48).
198. Finkelstein and Silberman, *The Bible Unearthed*, p. 352.

from the Beersheba valley in the south to the area just to the north of Jerusalem. They were also found in large quantities in the eastern Shephelah.'[199] Although they were also found outside of 'these traditional borders of Judah' in the lower Shephelah and the coastal plain, 'this can be a result of strong trade activity between Judah and this area'.[200] There seems to have been a strong trade activity, especially with Ekron.[201] They also use the distribution of rosette impression seals, which may have had some role in the administration of Judah at the time, to draw the boundaries. They note that the distribution of the rosette impression seals 'encompasses the highlands of Judah, from the Beersheba valley in the south to the area a bit to the north of Jerusalem, with the main concentration in the area of the capital'.[202] There are also clay figures that are considered Judaean. Almost all of the figurines of a standing woman supporting her breasts 'were found in the heartlands of Judah, between Beersheba and Bethel' and the figurines depicting a horse and a rider 'were found within the borders of Judah proper'.[203] They argue, 'When all these items are individually plotted on a map, their distribution is quite similar. It extends from the Beersheba valley to the plateau of Bethel north of Jerusalem, and from the Dead Sea and Jordan valley to the upper Shephelah.'[204] Although they conclude that 'a permanent and far-reaching annexation of new territories into the kingdom of Judah is simply not suggested by the archaeological finds', they leave the possibility of a short-lived drive outside of Judah's core territory, even to the north.[205]

Finkelstein and Silberman do not refute the expansion thesis. Josiah would have expanded his kingdom to the north if not for Egypt. The question is not necessarily about whether Josiah recovered the province of Samerina or not, but who had the right to occupy that province. Egypt is a foreign power, so

199. Finkelstein and Silberman, *The Bible Unearthed*, p. 352.
200. Finkelstein and Silberman, *The Bible Unearthed*, p. 351.
201. Na'aman states that 'Excavations at Tel Miqne (Ekron) have shown that a very large town, over 250 dunams in area, flourished there during the seventh century, and that its economy was principally based on the production of olive oil… Judah's obvious weakness along its western border following Sennacherib's campaign, no less than Ekron's rise to power, prevented Josiah from expanding westward' ('The Kingdom of Judah', p. 49).
202. Finkelstein and Silberman, *The Bible Unearthed*, p. 352.
203. Finkelstein and Silberman, *The Bible Unearthed*, p. 352.
204. Finkelstein and Silberman, *The Bible Unearthed*, p. 353.
205. Finkelstein and Silberman, *The Bible Unearthed*, p. 353. Na'aman also leaves room for the possibility, albeit a limited one, of northern expansion: 'In summary, it is definitely possible that Josiah expanded in the Samarian hill country, although the information on this is not sufficiently clear and there is no way to determine the actual extent of his activity in the area. On the other hand, his expansion certainly ran no further north than the central hill country, and there is no basis for the hypothesis that either Galilee or the Jezreel Valley was also included within the boundaries of his kingdom' ('The Kingdom of Judah', p. 44).

even if it had occupied it, it had no right to do so; Josiah had the right to occupy it. The fact that he was not able to do so is a moot point. Stern does not ask why Josiah was not able to expand to the north; he simply acknowledges that Josiah did not do so based on archaeological evidence. Why is it that they do not ask whether there was a people organized as a political entity that occupied the province of Samerina after the supposed retreat of Assyria (another foreign power)? If biblical scholars can envision the extent of Josiah's kingdom stretching as far north as Megiddo without any archaeological evidence, why can they not envision a political entity in Samaria after the supposed retreat of Assyria? For some the province of Samerina was 'empty', but for some reason, perhaps because of Egypt, Josiah was unable to expand to the north. If the province of Samerina was not 'empty', this may explain why Josiah was unable to expand to the north. Perhaps there was a politically organized people occupying the land even after the supposed retreat of the Assyrians.

In the end it really does not matter whether Josiah expanded his kingdom to the north or not; it really does not matter whether Josiah's reforms were actually implemented in the north or not. Boundaries change, but the stage and the actors remain the same. For the standard political 'map' of ancient Israel does not change.[206] Whether Josiah's kingdom was smaller than Judah proper or whether it extended beyond Judah proper does not matter. There exists 'Greater' Israel in the imagination of biblical scholars. It does not matter whether Josiah recovered a large portion of the former northern kingdom or a small portion. The region north of Jerusalem is still considered part of 'Greater' Israel. DH provides the official, political map of 'Greater' Israel. The political map gives Josiah the authority to claim the land for himself. Thus, the archaeological findings are framed within this political map. They may appear outside or inside Josiah's kingdom, but they are plotted on the political map of 'Greater' Israel. The borders of Josiah vary, but there is no change in the land as the stage on which the history of ancient Israel is enacted. The people within the borders of Israel proper are Israelites and the others are foreigners. The solid lines demarcating the political borders of 'Greater' Israel construct a stage on which Josiah's reforms are played out. Borders however are porous, not fixed. The idea of one culture per place is

---

206. According to DH, it was David who was supposed to have unified Palestine under his dynasty. Ideologically, the town lists in the book of Joshua serve as the map of ancient Israel. It does not matter whether they indicate the tribal allotment at the end of the period of Judges or the administrative districts of the united kingdom or the town lists of the southern tribes belonging to the time of Josiah. The town lists in the book of Joshua are the map that names the sites in 'Greater' Israel, thereby appropriating, defining, and capturing the land for Josiah to reunify the divided kingdoms, or to state his policy to reunify them.

fictional. Boundaries do not enclose a fixed culture or people. By closing the borders, by fixing the borders, we are creating an artificial view of the reality. This is no more than following the conceptual premise of the modern nation that conceived the principle of the congruence between the people and the polity: 'Rarely did the populace of a given territory have a more or less single and set language, culture, and political allegiance. This was not true for most of the world until the nineteenth century, and for much of it is still not true.'[207]

A Power Vacuum in the Province of Samerina?

We need now to examine the assumption that the province of Samerina, the land north of Josiah's kingdom, was 'empty' of power and people as soon as Assyria supposedly withdrew from that part of Palestine, clearing the stage for the history of ancient Israel to unfold. There is no direct evidence to prove that there were 'native' powers and peoples in the province of Samerina competing and coexisting with Josiah's kingdom. First, there is a growing consensus that Josiah did not annex the province of Samerina, and if Josiah did expand to the north, this expansion was very limited. Why did Josiah not annex or expand to the province of Samerina? The idea that Egypt might have filled the power vacuum is a viable option that needs to be examined. But the possibility that the province of Samerina remained intact even if the retreat of Assyria occurred and competed with Josiah's kingdom needs to be considered. Rather than looking for the 'roots' of the house of David in the former northern kingdom of Israel, we are looking for 'routes' people have taken in the land called the province of Samerina.

We need to examine first when the supposed retreat of Assyria from the province of Samerina might have occurred since that is when the supposed power vacuum occurred. We know that after conquering and securing the West by the beginning of the seventh century, Assyria under Ashurbanipal (668–627) reached the zenith of its power when Ashurbanipal invaded and conquered Thebes in 663. The great and mighty Assyria, however, would totally collapse and disappear from world history little more than fifty years later. When did Assyria retreat from or lose control of the southwest district of its empire? Was there a power vacuum in Palestine during Josiah's reign? There are many scholars who argue that Judah, under the leadership of Josiah, enjoyed full independence from foreign forces during the civil war between Nineveh and Babylon, between the time of Ashurbanipal's death or close to his death (c. 627) and the death of Josiah (609). There is no question that Judah was under the shadow of the Assyrian empire prior to Josiah's reign and that Judah fell quickly under the suzerainty of Egypt after Josiah's death

---

207. A remark Robert Coote made in his lecture on the term 'nations'.

for a short time (from 609 to 605), before bearing the yoke of Babylon when Nebuchadrezzar defeated Egypt in 605 at Carchemish. Was there an interruption of hegemony in Palestine for Josiah to expand his kingdom to the north in the two decades in question (c. 630–610)? Is there a reasonable explanation to support the claim that, although Assyria was considerably weakened during the two decades in question, there was no power vacuum for Josiah to fill?

Many scholars would agree with Tadmor's assessment that 'Assyria's supremacy in the West rapidly declined after the death of Ashurbanipal in 627'.[208] After the death of Ashurbanipal, Assyria was locked once again in an exhausting war with Babylon, which lasted until the end of Assyria. It was not only Babylon that preoccupied Assyria's attention and drained Assyria's strength. The Medes and the Cimmerians, and possibly the Scythians, were threatening them from the northeast. Unfortunately, there is no written source that states when Assyria actually relinquished its grip over the West. The last attested date for Ashurbanipal is 631 and there is no mention of what the situation in the West was like.[209] Cross and Freedman have tried to show that Josiah's reformation as described in 2 Chronicles 34–35 reflected the progressive decline of Assyrian authority.[210] Thus, Josiah's eighth (632), twelfth (628), and eighteenth years (622) represented Josiah's reactions to the political changes in Assyria and the steps in his political-religious reformation designed to overthrow the Assyrian rule and to re-establish the Davidic kingdom. Although Cross and Freedman's chronology needs adjustments, the suggestion that the Chronicler's account of Josiah's reformation has a genuine historical reflection is attractive. But I have my reservations in taking the Chronicler's account at face value.[211]

There is, however, no proof that Assyria lost control of Palestine after 630. Even in the southeastern region of the Neo-Assyrian Empire, Assyria seemed

---

208. Hayim Tadmor, 'Philistia under Assyrian Rule', *BA* 29 (1966), pp. 86-102 (101).

209. Joan Oates, 'Assyrian Chronology, 631–612 B.C.', *Iraq* 27 (1965), pp. 135-59.

210. Cross and Freedman, 'Josiah's Revolt Against Assyria'.

211. The Chronicler wants to portray Josiah as a 'reformist' even before the discovery of the 'book of the law' in the eighteenth year; this 'fact' may have more to do with the Chronicler's overall scheme in writing Chronicles rather than on historical fact. See Sara Japhet, *I & II Chronicles* (Louisville, KY: Westminster/John Knox Press, 1993), and H.G.M. Williamson, *1 and 2 Chronicles* (New Century Bible Commentary; Grand Rapids: Eerdmans, 1982), for some theological and schematic reasons for this. The scholarship on Chronicles has been fixated on the question of its historicity since the dawn of modern biblical scholarship. Its theological and schematic view of history has brought suspicion, more so than DH, on its reliability as a source of history, and for good reasons. See John W. Kleinig, 'Recent Research in Chronicles', *CurBS* 2 (1994), pp. 43-76, and M. Patrick Graham, Kenneth G. Hoglund and Steven L. McKenzie, *The Chronicler as Historian* (JSOTSup, 238; Sheffield: Sheffield Academic Press, 1997), for discussion on the Chronicler as historian.

to have maintained a firm control. Brinkman notes that the Babylonian documents show that the years 647–627 BCE were years of peace and economic growth for Babylonia and were characterized by continuous and uninterrupted Assyrian rule in Babylonia.[212] Furthermore, the northern district of the Neo-Assyrian Empire seemed to have been under Assyria's control until the end. Na'aman notes:

> In 609–607 BCE, when all the major cities of Assyria had already fallen into his hands, King Nabopolassar of Babylonia launched campaigns into districts south of the kingdom of Urartu; this leads us to conclude that, throughout its existence, the Assyrian empire maintained control of its northern districts, up to its border with Urartu.[213]

Thus Na'aman asks: 'Are we to assume that a different state of affairs prevailed on its southwestern front, and that Assyria had previously withdrawn from that front?'[214] Na'aman maintains that no one ousted Assyria from Syria and Palestine before Ashurbanipal's death and the revolt in Babylonia in 626 BCE led by Nabopolassar.[215] Na'aman, however, suggests that Josiah's cultic reform began in Josiah's eighteenth year (622) because it was only at that point that Josiah felt 'secure to carry out a comprehensive purge throughout his kingdom'.[216] But this does not mean that there was a power vacuum in the province of Samerina for Josiah to step into and fill. Na'aman argues that the Assyrian retreat from the West (Syria-Palestine) 'was implemented in coordination with Egypt, which could, from all possible standpoints, be considered as a sort of 'successor state' for the territories vacated by Assyria'.[217] Thus, Na'aman concludes that Josiah was a vassal of Assyria during the first half of his reign and a vassal or a junior ally of Egypt for the second half of his reign.[218] Na'aman points out that Josiah under Egypt had considerable freedom of action in the internal regions of his kingdom because Egypt was preoccupied with other obligations, especially securing the important trade routes and supporting Assyria against Babylon. Egypt left Judah

---

212. John A. Brinkman, *Prelude to Empire: Babylonian Society and Politics, 747–626 B.C.* (Philadelphia: The Babylonian Fund, University Museum, 1984), pp. 105-11. There are no historical documents from 639–626 BCE. The Babylonian Chronicles pick up with Nabopolassar's accession in 626 BCE. See D.J. Wiseman, *Chronicles of Chaldaean Kings (626–556 B.C.) in the British Museum* (London: British Museum, 1956), and A.K. Grayson, *Assyria and Babylonian Chronicles* (Locust Valley, NY: J.J. Augustin Publisher, 1975).
213. Na'aman, 'The Kingdom of Judah', p. 36.
214. Na'aman, 'The Kingdom of Judah', p. 36.
215. Na'aman, 'The Kingdom of Judah', p. 38.
216. Na'aman, 'The Kingdom of Judah', p. 38.
217. Na'aman, 'The Kingdom of Judah', p. 40.
218. Na'aman, 'The Kingdom of Judah', p. 40.

alone because it did not play an important role in the trade route, the *via maris*, that was crucial for Egypt and Assyria.[219]

The *via maris* played a crucial role in the Assyrian hegemony of Palestine. Assyria wanted to control Philistia, which straddled the *via maris*, the all-important road connecting Egypt in the south to the north (Palestine, Syria, and Mesopotamia); Samaria and Megiddo played important roles in the security of the route whereas Judah played no role in securing it. Tadmor remarks that the position of the *via maris* 'on the major international trade routes, and its possession of convenient ports and a developed maritime trade made it a natural target for conquest'.[220] Therefore, it is not surprising that Judah was left alone as a vassal state, whereas Philistia was controlled more tightly. Ashurbanipal had a firm control of Philistia when he started his reign. This is confirmed by his campaigns in Egypt, which required a full cooperation from Philistia in order to launch such campaigns. About a decade later, Assyria's dominance of Philistia is attested by two legal documents from Gezer, one of the main cities in Philistia, from the years 651 and 649. There is also a mention of an Assyrian governor at Samaria in 646.[221] Tadmor reasons, 'Ashkelon and Gaza paid tribute as long as Assyria prevailed in Ashdod and in Samaria'.[222]

Who, then, controlled the *via maris* after the 'retreat' of Assyria? Herodotus states, 'Psammetichus ruled Egypt for fifty-four years; for twenty-nine of these he sat before Azotus, the great city in Syria, and besieged it till he took it. Azotus held out against a siege longer than any city of which I have heard' (Herodotus 2.157). Tadmor suggests that Azotus—generally held to be Ashdod—was besieged in the twenty-ninth year of Psammetichus, 635, rather than for a period of twenty-nine years.[223] This is an attractive suggestion since Herodotus himself was puzzled by such a long siege. Anthony Spalinger acknowledges that a siege of twenty-nine years seems fictitious,

---

219. The *via maris* ('the Way of the Sea') was a major trade route that ran through Palestine along the coast; important cities along this route were Philistine cities, and, if a traveler wanted to turn eastward, Megiddo; this route by-passed the central Palestinian hill country (Judah).
220. Tadmor, 'Philistia under Assyrian Rule', p. 86.
221. Malamat, 'Josiah's Bid', p. 270.
222. Tadmor, 'Philistia under Assyrian Rule', p. 101.
223. Tadmor, 'Philistia under Assyrian Rule', p. 102. Na'aman argues that 'the "twenty-nine years of siege" grew out of chronological speculation on Herodotus's part: according to his calculations, the siege began when Psammetichus I set out to meet the Scythians on the coast of Philistia and persuaded them to retreat (I.105), and ended immediately after the Scythians' defeat by the Medes 28 years later, putting an end to their rule in Asia' ('The Kingdom of Judah', p. 40). According to this scheme, Psammetichus began the siege in 641 (for 29 years), encountered the Scythians in the following year (640), and the end of the siege (612) coincides with the defeat of the Scythians by the Medes in 612.

but he maintains that it is highly likely that Psammetichus did take Ashdod sometime prior to sending his army into Syria and to the Euphrates in 616.²²⁴ Spalinger maintains that prior to Egypt's activity along the Euphrates in 616 'some type of alliance existed between Josiah of Judah and Psammetichus', enabling Egypt to secure 'the *via maris* for herself as well as a pledge of neutrality (if not benevolent in nature) from Josiah…when the Assyrian influence receded from Syria and Palestine'.²²⁵ It was crucial to control Ashdod in order to control Philistia and in turn to control the *via maris*. And the likelihood that the fortress in Mesad Hashavyahu was Egyptian supports the view that it was used by Egypt to secure the route (*via maris*) to the north for the Egyptians.²²⁶ This was what both Egypt and Assyria wanted: to maintain the control of the *via maris* for their commercial interests. It seems that Egypt stepped in to maintain the control of the *via maris* when Assyria was busy at the other end of its empire.

There is another power, however, that needs to be considered in the political equation of the west. Herodotus describes the domination of the Scythians over 'Asia' and their encounter with Psammetichus I in Palestine at the start of their 'domination':

> [104]…the Medes met the Scythians, who worsted them in battle and deprived them of their rule, and made themselves master of all Asia. [105] Thence they marched against Egypt: and when they were in the part of Syria called Palestine, Psammetichus king of Egypt met them and persuaded them with gifts and prayers to come no further. So they turned back… [106] The Scythians, then, ruled Asia for twenty-eight years… The greater number of them were entertained and made drunk and then slain by Cyaxares and the Medes: so thus the

---

224. Anthony Spalinger, 'Egypt and Babylonia: A Survey (c. 620 B.C.–550 B.C.)', *SAK* 5 (1977), pp. 221-44 (223). Spalinger believes that the interval between 622 and 620 satisfies three sources for the end of the siege of Ashdod: the eighteenth year in 2 Kings, the Babylonian Chronicles (Egypt's activity in 616), and Herodotus (Psammetichus's siege of Ashdod and encounter with the Scythians). But he cannot rule out an earlier date for the end of the siege of Ashdod, for example, Tadmor's suggestion of 635 or Gitin's suggestion of c. 630 (see below).

225. Spalinger, 'Egypt and Babylonia', p. 223.

226. Redford, *Egypt, Canaan, and Israel*, supports the view that Egypt controlled this fort. He cites Psammetichus's policy of organizing his military into 'garrisons' and manning the garrisons with foreign soldiers. Redford characterizes Psammetichus as 'a highly desirable employer for Asiatics as well as Greeks' (p. 444), and suggests that it was a policy of Josiah to send Judaeans to Egypt, at least during the first two decades of Josiah's reign (p. 444). He agrees with Na'aman and Spalinger among others that there was a treaty, an alliance between Egypt and Judah: 'Whether Judah, already under Josiah, had signed a treaty with Psammetichus, whereby it suffered reduction to vassal status, is a moot point: the Bible does not mention such a treaty, but an understanding of some sort might well explain the exchange of Judaeans for military service in Egypt in return for horses and Greek garrison troops' (p. 444).

Medes won back their empire and all that they had formerly possessed; and they took Ninus [Nineveh]...and brought all Assyria except the province of Babylon under their rule.²²⁷

Richard P. Vaggione describes how Herodotus's description of the Scythian domination in conjunction with Jeremiah's prophecy concerning 'the foe from the north' (Jer. 1.13-14) presented a picture of a world empire that competed with the Assyrian empire and threatened to dominate Palestine.²²⁸ Vaggione argues that the Scythians' empire was limited to 'Upper Asia', which 'extended roughly from the Halys to the further border of Media, and was limited on the north and south by the width of Asia Minor'.²²⁹ Babylonia and Syria-Palestine were not only excluded from the Scythian empire but were simply irrelevant. Vaggione concludes:

> The picture which Herodotus presents to us is one in which the Scythians have used the confused political situation to seize control of a part of the disintegrating Assyrian Empire and are raiding the surrounding countries. In his account of the Scythians' descent into Palestine-Syria he gives us an example of such a raid.²³⁰

Redford speculates that there might be a connection between the raid by the Scythians described by Herodotus and the assassination of Amon in 640:

> Twenty-eight years before the fall of Nineveh in 612 would bring us to 641–640, the twenty-fourth year of Psammetichos I... Within months Amon...was assassinated... One can only suspect a connection between this precipitous action on the part of a populace filled with panic and the havoc caused by a recent raid of barbarians never seen before and possibly still roving the countryside.²³¹

---

227. Herodotus 1.104–106. Quotations from LCL. Redford describes the appearance of the Scythians in a dramatic fashion: 'If no other faction had been introduced into the political equation, Egypt and Assyria might, in the years following 650 BC, have tacitly agreed to maintain separate spheres of influence and have divided the ancient world between them. But a new element from an unexpected quarter was about to impinge on the weary old states of the river-valley civilizations: a whirlwind was arising out of the north' (*Egypt, Canaan, and Israel*, p. 438).

228. Richard P. Vaggione, 'Over All Asia? The Extent of the Scythian Domination in Herodotus', *JBL* 92 (1973), pp. 523-30.

229. Vaggione, 'Over All Asia?' p. 529. Anthony Spalinger, 'Psammetichus, King of Egypt: II', *JARCE* 15 (1978), pp. 49-57, agrees that by the term 'Asia' it is meant 'Upper Asia' in this context: 'According to Herodotus, the Scythians then gained control of "Asia" (I, 104), although from other passages (I, 95 and 130 with IV, 1) it is clear that "Upper Asia" is meant (i.e., Asia eastward from the Halys River to northwestern Media but not including Assyria)' (p. 49).

230. Vaggione, 'Over All Asia?', p. 530.

231. Redford, *Egypt, Canaan, and Israel*, p. 440.

Spalinger, however, argues that the encounter between the Scythians and Psammetichus occurred sometime after 623 BCE, but before 616 BCE when Psammetichus was already operating freely in the Levant.[232] Spalinger opines that the incursion of the Scythians into Palestine suggests the weakening of the Neo-Assyrian Empire, which perhaps led the Assyrians to form a new alliance or to renew an old one with Egypt: 'It is thus possible that Assyria originally allied herself to Egypt as a result of the Scythian threat or that she renewed the old alliance with Psammetichus—the one that Assurbanipal fixed with Sais in 664 BC'.[233]

It seems that the Scythians were a factor in Palestine during Josiah's reign, but to what extent they played a role in the political equation of Palestine is difficult to judge. Herodotus's account is the only source that describes the Scythian domination of 'Asia' and their encounter with Psammetichus in Palestine. Na'aman notes, 'No ancient Near Eastern documents now in our possession can confirm this hypothesis'.[234] There are no other documents to support the claim that the Scythians played a major role 'in the chain of events throughout Western Asia in the second half of the seventh century B.C.E.'[235] Na'aman questions the scenario in which 'a huge Scythian campaign, which reached as far as the Egyptian border, and yet, within a short time, retreated and disappeared into the north, leaving no impression on the region through which its vast forces supposedly passed' as implausible.[236] Na'aman concludes:

> It should be remembered that invasion by such nomad groups always leaves a distinctive mark, for they not only overthrow the ruling power in the area, but generate widespread havoc and destruction. Neither such an Assyrian defeat nor its disastrous consequences are attested to in either documents or material culture; accordingly, those scholars who cast doubt on Herodotus' tale of the Scythian invasion of Syria and Palestine appear to have been right.[237]

Even if the Scythians entered Palestine, Herodotus shows that Psammetichus was in charge of the region.

Gitin's work leaves little doubt as to who controlled the *via maris* after the supposed retreat of Assyria.[238] Gitin's excavation shows that Assyria build up

---

232. Anthony Spalinger relies on the date of the defeat and death of Pharaortes whose son, Cyaxares, was attacked by the Scythians. The Babylonian Chronicles are silent on the encounter.

233. Spalinger, 'Psammetichus, King of Egypt: II', p. 51.

234. Na'aman, 'The Kingdom of Judah', p. 37.

235. Na'aman, 'The Kingdom of Judah', p. 36.

236. Na'aman, 'The Kingdom of Judah', p. 37.

237. Na'aman, 'The Kingdom of Judah', p. 37.

238. S. Gitin, 'The Neo-Assyrian Empire and its Western Periphery: The Levant, with Focus on Philistine Ekron', in S. Parpola and R.M. Whiting (eds.), *Assyria 1995* (Helsinki: Neo-Assyrian Text Corpus Project, 1997), pp. 77-103.

Ekron, a Philistine city located between Mesad Hashavyahu (and Ashdod) and Jerusalem, into a major urban and industrial center upon reclaiming it after the revolt of 701.[239] Ekron 'which grew to 85 acres, eight times the size of its eighth century city, became a huge olive oil industrial center' at the expense of Judah which lost the Shephelah to Ekron.[240] In the seventh century, Ekron became an international industrial center within the Neo-Assyrian Empire. Gitin gives much evidence to indicate that there was a clear presence of the Assyrians at Ekron for the first two thirds of the seventh century, and the massive destruction of the city of Ekron is associated with the 603 campaign of the Neo-Babylonian king, Nebuchadrezzar.[241] There was, however, no interruption or disturbance of the trade and industry that went on at Ekron prior to Nebuchadrezzar's destruction. Gitin suggests that the Egyptians took over Ekron based on archaeological evidence found there:

> The western rooms adjacent to the throne room produced a number of Egyptian objects, supporting the conclusion that, around 630 BCE, when the Assyrians withdrew from the Levant because of military pressure on their eastern border, Egyptian hegemony was reinstated in Philistia.[242]

There seems to be no reason to doubt that Egypt controlled Ashdod and Ekron after Assyria retreated from the west; thus Egypt controlled the *via maris* after Assyria withdrew.

Furthermore, the fact that Necho I moved a large army across Palestine and Syria to wage a war against the Babylonians leads us to assume that Necho had a firm control of the route. For Egypt would not have risked a confrontation with the Babylonians without securing the *via maris* and without the support or control of the territories through which the route passed. Moreover, we have to keep in mind that the Egyptians operated military campaigns in Mesopotamia as early as 616, as attested in the Babylonian Chronicles, which imply that they had bases from which to send their troops.[243] When Necho used Riblah in Hamath as the basis of his operation against Babylon in 609, he did not conquer and make Riblah into a base at that time; instead, he used a base that had probably been used previously by his father. Therefore, I believe that Mesad Hashavyahu and Megiddo, along with Ashdod and Riblah, were under Egypt's control and served as important bases that secured the route for Egypt.[244]

239. Gitin, 'The Neo-Assyrian Empire and its Western Periphery', pp. 79-80.
240. Gitin, 'The Neo-Assyrian Empire and its Western Periphery', p. 84. It was Sennacherib who gave the Shephelah to Ekron and other Philistine cities.
241. Gitin, 'The Neo-Assyrian Empire and its Western Periphery', pp. 91-98.
242. Gitin, 'The Neo-Assyrian Empire and its Western Periphery', pp. 98-99.
243. Grayson, *Assyrian and Babylonian Chronicles*, p. 91.
244. Na'aman does not think Necho II moved the Egyptian army across Palestine through the *via maris*. He asks: 'Why did the Pharaoh and his army have to pass through

The important point is that the commercial and trade systems set up by the Assyrians were not disturbed even after Assyria supposedly retreated from the West. This suggests that there is no indication that Assyria retreated from the West. The *via maris* remained secure during this transition of power from Assyria to Egypt. There was a concerted and cooperative transfer of power between Egypt and Assyria prior to Josiah's eighteenth year (c. 622). The friendly alliance between Egypt and Assyria that began with Ashurbanipal and Psammetichus and the possible alliance between Egypt and Judah left Palestine without much change, including a politically organized people of the province of Samerina. There is no reason to believe that there was a power vacuum in the province of Samerina after Assyria transferred the duty of securing the *via maris* to Egypt during the second half of Josiah's reign.

Judah was situated within the Assyrian-Egyptian hegemony of the West during Josiah's reign: in the first half of his reign as a vassal of Assyria and in the second half as a vassal or a junior partner of Egypt. There are, however, many who believe that Josiah achieved independence and competed with Egypt for the control of Palestine. That is, Josiah stepped in to fill the power vacuum after the 'retreat' of Assyria from the region. Specifically, some say that Josiah filled the power vacuum in the province of Samerina. There is no evidence, except the ambiguous account in 2 Kings 23, to justify this claim. We have seen that based on archaeological evidence it was unlikely that Josiah annexed the province of Samerina. We have also seen that the time span between the 'retreat' of Assyria (c. 623) and the death of Josiah (609) was short and there might not have been a power vacuum in Palestine in general and Samaria in particular. The thesis that Assyria and Egypt might have formed an alliance throughout Josiah's reign and then transferred the

---

Palestine on their way to northern Syria? Why did Necho II not adopt the tactics of the Egyptian kings at the time of the New Kingdom, who often sailed as far as the Lebanese coast and launched campaigns from there…? In this way, Necho II could have gone by sea to the Lebanese coast and set out from there on foot, by way of his military base at Riblah on the Orontes, to northern Syria, shortening the travel time and refraining from exhausting his forces in a grueling forced march from the Egyptian border to the battlefield near the Euphrates' ('The Kingdom of Judah', p. 51). He suggests that Necho came to Palestine 'to administer an oath of fealty to his vassals, whose previous oath had become invalid on his father's death' (p. 52). Josiah reported to Necho but 'was suspected of disloyalty and slain on the spot' (p. 53). Na'aman notes that the fact that Necho was able to arrest Jehoahaz and replace him with Eliakim to rule Judah leads to the conclusion that 'as early as Josiah's day, Judah was at least formally subordinate to Egypt, and that the slaying of Josiah was intended to intimidate the Judeans into abiding by the Egyptian rulers' instructions' (p. 53). However, Spalinger suggests that Josiah did attack Necho at Megiddo in 609, but expresses the view that this 'must be regarded as extraordinary' ('Egypt and Babylonia', p. 225). Spalinger believes that 'Egypt's defeat in 610 BC at the hands of the Babylonians forced a reversal of policy by Josiah' ('Egypt and Babylonia', p. 225).

control of the *via maris* and Palestine as a whole peacefully needs further examination.[245] For if Palestine remained intact as it was before the retreat of Assyria, it would be reasonable to assume that the province of Samerina as a politically organized people remained intact.

Bright's understanding of the relationship between Assyria and Egypt is a good example of a prevailing understanding among many biblical scholars.[246] Bright saw Egypt as Assyria's vassal after Ashurbanipal's conquest and the relationship between Egypt and Assyria as hostile during the greater part of Psammetichus's reign (664–610). Bright's reconstruction was something like this: Psammetichus threw off Assyria's yoke in his early reign and unified Egypt, then maintained a hostile relationship with Assyria until the latter part of his reign; the relationship between Egypt and Assyria changed when Egypt recognized the Babylonians as a greater threat than the Assyrians. Thus, Egypt became an ally of Assyria during the last stage of Assyria's decline because Egypt wanted to stop the Babylonians' expansion into the West. When Necho II passed through Megiddo in 609, killing Josiah on the way, he was trying to stop the advancement of Babylon.

Spalinger challenges this reconstruction, and thinks that the relationship between Egypt and Assyria was friendly from the beginning of Psammetichus's reign until the very end of Assyria's collapse. In one article, Spalinger traces Assyrian-Egyptian relations by investigating numerous accounts of Ashurbanipal's military campaigns during the two Egyptian campaigns.[247] It was Ashurbanipal's father, Esarhaddon, who initially invaded Lower Egypt, but he did not have firm control over it. Esarhaddon died on his way to Egypt to quell another rebellion incited by Taharqa, king of Kush. As soon as Ashurbanipal took the throne, he sent his army to Egypt and defeated Taharqa who fled to Thebes. Ashurbanipal wanted to stamp out the Egyptian problem (more accurately, the Kush problem) once and for all by going to Thebes and capturing the instigator, the king of Kush. He quickly formed a new army consisting of Assyrian troops, native Egyptians, and other soldiers from his vassal states. But on the way to Thebes, the Assyrian army discovered the plot of Egyptian princes, who were with the army, to hand over the Assyrians to Taharqa. The Assyrians abandoned their mission to Thebes, turned back to Memphis, captured the Egyptian princes and sent them to Nineveh. Ashurbanipal executed them except for the prince of Sais, Necho I, the father of Psammetichus.

---

245. Among scholars who advocate the 'Alliance hypothesis' are Nadav Na'aman, John H. Hayes and J. Maxwell Miller, Gosta Ahlström, and Anthony Spalinger.

246. Bright, *A History of Israel* (Philadelphia: Westminster Press, 3rd edn, 1981), pp. 310-23.

247. Anthony Spalinger, 'Assurbanipal and Egypt: A Source Study', *JAOS* 94 (1974), pp. 316-28.

What was the reason for sparing Necho's life? Spalinger puts it this way:

> With the effective end of this revolt, Assurbanipal was faced with a major problem with regard to Egypt. The question was how could the Assyrians make a peaceful country out of Egypt with the Kushite threat still present.[248]

Ashurbanipal decided to support one of the leaders of the rebellion, namely, Necho, whom he treated as a friend and ally. Ashurbanipal sent Necho back with lavish gifts and placed him as ruler of Sais, as a major ruler of the still segmented Lower Egypt. Moreover, he made Necho's son, Psammetichus, ruler of a city, Athribis. This turned out to be a wise policy. For when Tanoutamon, new ruler of Kush, invaded Egypt, Necho fought on the side of the Assyrians and lost his life fighting against the Kushites. After defeating Tanoutamon, Ashurbanipal placed Psammetichus in his father's place. Mary Francis Gyles remarks that Psammetichus, the founder of the Saite Dynasty (the twenty-sixth), benefited from his own and his father's loyalty to Ashurbanipal, receiving Memphis, Sais and Arthribis and becoming 'the most powerful Egyptian prince in the Delta'.[249]

We need to look more closely at Ashurbanipal's policy towards Egypt. The Assyrians had no desire to annex Egypt, which probably was impossible considering the size of Egypt and the distance from Nineveh. What the Assyrians wanted was what they had wanted since the ninth century—a commercial domination over Phoenicia and Philistia. Although Assyrians maintained firm control over Phoenicia and Philistia, Egypt was meddling with Assyrian domination in those regions. Actually it was not Egypt per se, but the Kushites who wanted to rule Egypt and to break the Assyrian hegemony over the West. So the real culprit was Kush, not Egypt. And Spalinger emphasizes that the Assyrians never failed to make the distinction between Egypt and Kush. Ashurbanipal's attitude toward Egypt is best expressed by the phrase 'to uproot the Kushites'.[250] Thus, Ashurbanipal probably made a treaty with Necho, then with Psammetichus, to form an alliance against the Kushites. Furthermore, Psammetichus also saw the Kushites as his primary enemies.[251]

---

248. Spalinger, 'Assurbanipal and Egypt', p. 323.

249. Mary Francis Gyles, *Pharaonic Policies and Administration, 663 to 323 B.C.* (Chapel Hill: University of North Carolina Press, 1959), p. 16.

250. Anthony Spalinger, 'Psammetichus, King of Egypt: I', *JARCE* 13 (1976), pp. 133-47 (133).

251. Spalinger states that 'the Saite expansion in Egypt was based on two main policies: to remove the local Egyptian kings in the Delta one by one, either by force or by alliance; and to achieve domination over Upper Egypt without incurring another military invasion by Kush' ('Psammetichus, King of Egypt: I', p. 138). Spalinger notes that 'to the Saites, Kush was far more dangerous than Assyria' (p. 142).

4. *Whose Space is it Anyway?*

There is no question that Egypt's policy toward Assyria was friendly in the latter part of Psammetichus's reign and the beginning of his son's (Necho II) reign. The Babylonian Chronicles clearly attest to Egypt's involvement in the conflict between Assyria and Babylon in the year 616: 'In the month of Tisri the Egyptian army and the Assyrian army marched after the king of Akkad as far as the town of Qablinu but did not overtake the king of Akkad and then went back'.[252] This entry assumes that the alliance between Egypt and Assyria was formed previously. In other words, the Chronicles do not note this alliance as a novelty, but accept it as a given. And the fact that this skirmish against the king of Akkad (Nabopolassar) takes place in the heart of Mesopotamia strongly supports the view that Egypt was very much involved in helping Assyria and in honoring the alliance. In the entry for 610, Nabopolassar's seventeenth year, the Chronicles mention the Egyptian army that came to the aid of Ashur-uballit, the last king of Assyria. Then in 609 'in the month of Tammuz Assur-uballit, king of Assyria, a great Egyptian army… crossed the river and marched against the city of Harran to conquer it'.[253] We know that by 609 it was Necho who was ruling Egypt. We can see that Necho II continued his father's friendly policy toward Assyria.

So the question is whether Egypt's friendly policy toward Assyria at the last stage of Assyria's collapse was a continuation of Egypt's earlier policy or whether Egypt's policy from 616 to the end of Assyria was a change from Egypt's earlier hostile policy as many have suggested. Once again, John Bright's understanding will serve as a foil. After describing the unrest in Babylonia, Bright describes the situation in the West:

> At the opposite end of the realm, Egypt could not be effectively controlled. Psammetichus I (664–610), son of the Neco to whom the Assyrians had shown mercy, though nominally a vassal, gradually expanded his power until most of Egypt was under his sway. As soon as he felt strong enough (c. 655 or soon after) he presumably withheld tribute and made himself formally independent. With this the Twenty-Sixth (Saite) Dynasty began. Psammetichus had the support of Gyges, king of Lydia, another enemy of Assyria, who desired to stir up trouble for her in whatever way he could. Asshurbanipal [*sic*], occupied elsewhere, was in no position to take effective countermeasures.[254]

Bright makes several assumptions: (1) he assumes that Assyria wants to control Egypt. However, I have shown that Assyria was not interested in controlling Egypt but desired a friendly relationship that would leave Assyria's hegemony in Philistia alone. (2) He assumes that Ashurbanipal had imposed tribute on Psammetichus, and thus Psammetichus wanted to overthrow the Assyrian yoke. However, we have seen that Ashurbanipal wanted a trusted

---

252. Wiseman, *Chronicles of Chaldaean Kings*, p. 55.
253. Wiseman, *Chronicles of Chaldaean Kings*, p. 63.
254. Bright, *A History of Israel* (2nd edn), p. 313.

ally like Necho I and not a fearing vassal, who would rebel at the first sign of Assyria's weakness. (3) He assumes that Gyges was an enemy of Assyria and had helped Psammetichus achieve independence from Assyria. (4) He assumes that Ashurbanipal was too weak to counteract Psammatichus's rebellion during the 650s.

Spalinger addresses the latter two assumptions.[255] There are several Assyrian sources that describe how Assyria came into contact with Lydia (*ARAB*, 784-85). Gyges, king of Lydia, had a dream in which Assur, the patron god of Assyria, appeared and instructed him to seek the favor of Ashurbanipal. Gyges promptly sent his emissary to Ashurbanipal with tribute (gifts, not the annual tribute required by vassals) around 664–663 (the same time as Psammetichus's taking his father's place). Spalinger points out that no hostile activity occurred when they met, and that the encounter was not a result of any wrongdoing on the part of Gyges. It was a political move on the part of Gyges, who recognized the importance of having Ashurbanipal on his side. Shortly after the meeting, the Cimmerians invaded Lydia, but Gyges was able to defeat them without help from Ashurbanipal. Gyges was never a vassal of Assyria and was not dependent militarily on Assyria.

Sometime after the battle with the Cimmerians (c. 662–658), Gyges sent his troops to Psammetichus. Now the question is whether the troops were used to fight against the Assyrian force in Egypt, as assumed by Bright. Spalinger maintains that 'Gyges' military support was not used directly against Assyria' and that 'no vast anti-Assyrian alliance of Egypt and Lydia… directed against Assurbanipal can be reconstructed'.[256] Rather he suggests that 'Gyges' soldiers were employed in the unification of Egypt'.[257] Herodotus's account of Psammetichus's unification of Egypt supports this view (Herodotus 2.151–53). Herodotus tells a story of how Psammetichus came into contact with Greeks who landed on the Egyptian shores. He employed them to depose eleven kings of Egypt and to make himself king of all Egypt. There are two things in this account we need to point out: (1) the Greek soldiers were probably connected to the troops sent by Gyges and (2) there is no mention of using the soldiers against the Assyrians. In fact, there is no reference in Egyptian or classical sources to any rivalry between Egypt and Assyria during Ashurbanipal's reign.[258] Thus, the friendly relationship with Egypt left Assyria free to attend to other fronts closer to home.

---

255. Spalinger, 'The Date of the Death of Gyges and its Implications', *JAOS* 98 (1978), pp. 400-409.

256. Spalinger, 'The Death of Gyges', p. 402. See also Spalinger, 'Psammetichus, King of Egypt: I', p. 135.

257. Spalinger, 'The Death of Gyges', p. 402.

258. Na'aman states: 'The Assyrian, Egyptian and Greek sources tell us nothing about hostile relationships between Assyria and Egypt; it appears that the Assyrian retreat took

Moreover, Psammetichus preferred to use diplomacy rather than arms to unify Egypt.[259] His military strength came from the 'men of bronze' (most likely the Greek mercenaries sent by Gyges) and the support of Ashurbanipal.[260] Gyles maintains that Psammetichus was able to overcome the other Delta princes 'prior to the departure of the Assyrians, and that he had been recognized by Ashurbanipal as vassal king of all Egypt in return for his loyalty and assistance'.[261] Gyles continues that the adoption of Psammetichus's daughter, Nitocris, as the future God's Wife of Amun was negotiated from a position of considerable power and authority—this position of power arose from the backing of Ashurbanipal and a firm control of Lower and Middle Egypt; this event effectively unified the whole Egypt.[262] Gyles, contrary to Spalinger, maintains that Psammetichus used the mercenaries sent by Gyges to expel the Assyrian garrison from Egypt around 655–654. But she notes that 'no other information exists concerning Psamtik's [Psammetichus's]

place following the conclusion of an agreement with Psammetichus I, Assyria's protégé-turned ally' ('The Kingdom of Judah', p. 39).

259. Psammetichus was able to control Middle Egypt through diplomacy. K.A. Kitchen, *The Third Intermediate Period in Egypt* (Warminster: Aris & Phillips, 1986), states that 'thus, in Pediese and his son Somtutefnakht, Psammetichus I had powerful allies in Middle Egypt, leaving him a free hand in the Delta... So, in Year 1, with the whole Delta acknowledging his rule and with a strong ally in Middle Egypt, Psammetichus I could now look southwards towards Thebes' (p. 403). Psammetichus was able to merge Upper Egypt under his rule by presenting his daughter Nitocris as the future God's Wife of Amun, attested in the Adoption Stele of Nitocris. He was also a very patient man who changed the officials and administration in Thebes slowly, waiting for the 'mayor' of Thebes and the current God's Wife of Amun to die a natural death. Herodotus mentions how Psammetichus was able to turn back the Scythians without a fight. Psammetichus was a diplomat who was able to form alliances with various parties, including Assyria and Judah. Spalinger also states that 'in all, Psammetichus preferred to deal more diplomatically, than militarily' ('The Concept of the Monarchy', p. 17). This strategy is not only based on Psammatichus's style or personality but on the fact that Psammetichus came to power with the help of foreign mercenaries and Assyria's arms.

260. As mentioned above, Herodotus tells the story of how Psammetichus was banished by the eleven princes for using his bronze helmet to receive the libation but was able to make himself the sole ruler of Egypt with the help of 'men of bronze' (1.151–53). Gyles states that 'although Herodotus does not mention the Assyrians and later generations were probably genuinely ignorant of the Assyrians' role, or they were chauvinistic, it was the Assyrians who helped Psamtik unify Egypt with the help also of the bronze men' (*Pharaonic Policies*, p. 18).

261. Gyles, *Pharaonic Policies*, p. 19.

262. Gyles, *Pharaonic Policies*, p. 19. Kitchen describes the Adoption Stele of Nitocris as 'a splendid granite stele erected at Karnak' in commemoration of the adoption of Psammetichus's daughter, Nitocris, as the future God's Wife of Amum at Thebes (*The Third Intermediate Period*, pp. 403-404). Kitchen notes that, of course, this happened 'after suitable prior negotiations' (p. 403).

activities in the growing rebellion against Assyria' and she suggests that Psammetichus made peace with Assyria after the death of Gyges (c. 653).[263]

Spalinger also points out that 'Assurbanipal's acquiescence to the unification of Egypt cannot be explained away by any impotence on his part'.[264] There was no weakening of the Assyrian army during this time; if Ashurbanipal wanted to crush Psammetichus, he could have done so.[265] Thus it is better to understand Ashurbanipal's inaction as an indication that he approved Psammetichus's actions or that at least he did not see Psammetichus's actions as an indication of breaking the treaty between them. After all, this is exactly what Ashurbanipal wanted—a strong ally who could hold off the Kushites and who would cooperate in the control of the commercial routes and interests in the West.[266] Thus Gyles opines that Psammatichus undertook the siege of Ashdod as an ally of Assyria to quell a rebellion against Assyria around 650.[267] Gyles suggests that the alliance between Egypt and Assyria was made much earlier than 620; that is, there was no change in policy from the part of Egypt:

---

263. Gyles, *Pharaonic Policies*, p. 20. It is important to keep in mind that Gyges was not fighting against the Assyrians, but was killed by the Cimmerians.

264. Spalinger, 'The Death of Gyges', p. 406. Spalinger states that there was no anti-Assyrian alliance formed between Gyges and Psammetichus ('Psammetichus, King of Egypt: I'). However, there is a document (Prism A, written around 643/42) that specifically states: 'He [Gyges] placed his trust in his own strength and then became overbearing. So he sent his troops to the aid of Psammetichus, king of Egypt, who had overthrown the yoke of my kingship' (Prism A. II, 113-15). Spalinger explains the importance of Prism A: 'The account of Prism A demonstrates that, some time after 663 B.C., Psammetichus had become king of Egypt. The rather fluid bureaucratic set-up which Assyria had established in Egypt had ended. Implicit in A. II, 113-15 is a break between Psammetichus I and Assurbanipal, a revocation of the *adu* agreement which the two powers had signed. This alliance was some type of superior–inferior relation, but unfortunately none of the Assyrian sources details the arrangements. In A. II, 113-15 it appears more likely that the Assyrian king was angered not over Psammetichus's claiming to be king of Egypt (after ending the local native opposition), but instead by his revocation of that *adu*-agreement' ('Psammetichus, King of Egypt: I', p. 135). Spalinger continues that 'the split between Nineveh and Sais which Prism A claims cannot be determined from the Assyrian sources. The Greek historians stress the internal aspects of the rise of Sais to domination over Egypt, and they probably reflect the chauvinistic Egyptian viewpoint which disregarded the Assyrian presence' (p. 136).

265. Spalinger states that from Ashurbanipal's campaign against Ba'al of Tyre (654–646) and the fact that 'the Babylonian revolt had not flared up (652/1–648)' indicate that 'if, in fact, Psammetichus did oppose Assyria, the reason for Assurbanipal's military inaction could not have been due to his weakness' ('Psammetichus, King of Egypt: I', p. 142).

266. After Psammetichus unified Egypt around 654, the Kushites did not meddle in the affairs of the west, proving that Ashurbanipal's strategy worked.

267. Gyles, *Pharaonic Policies*, p. 21.

> The Assyrian records in the years from 650s onward, maintain 'a curious silence' about Egypt. Egypt is scarcely mentioned. Yet the loss of so rich a province should surely have been of grave concern to an Assyrian ruler. And the activities of Psamtik [Psammetichus] at Ashdod, unless undertaken in alliance with Assyria, would have increased the concern.[268]

Therefore, she concludes that Psammetichus's decision to send his troops to aid the Assyrians in 616 is 'more consistent with a long-standing and time-honored alliance than with a recent treaty which was of little or no value to Egypt'.[269]

In order for Ashurbanipal to maintain a firm control over the West, he needed a partner in Egypt who would support Assyria against the ever-present threat from the Kushites. He formed a friendly alliance with Necho I, then with his son Psammetichus I. This friendly policy between the Saite Dynasty and Assyria was to last for over fifty years until the very end of Assyria when the Egyptians fought side by side with the Assyrians. One could interpret Psammetichus's unification of Egypt by employing Gyges' armed forces as a change of policy on the part of Psammetichus.[270] However, it was not Assyria's intention to annex Egypt or even to control it as a vassal. Assyria probably welcomed a strong Egypt that was able keep the Kushites from interfering with its hegemony over Palestine. After all, they wanted to control not Egypt, but the *via maris* that was so important to their commercial and military interests.

Egypt was also interested in Palestine; Egypt, traditionally, considered 'Palestine and South Syria her first line of defense'.[271] Egypt always wanted to dominate the Palestinian states because 'dangers for Egypt, with the exception of the Ethiopian invasions, had always historically come from the north'.[272] This general policy to dominate Palestine was based on political

---

268. Gyles, *Pharaonic Policies*, p. 23.

269. Gyles, *Pharaonic Policies*, p. 23. Na'aman summarizes: 'Two questions now arise: when did the Egyptians enter Asia, and when had Egypt become so close to Assyria as to be willing to send its army to assist a sorely beset ally? These questions have no unambiguous answers. As it seems, the Egyptian entry into Asia was not a forcible conquest, but part of an Assyrian retreat by agreement, with Egypt (gradually or rapidly) taking the place of an Assyria in the evacuated areas. It appears that the alliance between the two powers became especially close during the reign of Sin-shar-ishkun, after he had crushed the rebellion of his general (end of the year 623 BCE), and was willing to pay a heavy territorial price in the west in order to overcome the severe danger facing him and his kingdom in the south and east. The renewed alliance between Assyria and Egypt may thus have been concluded in the late 620s; this, in turn, would mean that only then did Assyria retreat from (and Egypt enter) the territories beyond the Euphrates' (p. 39).

270. But we need to keep in mind that Psammetichus was able to unify Egypt with the help of the Assyrians as well.

271. Gyles, *Pharaonic Policies*, p. 11.

272. Gyles, *Pharaonic Policies*, p. 89.

reasons, but also equally on economic grounds.²⁷³ Gyles states that the two regions had maintained close trade relations for centuries:

> From Egypt poured linen, grain, papyrus, horses, leather goods, perfumes, ivory and ebony from the African hinterland coming down the Nile, gold and silver jewelry and other wares...stonework and varied luxury products. In return there flowed from Syria-Palestine timber and balsam from the Lebanese cedars, iron manufactures, dyes, wood textiles, blown glass, oils, wines, bronzewares and pottery.²⁷⁴

Of course, the trade could be easier and more profitable for Egypt if it controlled the area politically and 'the normal profits to be expected from any imperialism...in which both Pharaoh and Egyptian nationals could profit from economic exploitation of the region'.²⁷⁵

However, the Egypt of the Saite Dynasty struggled to build an empire in the face of its lack of a strong army of its own; as a result, 'the Saite monarchy could not operate the kingdom internally or externally without the support of foreigners'.²⁷⁶ Once again, Psammetichus came into power and unified Egypt with the help of foreign arms. Upon uniting Egypt, Psammetichus had to call upon the local leaders 'to supply him with troops—the monarchy did not have at its disposal a ready standing army' when Libya tried to invade Egypt.²⁷⁷ When Egypt stepped in to fill the role as the guardian of the *via maris*, Psammetichus 'immediately became entangled in a long siege at Ashdod and a Scythian war'.²⁷⁸ Egypt was able to fill the role of securing the *via maris*, but 'no massive expansion of Pharaonic arms into Palestine was attempted by Psammetichus'.²⁷⁹ Spalinger characterizes the Saite Dynasty as lacking 'imperialistic feeling':

> Egypt's policy in the Levant was commercial in intent, benevolent in application, laissez-faire in nature, and short in duration. Psammetichus I and Necho preferred to leave the international affairs of the northern states alone so long as they could secure sufficient economic advantage from them. These first two rulers maintained a strong and ready standing army composed of Greeks and Asiatics to oppose the threat of Babylonian opposition.²⁸⁰

---

273. Gyles, *Pharaonic Policies*, pp. 89-90.
274. Gyles, *Pharaonic Policies*, p. 90.
275. Gyles, *Pharaonic Policies*, p. 90.
276. Spalinger, 'The Concept of the Monarchy', p. 36.
277. Spalinger, 'The Concept of the Monarchy', p. 15.
278. Spalinger, 'The Concept of the Monarchy', p. 16.
279. Spalinger, 'Egypt and Babylonia', p. 223. Spalinger adds that Egypt was more interested in securing the *via maris* and avoiding a Hellenic commercial monopoly in the Levant, than he was with competing with a Judean power for control of Palestine (p. 223).
280. Spalinger, 'Egypt and Babylonia', p. 222.

Spalinger underscores the weakness of the Saite 'Empire':

> The so-called Saite Empire that many have wished to see was in reality nothing of the sort. At best, one can imagine that some type of commercial monopoly was exercised by the Egyptians over the Lebanon. Close relations existed between Psammetichus and the Philistine cities (undoubtedly through treaties), but the hinterland, now ruled by Josiah, was left alone.[281]

Spalinger and others pay no attention to whether the province of Samerina was also left alone by Egypt after the 'retreat' of the Assyrians. Perhaps Egypt, after taking over the fort in Megiddo to maintain control of the *via maris* between Egypt and Assyria, was supported by the province of Samerina to secure the route without interfering with their daily business. Egypt was not powerful enough to control the internal affairs of the Palestinian states, but it was strong enough to secure the trade route in cooperation with them. This picture fits the policy of Psammetichus who was a master diplomat. The continuing existence of the province of Samerina with a politically organized people occupying the land could be the main reason why Josiah was unable to expand into this region. There is no document to prove this claim, but there is circumstantial evidence to support it. As mentioned above: (1) Josiah was unable to expand into this region; (2) Egypt was not powerful enough to occupy and control the inland political powers, including Judah and the province of Samerina; and (3) there is no conclusive evidence of disruption in the province of Samerina during this period.[282]

---

281. Spalinger, 'The Concept of the Monarchy', p. 16.

282. Stig Forsberg, *Near Eastern Destruction Datings as Source for Greek and Near Eastern Iron Age Chronology: Archaeological and Historical Studies: The Cases of Samaria (722 B.C.) and Tarsus (696 B.C.)* (Uppsala: Uppsala University, 2nd edn, 1995), has argued, *contra* the earlier conclusion by K.M. Kenyon that the destruction level at Samaria in the Late Iron II is to be attributed to Assyria's siege of Samaria in c. 722–720 BCE, that 'The written evidence provides no ground for believing that Shalmaneser or Sargon inflicted a destruction on Samaria. On the contrary, the available evidence rather suggests a picture of events that did not include a devastation of the city' (pp. 49-50). Forsberg pushes the date to mid-seventh century and suggests three scenarios that are more viable alternatives: (1) Ashurbanipal was losing control of the west after the wars in the east against Babylon and Elam in the late 650s and early 640s and Samaria might have been involved in a rebellion; therefore, 'the possibility that the destruction belongs in this context, that Ashurbanipal's sending new settlers to Samaria reflects Assyrian efforts to restore strength and stability there after an insurrection and that these efforts involved also the tidying up in the citadel area producing the Period VII leveling can be hardly excluded' (p. 35); (2) Forsberg accepts the biblical account of destruction of 'the cities of Samaria' at face value and believes that Josiah was able to annex the province of Samerina: 'Such activities in the territory of Samaria presuppose the disappearance of Assyrian control there and the annexation of the former Assyrian province by Josiah' (p. 35); (3) the Scythians were responsible for the destruction level in Samaria, dating the Scythian invasion of Palestine to either the 630s or the beginning of the 620s (pp. 35-36). However,

There is a possibility that the province of Samerina remained in operation as it was before Assyria transferred the control of the *via maris* to Egypt. There is also a possibility that the people of Samaria (Israelites, various groups implanted by Assyria, and Judaeans who migrated to the region) as a politically organized people could have continued to occupy the province of Samerina; the governorship of Samerina would have continued. There are good reasons to believe that there was a transfer of power from Assyria to Egypt in the West, especially in order to maintain control over the *via maris*. The inland political powers were left alone to go about their business as usual. It would be a mistake to assume that there existed a power vacuum in the province of Samerina. The infrastructure and people that were in place for a hundred years remained intact; there is no reason to assume that the infrastructure and people would vanish whenever the king of Assyria was on the other side of his empire. The space between Jerusalem and Megiddo was not empty of power and people for Josiah to occupy.

What effect will this have in our understanding of DH if we take seriously the existence of a politically organized people in Samaria? If we can propose that the northerners were 'always' migrating to Judah, what about the possibility that the southerners, especially the descendants of those who migrated to Judah after the collapse of Samaria in 722, might have wanted to migrate to the north? Perhaps Josiah wanted to consolidate the people living in Judah, including the descendants of northern refugees, to prevent them from moving back to the province of Samerina.

Summary

Space is a physical–mental–social construction we measure, imagine, shape, transform, and live. It is used to maintain and control the 'difference' between the center and the periphery—the power differential between the center and the periphery—through the Firstspace–Secondspace construct that usually gives advantage to those in the center. At the same time, there are 'counterspaces'(space of liminality or Thirdspace) where 'difference' can be used as 'a basis for community, identity and struggle against the existing power

---

Ron E. Tappy, *The Archaeology of Israelite Samaria*. II. *The Eighth Century BCE* (HSS, 50; Winona Lake, IN: Eisenbrauns, 2001), cautions against attributing diverse layers of destruction '*en masse* to a single historical event' (p. 440). Tappy notes that had Forsberg known that 'no single, clear level of destruction debris exists across the floors and walls of the BP V house(s), the historical scheme that he inferred from the date of the pottery might have changed dramatically' (p. 440). Tappy concludes that 'I have not encountered a blanket of destruction debris across the BP V remains at the site; rather, diverse layers dating from many time periods and extending as late as the Late Roman period have emerged' (p. 440), therefore, 'in short, a direct correspondence between archaeological history and political history does not always exist' (p. 441).

relations at their source'.[283] It is at the margin (Thirdspace or space of liminality) where the hierarchy of center and periphery is thwarted and where resistance to hegemonic history and cultural imperialism can be nurtured and practiced. Thus, we must ask whose space we are dealing with when we speak about Josiah's kingdom—whether it is a space constructed exclusively from the center that wants to maintain the *status quo* and the existing power relations or from Thirdspace (space of liminality) that is open to new possibilities and relations. Berquist makes the following comment that captures the connection between how we speak about space and the position of the speaker:

> The question of 'where' always requires the question 'according to whom'. Space is not neutral or objective; there is no magical space to stand from which one can observe space without perspective. There is no terminology that one can use to speak of space neutrally. Thus, any talk of space is talk of meaning—the meaning that interpreters attach to space.[284]

Josiah's kingdom needs to be understood as a physical–mental–social construct. A Josiah's kingdom that is limited to a Firstspace–Secondspace construct continues to function to maintain the power differential between the West and the rest. Postcolonialism has critiqued the conception of space in terms of the Firstspace–Secondspace dualism. In particular, it has critiqued the understanding of space as a stage on which Western history is played out, often at the expense of the subjectivity of the 'natives'. The 'natives' have often felt 'unhomely' in their own land because the West has named the space as their own. Postmodern study of spatial history shows that the West was far more interested in searching for the 'roots' of Western civilization than the 'routes' that can be traced in the land. I examined how Asian Americans have been made 'unhomely' in North America—the land they call their home—because the land is viewed as belonging to a particular people according to the discourse of nationalism.

In light of the postcolonial critique on space and the experience of Asian Americans, I put to critique three assumptions related to Josiah's kingdom: (1) the understanding of 'Greater' Israel of David as a stage on which history unfolds and where Josiah represents the only legitimate power, (2) the boundaries of Josiah's kingdom are based on the nationalist principle that equates 'ethnic' artifacts with political sovereignty, and (3) the notion that after the supposed retreat of the Assyrian power in the north left the land 'empty' of power and people.

First, Josiah is caught on a stage constructed in part by biblical studies, which views the land north of Judah as part of an indivisible land belonging

---

283. Soja, *Thirdspace*, p. 89.
284. Berquist, 'Critical Spatiality', p. 22.

to 'Greater' Israel founded by King David. It belongs to the subsequent heirs of the house of David. Thus, Josiah is portrayed as a powerful king who attempted to recover the Davidic Empire. This view is supported by imperial history which views a space as a stage on which Western history is played out; Josiah is a hero portrayed in the image of the West, following the script written by the discourse of nationalism, which views a land as 'empty' unless it is occupied by a centralized political entity, especially by the nation-state. The Cross School in particular has advocated this thesis, exemplified recently by Gary N. Knoppers and others. However, this view is not limited to the Cross School or to Western scholars. Other scholars also follow the limited geographical imagination of modernist, imperial history. This view continues to give advantage to the center, often at the expense of those situated in the periphery.

Second, the debate on the extent of Josiah's kingdom—some opting for an extensive expansion and some arguing for a much more limited expansion—is no more than variations on the expansion thesis. The difference is the extent of Josiah's expansion, but the assumption that the province of Samerina belongs to the 'Greater' Israel remains. Biblical scholars use the principle of equating 'ethnic' artifacts with political sovereignty to draw political maps of Josiah's kingdom. However, borders are porous, not fixed. The idea of one culture per place is fictional. Boundaries do not enclose a fixed culture or people. By closing the borders, by fixing the borders, we are creating an artificial view of the reality. By seeing Josiah's kingdom through the lens of Firstspace–Secondspace dualism (as political maps), we are limiting ourselves from seeing Josiah's kingdom and the province of Samerina as lived space where people as inhabitants and users of these spaces experienced 'real and imagined' spaces simultaneously. We are ignoring hybrid people and culture that are common features in real lived space.

Third, I examined whether the land north of Judah, commonly referred to as the former kingdom of Israel, but known during the time of Josiah as the province of Samerina, was 'empty' after the supposed retreat of the Assyrians. There seems to be a consensus among biblical scholars that Josiah was unable to annex the province of Samerina after the 'retreat' of the Assyrians. Some argue that Egypt stepped in to take the place of the retreating Assyrians in a concerted transference of power. Egypt, however, was not powerful enough to control the inland Palestinian states; besides, Egypt was far more interested in controlling the *via maris* than with meddling in the affairs of commercially unprofitable inland states. This leads me to conclude that the province of Samerina remained intact even after the Neo-Assyrian Empire weakened greatly after Ashurbanipal's death, and that it continued to function as a politically organized people. The subalterns in Josiah's reform were the people of Samaria who felt 'unhomely' in the land, where they have been living for a hundred years. The question I raised was whether—if there was no power vacuum in the north and if Josiah was unable to expand to the north—Josiah was addressing the problem of some people migrating to the province of Samerina. There is a possibility that perhaps Josiah was addressing the problem of the Israelite Judeans who might have wanted to move back to the north, to their homeland. There is no written proof of such a concern. But we must attempt to hear the voices of those who were unable to leave documents, such as the people of the province of Samerina and the Israelite Judeans. It is the limited imagination of biblical scholars based on the discourse of nationalism that cannot envision the 'natives' and hybrid people in Josiah's kingdom and the province of Samerina. To imagine the route of people in one direction (from the north to Judah) is a geographical imagination that ignores the lived space of people of the past as well as of today.

5

THE *REALPOLITIK* OF LIMINALITY IN JOSIAH'S KINGDOM

A postcolonial reading of Josiah takes account of the lived experience of those who are located in the space of liminality. We also need to imagine the lived space of the people of Josiah's kingdom, taking into account of the fact that Josiah's kingdom was located in an ideological, political landscape shaped by Assyrian imperialism, where they were viewed as one of the Others. There was a rise in ethnic sentiments during the Sargonid Dynasty, which contributed to seeing others as inferior enemies. Judah undoubtedly experienced the *Realpolitik* of liminality, the danger of being located in a space not of one's own making.[1] Judah witnessed first hand the military might of the Neo-Assyrian Empire. Moreover, the story of Josiah is framed within two accounts of death (2 Kgs 21.19-26 and 23.28-30), which best illustrate the *Realpolitik* of liminality experienced by Josiah's kingdom. However, in spite of being located in a political landscape not of their own making, Josiah's court wrote DH, in part, as an attempt to construct 'a history of their own' independent from imperial forces. The story of Josiah illustrates the effort of Josiah's court to retrieve lost 'inscriptions' and customs that may have been erased and overwritten during the Assyrian domination. In this chapter I will read the story of Josiah intercontextually with the lived experience of Asian Americans and their efforts to write 'a history of their own' by retrieving lost 'inscriptions' in order to define and develop their identity and destiny.

The Realpolitik *of Liminality in North America*

Asian Americans know all too well what it is to be viewed as the Other in the racialized landscape of North America. We all know the common experience of being asked by other Americans, 'Where are you from?' It is not about our

---

1. Although the term 'liminality' is normally defined as 'being in a state of "in-between" two or more worlds', for my work I want to narrow the definition to 'being in a location not of one's own making'.

hometowns that the inquirers are searching to know. If we respond by naming our hometowns in North America, they are not satisfied until they find out where we are 'originally' from. The inquirers may or may not be aware that their investigation is based on the premise that Asians or people of Asian descent are aliens in this nation. Their investigation follows the logic of identity politics and the contour of the racialized landscape of North America.

Henry Yu traces how American sociologists have studied Asian Americans in the framework of the 'Oriental Problem' in the first half of the twentieth century and how this legacy still shapes much of how Asian Americans are studied and viewed today.[2] Asian Americans as 'Orientals' were studied as objects:

> Throughout the history of the United States, Asian Americans have been objectified, in all the senses which that word connotes. Who has treated them as objects, and what about them as objects has made them interesting or valuable, and how they have responded to their treatment as objects.[3]

Orientals are viewed as a problematic object that needs to be managed and controlled; they are advantageous and desirable if they would just stay in their place and play the subordinate role they are assigned in America; they are undesirable and dangerous if they refuse to stay in their place and play the role assigned to them and demand to be accepted as full Americans. The problem is related to identity and race politics in North America. The descendants of white Europeans are the rightful inhabitants of the land, but Asian Americans are lumped together as aliens in this land. As Chan notes:

> Though it is often thought that these various groups are lumped together as 'Asian Americans' because they or their ancestors have all come from Asia, there is a more important reason for treating them as a collective entity: for the most part, the host society has treated them all alike, regardless of what differences might have existed in their cultures, religions, and languages, or in the status of their homelands in the family of nations.[4]

The assimilation model that was developed out of the experience of European immigrants does not work with Asian Americans due in large part to the politics of race and identity in North America. Chan remarks that Asian Americans know,

---

2. Okihiro also notes that the 'Anti-Asianists' in writing the history of Asian Americans established the terms, questions, and objects of research on Asian Americans as 'a problem for American society as aliens both abroad and at home' (*Columbia Guide*, p. 225). Okihiro describes 'liberals' (the sociologists Henry Yu examines would fit into this category) as those who responded to the charge by the Anti-Asianists as a problem: 'liberals framed their rebuttals similarly, as problems but also as affirmations of American democracy' (*Columbia Guide*, p. 225).
3. Yu, *Thinking Orientals*, p. ix.
4. Chan, *Asian Americans*, p. xiii.

> Even as they acquired the values and behavior of Euro-Americans, they simultaneously had to learn to accept their standing as racial minorities—people who, because of their skin color and physiognomy, were not allowed to enjoy the rights and privileges given acculturated European immigrants and native-born Americans. In short, if they wished to remain and to survive in the United States, they had to learn to 'stay in their place' and to act with deference toward those of higher racial status.[5]

In the racialized landscape of North America, Asian Americans are colored yellow.[6] The racial politics in America defines yellow in opposition to white but also as different from black. This sets up a peculiar problem for Asian Americans: Is yellow white or black? Okihiro notes that this question is multilayered: 'Is yellow black or white? is a question of Asian American identity. Is yellow black or white? is a question of Third World identity, or the relationships among people of color. Is yellow black or white? is a question of American identity, or the nature of America's racial formation.'[7] Okihiro argues that the position of Asian Americans caught in-between two racial poles (black and white) has caused unique disabilities as well as special opportunities: Asian Americans were often used by whites to punish blacks and other minorities and were also given opportunities to work because they were not black.[8] Being yellow, being in the middle, produces a state of liminality, which is desirable at times, but can also be dangerous as well. Okihiro summarizes this problem of being colored yellow: 'Asians have been marginalized to the periphery of race relations in America because of its conceptualization as a black and white issue—with Asians, Latinos, and American Indians falling between the cracks of that divide. Thus, to many, Asians are either "just like blacks" or "almost whites".'[9]

Robert Lee looks at the ways in which Asian Americans have been made into a race of aliens by examining how the racial category of Oriental is represented in popular culture. Lee examines the representation of the Oriental in popular culture as a site where the common understanding of who Asian Americans is formed and maintained. It is in the realm of popular culture 'where struggles over who is or who can become a "real American" takes place and where the categories, representations, distinctions, and markers of race are defined'.[10] He argues that 'the representation of the Oriental

---

5. Chan, *Asian Americans*, p. 187.
6. Lee, *Orientals*, describes how Asian Americans are depicted as having yellowfaces: 'Yellowface exaggerates "racial" features that have been designated "Oriental", such as "slanted" eyes, overbite, and mustard-yellow skin. Only the racialized Oriental is yellow; Asians are not. Asia is not a biological fact but a geographical designation. Asians come in the broadest range of skin color and hue' (p. 2).
7. Okihiro, *Margins and Mainstream*, p. 33.
8. Okihiro, *Margins and Mainstreams*.
9. Okihiro, *Margins and Mainstream*, p. xi.
10. Lee, *Orientals*, p. 5.

constructs the alien as a racial category' and 'the concept is deeply imbedded in American ideologies of race, class, gender, and sexuality'.[11] He maintains that throughout American history Asian Americans are always vulnerable to being viewed as pollutants—objects or persons perceived to be out of place— and as the alien minion of a foreign power.

Lee examines six representations of the Oriental in American history: the pollutant, the coolie, the deviant, the yellow peril, the model minority, and the gook:

1. The representation of the pollutant originated in mid-nineteenth-century California when white settlers from the east coast viewed the Chinese settlers as a disruption to their westward expansion and a threat to their desire to create a racially pure state free from the national debate over slavery and abolition.[12]
2. The representation of the Chinese immigrant workers as coolies came about as the US working class was formed in the 1870s and 1880s; they were represented as a threat to the white working man's family.[13]
3. The representation of the Oriental as deviant arose when thousands of Chinese immigrant men were hired into middle-class households as domestic servants in the 1860s and 1870s; the representation of the Oriental as deviant, in the person of the Chinese household servant, justified a taboo against intimacy through which racial and class stability could be preserved.[14]
4. The representation of Asian immigrants as the yellow peril as a threat to nation and race appeared by the turn of the nineteenth century when the US acquired territories and colonies, bringing a renewed threat of 'Asiatic' immigration, an invasion of 'yellow men' and 'little brown brothers'.[15]
5. The representation of Asian Americans as a model minority originated in the Cold War liberalism of the 1950s; the image of Asian Americans as a successful case of 'ethnic' assimilation helped to contain three spectres that haunted Cold War America: the red menace of communism, the black menace of racial integration, and the white menace of homosexuality; by the late 1960s, an image of a 'successful' Asian-American assimilation could be held up to African Americans and Latinos as a model for nonmilitant, nonpolitical upward mobility.[16]

11. Lee, *Orientals*, p. xi.
12. Lee, *Orientals*, Chapter 1.
13. Lee, *Orientals*, Chapter 2.
14. Lee, *Orientals*, Chapter 3.
15. Lee, *Orientals*, Chapter 4.
16. Lee, *Orientals*, Chapter 5.

6. Since the 1970s, after the bitter defeat in the Vietnam War, the model minority image has coexisted with and reinforced a representation of the Asian American as the gook; the Asian American is represented as the invisible enemy and the embodiment of inauthentic racial and national identities.[17]

Lee argues that these representations need to be contextualized and understood within the discourse of race and identity in America. These representations portray Asian Americans as 'the Oriental as an alien body and a threat to the American national family'.[18] He argues that these faces of the Oriental are not arbitrary but are connected to economic changes, particularly during the periods of 'transformations of the structure of accumulation', and social crises, particularly during identity crises among white Americans, in American history. It is during times of change and crisis in America that a particular representation of the Oriental arises in order to help define who real Americans are. In other words, it is framed within the discourse of race and identity in America. Lee states: 'What produces these stereotypes is not just individual acts of representation, but a historical discourse of race that is embedded in the history of American social crises'.[19]

Lee states that the representation of Asian Americans both as a model minority and the gook reflects 'the deeply contradictory and contested representation of the Asian American as permanent alien'.[20] Asian Americans have two faces—a model minority and the gook: the model minority stereotype presents Asian Americans as 'silent, disciplined; this is their secret to success', but, at the same time, 'this silence and discipline is used in constructing the Asian American as a new yellow peril'.[21] Even without the representation of the Oriental as the gook, the model minority stereotype reflects the 'ambivalence' that the dominant group feels toward Asian Americans: it refers to a simultaneous attraction and repulsion from what the dominant group sees as Asian Americans' 'mimicry' of the American identity. Okihiro

---

17. Lee, *Orientals*, Chapter 6. Lee explains the term 'gook': it 'has a long history in the American vocabulary of race and in the American imperial career in Asia and the Pacific. A bastardization of the Korean *hankuk* (Korean), or *mikuk* (American), it was used by Americans in the Korean War to refer to North and South Koreans and Chinese alike. The term also has links to "goo-goo", used by American soldiers used to describe Filipino insurgents at the turn of the century' (p. 190). Lee continues that 'the supposed invisibility of the Viet Cong led to the racialization of the Vietnam War. "Gook" became the most common racial epithet used by Americans to describe Vietnamese, enemy and ally alike' (p. 190).

18. Lee, *Orientals*, p. 8.
19. Lee, *Orientals*, p. 12.
20. Lee, *Orientals*, p. 180.
21. Lee, *Orientals*, p. 190.

states that whites desired to lift up Asian Americans as a 'model' of themselves: 'The concept of the model minority posits a compatibility, if not identity, between key elements of Asian and Anglo-American culture, and thus, instead of deconstructing the European identity, Anglicized Asian culture... reifies and attests to its original'.[22] However, the model minority stereotype functions in a way similar to other representations of the Oriental, especially with that of the yellow peril.[23] The model minority stereotype is used to uphold Asian Americans as 'near-whites' or 'whiter than whites' in bipolar racial politics, but it ignores the white racism that Asian Americans continue to face; moreover, this stereotype is used to 'discipline' African Americans and other minority groups.[24] Okihiro notes the similarity between the two stereotypes:

> Like those pliant and persistent constructions of Asian culture, the concepts of the yellow peril and the model minority, although at apparent disjunction, form a seamless continuum. While the yellow peril threatens white supremacy, it also bolsters and gives coherence to a problematic construction: the idea of a unitary 'white' identity. Similarly, the model minority fortifies white dominance, or the status quo, but it also poses a challenge to the relationship of majority over minority. The very indices of Asian American 'success' can imperil the good order of race relations when the margins lay claim to the privileges of the mainstream.[25]

The ambivalence of Asian Americans in the eyes of the dominant group has put Asian Americans in a state of liminality, resulting in discrimination,

---

22. Okihiro, *Margins and Mainstreams*, pp. 139-40. According to the model minority thesis, the common elements between Asian culture and Anglo-American culture—namely, the work ethic, education, family value, and self-reliance—enabled Asian Americans, like all of America's white immigrants, to move from the margins to the mainstream.

23. Okihiro argues that the yellow peril stereotype functioned to maintain the social order in the midst of a fear of change in the relationship between whites and Asians: 'The idea of the yellow peril...helped to define that challenge posed by Asia to Europe's dominance and was inscribed within the colonialist discourse as a justification for the imposition of whites over nonwhites, of civilization/Christianity over barbarism/paganism... The fear, whether real or imagined, arose from the fact of the rise of nonwhite peoples and their defiance of white supremacy. And while serving to contain the Other, the idea of the yellow peril also helped to define the white identity, within both a nationalist and an internationalist frame' (*Margins and Mainstreams*, pp. 137-38).

24. The model minority stereotype has been thoroughly criticized. Takaki, *Strangers*, argues that it is used to affirm the American Dream and to admonish and discredit other minorities for not achieving such success as Asian Americans (pp. 475-79). Chan, *Asian Americans*, lists six criticisms against the model minority 'myth' by showing that the statistics used to depict a rosy picture of Asian-American existence are misleading and that many Asian Americans still suffer discrimination in many areas of American life (pp. 167-69).

25. Okihiro, *Margins and Mainstreams*, p. 141.

betrayal, and violence against them. Asians, understood as a race of aliens in opposition to whites, were victimized by the institutionalized racial immigration policies. The well-known Chinese Exclusion Act of 1882 prohibited the Chinese from immigrating to the US and prevented foreign born Chinese already living in the US from citizenship for 10 years (renewed indefinitely in 1902 by the Congress). The Chinese were the only group of people singled out on a racial basis from entering the US. They were excluded from the US because of identity politics in America that defined the Chinese as undesirable pollutants to white America. Another tragic moment in American history was when President Franklin D. Roosevelt set aside the Constitution of the United States and issued Executive Order 9066, which resulted in the incarceration of Japanese Americans in internment camps by the federal government. Although two thirds of the 120,000 internees were American citizens by birth, 'even the possession of US citizenship did not protect rights and liberties guaranteed by the Constitution'.[26] Japanese Americans were betrayed by their own government.[27]

These moments in American history are reminders that Asian Americans are only a step away from experiencing the *Realpolitik* of liminality, from being viewed as aliens within their own land, which could result in discriminations and violence against them. The LA Riots that occurred between 29 April and 2 May 1992 is one of the latest events that remind Asian Americans of the danger in being in a state of liminality. Asian Americans suspect that the predominantly 'colored' neighborhoods of Los Angeles became free-fire zones after the (mis)verdict of the Rodney King case: 'The LAPD sealed off the "colored" zones of the city from White LA and let them burn. The LAPD's strategy of containment was effective in protecting White LA; it brought massive destruction and death to LA's "Third World".'[28] The damage done to ethnic neighborhoods was mere collateral damage in the attempt to protect real Americans. In particular, Korean Americans suffered about half the estimated $850 million in material losses.[29] Lee remarks:

26. Takaki, *Strangers*, p. 15.
27. Unfortunately, Arab Americans are facing similar discriminations and tactics from the federal government after 9/11; the Patriot Act and the Homeland Security make Arab Americans targets of surveillance and investigation as potential 'terrorists' within America.
28. Lee, *Orientals*, p. 204.
29. Elaine Kim, 'Home is Where the *Han* Is?', in Wu and Song (eds.), *Asian American Studies*, pp. 270-89, examines the psychic damage incurred by Korean Americans. She suggests that in order to survive and overcome the brutal psychological damage that creates *han*, Korean Americans need to hold on to Korean national consciousness that create 'a new kind of nationalism-in-internationalism to help us call forth a culture of survival and recovery, so that our *han* might be released and we might be freed to dream fiercely of different possibility' (p. 284).

The outbreak of mass violence in Los Angeles could, however, also be called a pogrom. Although stores owned by many blacks, whites, Latinos, and other Asian Americans were also wrecked, Korean immigrant merchants sustained fully one half of the $850 million of property loss in the three days of looting and arson. An estimated 2,300 Korean-owned businesses were destroyed.[30]

Lee argues that although the reasons for targeting Korean Americans are complex and local, they were, however, merely the gook of the moment: the people who were targeting Koreans were following the mere gook rule—the rule that says that any dead Vietnamese could be counted as a dead enemy during the Vietnam War—'Koreans were the closest and most vulnerable Asian Americans in sight'.[31] Lee gives examples of the danger of looking like an Asian:

> In several of these cases and in many others, it did not matter that the victim was Chinese, or Korean, or Vietnamese; the mere gook rule overrode ethnicity. Vincent Chin, a Chinese American, was taken to be Japanese and killed by two white, furloughed autoworkers in Detroit. Jim Loo, also a Chinese American, was killed by two white men who thought he was Vietnamese. In 1990, Tuan Ana Cao, a Vietnamese American, was beaten and severely injured by a group of black men who though he was Korean. In January of 1996, Thien Minh Ly, a Vietnamese American, was killed by two White drifters who called him a Jap. In these cases it didn't matter what ethnicity or nationality the victims really were; the only significant issue was that they were the gook.[32]

A poem written by a college student expresses powerfully the *Realpolitik* of liminality experienced by Asian Americans in North America:[33]

> June 19, 1982, Detroit
> Vincent Chin
> young Chinese American
> engineer during the week, Chinese restaurant waiter on the weekend
> celebrating upcoming wedding
> chased and hunted down
> then bloodied and bludgeoned to death with a Louisville Slugger
> outside a crowded McDonald's
>
> two auto-workers
> a plant superintendent at Chrysler and his laid-off stepson
> *'It's because of you Mother fuckers we're out of work'*[34]

30. Lee, *Orientals*, p. 205.
31. Lee, *Orientals*, p. 216.
32. Lee, *Orientals*, p. 217. See my 'Uriah the Hittite' where I use Vincent Chin's death as an example of the dangerous side of liminality within US identity/race politics.
33. This poem entitled 'I will be free in my own country!' was written by Deborah Lee, a friend and a colleague at Pacific School of Religion, when she was in college.
34. The incriminating phrase uttered by Ronald Ebens overheard by a worker at the striptease bar, who gave evidence to the racial motivation behind the murder.

Unemployed, Made in Japan.
Once a Jap, always a Jap.

both men released
not a day in prison
'These aren't the kind of men you send to jail.
You fit the punishment to the criminal, not the crime.'[35]

3 years probation
$3,000 fine and $780 court fees
the price of a used American car

Forget Pearl Harbor, Remember Detroit
In North Carolina
happens again
this time
victim: Jim Lu
killed in a bar
crime: mistaken for being Vietnamese

Stockton,
Patrick Edward Purdy
hated Vietnamese
they don't belong in this country
taking American jobs
able to come into our country
taking over everything
slant eyes everywhere

January 17, 1989
Cleveland Elementary School, Stockton
a school where 7 out of 10 students
Cambodian, Lao, Vietnamese
Asian refugees
400 kids playing the schoolyard
recess
Purdy walks out of his Chevy wagon
fires 105 rounds
with an AK-47

Matter-of-factly
sweeps playground
leaving 34 children shot
bleeding, wounded and dead
Thuy Tran, six-year-old Cambodian girl is
dead.

---

35. Quote from presiding Judge Charles Kaufman explaining the light sentence. Helen Zia, *Asian American Dreams: The Emergence of an American People* (New York: Farrah, Strauss & Giroux, 2000), p. 60.

5. *The* Realpolitik *of Liminality*

> Sokhim Ang, six-year-old Cambodian girl,
> dead.
> Oeum Lim, eight-year-old Cambodian girl,
> dead.
> Rathanan Or, nine-year-old Cambodian boy,
> dead.
> Ran Chun, eight-year-old Cambodian girl,
> mortally wounded,
> dies on way to hospital.
>
> This is not the case of a crazy man
> this is not new to me
> this is very, very old
> victims are not accidental.

This poem reminds us that Asian Americans are always a short step away from being viewed as aliens, which often results in violence against them. Asian Americans experienced the *Realpolitik* of liminality throughout their history because they were viewed as the Oriental—a racial category that falls in-between the stratifications—in the discourse of identity and race in the US.

In spite of being viewed as the Oriental—as a race of aliens, as permanent strangers, as foreigners—Asian Americans have been writing a history of their own. In spite of being represented as the pollutant, the coolie, the deviant, the yellow peril, the model minority, and the gook, Asian Americans have been writing a history of their own. In spite of experiencing the *Realpolitik* of liminality—discrimination, betrayal, and violence by being placed at the margins of the racialized landscape shaped and maintained by the politics of race and identity grounded in Orientalism and the discourse of nationalism in North America—Asian Americans have been writing a history of their own. They are writing a history of their own by refusing to view their history as an insignificant footnote in the national history of the US. They are writing a history of their own by rejecting the assimilationist model that requires relinquishing their own unique identity and history. They are writing a history of their own by rejecting the model minority thesis that requires Asian Americans to imitate the dominant group. They are writing a history of their own by seeing themselves as agents of their own history and destiny. They are writing a history of their own by recovering their past and imagining an alternate view of America.

Asian Americans have turned Orientalism on its head.[36] They rejected the connotation of the term 'Oriental'—an objectification of Asians in America—

---

36. Yu, *Thinking Orientals*, asserts that Asian Americans, reacting in the 1960s and 1970s against the objectification of Asians, exemplified by the exotic connotations of the term 'Orientals', valued a past that had its roots in Asia, but at the same time, were 'emphatically sounding a right to be treated as Americans, Asian American activists turned Orientalism on its head' (p. viii).

and began to use the term 'Asian American' in the 1960s. 'Orientals are rugs, not people. Asian Americans are people.'[37] Takaki's *Strangers from a Different Shore* treated Asian Americans not as objects for study but as agents of their own histories. This means that Asian Americans' shared history, experience, and aspirations cannot be framed within the Oriental Problem, which is based on why Asian Americans, unlike European immigrants, have problems assimilating into the mainstream. Asian Americans reject the assimilationist approach that requires Asian Americans to relinquish their unique identity and experience and to mimic the dominant culture. But this does not mean that Asian-American communities are to create exact replicas of those in Asia, as if that were possible. Chan suggests that Asian-American communities 'are components of an increasingly multiethnic American landscape and can best be understood and appreciated as such'.[38] Asian Americans need to form more than a synthesis of Asia and America; they need to form an interstitial community, refusing to disconnect with any community, but not assimilating into a community to the extent that they lose their own unique identity and history.

Okihiro offers a new lens, a new framework in which to view the history of Asian Americans. He changes the place of Asian Americans from the margin to the mainstream.[39] Asian Americans have been viewed and treated as being at the margins of American society throughout American history, but Okihiro contends that Asian Americans were in fact part of the mainstream that made the US into a more equal and just society. Okihiro argues that the standard approaches to Asian-American history miss the deeper significance of experience and history of Asian Americans. The 'Asians as victims' approach highlights the suffering incurred by Asian Americans due to discriminatory laws and racism in America to the extent that, as Roger Daniel puts it, 'Asians have been more celebrated for what had happened to them than for what they have accomplished'.[40]

---

37. This is an often used statement to illustrate the difference between 'Oriental' and 'Asian American'. Okihiro explains that the term Asia 'was a European invention that named the Orient as spaces east of Europe and assigned natures, Orientalism, to its peoples. Accordingly, from 1850 to World War II, US laws governing immigration, citizenship, and civil and property rights and social convention and practice lumped together Chinese, Japanese, Koreans, Asian Indians, and Filipinos as an undifferentiated group. But that essentializing name was also made in America by Asians during the late 1960s, when they sought a pan-Asian identity premised upon a common past in the United States and upon a racialized politics that they would enable and lead to mobilization and empowerment' (*Columbia Guide*, pp. xiv-xv).

38. Chan, *Asian Americans*, p. xiv.

39. Okihiro, *Margins and Mainstreams*.

40. Roger Daniels, *Asian America* (Seattle: University of Washington Press, 1988), p. 4, quoted in Okihiro, *Margins and Mainstream*, p. 152.

The 'Asian contribution to American history and culture' approach celebrates Asian labor in building America, but 'when compared with the centrality of the founding fathers, the framers of the Constitution, the shapers of American letters and culture, the movers and shakers in the worlds of industry and government, Asian contributions seem trivial, and rightfully so'.[41] Okihiro suggests that the deeper significance of Asian-American history lies in Asian Americans' struggles for inclusion and equality, which 'helped to preserve and advance the very privileges that were denied to them, and thereby democratized the nation for the benefit of all Americans'.[42] It was their effort to resist the power that repeatedly denied the full inclusion within the American community and the rights to 'the promise of American democracy' that enlarged the range and deepened the meaning of American democracy'.[43] Moreover, Asian Americans helped 'to redefine the meaning of the American identity, to expand it beyond the narrower idea of only white and black, and to move it beyond the confines of the American state and the prescribed behaviors of loyalty and patriotism'.[44] Thus, he concludes: 'The margin has held the nation together with its expansive reach; the margin has tested and ensured together the guarantees of citizenship; and the margin has been the true defender of American democracy, equality, and liberty. From that vantage, we can see the margin as mainstream.'[45] Okihiro's thesis succeeds in attempting 'to move the pivot, by fracturing the universalism of white men and by repositioning gender, class, race, and sexuality from the periphery to the core, decentering and recentering the colors and patterns of the old fabric'.[46]

First, Asian Americans are recovering overwritten or forgotten 'inscriptions' from the past in order to write 'a history of their own'. The discovery of the 'inscriptions' from the barracks of the Angel Island Immigration Station illustrates the efforts of Asian Americans in recovering overwritten or forgotten memories and histories from the past. The story of the Angel Island Immigration Station, also dubbed 'the Ellis Island of the West', was a forgotten story in the collective memory of American immigration history.[47] It was assumed that its story was like that of its counterpart in New York harbor.

41. Okihiro, *Margins and Mainstreams*, p. 154.
42. Okihiro, *Margins and Mainstreams*, p. 151.
43. Okihiro, *Margins and Mainstreams*, p. 156.
44. Okihiro, *Margins and Mainstreams*, p. 155.
45. Okihiro, *Margins and Mainstreams*, p. 175.
46. Okihiro, *Margins and Mainstreams*, p. 151.
47. My reflection is based on my personal visit to Angel Island, PBS programs 'Becoming American: The Chinese Experience' in 3 parts (25–27 March 2003), the Angel Island Immigration Station Foundation web site (<http://www.aiisf.org>) and brochures, Takaki's *Strangers* (especially pp. 231-39), and H. Mark Lai, *Island: Poetry and History of Chinese Immigrants on Angel Island, 1910–1940* (San Francisco: HOC DOI, 1980).

We might have known that an estimated 175,000 Chinese immigrants had passed through Angel Island between 1910 and 1940, but we might not have known that their experience and stories were very different from that of their counterparts on the east coast if not for an accidental discovery of hundreds of poems carved on the walls of the barracks; there Chinese immigrants were imprisoned anywhere from a few weeks to 22 months (the longest stay that is documented).[48] This forgotten chapter in American history was unknown even to the Chinese-American community because Chinese immigrants who were imprisoned in Angel Island did not talk about their experience to their children. The barracks where Chinese immigrants were detained were scheduled to be burned for a scene in a movie.[49] But a park ranger was exploring the wooden barracks when he discovered the Chinese poetry carved on the walls.[50] The park ranger told Asian-American student activists and scholars about his discovery.[51] They recognized immediately the importance of the writings on the walls.

The discovery of the wooden barracks of Angel Island and hundreds of poems carved in Chinese characters on the walls came as a large shock to the Asian-American community.[52] The experience, voices, and history of Chinese men, women, and children who were detained on Angel Island would have been lost forever if not for the 'accidental' discovery. The archive of poems preserves the memories of their experience and thoughts. It is believed that underneath several layers of paint on the walls thousands more poems are waiting to be discovered and read. I believe the discovery of the writings in Angel Island illustrates the efforts of Asian Americans to write a 'history of their own' by recovering 'inscriptions' of Asian-American experience and

48. The Chinese Exclusion Act of 1882 stopped new Chinese immigrants and Chinese men living in the US but who were not US citizens from bringing their families to the US. The great earthquake of San Francisco in 1906, which destroyed almost all of the municipal records, including citizenship records, opened the way for Chinese men to claim that they were US citizens; as a result they could bring their families to the US. The new immigrants were detained and imprisoned at the immigration station in Angel Island where they were interrogated and examined until they could prove their paperwork was authentic.

49. The Chinese were separated from all other ethnic groups. The barracks were to be burned for a scene in the movie *The Candidate* starring Robert Redford in the late 1960s.

50. See the 'rediscovery' webpage at <http://www.aiisf.org>.

51. This was the time of the Asian-American movement begun by the student strikes at San Francisco State University in the late 1960s.

52. See the 'rediscovery' webpage at <http://www.aiisf.org>. Now the immigration station (the barracks with the 'archive' of poems) is a National Historic Landmark and listed as one of 'America's 11 Most Endangered' historic places by the National Trust for Historic Preservation, due to the dilapidated condition of the buildings. 'This irreplaceable site is destined to become a powerful place for healing and learning, a lens through which the broad contemporary issues of race, culture, and class conflict can be examined' (from the Angel Island Immigration Station Foundations' brochure).

history that have been hidden or forgotten underneath several layers of paint and other writings. Otherwise, we would have believed that the story of the Angel Island Immigration Station was no different from the story of Ellis Island and the story of Chinese immigrants in the west was no different from the story of European immigrants in the east.

Second, Asian Americans are writing a history of their own by remembering injustice and violence they have incurred through participating in pilgrimages. Joanne Doi's article on the Tule Lake Pilgrimage exemplifies the efforts of Asian Americans in trying to keep alive experience and memory that are being forgotten and silenced.[53] Japanese Americans who were interned are reluctant to talk about their experience at the camps; this chapter in American history has been cloaked in silence until recently.[54] Doi states that to revisit the former internment campsites gives 'voice to a complex silence'.[55] She continues that 'the magnitude of the silence of the Nisei [second generation] helped form the voice of the Sansei [third generation]; the Nisei's absence of outward emotional response mobilized the Sansei to begin to speak out'.[56] The Tule Lake Pilgrimage began in 1969 and there have been thirteen subsequent pilgrimages through the year 2002.[57] Doi describes her journey to Tule Lake as a postcolonial pilgrimage 'that continues to re-weave fragments of identity, family, community, memory, and history'.[58] It is 'a journey to the specific place' in the twenty-first century that 'evokes memories of that time' more than fifty years ago when a community of Americans had to struggle to survive in America.[59] Doi summarizes the importance of going on pilgrimages to the places that hold 'memories' of injustice and violence:

> These pilgrimages emphasize the significance of this ongoing movement back in time for the construction of meaning and identity for Japanese Americans and the multicultural reality of the US that is part of American history. A reconnection to a pivotal time in the past, a reconnection to the lives of those who passed through barbed wire fences into a permanent sense of displacement reveals the painful liminal reality that pervades subsequent generations.[60]

---

53. Joanne Doi, 'The Lake Pilgrimage: Dissonant Memories, Sacred Journey', in Jane Iwamura and Paul Spickard (eds.), *Revealing the Sacred in Asian and Pacific America* (London: Routledge, 2003), pp. 273-89.
54. Joy Kogawa, *Obasan* (New York: Anchor Books, 1994), has been instrumental in articulating the complexity of silence around the internment experience.
55. Doi, 'The Lake Pilgrimage', p. 275.
56. Doi, 'The Lake Pilgrimage', p. 277.
57. Doi, 'The Lake Pilgrimage', p. 275. The internment camp is located in Newell, CA, near the border of Oregon. It is one of the ten internment camps. Tule Lake is the name of a lake near there.
58. Doi, 'The Lake Pilgrimage', p. 273.
59. Doi, 'The Lake Pilgrimage', p. 275.
60. Doi, 'The Lake Pilgrimage', p. 275.

Doi distinguishes the postcolonial understanding of pilgrimage from the standard understanding. Pilgrimage is normally understood as a movement to the center, a quest of a place that embodies 'the source of the social-moral order of the cosmos'.[61] However, 'the Tule Lake Pilgrimage could be seen as moving away from the center as it enters into the chaos of suffering, that which has torn apart our webs of significance'.[62] She explains the postcolonial understanding of the Tule Lake Pilgrimage:

> The Tule Lake Pilgrimage as sacred journey can be understood as an attempt to regain our center as human person and community by reconnecting to our history and each other on the periphery, on the margins. It is a sacred journey to our own otherness that brings us home to ourselves. It is not escape but a return to the center of our history, the pivotal events that have marked us as Japanese Americans. In a paradoxical way, the center of our history located on the margins recreates and revitalizes as the truth of who we are shifts into place.[63]

It is a pilgrimage to the periphery that will keep alive the memory, experience, and history of those who have been silenced and placed on the margins, where we will find the ground of our being and identity. We must revisit the sites of struggle and suffering and predicament, for these sites also offer hope and promise and contest the American narrative that suppresses, ignores, and neglects the stories from the margin.

Third, Asian Americans are writing a history of their own by reinventing or making a culture of their own. Asian Americans are not only looking to the past for an aid in holding the Asian-American community together; they are also looking to create the future in which there are safe spaces and viable means to express their experience, aspirations, and history. They need cultural spaces in which Asian Americans can be authentic to themselves, without homogenizing the richness and complexity of Asian Americans.

Helen Zia acknowledges that there is no Asian-American monolithic culture but many cultures within the Asian-American community: 'The question of identity and culture have become more faceted and complex as newly emerging populations of Asian Americans push against ethnic, racial, generational, and class boundaries'.[64] As an example, she draws the complex picture of an emerging Asian-American group, the Hmong American community in Minnesota, coming to terms with being a minority ethnic group in America while struggling to create cultural space in which to articulate their own stories, experience and culture.[65] The Hmong community and 'other Asian

---

61. Doi, 'The Lake Pilgrimage', p. 280.
62. Doi, 'The Lake Pilgrimage', p. 280.
63. Doi, 'The Lake Pilgrimage', p. 280.
64. Zia, *Asian American Dreams*, p. 265.
65. Zia, *Asian American Dreams*, pp. 252-80.

American cultural workers in the Twin Cities and elsewhere are creating new images of Asian Americans and the culture that makes us uniquely American'.[66] She also notes that *hapas* (children of Asian and white marriages) and inter-ethnic marriages are expanding and complicating who is Asian American and what is Asian-American culture. Zia summarizes that 'as new and self-identified communities develop and seek their places in the Asian American community, they extend the boundaries of what it means to be Asian American and open up the range of Asian American culture'.[67] As a result, Asian Americans are asserting their own visions of what Asian-American cultures are.

By moving away from the essentialist view of culture, Asian-American cultures are being hybridized and reinvented toward the future. Zia asks: 'Is it possible to create cultural symbols and expressions that can convey the richness and complexity of Asian Americans?'[68] Asian-American cultural artists are forging authentic Asian-American cultures:

> Despite authenticity debates, distinction between 'pure' Asian art and Asian American hybrids are blurring as global influences affect both Asian and Western forms. Asian American artists, at the forefront of creating synergies between Asian and Western culture, are themselves influencing artists in Asia... Asian Americans are providing creative inspiration to Asia as well as America.[69]

Asian Americans also need something akin to what the African-American community invented: the Kwanza festival. We need the Lunar New Year festival that lasts for several days for all Asian-American communities to participate in. Instead of holding ethnic parades separately, we should have an Asian-American parade, each group being represented distinctively within the overall parade during the Lunar New Year festival. The point is that we need some cultural event, a festival, for all Asian-American groups to share in common. I think this will be vital for the Asian-American community to remain an identifiable group, as a unique American community.

Josiah's Kingdom in a Space of Liminality

Josiah's kingdom was located in a landscape not of its own making. Judah was under the shadow of Assyria for sixty years when Josiah came to the throne. Assyria saw Judah as no more than a member of the 'Wicked Hittites'. Josiah and his people were viewed as the enemy/Other in the ideological

---

66. Zia, *Asian American Dreams*, p. 255.
67. Zia, *Asian American Dreams*, p. 268.
68. Zia, *Asian American Dreams*, p. 268.
69. Zia, *Asian American Dreams*, p. 272.

landscape of the Assyrian Empire. Perhaps it was in such an ethnically charged landscape that Josiah began his reforms in his eighteenth year.

E. Theodore Mullen suggests that DH functioned to respond to the crisis of assimilation in the exile by providing a means to form an ethnic group identity.[70] Mullen analyzes several major 'narrative events' in DH, including Josiah's reform, and offers the following conclusion:

> The narrator of those stories has organized them as a series of 'social dramas' of ritual creation/reenactment which produce or reinforce certain ethnic boundaries that define the people 'Israel'. From the fabric of traditional stories, some ancient and some invented, the author 'imagined' the form and content of a community and then gave it a 'history' designed to define and preserve selected aspects that might be understood as unique and meaningful to the community being addressed.[71]

It is the book of Deuteronomy, Mullen argues, that provides the vision, the manifesto that defines the Israelite identity as the people who were separated for YHWH and as the followers of the Deuteronomic code. The community in the exile could participate in the establishment of the Deuteronomic community by re-enacting the renewal of the covenant, by drawing the boundaries according to the manifesto in Deuteronomy.[72] Mullen maintains that the account of Josiah represents 'a thematic high point in the deuteronomistic history'.[73] The reason is that although there are other reforms attributed to selected kings, 'it is only Josiah who acts in such a way to reunify, and hence recreate, the ideal of Israel', and thus 'his actions enforce the group identity formulated in the deuteronomic corpus' both religiously and nationally.[74] The account of Josiah as a history-like narrative confirms the belief that it is

---

70. E. Theodore Mullen, *Narrative History and Ethnic Boundaries: The Deuteronomistic Historian and the Creation of Israelite National Identity* (Atlanta: Scholars Press, 1993). It is closer to a final-form reading done by literary critics than the work of historical-critical scholars on the DH. Although his decision to work with an exilic edition and to investigate its function in the community in the Exile places him in line with Noth and the Smend School, his work is more in tune with the Cross School.

71. Mullen, *History and Ethnic Boundaries*, pp. 15-16.

72. Mullen summarizes this point: 'this covenantally based concept of renewal constituted a type of narrative charter by which restored blessing and the reestablishment of order might be effected at those times of crisis perceived as the result of the violation of the deuteronomic code. This ideological charter provides for the way in which the failures of the people, and hence the threat of destruction, might be redirected and reconstituted so as to avoid dissolution and chaos' (p. 76).

73. Mullen, *History and Ethnic Boundaries*, p. 76. Mullen more or less follows the Cross School in that Josiah's reform is still the climax of DH; the ending that follows Josiah's reformation is not important at all.

74. Mullen, *History and Ethnic Boundaries*, p. 77.

possible to recreate this national ethnic group based on the manifesto in Deuteronomy: 'A people ethnically and religiously defined in terms of the stipulations of the deuteronomic corpus could be ritually recreated by the proper enactment of the covenant ceremonies prescribed therein'.[75] Mullen highlights the importance of Josiah again:

> In this way, the deuteronomistic author created a partial frame around the history of 'Israel' in the land that was constructed of the ethnic group 'Israel', defined as an ideal in Deuteronomy, and the reconstitution of that ideal near the very end of that history in the account of the actions of Josiah. The stories of the actualizations of that identity and its loss are contained within this frame.[76]

Now the community in the exile is ready to begin a new history by recreating the Deuteronomic community: 'A new history would begin, understood now in terms of the ideal past that had been forfeited by the people's failure to recognize and maintain their distinctive relationship with their god'.[77]

Although Mullen seeks to develop an alternate model of interpretation of DH by examining the function of DH in the community rather than focusing on the meaning and composition of DH, once one strips away such terms as 'ethnicity' and 'identity formation', his approach, in many ways, is no different from that of the two schools. Mullen does not deal with ethnicity.[78] In Mullen's analysis, ethnicity plays no part in identity formation. He also does not elaborate on what the crisis of assimilation is. He works with a general

---

75. Mullen, *History and Ethnic Boundaries*, pp. 83-84; according to Mullen, this is exactly what Josiah did. Mullen states that 'the greatness of Josiah was to be found in the fact that despite the absolute confirmation of the disaster that was to befall Judah, he continued his reform. Following the guidelines of "the book", by which the writer clearly seems to have intended Deuteronomy, Josiah engaged in a covenant renewal, a complete cleansing of the cultus of any non-Yahwistic practices, and defiled *bamot* that dated back to the days of Solomon ([2 Kgs] 23.13). More importantly, he fulfilled the prophecy against the altar at Bethel (23.15-20). The newly recreated covenantal "Israel" then celebrated the Passover in a manner unequaled since the time of the judges (23.22). In ritual terms, "Israel" had been redefined in the days of Josiah by the deuteronomic boundaries provided in this "book of the torah"; because of that same covenantal charter, this recreation could not last. Despite Josiah's efforts, Judah had been condemned by Yahweh's prophets. Yahweh would not fail to bring their proclamations to fruition (23.26-27)' (pp. 280-81).
76. Mullen, *History and Ethnic Boundaries*, p. 84.
77. Mullen, *History and Ethnic Boundaries*, p. 281.
78. Kenton Sparks, *Ethnicity and Identity in Ancient Israel: Prolegomena to the Study of Ethnic Sentiments and their Expression in the Hebrew Bible* (Winona Lake, IN: Eisenbrauns, 1998), critiques Mullen on this point: 'Mullen's work tends to focus much more on the definition of the Israelite community than on the place and function of ethnic sentiments within that definition. Because of this, although Mullen provides a careful analysis of religious identity in Deuteronomy, one will notice his rather thin treatment of some important issues that are integrally related to ethnicity' (p. 272).

notion of oppressive context, which includes the pressure to assimilate, but this is not helpful in understanding why ethnic sentiments became strong during the exile. There is also no need to start the investigation from the Exile just because DH ends there. One can argue that the formation of ethnic group identity started during the time of Josiah. In fact, it was during Josiah's time that the need for forming ethnic group identity became strong. Still, Mullen introduced something important to the scholarship on DH: DH as history writing that functioned to help form ethnic group identity.

Kenton Sparks deals more extensively with ethnicity in relation to formation of group identity. He uses six principles to help his investigation in the connection between ethnicity and identity formation in ancient Israel:[79]

1. Ethnicity is one of the many varieties of human behavior and is perceptible only in certain cultural contexts.[80]
2. Ethnicity is a phenomenon of genetic perception.[81]
3. Ethnic sentiments do not arise in a vacuum but arise most intensively in the context of multicultural contact.[82]
4. Phenotypical characteristics play an important role as ethnic *indicia*.[83]
5. Ethnicity must be considered in its political, social-structural, and economic setting.[84]
6. Ethnic identities are highly fluid.[85]

---

79. Sparks prefers to talk about 'ethnic sentiments' in biblical writings and in the contexts in which they were written, rather than ethnicity, because of the difficulty of defining the term and identifying it in the text and in the context. Generally, a group identity is formed by 'genealogy' (Who are your ancestors?) and 'geography' (Where are you from?).

80. Sparks, *Ethnicity and Identity in Ancient Israel*, p. 18. This means that ethnicity is perceptible when a given community attempts (or is pressured) to define itself by distinguishing itself from other communities; or a given community is defined by other communities.

81. Sparks, *Ethnicity and Identity in Ancient Israel*, p. 18. Sparks explains that this principle 'includes the idea that the group in some way shares a common ancestry, and this is quite apart from the question of whether the individuals in the group are actually related' (p. 18). Sparks sees this principle in biblical narratives—a creation of fictive kinship. Ethnicity is one aspect of identity. Sparks concludes that ethnicity is secondary to religious identity in Deuteronomy.

82. Sparks, *Ethnicity and Identity in Ancient Israel*, pp. 19-20. Sparks agrees to a certain extent with the theory that ethnic sentiments intensify when 'peripheral' groups live under the domination of a powerful 'core' civilization.

83. Sparks, *Ethnicity and Identity in Ancient Israel*, p. 21. Sparks notes that this principle played a small role in forming Israelite identity; there is no evidence of phenotypical differences between Israelites and other West Semitic peoples.

84. Sparks, *Ethnicity and Identity in Ancient Israel*, p. 22.

85. Sparks, *Ethnicity and Identity in Ancient Israel*, p. 22. Sparks notes that 'attention must be given to the kinds of changes that occur in a given, concrete historical situation' (p. 22).

Using these principles Sparks investigates the expressions of ethnic sentiments in the biblical narratives and the possible contexts in which they arose. Sparks agrees with Mullen about the importance of focusing on Deuteronomy for the definition of Israel's group identity and the primacy of religious identity:

> Mullen's emphasis on the essentially religious boundaries that define Deuteronomic identity is fundamentally correct, because my study also suggests that Deuteronomy's primary concern was religious and Yahwistic, with ethnic sentiments playing a secondary role in support of those priorities.[86]

Sparks makes the following conclusions: (1) Deuteronomy had a supportive stance toward foreign 'sojourners', which was an effort to protect the refugees/immigrants from the former northern kingdom; (2) the primary criterion for community membership was religious (a commitment to YHWH); and (3) there were no clear and useful *indicia* that could serve to draw boundaries between insiders and outsiders. These findings support his thesis: 'Deuteronomy's ethnic concern was much more the establishing of a sense of ethnic kinship among Israelites and Judeans than it was the excluding of foreigners from participation within the community'.[87]

He concludes, however, that ethnic sentiments expressed in Deuteronomy and in the other biblical texts he investigates relate more closely to Greek materials than to any other ancient Near Eastern materials (Egypt and Mesopotamia). He maintains, 'For the Egyptians and Assyrians, identity was political and cultural, not ethnic, and was linked with kingship, the king's relationship to the deity, and the deity's role in extending the national borders and the native empire to the "ends of the earth"'.[88] In contrast, Sparks states that the Greeks showed greater ethnographic interests than imperial or religious interests: 'Greek identity...was quite distinct from both of its neighbors, being primarily concerned with ethnic varieties of social identity and with

---

86. Sparks, *Ethnicity and Identity in Ancient Israel*, p. 272. Sparks points out that much more work needs to be done on the issue of ethnic identity and its place in DH because Mullen's treatment is characterized by the tendency to generalize without dealing with important issues related to ethnicity. Sparks also limits himself to Deuteronomy but acknowledges the need for further investigations of ethnic sentiments in DH as a whole.

87. Sparks, *Ethnicity and Identity in Ancient Israel*, p. 283. This supports my suggestion that Josiah's reforms were oriented toward the Judeans (native Judeans and Israelite immigrants/refugees) rather than the people living in the Samerina province. But Sparks, after noting that two primary purposes of the older, pre-Josianic core of Deuteronomy composed after the fall of Samaria were 'first, to preserve the mono-Yahwist agenda of the proto-Deuteronomic movement, and second, to employ its ethnic sentiment in support of Northern and Southern unity, especially with regard to the integration of the North's refugees' (p. 327), seems to assume that the Josianic core continues these purposes; the proof seems to be Josiah's campaign to the Samerina province.

88. Sparks, *Ethnicity and Identity in Ancient Israel*, p. 91.

various standards of "civilized" behavior'.[89] He argues that the Greek materials showed many similar interests to that of the Hebrew Bible: the origins of different peoples (humanity); how the past is connected with the present; the notion of a 'Golden Age'; the primeval period of history featuring superhuman figures; human population groups originating via eponymous ancestors or territorial migration, and so on. Sparks suggests that it was when Persia threatened Greek states—when the Greeks put aside their differences—that 'a new sense of collective Hellenic identity' was developed.[90] Sparks, following John Van Seters, understands Deuteronomy as a postexilic document and suggests that it is closer to the writings represented by Herodotus and other Greeks.[91] He speculates that there was a much earlier contact between Israel and Greece and the exchange of ideas was more active. Thus he concludes:

> Deuteronomy (especially in its Deuteronomistic sections) shows signs of influence from Greece or perhaps from a common cultural arbiter [i.e. Phoenicia] between Israel and Greece. Such an exchange of ideas should be viewed as more likely in the case of Deuteronomy…because Deuteronomy comes later in the period of growing contacts between Greece and the Levant.[92]

But he does qualify his conclusion by remarking that 'there is sufficient subtlety in the evidence to suggest that we are talking about probabilities rather than about practical certainties'.[93]

In contrast to Sparks, there are good reasons to view ethnic sentiments in DH (including Deuteronomy) as having arisen from the context of the Neo-Assyrian period rather than the later Hellenistic period. In fact, Sparks himself provides much evidence for this in his investigation—his work shows that ethnic sentiments intensified in the Sargonid Dynasty—so it is strange that he insists that 'one of the more important features of the Assyrian materials is how little they reflect ethnic sentiment on the part of the Assyrians, either in terms of their own identity or in terms of their conceptions about other groups'.[94] Sparks points out that there are several features in Sargon's royal inscriptions that are helpful in understanding the change in Assyrian identity during the Sargonid Dynasty. He notes that the stereotyped phrase *ana/itti nišē Aššur amnušunūti* ('with the people of Assyria I counted them'),

---

89. Sparks, *Ethnicity and Identity in Ancient Israel*, p. 92.
90. Sparks, *Ethnicity and Identity in Ancient Israel*, p. 93.
91. Van Seters sees DH as a late production and connects it with the writing of Herodotus.
92. Sparks, *Ethnicity and Identity in Ancient Israel*, p. 261.
93. Sparks, *Ethnicity and Identity in Ancient Israel*, p. 261.
94. Sparks, *Ethnicity and Identity in Ancient Israel*, p. 25. Sparks differentiates Assyrian identity as religious and political and Greek identity as more ethnographical, but he and Mullen have argued that identity definition in Deuteronomy is primarily religious.

which was in common use to refer to the subject peoples of Assyria prior to Sargon II, was replaced during Sargon's reign by the phrase *biltu maddatu kī ša Aššurī ēmissunūti* ('tribute, tax, I imposed upon them as upon Assyrian'), which continued to be used throughout the Sargonid Dynasty.[95] The old phrase reflects a more positive attitude toward non-Assyrians with the possibility of non-Assyrians becoming Assyrians.[96] But the new phrase, according to Sparks, 'seems to reflect a discourse strategy aimed at generating firmer boundaries between Assyrian identity and that of its vassals'.[97] He continues that 'following Sargon's reign, phrases that equate imperial subjects with Assyrians are lacking entirely and were replaced with a marked tendency to describe conquered peoples as foreign booty or as a source of corvée labor'.[98] He credits the Sargonid Dynasty's view of the smaller political entities as no more than a group of inferior vassals, using derogatory terms like 'the wicked Hittites' to refer to the Western states (including Judah), to the formation of Assyrian 'national' identity based on 'imperialistic expansion of the kingdom of the god *Aššur* and his high priest, the king', that is, it was political and monarchic rather than ethnic.[99] Therefore, although he acknowledges that during the period of Assyrian domination 'a marked intensification of ethnic boundaries in Judean society' became visible and had an impact on biblical texts like Deuteronomy, he maintains that Assyrian identity was not ethnic in character.[100]

Sparks wants to argue that the evidence of ethnic sentiments in the biblical texts are related to the Greek writings on identity rather than to Assyrian

---

95. Sparks, *Ethnicity and Identity in Ancient Israel*, pp. 25-51. Sparks notes that the old phrase 'disappeared entirely from the inscriptions of Sennacherib, Esarhaddon, and Assurbanipal' (p. 32).

96. Sparks explains that there was 'a perceived difference between the new imperial subjects, those counted as Assyrians, and true Assyrians more closely associated with Assyrian politics, rule, and culture, but this distinction did not preclude the use of the term *Assyrian* to refer to these new subjects' (p. 50).

97. Sparks, *Ethnicity and Identity in Ancient Israel*, p. 32. B. Oded, *Mass Deportations and Deportees in the Neo-Assyrian Empire* (Wiesbaden: Reichert, 1979), states: 'The impressive victories of Tiglath-pileser III and Sargon II, in the course of two generations (745–705), gradually fostered a sense of superiority of the Assyrian people over other nations. The old ideology of Assyrian domination of the whole world...started to become an apparent reality during the eighth century B.C.... This deep-rooted feeling of superiority led to a sterner attitude towards deportees, and sharpened the differentiation between Assyrians...and non-Assyrians... This is, we believe, one of the underlying reasons for the disappearance of the formula *ana/itti nišē Aššur amnušunūti*' (*Mass Deportation*, pp. 89-90).

98. Sparks, *Ethnicity and Identity in Ancient Israel*, p. 33.

99. Sparks, *Ethnicity and Identity in Ancient Israel*, pp. 49-50.

100. Sparks, *Ethnicity and Identity in Ancient Israel*, p. 224.

writings. Thus, Sparks hesitates to accept Wallerstein's periphery/core theory and qualifies it: 'Wallerstein is correct to suppose that the peripheral experience intensifies *identity* but is wrong that it tends to create *ethnic sentiments*'.[101] Thus, Assyrian domination intensified identity formation in 'Israel', but not necessarily ethnic sentiments or ethnic identity. Sparks dismisses the idea that the use of the term *ṣalmāt qaqqadi* ('black-headed men') had ethnic connotations.[102] He reasons that it was used without ethnic content: 'the only prospect for an ethnic component in Assyrian identity is their use of the ancient Sumerian designation, the *black-headed people*. It is now clear, however, that this was probably not an ethnic term but a general reference to the Mesopotamian peoples'.[103] The term, however, had a more specific reference. It was used by the Assyrians and Babylonians deliberately—politically, culturally, ethnically—to identify themselves as the inheritors of the ancient civilization of Sumer and Akkad in contrast to those who were perceived as Others.[104]

There was a heightened awareness of ethnic sentiments during the Sargonid Dynasty in the Neo-Assyrian Empire that may have intensified the formation of ethnic identity among peripheral states. Carlos Zaccagnini observes that the bearing of 'ethnographic' observations within the complex of the Neo-Assyrian textual material begins with Sargon II.[105] Before Sargon's time the only ethnographic remark to be found is the stereotyped phrase 'Place Name X, which they (i.e. the enemies) call Place Name Y'.[106] Sargon and his successors replaced such a stereotypical phrase with more detailed and interesting ethnographic descriptions of the Others. Zaccagnini argues that the Assyrian ethnographic vision of the Others is based on a simple dualism that is rooted in the ideology of Assyrian imperialism, which is an expression of the Neo-Assyrian hegemonic class. He summarizes his main points as follows:

101. Sparks, *Ethnicity and Identity in Ancient Israel*, p. 328 (emphasis mine).
102. A phrase that originated with the Sumerians and was used by Assyrians and Babylonians throughout their histories to refer to themselves.
103. Sparks, *Ethnicity and Identity in Ancient Israel*, p. 37.
104. I am not implying that the Assyrians had black hair and that they used it as their ethnic marker. However, there was a sense of superiority, ethnic pride if you will, in using the term *black-headed people* to identify themselves as the descendants of the ancient civilization of Sumer and Akkad.
105. Carlos Zaccagnini, 'The Enemy in the Neo-Assyrian Royal Inscriptions: The "Ethnographic" Description', in Hans-Jörg Nissen and Johannes Renger (eds.), *Mesopotamien und seine Nachbarn: Politische und kulturelle Wechselbeziehungen im Alten Vorderasien vom 4. bis 1. Jahrtausend v. Chr. XXV. Rencontre Assyriologique Internationale Berlin 3. bis 7. Juli 1978* (Berliner Beiträge zum Vorderen Orient, Band 1, Teil 2; Berlin: Deitrich Reimer Verlag, 1982), pp. 409-24 (412).
106. Zaccagnini, 'The Enemy in the Neo-Assyrian Royal Inscriptions', p. 412.

[1] In general, we may observe that the Neo-Assyrian imperialistic ideology expresses itself through the recurrent use of the *topos* of the enemy, who is viewed as an alien and 'other' reality, as a necessary dialectical term for the Assyrian reality, in its historical being and becoming. [2] Within the framework of this ideology, the figure and role of the enemy are the necessary counterparts to the reasserting of the Assyrian entity over the whole of its opponents. The identity of the Assyrian power comes out in its true character, i.e. its own deep consciousness of being the hegemonic strength among all the cultures and political organizations of the Near East of the time. [3] Moreover, it is important to stress that the theme of the enemy, in its various articulations, is a direct expression of the ideology of the Neo-Assyrian hegemonic class.[107]

Zaccagnini points out that the Sargonid Dynasty's dualism is a very basic and somewhat crude binary scheme in which everything pertaining to Assyria is good and everything pertaining to the outer world is bad. The scheme sees 'the others', non-Assyrians, as the enemies who are morally and culturally inferior to the Assyrians. Zaccagnini argues that this scheme becomes most apparent when we recognize that the royal inscriptions use a fixed set of often-repeated *topoi* in describing the enemies, regardless of the differences in these enemies and their historical situations. This binary scheme is based not only on typical ethnocentrism, but also on Assyria's peculiar ideology of imperialism. Zaccagnini explains that 'the Assyrian representation of the "other" is a direct and consequent expression of this imperialistic ideology'.[108] This is most apparent in the ample descriptions of the military aspects of war campaigns in the Assyrian royal inscriptions. They depict the enemy 'as a passive agent, incapable of military initiatives', and we are privy to their 'fear, terror, impotence, after which inevitably follows flight and/or defeat, annihilation, etc.'[109] The message to the enemies is: If they foolishly choose to resist, they had no chance since the Assyrians always managed to overcome and defeat them.

Frederick Fales agrees with Zaccagnini's assessment of the role played by the enemy in the Assyrian binary scheme.[110] He points out that although there are many different enemies attested in the Assyrian royal inscriptions, 'there is only one Enemy—with a capital letter' who serves as the antagonist to the Assyrian king.[111] The royal inscriptions portray the various kings and rebellious vassals as separate manifestations of a unitary ideology of enmity. Fales describes the king and the enemy as two actors on stage, strictly following their scripts; the Enemy has to play

---

107. Zaccagnini, 'The Enemy in the Neo-Assyrian Royal Inscriptions', p. 410 (numbering mine).
108. Zaccagnini, 'The Enemy in the Neo-Assyrian Royal Inscriptions', p. 410.
109. Zaccagnini, 'The Enemy in the Neo-Assyrian Royal Inscriptions', p. 414.
110. Frederick Fales, 'The Enemy in Assyrian Royal Inscriptions: "The Moral Judgment"', in Nissan and Renger (eds.), *Mesopotamien und seine Nachbarn*, pp. 425-35.
111. Fales, 'The Moral Judgment', p. 425.

the part of the antagonist to the king: He has...become the present bearer of a sort of 'theatrical mask' of the nakru [enemy], and—as such—part of the eternally revolving mechanism of nakrus and šarrus [kings] confronting themselves on the 'stage' of the cuneiform texts... For the šarru has a role similar to his, although opposite: the function of both is to fight unendingly, but the function of the šarru is to win every single time, and thereby await the arrival onstage of the next nakru.[112]

Fales also adds that there is a moral evaluation and judgment involved in the description of the enemy. By examining the *topoi* used to describe the enemy, Fales reaches the conclusion that 'the "senseless", "plotting", and "wicked" enemies become, in brief, standard characters of the Sargonids' view of nakrūtu'.[113]

Zaccagnini argues that the ethnographic vision in the Sargonids' royal inscriptions is the typical approach of a hegemonic culture toward the 'others' and subordinate cultures; in this case, it represents the viewpoint of the Neo-Assyrian hegemonic class.[114] There is, in general, no genuine desire to know the 'other' cultures when describing the outer world in the inscriptions. The ethnographic descriptions express the viewpoint of a typical hegemonic class: the foreign people are not only charged with a long series of faults and imperfections, but even their lands are viewed as a deviation from the norm, that is, from the Assyrian landscape.[115] He concludes that 'the Assyrian attitude in depicting the "other cultures" is well aligned with the propaganda purposes of the Assyrian hegemonic class'.[116] The ethnographic vision of the enemy serves as a pedestal on which the Assyrian hegemonic class stands 'to celebrate the Assyrians' self-legitimation as a hegemonic and unique power over the rest of the world'.[117]

The Experience of the Realpolitik *of Liminality*

Josiah's kingdom was located in the ideological landscape of Assyrian imperialism where it was viewed as an Other. Josiah's people were located in a space of liminality, in an ideological space not of their own making where they experienced the *Realpolitik* of liminality. Judah was no more than a petty state caught in the political, commercial matrix shaped by the Assyrian Empire, driven by its ideology of expansion. It was located at the margin of the Assyrian Empire, where it experienced an ambivalent relationship with Assyria, usually as a victim or a witness of violence and exploitation. The

112. Fales, 'The Moral Judgment', p. 426.
113. Fales, 'The Moral Judgment', p. 431.
114. Zaccagnini, 'The Enemy in the Neo-Assyrian Royal Inscriptions', pp. 411-12.
115. Zaccagnini, 'The Enemy in the Neo-Assyrian Royal Inscriptions', p. 413.
116. Zaccagnini, 'The Enemy in the Neo-Assyrian Royal Inscriptions', p. 417.
117. Zaccagnini, 'The Enemy in the Neo-Assyrian Royal Inscriptions', p. 418.

presence of the Assyrian arms left no doubt as to whose political landscape Judah was located in.

The Neo-Assyrian dynasty's intrusion into the West, the region west of the Euphrates River referred to as 'Hatti' in the royal inscriptions of the Neo-Assyrian kings, began with Ashurnasirpal II's (883–859 BCE) desire for military expeditions across the Euphrates River.[118] Shalmaneser III (858–824), son of Ashurnasirpal, not only continued his father's intrusions, but also conducted more systematic annual campaigns in the West designed to secure Assyrian commercial interests and to expand Assyrian borders. When Shalmaneser annexed Bit-Adini in 856, he 'introduced a new stage in Assyrian domination of the West. For the first time a major western state...was subdued and became a regular Assyrian province.'[119] Thus, Shalmaneser set the policy that was to direct Assyria's relationship with the West for the next two hundred years. It was, however, not until the reign of Tiglath-pileser III (744–727) in the middle of the eighth century that Assyria was able to carry out Shalmaneser's policy on a grand scale.[120] Tiglath-pileser conquered all of Syria and advanced farther and farther down Palestine in order to control the *via maris*, which was crucial to Assyria's expanding commercial interests.[121] Then, finally, Sargon II and his dynasty dominated and controlled the entire West for almost the next one hundred years.

Tadmor states that the political-ideological factor that shaped the Neo-Assyrian Empire's territorial expansion was the view that the primary duty of every Assyrian king was to expand the borders of his land.[122] The command—'With your just scepter, extend your land!'—attested first with Tulkuti-Ninurta I, is again attested six hundred years later in Ashurbanipal's reign—'Extend your land at your feet!'[123] Tadmor also points out that, with this principle of perennial expansion, there is a recurrent motif, the 'heroic priority', in which 'the king boasts that he has traversed a land none of his forefathers had heard of'.[124] Sargon II boasts after defeating the Cypriote

---

118. Hayim Tadmor, 'Assyria and the West: The Ninth Century and its Aftermath', in Hans Goedicke and J.J.M. Roberts (eds.), *Unity and Diversity: Essays in the History, Literature, and Religion of the Ancient Near East* (Baltimore: The Johns Hopkins University Press, 1975), pp. 36-48.

119. Tadmor, 'Assyria and the West', p. 39.

120. Tadmor, 'Assyria and the West', p. 37.

121. Tadmor, 'Philistia under Assyria Rule'.

122. Hayim Tadmor, 'World Dominion: The Expanding Horizon of the Assyrian Empire', in L. Milano, S. de Martino, F.M. Fales and G.B. Lanfranchi (eds.), *Landscape: Territories, Frontiers and Horizons in the Ancient Near East: Papers Presented to the XLIV Rencontre Assyriologique Internationale Venezia, 7–11 July 1997* (History of the Ancient Near East Monographs, 3/1; Padova: Sargon, 1999), pp. 55-62.

123. Tadmor, 'World Dominion', p. 55.

124. Tadmor, 'World Dominion', p. 56. Tadmor also comments that this heroic principle of royal omnipotence is the *leitmotif* of the accounts of campaigns.

kings that he had expanded the horizon of Assyria even though he hardly added any territory beyond the borders established by Tiglath-pileser III. Tadmor explains Sargon's expansion: 'What emerges from these boasts of heroic priority is that Sargon expanded the horizons of the Empire one step beyond the limits set by Tiglath-pileser III. These horizons no longer extended merely from sea to sea, but to the islands in the midst of the seas.'[125]

Although Sennacherib did not expand his borders, he continued to use the heroic priority of the Assyrian monarch in the descriptions of his campaigns; that is, he saw himself as a powerful king who devastates, destroys, and burns the cities of his enemies. Julian Reade remarks that 'architecture, sculpture and iconography in Sennacherib's reign are imperial and cosmopolitan in a way foreshadowed but never rivalled previously'.[126] Esarhaddon continued Sargon's imperial policy of expansionism by entering Egypt. Ashurbanipal then invaded Egypt twice, conquering Thebes in 664, and strengthened his control over Egypt; in the process he unified the ancient Near East. Giovanni Lanfranchi summarizes the importance of the Neo-Assyrian Empire's hegemony:

> The empire which emerged after Sargon's death was stable and strong after a pause during Sennacherib's reign...the expansion progressed with Esarhaddon, who was finally able to crush Egypt... In a wider sense, and in a *longue durée* perspective, the unification of the Near East which was achieved by the Neo-Assyrian empire was to last—though occasionally disturbed by short-lived fragmentation—as a structural characteristic down to the end of the fourth century B.C., right to the end of Persian rule—and even later.[127]

The method of expansion, however, was not limited to conquest. Lanfranchi draws the image of a two-faced king, the traditional image of an awesome and fierce king together with the image of a kind and solicitous king, which seemed to have been an innovation begun during the reign of Sargon II.[128] Lanfranchi states that 'policies other than war and repression also must have been employed to enlarge, strengthen and maintain the expanding imperial structure'.[129] Sargon and his successors sought alliance and cooperation with their subjects as well as with their competitors. The existence of faithful and good allies of Assyria attests to this policy of alliance and cooperation. The

125. Tadmor, 'World Dominion', p. 57.
126. Julian Reade, 'Neo-Assyrian Monuments in their Historical Context', in Frederick M. Fales (ed.), *Assyrian Royal Inscriptions: New Horizons in Literary, Ideological, and Historical Analysis* (Rome: Instituto per l'Oriente, 1980), pp. 143-67 (163).
127. Giovanni Lanfranchi, 'Consensus to Empire: Some Aspects of Sargon II's Foreign Policy', in H. Waetzoldt and H. Hauptmann (eds.), *Assyrien im Wandel der Zeiten* (Heidelberg: Heidelberger Orientverlag, 1997), pp. 81-87 (81).
128. Lanfranchi, 'Consensus to Empire', p. 86.
129. Lanfranchi, 'Consensus to Empire', p. 82.

subjects wanted to be independent, but, at the same time, they realized the advantage of remaining as Assyria's allies.[130]

The Assyrian kings used two tactics to maintain their control over their subjects. The use of terror by the Assyrians is a well-known fact. Zaccagnini suggests that the royal inscriptions' purpose was very specific: 'They were an optimal instrument for conveying (ideological) messages to serve a practical purpose: e.g. terror to be inspired upon inner or outer "subject"'.[131] If we accept the royal inscriptions' descriptions of what the Assyrians did to their enemies at face value, it is truly terrifying—flaying alive, impalement, cutting or excising, burning alive, smashing, heaping up of corpses or of heads, and so on. The king would conduct exemplary punishments on those enemies 'who have shown a stiffer resistance'.[132] Furthermore, Younger points out that 'the more specific punishment of flaying alive seems to have been reserved for Assyrian traitors and usurpers'.[133] These punishments were used as psychological warfare to instill fear in their enemies and subjects, in order to deter them from rebellion and to give the Assyrians a psychological edge over their subjects.

The Sargonid kings also used acts of kindness in dealing with their enemies and rebellious vassals in order to maintain their empire. Lanfranchi suggests that Sargon's image as a kind and solicitous king was drawn in order to elicit consensus (i.e. cooperation in order to gain hegemony) to his empire from the ruling classes of his subject vassals and competing powers. Sargon used various tactics including promotions, gifts, rewards, and so on, to win over his enemies and to gain the loyalty of his vassals. Lanfranchi states that 'the first feature to be noted is Sargon's reward of the loyal vassals, which is amply stressed in his Royal Inscriptions'.[134] Sargon is also portrayed 'as a promoter of the loyal ruler to a ideologically higher rank of kingship'.[135] He also promoted soldiers belonging to subjugated kingdoms by incorporating them to the Assyrian army, 'which was clearly meant to show a benevolent attitude towards local military aristocracies'.[136] Sargon wanted his

---

130. The relationship between colonizer and colonized is not one-dimensional, but characterized by 'ambivalence'. Ashcroft, Griffiths, and Tiffin explain that it is a term psychoanalysts use to describe 'a continual fluctuation between wanting one thing and wanting its opposite', and it has been adapted by Homi Bhabha to describe 'the complex mix of attraction and repulsion that characterizes the relationship between colonizer and colonized' (*Key Concepts*, p. 12).

131. Carlos Zaccagnini, 'An Urartean Royal Inscription in the Report of Sargon's Eighth Campaign', in Fales (ed.), *Assyrian Royal Inscriptions*, pp. 259-95 (262).

132. Younger, *Ancient Conquest Accounts*, p. 76.

133. Younger, *Ancient Conquest Accounts*, p. 76.

134. Lanfranchi, 'Consensus to Empire', p. 82.

135. Lanfranchi, 'Consensus to Empire', p. 83.

136. Lanfranchi, 'Consensus to Empire', p. 84.

subjects to believe that 'even kings who had been dismissed for their disloyalty had the possibility of regaining their former status'.[137] We have seen Ashurbanipal practice such tactics with Necho I and Psammetichus I, and perhaps with Manasseh as well. Sargon would even offer a prestigious appointment to the most bitter enemy in order to gain his friendship and cooperation. Sargon used the double-edged policy of terror and benevolence in order to maintain his control over his subjects.

M. Liverani argues that Assyrian ideology was of the imperialistic type with the purpose of supporting 'an ideology of unbalance', which has the aim

> of bringing about the exploitation of man by man, by providing the motivation to receive the situation of inequality as 'rights', as based on qualitative differences, as entrusted to the 'right' people for the good of all... Ideology has the function of presenting exploitation in a favourable light to the exploited, as advantageous to the disadvantaged.[138]

Lanfranchi also argues that 'it was necessary to show that the Assyrian system' during Sargon's reign 'was working *in favour* of its neighbors'.[139] Lanfranchi continues that 'a widespread consciousness had developed that success depended on the cohesion of the Assyrian Empire, that is of the various forces which cooperated to keep its unity'.[140] Sargon and his successors had to maintain this ideology in order to benefit from economic exploitation, namely, an unbalanced trade relationship.

The economic advantage was essentially exploited in two ways. The more direct and crude means was to impose taxes and tributes; this is a form of unbalanced trade relationship. Sometimes the Assyrian king would demand that his subject rulers bring certain items for his building projects and other needs. However, the more sophisticated and systematic means of creating and maintaining an unbalanced economic relationship is through 'the aggressive policy of economic exploitation, by means of which the core area, Assyria, dominated its contiguous periphery in the eastern Mediterranean basin'.[141] Israel and Judah were victims of such a policy. Gitin points out that Assyrian policy had a dramatically negative impact on the northern kingdom of Israel after the conquest of Tiglath-pileser III; the inhabitants of the hill country of Ephraim were either decimated by deportation or fled to Judah.[142] If we understand human labor as economic commodity, the Assyrians moved the local

---

137. Lanfranchi, 'Consensus to Empire', p. 83.
138. M. Liverani, 'The Ideology of the Assyrian Empire', in M.T. Larsen (ed.), *Power and Propaganda: A Symposium in Ancient Empires* (Mesopotamia, 7; Copenhagen: Akademisk Forlag, 1979), pp. 297-317 (298).
139. Lanfranchi, 'Consensus to Empire', p. 86.
140. Lanfranchi, 'Consensus to Empire', p. 87.
141. Gitin, 'The Neo-Assyrian Empire and its Western Periphery', p. 78.
142. Gitin, 'The Neo-Assyrian Empire and its Western Periphery', p. 82.

population to another region that was more profitable to them. Consequently, 'the Assyrians did not repopulate this area with deportees from other regions since...it was neither suitable for producing raw materials and surpluses, nor was it strategically located on one of the major trade routes'.[143] Judah was also relegated to 'a rather insignificant role in the broad economic policy of Assyria in the 7th century'.[144] As a result, Judah had to establish its own self-sufficient economy while paying tributes to Assyria; this was an unbalanced economic relationship.

On the other hand, Philistia and its capital cities (Gaza, Ashdod, Ashkelon, Ekron, and Gezer) benefited from Assyria's economic policy. Gitin explains that these cities were targeted for growth by the Assyrians, each with a different focus. He explains Ekron's phenomenal growth as a huge olive-oil industrial center as a direct result of Ekron's incorporation into the Assyrian international trading network. Some regions and subjects benefited from Assyria's economic policy, which targeted certain areas for economic development, while other regions suffered under the same economic policy. But more importantly, Assyria benefited from this policy.

The Neo-Assyrian hegemony over the West was maintained and expanded throughout the Sargonid Dynasty: Sargon II, Sennacherib, Esarhaddon, and Ashurbanipal. The following discussion will not be an attempt to reconstruct the history of Judah during the Sargonid Dynasty, but rather to sketch the location of Judah within the political landscape shaped by the Sargonid Dynasty. To put it simply, Judah was one of several states in Syria-Palestine caught between Assyria and Egypt, in a bi-polar system dominated by Assyria for the duration of the reign of the four kings.[145] After the death of Ashurbanipal in conjunction with the rise of the Neo-Babylonians and Medes, the power shifted from the Egypt–Assyria alliance to the Babylonia–Medea alliance.[146] The status of Judah, however, remained the same; it was a small

143. Gitin, 'The Neo-Assyrian Empire and its Western Periphery', p. 82. This may explain Josiah's expansion to Bethel. However, Samaria was repopulated.

144. Gitin, 'The Neo-Assyrian Empire and its Western Periphery', p. 84.

145. Malamat, 'The Kingdom of Judah between Egypt and Babylon', describes Judah as a small state caught between Egypt and Babylon and how the fate of Judah was determined by Judah's vacillating foreign policy, alternating loyalty between Egypt and Babylon. Although Malamat lists six critical turning points, starting with Josiah's death in 609, we can assume that Judah was in a similar situation prior to the rise of the Babylonians; that is, Judah was caught between Egypt and Assyria. Tae Hun Kim, 'Assyrian Historical Inscriptions and the Political and Economic Relations among Assyria, the Syro-Palestinian States, and Egypt in the Eighth–Seventh Centuries BCE' (PhD dissertation, The Graduate Theological Union, 2001), summarizes that during the reigns of the four kings 'the Assyrian empire continued to be the dominant power in Syria-Palestine, and it succeeded in intensifying its influence over the region, extending its power to Egypt' (p. 324).

146. In my historical reconstruction, Egypt (actually the Kushites) play(s) the viable but weaker alternative to Assyria during the Sargonid Dynasty until Ashurbanipal, in

state located in a political landscape shaped first by the Neo-Assyrians and maintained as a unified whole by subsequent imperial forces.

Sargon II (722–705) claimed that he had conquered Samaria in his first campaign: 'I besieged and captured Samaria' (*ARAB*, 55). The Babylonian Chronicles, however, attribute the conquest of Samaria to Shalmaneser V.[147] Tadmor points out that one of the ideologies expressed in the royal inscriptions is the idea that the king would perform a military feat immediately upon his accession; this sometimes conflicts with reality:

> The conflict between the stereotyped formula and reality is especially apparent in the reign of Sargon, whose first regnal year (721), was devoted to the consolidation of his rule rather than to major military campaigns. The solution was...to usurp for himself the conquest of Samaria, the last achievement of Shalmaneser V, his predecessor.[148]

But there is no question that it was Sargon who turned Samaria into an Assyrian province. In his second campaign, he crushed a rebellion in which Samaria was involved (*ARAB*, 5). He claims that 'I plundered the city of Shinutu, Samirira (Samaria) and the whole land of Bît-Humria (Israel)' (*ARAB*, 80). Furthermore, in his seventh campaign Sargon defeats the Arabs and 'the remnant of them I deported and settled them in Samaria' (*ARAB*, 17). He also deported the remnant of the people from other regions and settled them 'in the midst of Bît-Humria' (*ARAB*, 118). Thus, Sargon had turned Samaria into an Assyrian province. It is also important to note that Sargon had also turned Ashdod, an important Philistine city, into a province in his eleventh year.[149] A formulaic saying is used to describe the provincialization of Ashdod: 'My official I set over them as governor, I counted them with the people of Assyria and they drew my yoke' (*ARAB*, 30). With Samaria and Ashdod serving as provinces, the *via maris* and Palestine were under Sargon's firm control.

---

alliance with Psammetichus I, eliminates the Kushite problem. After removing the Kushites, Egypt and Assyria remained as allies until the end of Assyria, when the emerging powers in the east (the Babylonians and the Medes) threatened their hegemony over the West.

147. The Babylonian Chronicles do not give credit to Sargon for sacking Samaria; instead they credit Shalmaneser V with having 'ravaged' Samaria; see Grayson, *Assyrian and Babylonian Chronicles*, p. 73.

148. Hayim Tadmor, 'History and Ideology in the Assyrian Royal Inscriptions', in Fales (ed.), *Assyrian Royal Inscriptions*, pp. 13-33 (14). T.H. Kim concludes that Sargon II conducted three campaigns (720–719, 716–715, and 712–711) in the West ('Assyrian Historical Inscriptions', p. 326).

149. Kim states that Ashdod, an important Philistine city on the coast that was vital to controlling the *via maris*, was made into an Assyrian province in 712 ('Assyrian Historical Inscriptions', p. 327).

During Sargon's reign, Judah was no more than a remote vassal in Assyria's vast imperial network. The list of epithets for Sargon in the Nimrud (Calah) Prism, includes this epithet: 'subduer of the land of Iauda (Judah), which lies far away' (*ARAB*, 137). Judah, due to its location, did not feature prominently in Sargon's economic development, but it had to pay tribute and taxes to Assyria (*ARAB*, 195). After the fall and provincialization of Samaria, Judah was no more than a tax and tribute paying vassal. It seems that the reason Sargon did not provincialize Jerusalem or try to control it more tightly is that it did not play any significant role in Assyria's economic and trade interests.[150] Judah had an unbalanced trade relationship with Assyria and this relationship in conjunction with witnessing the demonstrations of Assyria's arms against its neighbors made it clear in whose political landscape Judah was situated.

Sennacherib's reign (705–681) is considered a 'pause' in Assyria's policy of perennial expansion. This should not, however, be interpreted as a sign of weakness on the part of Sennacherib or Assyria. The fact that Sennacherib did not receive any serious threat (except for the short-lived Babylonian revolt) is an indication that the status quo established by Sargon was firmly in control during Sennacherib's reign.

Sennacherib's third campaign may be the best known of all the Assyrian campaigns. When Sennacherib had approached Palestine, the rebellious vassals 'became afraid and called upon the Egyptian kings' (*ARAB*, 280). It is necessary to point out that no vassal would dare rebel on his own, due to the imbalance of power between the Assyrian army and that of any vassal. Consequently, 'disloyalty and enmity implied often requests for help addressed to other competing empires, or formal alliance… [T]he defense of autonomy… merely appears as a conscious adhesion to another imperial system.'[151] Hezekiah had rebelled in alliances with other neighboring states and relied on Egypt for help. This, however, was to no avail. Sennacherib claimed that he had diminished Hezekiah's lands, surrounded and besieged Jerusalem, and retreated only after receiving a large amount of gifts.

Some believe that Hezekiah did not surrender because the inscriptions do not say that he went to Nineveh himself, but that he sent his messengers instead. Some believe that Sennacherib's inscription hides the fact that he was not able to besiege Jerusalem successfully. This way of thinking derives

---

150. Kim shows that Sargon pursued various forms of relations with the states in Palestine. In contrast to Judah, for example, 'Ekron not only survived, but also became a powerful city-state for Assyria, experiencing great growth and wealth, due to its production of olive [*sic*] and its ideal location for easy access to international markets by sea' ('Assyrian Historical Inscriptions', p. 327).

151. Lanfranchi, 'Consensus to Empire', p. 82.

from an overly mechanical understanding of three stages of destruction of a politically independent state. Cogan summarizes the three stages:

> [1] a vassal relationship was established, marked by the payment of annual dues and tribute...; [2] upon the discovery of disloyalty, military action to remove the unreliable vassal was undertaken, followed by his deportation and that of his supporters; a new ruler over a reduced territory...was appointed; [3] in the end, and after further rebellion even this vassal might be removed, his kingdom [was] incorporated and provincialized after Assyrian fashion.[152]

Samaria is a good example of this three-step process. But, in the case of Jerusalem, Sennacherib did not follow the second step in dealing with Hezekiah; that is, Sennacherib did not replace Hezekiah after his rebellion. This does not necessarily indicate that Sennacherib's first (and only) campaign against Jerusalem was not successful. This is one of the reasons why some argue for two invasions against Hezekiah.[153] Apparently the Assyrians did not always follow this three-step process; in the case of Jerusalem, Hezekiah's capitulation satisfied Sennacherib. Tae Hun Kim states that Sennacherib had a lenient policy toward the disloyal states; instead of practicing complete destruction of the rebellious states, Sennacherib 'adopted the strategy of expelling the anti-Assyrian factions in the region, leaving the states to be semi-independent'.[154] Kim continues that Sennacherib attempted to balance the power among the states in Palestine by reducing the territory of Judah and increasing the territories of the other states, including the Philistine states Ashdod, Ekron, Gaza, and probably Ashkelon, at the expense of Judah.[155] Although Sennacherib stopped short of conquering Jerusalem, Judah experienced first hand the power of Assyrian arms, and learned a lesson it never forgot—a rebellion would not be tolerated by Assyria.

Esarhaddon (680–669), with renewed vigor, continued Assyria's desire to dominate the West for its commercial and political gains. His reign is characterized by the desire to eliminate the Kushites' meddling in the affairs of Syria-Palestine.[156] Tae Hun Kim notes a change in Esarhaddon's policy:

---

152. Mordechai Cogan, 'Judah under Assyrian Hegemony', *JBL* 112 (1993), pp. 403-14 (406).

153. For a recent debate over whether Sennacherib attacked Jerusalem twice, see William H. Shea, 'Jerusalem Under Siege: Did Sennacherib Attack Twice?', *BARev* 25 (1999), pp. 36-44, 74. See also William R. Gallagher, *Sennacherib's Campaign to Judah* (Leiden: E.J. Brill, 1999), especially pp. 1-21 for a summary of the debate. Gallagher states that there is no problem serious enough 'to justify postulating of a second major invasion of Judah' (p. 9). Kim also concludes that Sennarcherib conducted only one campaign.

154. Kim, 'Assyrian Historical Inscriptions', p. 327.

155. Kim, 'Assyrian Historical Inscriptions', p. 329.

156. Kim concludes that Esarhaddon's policy is closely tied to the rise of the Kushite ruler, Tirhakah. Kim states that 'Tirhakah wanted to expel Assyrian domination from Syria-Palestine, and to solidify his commercial relationship with the coastal states. The

Esarhaddon abandoned the lenient policy of Sennacherib toward the rebellious states and 'responded to the disloyal states immediately and severely'.[157] After Esarhaddon defeated Egypt (the Kushites), which was the sole power competing with Assyria for the control of Palestine, Assyria's hegemony over Palestine was unchallenged during his reign and much of his son's reign as well. But even prior to his campaign against Egypt in his tenth campaign, there was no question that Assyria was in full control of the *via maris* and the West. Esarhaddon twice summoned groups of kings for his building projects. On one occasion, he summoned 'the kings of Hatti and the seacoast' in order to build a new city (*ARAB*, 512, 527). Apparently the term 'the kings of Hatti and the seacoast' is a technical term for a fixed group of kings situated along the *via maris*, including the king of Judah. On another occasion Esarhaddon summoned two groups of kings to restore the palace at Nineveh. Manasseh is named among the twelve kings of the Hittite land, along the *via maris*. Esarhaddon also summoned 'ten kings of the land of Iatnana (Cyprus), of the midst of the sea'. And the inscription notes that 'a grand total of 22 kings of the Hittite-land, the seacoast and the (islands) in the midst of the sea, all of them, I gave them their orders and great beams' (*ARAB*, 690; also 697). These two groups of kings were moved about as fixed units. Apparently Manasseh was a member of the twelve kings along the *via maris* who obeyed the bidding of Esarhaddon. We can also assume that Esarhaddon summoned the twenty-two kings for his campaign against Egypt just as his son, Ashurbanipal, did when he led two campaigns against Egypt. Ashurbanipal boasts:

> In the course of my march, 22 kings of the seacoast, of the midst of the sea and of the mainland, servants, subject to me, brought their rich (heavy) presents before me and kissed my feet. Those kings, together with their forces, on their ships by sea, on the dry land with my armies, I caused to take path and road (*ARAB*, 771).

During Esarhaddon's reign, the West was firmly under the hegemony of Assyria, and Judah was fully entrenched in Assyria's imperial matrix.

Ashurbanipal (668–627) continued his father's policy of maintaining a political status quo in the West by fighting against the Kushite rulers of Egypt who were meddling in Syria-Palestine in order to have full control over the trade routes through the *via maris*. Assyria reached the zenith of its power with Ashurbanipal's two invasions of Egypt, finishing what his father, Esarhaddon, had started. He summoned the twenty-two kings, including Manasseh, to help him with his first campaign against Tirhakah of Egypt in

appearance of Tyre, Ashkelon and Tirhakah as the object of Esarhaddon's campaigns indicates that the cooperation of Tyre/Kushites against Assyria or Ashkelon/Kushites against Assyria is deeply related to commerce in the eastern Mediterranean' ('Assyrian Historical Inscriptions', pp. 330-31).

157. Kim, 'Assyrian Historical Inscriptions', p. 330.

667 BCE (*ARAB*, 771).¹⁵⁸ Tae Hun Kim summarizes the first campaign as follows: 'The first campaign of Ashurbanipal was conducted against Tirhakah, who captured Memphis, killing governors and removing the local rulers whom Esarhaddon had instated in Egypt. After a huge battle, Tirhakah was driven out of Memphis and fled to Thebes.'¹⁵⁹ After taking control of Memphis and Thebes, Ashurbanipal reinstalled those kings, including Necho, who had been appointed as prefects and governors by his father, Esarhaddon (*ARAB*, 771). When Ashurbanipal returned to Nineveh, there was a conspiracy by the reinstalled kings against the Assyrians; however, it was quickly discovered by the Assyrians who brought the conspirators to Nineveh into the presence of Ashurbanipal (*ARAB*, 772). Ashurbanipal practiced a two-faced policy toward the conspirators, executing everyone except Necho I (*ARAB*, 774). He poured gifts on Necho and promoted him to be in charge of Sais. In the second campaign against Egypt in 663, Ashurbanipal defeated Tandamane, the nephew of Tirhakah who had invaded Egypt, and retook the city of Thebes (*ARAB*, 776–778). Ashurbanipal ended the Kushites' meddling in Syria-Palestine permanently. There is no reason not to assume that Ashurbanipal had summoned the twenty-two kings, including Manasseh, again during this campaign.¹⁶⁰

Manasseh was a loyal vassal of Assyria throughout his long reign, although there seems to be a tradition (2 Chron. 33.10-13) that suggests that Manasseh was taken captive to Babylon; perhaps he was part of a failed rebellion. Tae Hun Kim accepts this tradition: 'In 652 BCE, Ashurbanipal confronted an upheaval from various parts of his empire. Shamash-shum-ukin, king of Babylonia, revolted against Ashurbanipal. Judah was involved in this incident and fell under suspicion. Manasseh was deported to Babylon.'¹⁶¹ Ashurbanipal, however, dealt with Manasseh in the same way that he dealt with Necho I and Psammetichus I; he reinstalled Manasseh to his throne, following his policy of maintaining the political *status quo*.¹⁶² Rainey suggests that

---

158. Kim states: 'During his first campaign against Tirhakah, the western kings supported Ashurbanipal with their heavy tribute, auxiliary forces and ships' ('Assyrian Historical Inscriptions', p. 332).

159. Kim, 'Assyrian Historical Inscriptions', p. 331.

160. The fact that the Philistine states supported Ashurbanipal in the second campaign supports this assumption. Kim states: 'Four Philistine states, Gaza, Ashkelon, Ekron and Ashdod, supported Ashurbanipal in his campaign against Egypt by land and sea and opened the road to Ashurbanipal in his second campaign. This meant that Philistia was still working as a money-maker for Assyria during the reign of Ashurbanipal' ('Assyrian Historical Inscriptions', p. 323).

161. Kim, 'Assyrian Historical Inscriptions', p. 331.

162. However, according to T.H. Kim, Ashurbanipal took punitive actions against any power who threatened 'the political domination and commercial structures of Assyria' ('Assyrian Historical Inscriptions', p. 333).

5. *The* Realpolitik *of Liminality*   217

after Manasseh was shown mercy by Ashurbanipal, he became more loyal to Assyria.[163] Rainey, however, disagrees with the view that Manasseh benefited from the *pax assyriaca*:

> The primary goal of Assyrian policy in the west was complete, uncontested mastery of the rich commerce that flourished in the eastern Mediterranean basin. To achieve their aims, the Assyrians had to maintain their domination over the maritime states of the Phoenician and Philistine coast and also to control the caravan trade coming from north and south Arabia to the sea coast and to Egypt.[164]

In other words, there was no room for Manasseh to expand his territory or commercial interests. Manasseh remained a loyal vassal to the end. He had no choice. The last record of Ashurbanipal in the west is from around 644–643, when he campaigned against the Arab tribes. Tae Hun Kim states that 'Ashurbanipal's inscriptions do not provide any information about the activities of Ashurbanipal in Syria-Palestine or Egypt after his campaign' in 644–643.[165]

Judah continued to experience the *Realpolitik* of liminality during Josiah's reign as well. There is no reason to believe otherwise. But the most telling indication is not the witness of Assyrian inscriptions or the political situation at the time of Josiah's reign. The *Realpolitik* of liminality is illustrated most powerfully in the way Josiah's story is framed within two accounts of death: the account of Amon's death in 2 Kgs 21.19-26 and the account of Josiah's death in 2 Kgs 23.28-30. On one side of Josiah's story, Amon's death attests to the danger of maintaining the *status quo*. On the other side of Josiah's story, Josiah's death attests to the danger of resisting imperialism. Either way, it is a reminder of the *Realpolitik* of liminality, the danger of being in a location not of one's own making.

Amon followed his father's ways: 'He did what was evil in the sight of the Lord, as his father Manasseh had done. He walked in all the ways in which his father walked, served the idols that his father served, and worshiped them' (2 Kgs 21.20-21).[166] Presumably he followed his father's decision to remain a loyal vassal to Assyria. Amon wanted to maintain the political *status quo* that his father had established. But this stance cost him his life. Malamat questions the view that Amon's assassination had a religious origin, which asserts that the 'Religious Reform Party' killed Amon because they wanted to

---

163. Anson F. Rainey, 'Manasseh, King of Judah, in the Whirlpool of the Seventh Century B.C.E.', in *idem* (ed.), *Raphael Kutscher Memorial Volume* (Journal of the Institute of Archaeology of Tel Aviv University, Occasional Publications, 1; Tel Aviv: Institute of Archaeology of Tel Aviv University, 1993), pp. 147-64.
164. Rainey, 'Manasseh', p. 152.
165. Kim, 'Assyrian Historical Inscriptions', p. 320.
166. The Chronicler thinks even less of Amon than Manasseh (2 Chron. 33.22-23).

remove Assyrian influence on religious practices in Judah, but then the 'people of the land' killed the assassins because they wanted to restore the *status quo*.[167] Malamat instead sees the rebellion of Arabs against Assyria during Amon's reign as the political and military background for the assassination and the subsequent retaliation.[168] He assumes that 'the coup d'état in Jerusalem was aimed against the pro-Assyrian policy of Amon and that the conspirators wanted to join the general uprising against Ashurbanipal'.[169] But, Ashurbanipal was successful in punishing the rebellion. Malamat suggests that when it was certain that Assyria would punish Judah for removing the pro-Assyrian king, 'those forces in Judah who wished to prevent a military encounter with Assyria gained the upper hand' and 'a counter-revolution was achieved and the nobles, who had wished to throw off the yoke of Assyrian rule, were exterminated'.[170] Malamat suggests that the fact that there is no record of Assyria taking punitive actions against Judah indicates that the counter-revolution was able to placate the Assyrians.[171]

Cho suggests that Amon's death is a result of factional infighting among Judean elites. He adds more details from his analysis of factionalism to Malamat's view that Amon was killed because of his pro-Assyrian policy. He suggests that there were severe factional struggles among elites within the court of Judah; namely, anti- and pro-Assyrian factions that coexisted during the time of Amon and Josiah due to the Judean kings' vacillating foreign policies in relation to the Assyrian hegemony.[172] He notes that this factional infighting is an attestation to the fact that 'Assyria influenced the shape and dynamics of Judahite policy'.[173] Amon was assassinated by the anti-Assyrian servants in his court, but they in turn were killed by the pro-Assyrian elite called 'the people of the land'.[174] The counter-revolution might be a result of Assyria's tactic to use factions within a minor power to maintain a *status quo*

---

167. Malamat, 'Amon'.

168. Malamat dates Ashurbanipal's campaign against the Arabs to c. 640, that is, during Amon's reign; see also Cross and Freedman, 'Josiah's Revolt against Assyria'. But now the date of 644–643 for the rebellion of the Arabs is accepted (see T.H. Kim, 'Assyrian Historical Inscriptions').

169. Malamat, 'Amon', p. 27.

170. Malamat, 'Amon', p. 27.

171. Malamat, 'Amon', p. 27. Although Malamat's 'wrong' dating diminishes his argument, the point that the court was responding to Assyria seems still valid.

172. Cho, 'Josianic Reform', pp. 228-29. He suggests that Ahaz was pro-Assyria along with the ruling political elite, but that the religious elite was anti-Assyria; Hezekiah was anti-Assyria; Manasseh was pro-Assyria; Amon was pro-Assyria; and Josiah was anti-Assyria at the start of his reforms.

173. Cho, 'Josianic Reform', p. 229.

174. Cho states that a factional struggle is normal in the time of a suzerain state's decline. Cho assumes that Assyria was declining at this time; but there is no evidence for this assumption at this time.

5. *The* Realpolitik *of Liminality*

or, in this case, to counter the change in policy toward Assyria. Whether Amon died simply because of his pro-Assyrian policy or because of the factional infighting, it was Judah's location within the Assyrian hegemony that resulted in the assassination of Amon and the killing of the assassins. It was a reminder and a good illustration of the *Realpolitik* of liminality.

It is a common understanding that Josiah died at Megiddo in a battle against Necho II. But there is a minority voice that questions this view and suggests that Josiah was a victim of *Realpolitik*. At the time of Josiah's death, the political situation had changed from the beginning of his reign. Assyria became only a shadow of its dominating self; only a weak remnant of the once most powerful empire that dominated the ancient Near East for over a hundred years was encamped at Carchemish. Egypt under the leadership of Necho II was on its way through Palestine to help its ally, Assyria, against the Babylonians. At Megiddo, Necho II met Josiah. What happened at Megiddo? Was Josiah killed in a battle or was he a victim of the *Realpolitik* of liminality?

There are several written sources that bear witness to Josiah's death: 2 Kgs 23.29-30 and LXX parallel, 2 Chron. 35.20-27 and LXX parallel, 1 Esd. 1.25-31, and Josephus, *Ant.* 10.74-83. There seems, however, to be basically two versions of the event: 2 Kings gives one version and the other sources give another version. Josiah's death is recounted in one verse in 2 Kgs 23.29. There are a couple of ambiguous terms that we need to look at. The preposition על is ambiguous. It can mean either 'against' or 'for'.[175] We know from other sources that Necho went up to the king of Assyria to help him. The all-important phrase וילך המלך יאשיהו לקראתו is not clear about whether Josiah went out to meet Necho in order to wage a war or with friendly intentions. Welch and others argue that הלך is not usually used to describe kings going out to do battle, but rather יצא is used to describe this.[176] There is no clear evidence of any battle having taken place.

The Chronicler's account of Josiah's death at Megiddo is far more detailed and much longer than the Kings' version. Sara Japhet remarks that in comparison to the account in Kings, which is rather laconic, the Chronicler's version is formulated as a story, with a series of protagonists, changing scenes, two monologues, and a plot developing through a dramatic turn of events to a tragic conclusion.[177] The most intriguing change or clarification that the Chronicler makes is the detail of Josiah getting killed in a battle while trying to prevent Necho from passing through Megiddo. How did the Chronicler come up with the additional details? There are several possibilities: (1) the Chronicler was using other sources in addition to Kings; (2) the Chronicler

---

175. Welch, 'The Death of Josiah', p. 257.
176. Welch, 'The Death of Josiah', p. 256.
177. Japhet, *I & II Chronicles*, p. 1041.

was using only Kings but creatively expanded and changed Kings' version according to his theology; or (3) he was following a different version of Kings.

There are many scholars who believe that the Chronicler's version is a more accurate one. Their argument is based on the historical details that the Chronicler's version adds. Actually, only one additional historical fact is given: Carchemish as the destination of Necho's journey. Necho did go up to Carchemish to help Ashur-uballit retake Haran, which lay across the Euphrates River. Cross and Freedman give more weight to the Chronicler's version based on chronological markers in Josiah's story that seem to correspond with significant events that happened in Mesopotamia during that period.[178] Japhet cautions that the Chronicler followed Kings' version while adding new elements of his own according to his theology. Japhet summarizes the Chronicler's version as follows:

> In spite of all the clear differences in context and genre between the parallel passages, it is apparent that the Chronistic story is erected on the Deuteronomistic one; the original passage is fully represented in Chronicles, with all its textual elements utilized, and the new elements are woven into the borrowed ones along the original continuum.[179]

Williamson offers a hypothesis that the Chronicler's version of Josiah's death is based not on the Kings version (the Deuteronomic one) nor his own fictive imagination nor is it a composition based on some independent source, but rather its based on a version intermediate between Kings and Chronicles.[180] Therefore, he concludes that 'it would thus appear that the passage has been composed by someone who was aware of the difficulties of the narrative in Kings and who reflected on them within the wider context of the Deuteronomic History as a whole, and probably also with fuller knowledge of the actual course of events'.[181] The point is that because the Chronicler probably had fuller knowledge, his account is probably more accurate.

Other sources follow the Chronicler's version. 1 Esdras offers no new historical facts; instead, it is a later elaboration on the completed work of the Chronicler.[182] It is more theologically correct than the Chronicles version because it takes the word of God from Necho's mouth (as it is in Chronicles) and puts it in Jeremiah's mouth.[183] Josephus's version (*Ant.* 10.73-77) offers more details that are indeed accurate. He spells out that Necho went up to fight the Babylonians and the Medes who overthrew Assyria (*Ant.* 10.74).

---

178. Cross and Freedman, 'Josiah's Revolt against Assyria'.
179. Japhet, *I & II Chronicles*, p. 1041.
180. Williamson, 'The Death of Josiah'.
181. Williamson, 'The Death of Josiah', p. 246.
182. Talshir, 'The Three Deaths of Josiah', p. 234.
183. Talshir, 'The Three Deaths of Josiah', p. 232.

Necho wanted to pass through Josiah's territory, but Josiah would not let him (*Ant.* 10.75). Josephus blames Fate/Destiny for Josiah's death (*Ant.* 10.76). Even the LXX parallel to 2 Kings seem to suggest that Josiah went to meet Necho with a hostile intention. Thus, all the other sources, following the lead of the Chronicler, describe Josiah's death as a result of battle.

Some scholars blame the Chronicler for leading readers astray with his tale of fictitious battle and claim that Kings' account does not intend to record a battle at Megiddo at all. It is true that the Chronicler's version gives one additional historical piece of information. It tells where Necho was going up to fight (Carchemish), but it does not say whether he was helping out the king of Assyria or whom he was fighting against. The Chronicler also changes הלך to יצא. On philological grounds, Talshir argues that 'the account in Chronicles is more plausibly explained as a secondary elaboration on the short report in Kings'.[184] She continues that 'the Chronicler misunderstood the political situation and created a fictitious war'.[185] The Chronicler's account is like a midrashic interpretation of the report in Kings. Welch points out that the Chronicler's account of Josiah's battle with Necho has 'a suspicious resemblance to the fight at Ramoth-Gilead in which Ahab fell. So close is the likeness that the one account has evidently been modelled on the other.'[186] The Chronicler also gives a theological reason for the unexpected death of a righteous king: 'He did not listen to the words of Necho from the mouth of God' (2 Chron. 35.22).

What happened at Megiddo was not so much a battle between rivals but a court-martial based on sovereign–vassal relations. Nelson thinks that 'the best explanation for the narrator's reticence in describing the event itself' is treachery.[187] Therefore, the Kings' version may not tell much about how or why Josiah died, but it is more historically reliable because it, at least, does not embellish his death with a fictitious war. The account in 2 Kings is a dispassionate account that leaves a lot of questions unanswered, but it seems to express the sentiment of shock and disbelief at the sudden death of a righteous king.

Josiah's death in 2 Kgs 23.29-30, though it is outside of the Josianic edition of DH, tells much about the *Realpolitik* of liminality. Josiah was a victim of being located in the middle of the confrontation of the two powers (Egypt–Assyria and Babylonia–Medes) competing to control the Near East unified by the Sargonid Dynasty. Josiah's death was a reminder of Judah's position in the political and ideological landscape shaped by imperialism.

    184. Talshir, 'The Three Deaths of Josiah', p. 216.
    185. Talshir, 'The Three Deaths of Josiah', p. 219.
    186. Welch, 'The Death of Josiah', p. 255.
    187. Nelson, 'Realpolitik in Judah'. According to Nelson, Necho II tricked Josiah to come to Meggido and killed him because he wanted to secure his rearguard while he was battling the Babylonians, and also he was suspicious of Josiah's reforms.

Writing 'a History of their Own'

In spite of being viewed as insignificant 'others' and being located in the ideological landscape where they experienced the *Realpolitik* of liminality, Josiah and his court wrote DH, in part, to assert their subjectivity and to form their identity through 'a history of their own' independent from or without always referencing the imperial force. They were attempting to recover their subjectivity although they were perceived as no more than a small factor in the political and economic equation of the Neo-Assyrian Empire. But they refused to be pushed to the margin. They tried to recover their history that had been overwritten or erased during the Assyrian domination. Josiah's 'pilgrimage' to the province of Samerina was an attempt not only to discredit the cult of the former northern kingdom, but was perhaps also a symbolic act designed to dissuade his subjects from migrating to the province of Samerina. Moreover, the reinstitution of the Passover was perhaps an attempt to consolidate the various groups of people in Judah as one people as part of a strategy to stop some people from moving back to the north.

Although Josiah's kingdom was located at the margin of the political/ideological landscape shaped by Assyrian imperialism and was a victim of the *Realpolitik* of liminality throughout the reign of the Sargonid Dynasty—which resulted in erasure or overwriting of their history and culture during the Assyrian hegemony—it refused to be framed within the narrative of the powers that be. Josiah refused to be viewed as one of the Others. The Josianic editor(s) ignored the presence of Assyria after the siege against Jerusalem during Hezekiah's reign although Assyria's power had reached its apogee during the reigns of Manasseh, Amon, and the first half of Josiah's reign. By omitting the presence of Assyria, and also Egypt, the Josianic editor(s) attributed agency to the people of Judah, rather than to the imperial powers. They wrote a history of their own in which imperial powers played no part. They wrote a history of their own in which they were the subject of history, with YHWH as the divine agent controlling their history, destiny, and aspirations. The story of Josiah illustrates the Judeans' attempt to write a history of their own by refusing to be framed within the political/ideological landscape shaped by the imperial powers; they framed themselves within a history of their own making. First, they wrote a history of their own by recovering the overwritten or forgotten 'inscriptions' of their past. Second, they wrote a history of their own by remembering what went wrong in the past. Third, they wrote a history of their own by reinstituting or reinventing their own culture.

There has been a long-accepted assumption that the reform of Josiah removed elements of the Assyrian state religion from the Jerusalem temple, and this is understood as Josiah's attempt to throw off the yoke of Assyria, as a revocation of the vassal relationship, since Assyria obliged vassal states to accept the Assyrian state religion. John McKay and Mordechai Cogan refuted these assumptions in the early 1970s.[188] They had argued that there was no direct connection between Josiah's removing of 'foreign' cultic elements from Jerusalem and his attempt at independence from Assyria, because Assyria did not require vassal states to adopt the state cult of Assyria. However, both authors agreed that although Assyria did not coerce vassal states to adopt its religion as a policy, Judah's religion was greatly influenced by Assyria during the Assyrian hegemony that lasted over a hundred years.

John McKay argued that most of the gods worshipped in Judah (mentioned in 2 Kgs 23.4-14) during the Assyrian domination can be identified with local Palestinian deities, rather than with Assyrian deities. McKay concluded the following in his study:

> The various deities worshipped in Judah during the period of Assyrian domination lack the definitive aspects of the Assyrian gods and generally exhibit the characteristics of popular Palestinian paganism. Furthermore, many of the deities hitherto regarded as Assyrian, for example, the Queen of Heaven, were worshipped, not as official representatives of the overlord in the Temple, but in the local cults of the Judaean populace.[189]

McKay's argument was based on a simple but convincing principle: 'The likelihood that any god whose worship was officially required would have been known by its Assyrian name in Israel. Hence the natural presupposition is that a god with a Canaanite name was Canaanite, unless it can be shown to have been otherwise.'[190] Then, he argued that there was no clear evidence in Kings that 'Assyrian cults were to be found amongst those that Josiah abolished from the Jerusalem Temple, let alone that they had been introduced under obligation'.[191] In addition, the fact that the biblical accounts do not mention Assyrian gods specifically undermines the view that Josiah's reform was tied to his attempt to overthrow his vassalship. He conlcuded as follows: 'The very fact that the Assyrian gods were not considered worthy of special mention in the account of the reforms suggests that they neither enjoyed a privileged status in the Judaean cult, nor formed a peculiar focus for the reformation'.[192] Throughout his study he maintained that 'the Old Testament

---

188. John McKay, *Religion in Judah under the Assyrians 732–609 B.C.* (SBT, 2/26; London: SCM Press, 1973). Mordechai Cogan, *Imperialism and Religion: Assyria, Israel and Judah in the Eighth and Seventh Centuries B.C.E.* (SBLMS, 19; Missoula, MT: Scholars Press, 1974).

189. McKay, *Religion in Judah under the Assyrians*, p. 67.

190. McKay, *Religion in Judah under the Assyrians*, p. 31.

191. McKay, *Religion in Judah under the Assyrians*, p. 36.

192. McKay, *Religion in Judah under the Assyrians*, p. 43.

contains no evidence to support the theory that Judah was under obligation to introduce the cult of Assyrian gods'.[193]

Then McKay examined Assyrian and other Near Eastern writings and concluded that there was no evidence 'to support the thesis that imposition of the cult of Ashur was a regular feature of any importance in the Assyrian religio-political ideal'.[194] The strongest case for the thesis that imposition of the cult of Ashur was a regular policy of Assyria was the suggestion that the cult of the Host of Heaven represented the Assyrian official presence. McKay summarized this view as follows:

> It is argued that this must be the case, since the many references to the worship of the Host of Heaven, the record of the worship of the Queen of Heaven and the possible allusion to astrology in the Old Testament are all limited to the period of Assyrian domination; and it is well known that there was plenty of astral learning in Assyria.[195]

However, McKay argued that 'wherever the Israelites obtained their astral lore, it was to a significant degree independent of its Mesopotamian counterpart and may indeed well have been largely indigenous to the land of Canaan'.[196] He concluded that 'Israel's astral beliefs were nearer to those of her western neighbours than to those of Mesopotamia, even after the period of Assyrian domination'.[197] His study showed that there is no clear evidence to support the claim that the Assyrians required their vassals to introduce the cult of Ashur to their state sanctuaries.

McKay was not denying that Judah's religion was influenced by Assyria during the Assyrian domination or claiming that the Assyrians never enforced the worship of Ashur on defeated people. He acknowledged that there was Assyrian influence during this period: 'Indeed, the Old Testament clearly indicates that a number of Mesopotamian gods were known and worshipped in Judah both before and after the time of the nation's vassaldom'.[198] But his point was that 'there is no indication whatsoever that these represented an official Assyrian presence in the land'.[199] It was not the policy of the Assyr-

---

193. McKay, *Religion in Judah under the Assyrians*, p. 60. Cogan agrees: 'Our review of Judahite cultic practices during the eight and seventh centuries B.C.E. uncovered no evidence of Assyrian cults imposed upon Judah in any biblical source' (*Imperialism and Religion*, p. 88).
194. McKay, *Religion in Judah under the Assyrians*, p. 67.
195. McKay, *Religion in Judah under the Assyrians*, p. 45.
196. McKay, *Religion in Judah under the Assyrians*, p. 56. Cogan agrees: 'astral cults were not the exclusive patent of Assyrian religion… The reverence of celestial bodies can, in fact, be traced back to the second millennium B.C.E. in Syria-Palestine as part of common Semitic tradition' (*Imperialism and Religion*, p. 85).
197. McKay, *Religion in Judah under the Assyrians*, p. 58.
198. McKay, *Religion in Judah under the Assyrians*, p. 68.
199. McKay, *Religion in Judah under the Assyrians*, p. 68.

ians to force their vassals to adopt their state religion. McKay suggested two reasons for the Assyrian religious influence on Judah. First, McKay proposed, there was an infiltration of Assyrian influence via the province of Samerina. Second, the fact that the Assyrian gods, as well as other foreign gods, were brought to the province by settlers from other regions of the Neo-Assyrian Empire led to the conclusion that 'the upsurge of Mesopotamian heathenism in the North must have resulted in its infiltration into Judah, particularly during the reign of Manasseh'.[200] However, McKay credited the Assyrian influence on Judah to its voluntary adoption on the part of the Judeans because of 'the failure of Yahweh to protect against the might of Ashur'.[201]

Mordechai Cogan came to the same conclusion that the Assyrians did not force their vassals to adopt their state religion—therefore, the cult reforms of Josiah can 'no longer be thought of as expressions of political rebellion directed against Assyrian rule'.[202] Cogan made a significant contribution by showing that Assyrian administrative policies distinguished between provincial and vassal territories.[203] He showed that 'only in territories formally annexed as provinces was an Assyrian cult introduced, the planting of "Ashur's weapon" in the provincial center serving as its focal point', without, however, disturbing native cults.[204] Cogan continued that 'such cultic impositions obtained only within the territorial confines of the Assyrian state; vassal states bore no cultic obligations whatsoever... There is no record of the imposition of Assyrian cults upon vassal states.'[205] His study attempted to find the genesis of foreign innovations in the Judahite cult during the Assyrian domination in other areas rather than as impositions of the Assyrian empire.[206] He credited the natural process of acculturation for the Assyrian cultural influence on Judah. He agreed with McKay that the province of Samerina played a part in the acculturation process: 'The penetration of foreign cults was accelerated, this time at the hands of the Assyrian colonists resettled in Samaria, though once again we found evidence of the non-coercive imperial policy'.[207] However, for Cogan, the process of acculturation played the primary role in Judah's adoption of foreign cults. The wealthy class of Judah was attracted to art, architecture, and the commodities of Assyria, and Judah's leadership was disenchanted with YHWH, speeding up the process of assimilation.[208] Cogan described the context in which acculturation was favorable:

200. McKay, *Religion in Judah under the Assyrians*, p. 69.
201. McKay, *Religion in Judah under the Assyrians*, p. 59.
202. Cogan, *Imperialism and Religion*, p. 113.
203. Cogan, *Imperialism and Religion*, pp. 9-64.
204. Cogan, *Imperialism and Religion*, p. 112.
205. Cogan, *Imperialism and Religion*, p. 112.
206. Cogan, *Imperialism and Religion*, p. 72.
207. Cogan, *Imperialism and Religion*, p. 113.
208. Cogan, *Imperialism and Religion*, pp. 92-95.

> Among the populace, acculturation proceeded apace. Judahite soldiers joined other Westerners levied for the Egyptian campaigns of Ashurbanipal... These soldiers were certainly exposed to customs and languages other than their own. In the countryside of Judah, the intermingling of populations went much further, with foreigners settled to the immediate west and north of Judah in Assyrian provinces.[209]

Judah was surrounded on all sides by the cultural patterns dominant in the Assyrian empire and the Judeans were not only exposed to them but welcomed them as better than their own cultural patterns. Cogan concluded that 'although Assyria made no formal demands for cultural uniformity among its subjects, one of the by-products of political and economic subjugation was a tendency toward cultural homogeneity'.[210]

Two decades later, Mordechai Cogan re-examined the conclusion, which John McKay also reached, that a religious reformation was not an indication of rebellion against Assyria since the Neo-Assyrian Empire did not impose and coerce their vassal states to adopt their state religion.[211] Cogan states that a new stage in the discussion was reached with the publication of H. Spieckermann's re-examination of the issues, which concluded that 'there is no distinction between provinces and vassal states as far as religious practice is concerned; all areas under Assyrian hegemony were constrained to worship Assyria's gods'.[212] Cogan points out that several commentaries have quickly and joyfully reverted to this view.[213] After examining Spieckermann's work, Cogan calls for a more nuanced reading of the Assyrian royal inscriptions and the biblical texts, though he adheres to his earlier thesis:

209. Cogan, *Imperialism and Religion*, p. 93.
210. Cogan, *Imperialism and Religion*, p. 95.
211. Cogan, 'Judah under Assyrian Hegemony'.
212. Cogan, 'Judah under Assyrian Hegemony', pp. 404-405. Hermann Spieckermann, *Juda unter Assur in der Sargonidenzeit* (Göttingen: Vandenhoeck & Ruprecht, 1982), refutes McKay and Cogan, and supports the earlier thesis that cultic elements destroyed by Josiah were Assyrian and that the Assyrians forced their state religion on their subjects. Spieckermann argues that Josiah's reform was an attempt to overthrow the yoke of Assyria. He does this by showing that the gods mentioned in 2 Kgs 23.4-14, especially Baal, Asherah, and the Host of Heaven can be identified with Assyrian deities (*contra* McKay), and by demonstrating that the Assyrians did impose religious obligations on vassal states as well as on provinces (*contra* Cogan).
213. Cogan, 'Judah under Assyrian Hegemony', p. 405. For example, Rainer Albertz, *A History of Israelite Religion in the Old Testament Period. I. From the Beginnings to the End of the Monarchy* (trans. John Bowden; Louisville, KY: Westminster/John Knox Press, 1994), in his reconstruction of Israelite religion accepts Spieckermann's conclusions: 'On this hypothesis it can be recognized that the so-called Josianic reform was far more than a mere reform of the cult [referring to Cogan]; it was at the same time a broad national, social and religious renewal movement which sought to use the historical opportunity offered by the withdrawal of Assyria to reconstitute the Israelite state fully' (p. 199).

> No Assyrian text states or implies that conquered peoples were required to worship the gods of Assyria. Furthermore, no single paradigm can explain the mosaic of political and social relationships that developed between Assyria and its dependents. Biblical texts of the period focus on religious apostasy, as was their wont. There is not the slightest hint anywhere that the adoption of foreign ways were imposed.[214]

He maintains his earlier conclusion that it was due more to the process of cultural assimilation rather than to political coercion that Assyrian dominance left on the West, including Judah.[215] What is clear is that, whether Judah was affected by cultural imperialism or political coercion or both, Judah's history and culture had been overwritten, erased, or ignored during the Assyrian domination. Therefore, Josiah's reform, in part, was an attempt to recover Judean 'inscriptions', which had been forgotten during the Assyrian domination.

First, the discovery of the 'book of the law' was the catalytic event that launched Josiah's reform and, at the same time, began the recovery of forgotten or overwritten 'inscriptions' during the Assyrian domination. Josiah's court not only recovered 'the book of the law', but also many writings that may have had nothing to do with Josiah's reform but much to do with the identity of the people living in Judah at the time. In forming the first edition of DH, Josiah's court recovered much material that may have been ignored or overwritten during the Assyrian domination.

I agree with Robert and Mary Coote that 'scriptures were interpreted in and acquired their authority from the individual, organization, or institution to which they in return gave authority'.[216] In particular, the Cootes conclude that the purpose of the temple and its scriptures and cult, for our purpose the content of DH, was 'to legitimate the ruling house of David'.[217] Josiah's court was active in writing propaganda or an apologia directed toward the powerful few whose support Josiah needed.[218]

---

214. Cogan, 'Judah under Assyrian Hegemony', p. 412.

215. Cogan notes that Judah was also affected by the assimilatory process and the elements of foreign cults, including the Assyrian state cult, which 'bear witness to the cultural wave that inundated Judah from all sides' ('Judah under Assyrian Hegemony', p. 413).

216. Robert B. Coote and Mary P. Coote, *Power, Politics, and the Making of the Bible* (Minneapolis: Fortress Press, 1990), p. 3.

217. Coote and Coote, *Power*, p. 3.

218. The Cootes make it clear that scriptures were not written for popular consumption at the time, 'literacy being limited to a few wealthy and the scribes in wealthy employ' (*Power*, p. 28). But Finkelstein and Silberman suggest that 'in the seventh century BCE, for the first time in the history of ancient Israel, there was a popular audience for such works. Judah had become a highly centralized state in which literacy was spreading from the capital and the main towns to the countryside. It was a process that had apparently started

It is usually the case that during significant political changes the scribes of the scriptures become particularly active.[219] The discovery of the 'book of the law' played a key role in Josiah's attempt to consolidate the powerful few to side with him since 'the first and foremost of the discovered laws required that the cult of Yahweh…be conducted at only one shrine (Deut. 12.1-14), the temple—where Yahweh would place his name, the basis of judicial oath'.[220] Once again, I agree that this was probably one of the main purposes, if not the primary purpose, of producing DH. However, we should not let this fact limit us from seeing other purposes in DH. In the process of writing a full-scale history of the house of David, Josiah's court incorporated other writings that are not related to Josiah's reforms or the legitimation of the house of David. Josiah's court recovered more than the 'book of the law'. It recovered memories and histories that had been forgotten or overwritten during the Assyrian domination. The discovery of the book in the temple, which also served as an archive, illustrates the importance of recovering forgotten or neglected memories and histories in the archive.

Finkelstein and Silberman claim that 'archaeology has provided enough evidence to support a new contention that the historical core of the Pentateuch and DH was substantially shaped in the seventh century BCE' in the court of Josiah.[221] This assertion is really based on Finkelstein's theory that Judah developed into a full-blown state during the late eighth century to seventh century, that is, during the Assyrian domination of the Sargonid Dynasty. They state this premise as follows:

> It is now clear that phenomena like record keeping, administrative correspondence, royal chronicles, and the compiling of a national scripture…are linked to a particular stage of social development. Archaeologists and anthropologists working all over the world have carefully studied the context in which sophisticated genres of writing emerge, and in almost every case they are a sign of state formation, in which power is centralized in national institutions like an official cult or monarchy.[222]

in the eighth century, but reached a culmination only in the time of Josiah. Writing joined preaching as a medium for advancing a set of quite revolutionary political, religious, and social ideas' (*The Bible Unearthed*, p. 284).

219. In Josiah's case, on the one hand, there were drastic changes in politics on the international level (the decline of Assyria and the rise of Egypt and Babylonia), and, on the other hand, Josiah was trying to re-establish the house of David through the cult centralization.

220. Coote and Coote, *Power*, p. 61. See also Cho, 'Josianic Reform', for an exhaustive treatment of Josiah's attempt to consolidate different factions within the ruling class.

221. Finkelstein and Silberman, *The Bible Unearthed*, p. 14. They also side with the Cross School that 'the Deuteronomistic History was compiled, in the main, in the time of King Josiah, aiming to provide an ideological validation for particular political ambitions and religious reforms' (p. 14).

222. Finkelstein and Silberman, *The Bible Unearthed*, p. 22.

5. *The* Realpolitik *of Liminality*

One does not have to accept their premise to accept the theory that DH, in particular, was a literary masterpiece that was woven together from 'a rich collection of historical writings, memories, legends, folk tales, anecdotes, royal propaganda, prophecy, and ancient poetry'.[223] DH's purpose was, at the least, to be propaganda for Josiah's reforms, and then some.[224] Finkelstein and Silberman allude to this when they remark that few other cities have matched Jerusalem in any historical eras that 'have been so tensely self-conscious of their history, identity, destiny, and direct relationship with God'.[225] They claim that although the kingdom of Josiah remained basically the same as Manasseh's and is a direct continuation of Manasseh's Judah, 'in terms of its religious development and literary expression of national identity, the era of Josiah marked a dramatic new stage in Judah's history'.[226] The discovery of the book of the law, which they believe was written before or during Josiah's reign, rather than being an older book, 'sparked a revolution in ritual and a complete reformulation of Israelite identity'.[227] Once again, the point I want to suggest is that the discovery of the book illustrates the desire to recover histories and memories of the people that may have been forgotten or overwritten during the Assyrian domination, and that Josiah's court not only composed DH to support Josiah's reforms but also to recover their history and experience in order to formulate their identity.

Mullen is right in suggesting that it is important to examine the function of DH in the formation of group identity. He suggests an interpretive model that understands DH as a response to the crisis of identity, and that investigates narratives as 'social dramas of ritual creation/reenactment which produce or reinforce certain ethnic boundaries that define the people "Israel"'.[228] Mullen suggests that the book of Deuteronomy provides the manifesto that defines Israelite identity based on allegiance to YHWH (as a special people chosen by YHWH), and differentiated from all other peoples. Although Mullen claims that the book of Deuteronomy defines 'ethnic' group identity, ethnicity plays little role in defining Israelite group identity. Kenton Sparks's conclusion that the book of Deuteronomy defines religious rather than ethnic identity (playing a secondary role at best) seems to describe Mullen's understanding also. Sparks calls for others to look for ethnic sentiments in the biblical literature in the future.

---

223. Finkelstein and Silberman, *The Bible Unearthed*, pp. 1-2.
224. Once again, Josiah's reforms could have launched the whole project of writing a full-scale history, in large part to support Josiah's reforms and to legitimate the house of David.
225. Finkelstein and Silberman, *The Bible Unearthed*, p. 3.
226. Finkelstein and Silberman, *The Bible Unearthed*, p. 289.
227. Finkelstein and Silberman, *The Bible Unearthed*, p. 276.
228. Mullen, *Narrative History*, p. 15. However, I stated above that I disagree with Mullen's suggestion that the location of DH is the Babylonian Exile.

I think it is worthwhile to investigate DH to see whether Josiah's court incorporated materials (either in original form or by editing) in order to help define Israelite identity, ethnically as well as religiously. Once again, I am not saying that this was the primary purpose of writing a full-scale history of the house of David, but it is something worth investigating. The recovery of the book of the law and other documents and memories not only helped launch Josiah's reform, but also helped in reformulating Israelite identity after the Assyrian domination. Of course, it is beyond the scope of this work to investigate the entire DH for these clues. Rather, I would like here to give one example of ethnic identity formation in DH.[229]

There are hints of ethnic sentiments in DH that help to define Israelite identity. Although circumcision was a common practice among West Semitic peoples, the practice has a special importance in the Hebrew Bible.[230] According to Coote and Ord, the practice of circumcision functioned to maintain the male's power by securing men's loyalty to 'one huge fraternal interest group' during the tribal period, long before the Exile when the Priestly writer (P) writer set the practice in a theological framework.[231] They argue against those who believe that the priestly tradition placed great importance on circumcision as a mark of identity in the exile.[232] This well-established social

---

229. My article 'Uriah the Hittite' examines the role of ethnic identity in the story of David and Bathsheba (and Uriah) in 2 Sam. 11. The story struggles to define who the real Israelite is: Uriah the Hittite who is an ethnic 'other' but is a faithful Yahwist, or David who is an Israelite but does not follow the way of YHWH; Bathsheba is caught in the middle as the wife of an ethnic 'other' and the future mother of King Solomon. The scribes side with David and reject Uriah the Hittite who is an ethnic 'other' and give Bathsheba a double identity to mark her as an ethnic Israelite. In this case, the ethnic identity of the characters is more important than the religious identity.

230. Robert G. Hall, 'Circumcision', in *ABD*, I, pp. 1025-31. Especially in P, circumcision is the mark of the second 'everlasting covenant' (Gen. 17.9-14) which is made with Abraham in Gen. 17.1-14. God warns that if anyone does not practice circumcision they will be 'cut off' from the people (17.14).

231. Robert B. Coote and David Robert Ord, *In the Beginning: Creation and the Priestly History* (Minneapolis: Fortress Press, 1991), pp. 67-75. They argue that political power in the ancient world was 'dependent on the number of males who were available to defend the clan' (p. 68). Therefore, the strength of such a strong fraternal interest group depended on the loyalty of each member of the group. There was always a danger of a man breaking off from the group by starting his own group. Coote and Ord claim that the ritual of circumcision functioned to deal with this tension; by presenting his son to this ritual, a man was showing his loyalty to his clan by risking his son's reproductive organ, which represented future political power, thereby receiving the trust of his kinsmen, which increases the strength of the fraternal interest group (pp. 68-70). Women had no part in this ritual; they were excluded from the political structure.

232. Coote and Ord make a valid point that 'if circumcision functioned as a sign of identity, it was not exactly conspicuous, considering the Judahites wore clothes in public' (*In the Beginning*, p. 67). Instead, they argue that P's motivation for framing the practice

practice may not have been a mark of identity in practice (whether prior to the Exile or during the Exile), but in the biblical narratives it functions to define who the Israelites are in contrast to other peoples. The practice of circumcision is not a prominent element in DH; however, it plays a role in defining Israelite ethnic identity, in opposition to the 'uncircumcised'.

After the crossing of the Jordan River, the Israelites were commanded to be circumcised 'a second time' because those who were born in the wilderness were not circumcised (Josh. 5.1-8). Those men who came out of Egypt, who were not fit to take the land because of their disobedience, were presumably dead, and now the new generation of the circumcised would be given the land. Here the practice of circumcision functions to support religious identity, that is, the practice of circumcision as an act of obedience to YHWH's command. But in v. 9 it is stated that through this ritual the 'reproach of Egypt' has been rolled away.[233] By contrasting Egypt with the new land, the practice of circumcision is hinted at as an ethnic identity marker. This becomes more clear in portraying the uncircumcised, the Philistines, as the Other.[234] The Philistines are the only ones to be marked as the uncircumcised (Judg. 14.3; 15.8; 1 Sam. 14.6; 17.26, 36; 31.4; 2 Sam. 1.20). The Philistines were not only the archenemy during the days of Saul and David, they were also competing powers during Josiah's days. By marking the Philistines as the uncircumcised, the 'reproach' to Israel (1 Sam. 14.6), circumcision functions as an ethnic marker, a cultural practice that distinguishes Israelites from the Philistines. Josiah's court incorporated these stories into DH, and in the process helped to define the Israelites ethnically— as a group practicing circumcision—in contrast to the Other, the Philistines— who did not practice circumcision.

Second, could it be that the descendants of immigrants/refugees from the northern kingdom of Israel who came to Jerusalem after the fall of Samaria wanted to go back to the province of Samerina after the 'retreat' of Assyria? Is it possible that Israelite Judaeans were going on pilgrimages to the sanctuaries in the province of Samerina? Josiah wanted to stop them from making pilgrimages to the northern cult sites—Bethel and Samaria. Josiah's campaign to Samaria can be seen as an anti-pilgrimage, reminding the 'Judaeans' of the evil of the former northern kingdom. The account of Josiah's campaign against Samaria can be understood not as a historical account, but as a ritualized anti-pilgrimage, as a ritual of identity formation. Josiah's 'campaign'

---

of circumcision in theology was to exclude women from the cultic institution as well as from the political institution (pp. 70-75).

233. Hall, 'Circumcision', suggests that they were circumcised first according to the Egyptian practice, which left the foreskin hanging, but then they cut off the foreskin according to their new practice.

234. The term 'circumcised' does not appear again in DH, nor is there any reference to the practice of circumcision

narrative was a depiction of a pilgrimage to the province of Samerina to bring solidarity among the Judeans and the descendants of refugees/immigrants from the former northern kingdom living in Judah rather than as an attempt to recover the northern kingdom. It is a ritualized anti-pilgrimage that remembers the injustice/tragedy of the past and helps to form a common identity and destiny among various constituents living in Josiah's kingdom.

The initial entrance to the land of the Canaanites (the crossing of the Jordan and pitching camp at Gilgal), as described in Joshua 3–5, is more like a ritualized procession within the mythic/cognitive matrix of ancient Canaan than like a historical narrative.[235] Mullen states that 'the initial entry into the land, like the initial military conquest of Jericho, is couched in the form of a religious performance'.[236] This 'social drama' gives an opportunity for the future 'Israelites' to participate in the entering of the land (and eventually its conquest, symbolized by the conquest of Jericho, which is also depicted as a ritualized procession) through re-enactment of the ritual, thereby participating in forming their group identity. Mullen notes that the setting up of the commemorative stele (Josh. 4) and the celebration of the Passover (Josh. 5.10-12) after crossing the Jordan function, in ritual terms, to identify the people of the 'conquest' and the future generations with those who were delivered from Egypt: 'It is this type of infusion of metaphoric meaning into the narrated events that, in synchronic terms, ritually bridges the generations that have preceded and those that will follow'.[237] Mullen explains:

> This is part of the function and purpose of this type of narrative ritualization of communal tradition. It is precisely the 'frozen' character of literary presentations that allows a responding community to participate, in psychological and ritual terms, in situations that no longer exist and to reconstruct their identities in terms of those events.[238]

235. For a discussion on similarities between the crossing of the Jordan with the crossing of the Reed Sea, see Jan A. Wagenaar, 'Crossing the Sea of Reeds (Exod 13–14) and the Jordan (Josh 3–4): A Priestly Framework for the Wilderness Wandering', in Marc Vervenne (ed.), *Studies in the Book of Exodus* (Leuven: Leuven University Press, 1996), pp. 461-70. See also Bernard F. Batto, *Slaying the Dragon* (Louisville, KY: Westminster/John Knox Press, 1992); in Chapter 5, Batto argues that 'the motif of crossing dry shod originally was associated with the conquest tradition about the Israelites crossing over the Jordan River at Gilgal to take possession of the land of Canaan. But gradually over the course of several centuries, through their use in cultic celebration at the sanctuary at Gilgal, the motif of crossing dry shod was transferred to the exodus tradition, until eventually the motif of crossing dry shod came to be associated more closely with the exodus and the Red Sea than with the conquest and the Jordan. A powerful influence in this transformation of the motif was the linking of River and Sea in the Canaanite version of the Combat Myth (the Baal myth)' (p. 128).

236. Mullen, *Narrative History*, p. 107.
237. Mullen, *Narrative History*, pp. 107-108.
238. Mullen, *Narrative History*, p. 108.

5. *The* Realpolitik *of Liminality*

The setting up of the monument establishes it as a pilgrimage site for future generations to remember the miraculous entry into the land and the exodus out of Egypt and to participate in the formation of a community, with being faithful and obedient to God's commands as an identity boundary. The ritualized procession into the land (the initial entry to the land) concludes with the celebration of the Passover. Mullen notes the importance of the celebration of the Passover:

> The central significance of the brief mention of the Passover celebration is to be found in the final two verses of this section, which provide a transition from the 'period' of the wilderness...during which the people were fed with 'manna'... to the 'period' of the consumption of the produce of the land... The sanctification of the people and the ritual entry into the land, led by the announcement of Yahweh and the ark of the covenant, now culminated in the ritual circumcision of all the males, who were then qualified as members of the community to celebrate the Passover meal. With the 'reproach of Egypt' having been removed, the people could eat of the produce of the land, enjoying the benefits that were promised by Moses.[239]

The point is not whether it happened the way it is recounted, but that the narrative is clothed in ritual terms that function for future generations to participate in the formation of group identity.

Bernard F. Batto points out that the climax of the ritual was the ceremonial crossing of the Jordan, with the worshipers in a solemn liturgical procession: 'This portion of the ritual was designed to recall for the participants the belief that their God had literally laid open the land to them, for Yahweh temporarily caused the waters of the Jordan to stop flowing so that his people might cross dry shod into the Promised Land'.[240] Batto notes that the narrative emphasizes the 'cutting' of the waters and argues that the account of the crossing of the Jordan is framed within the common Semitic Combat Myth.[241] He observes that 'the River Jordan was personified as the chaos dragon, which had turned and fled from the awesome presence of the divine sovereign. Yahweh's victory over "River" was manifested in the Jordan being "split" and Yahweh's sovereignty being established by planting his people in his land.'[242] YHWH (represented by the ark of the covenant) is the divine warrior that defeats the serpent (the names of the opponent vary: Tiamat;

---

239. Mullen, *Narrative History*, pp. 114-15.
240. Batto, *Slaying the Dragon*, p. 139.
241. Batto is referring to the account of Marduk's accession to kingship in 'The Epic of Creation' (Stephanie Dalley, *Myths from Mesopotamia* [Oxford: Oxford University Press, 1989], pp. 233-77) and Baal's rise to kingship according to the Ugaritic versions (Michael David Coogan, *Stories from Ancient Canaan* [Philadelphia: Westminster Press, 1978], pp. 86-115).
242. Batto, *Slaying the Dragon*, p. 151.

Mot; Yam [Prince Sea or Judge River]) and establishes his domain. Thus, by framing the account of the crossing within the common Semitic Combat Myth, the narrative functions to justify the taking of the land.[243]

Batto agrees that 'the story of a miraculous crossing of the Jordan provided justification for the "Israelite" occupation of the land. YHWH, the "lord of all the earth", himself had "split" the Jordan before them and allowed them to cross dry shod as a sign that their seizing of Canaanite territory had divine approbation'.[244] The account is a ritualized procession couched in the cognitive matrix of the Semitic Combat Myth that functions to justify the possession of the land. This may have appealed to Josiah's court. The point is that the account of Josiah's campaigns may have been similar to such a ritualized account. Josiah's campaigns function to legitimize his authority over the region around Bethel, but, more importantly, they function to negate Samaria as a competing source of power and identity among Israelite Judeans and other various constituents in Judah.

In 2 Samuel 6 we have another ritualized account of the procession of the ark, this time led by David. David's strategy to place the ark in the new capital (Jerusalem) marks an important turning point in the history of Israelite religion and politics. C.L. Seow remarks that 'scholars hail David's initiative as a brilliant maneuver that effectively galvanized the loose confederation of Israelite tribes into a monarchical state. The procession was, first and foremost, of great political significance inasmuch as it legimated David and his successors.'[245] Seow suggests that David's procession of the ark should be understood as a synthesis of the two theses—a religious ritual rooted in ancient Near Eastern myth or a historical event of great political significance—that attempts to understand 'the historic procession in the cognitive matrix of ancient Canaan'.[246] Seow shows that the procession was 'a religio–political drama celebrating the victory of YHWH as the divine warrior of Canaanite mythology and his consequent accession as king'.[247] The narrative of the ark of the covenant rejects other cult sites (Shiloh and Qiriath-jearim) and legitimates Jerusalem as the center of David's kingdom and Israelite cult.[248] In addition to legitimating the house of David, '2 Samuel 6 has to do

---

243. Batto suggests that 'the theme of crossing dry shod was extended to apply to the exodus tradition as well, in part because of the influence of Canaanite myth in which Sea and River were linked as parallel concepts. Thus did the story of deliverance at the sea became a story of crossing dry shod through the sea, with all the mythic implications inherent in the common Semitic Combat Myth' (*Slaying the Dragon*, p. 151).

244. Batto, *Slaying the Dragon*, p. 151.

245. C.L. Seow, *Myth, Drama, and the Politics of David's Dance* (HSM, 46; Atlanta: Scholars Press, 1989), p. 1.

246. Seow, *Myth*, pp. 4-5.

247. Seow, *Myth*, pp. 7-8.

248. C.L. Seow, 'Ark of the Covenant', in *ABD*, I, pp. 386-93.

with the inauguration of the new city and is, thus, comparable with similar religio-political rituals performed elsewhere in the ancient Near East'.[249] Specfically, it was patterned after the divine warrior's rise to supremacy.[250] The purpose of the procession was to dramatize the accession of YHWH as king after victories over the enemies. This pattern may have been adopted by Josiah's court to depict Josiah as the new David who conquered Samaria—in ritual terms, to re-establish Jerusalem, once again, as the center of Josiah's kingdom and cult. Josiah 'defeats' the enemies (foreign cults and cult personnel within his domain and in Samaria) before returning to Jerusalem to celebrate the Passover.

David ends the procession with the banquet (2 Sam. 6.17-19) just as Baal's rise to the position of king climaxes with the banquet 'after his victory over his enemies and the completion of his temple'.[251] Josiah also ends his reformation after defeating his 'enemies' and then proclaiming, presumably at the newly renovated temple, the celebration of Passover. Seow concludes that 'the climax of the celebration was a ritual banquet' which 'corresponds to the victory banquet which the victorious warrior hosts'.[252] Seow continues that 'for David, as well as for his descendants, the procession marked a turning point in history. David had succeeded in establishing a place for YHWH and, in doing so, had assured a place for himself and his posterity.'[253]

I am suggesting that Josiah's campaign in 2 Kgs 23.15-20 is a ritualized anti-pilgrimage that negates Bethel and Samaria as centers of cult and culture and re-establishes Jerusalem as the center of cult and culture for the Judeans after the Assyrian domination. Josiah symbolically destroys the competing

249. Seow, *Myth*, p. 140.
250. Seow, *Myth*, p. 140.
251. Seow, *Myth*, p. 133.
252. Seow, *Myth*, p. 142.
253. Seow, *Myth*, p. 210. Josiah, a scion of David, was supported by the Zion theology developed by the house of David; see J.J.M. Roberts, 'The Davidic Origin of the Zion Tradition', *JBL* 92 (1973), pp. 329-44, and *idem*, 'Zion in the Theology of the Davidic–Solomonic Empire', in Tomoo Ishida (ed.), *Studies in the Period of David and Solomon: Papers Read at the International Symposium for Biblical Studies, Tokyo, 5–7 December, 1979* (Winona Lake, IN: Eisenbrauns, 1982), pp. 93-108. The Zion theology emphasizes that (1) YHWH is the King, (2) YHWH chose Jerusalem as his [Yahweh is a male god] dwelling place, and therefore, (3) YHWH will defend Jerusalem as a Mighty Warrior. A corollary to the Zion theology is the Judean royal theology, which insists that YHWH chose David (and his dynasty) as the king and the temple atop Zion as the locus of YHWH's dwelling. During Hezekiah's reign, the Zion theology played a crucial role via Isaiah. As Josiah attempted to centralize sacrifice in Jerusalem, the Zion theology would have been more important. Just as the Sargonid Dynasty's deeds were narrated according to the ideology of expansion, Josiah's deeds were narrated according to the Zion theology. However, the Zion theology is not an ideology of an empire; there is no sense of call to expand, rather it is a call to preserve or to defend Jerusalem.

powers and cult sites in the province of Samerina in order to maintain hegemony over his kingdom. Josiah's anti-pilgrimage remembers the domination of Samaria over Jerusalem prior to the Assyrian domination, as well as during the Assyrian domination. It is a pilgrimage to Jerusalem, the center, through the anti-center, Samaria. It is an anti-pilgrimage because it reminds the people of the 'evil' that has happened in Samaria; and it marks the end of Samaria in the worldview of Josiah's court. There is no more Samaria—therefore, the people should stay. It is a symbolic account of Josiah's attempt to consolidate the Judeans to prevent the Israelite Judeans from going back to Samaria. The account invites all to participate in the formation of a community through the celebration of the Passover at Jerusalem.

Third, the narrative says that Josiah reinstituted the Passover, not held since the days of the judges (2 Kgs 23.21-23). However, it was not exactly a continuation of a forgotten custom. The Passover did not discontinue after the days of the judges. It was probably practiced as a family festival prior to Josiah's reinvention of it. The reinvention of the Passover as a Jerusalem-centered festival, as a pilgrimage, as a state-wide festival, helped consolidate the various groups living in Judah. It homogenized an already existing festival as a means to construct their common heritage and identity, as a group of people who were delivered from Egypt by YHWH. By participating in the Passover, even those who have no direct link to the exodus event (who did at the time?) can participate in the community. It is similar to the way Thanksgiving functions in the United States: all Americans, regardless of when or where one's family entered America, celebrate Thanksgiving and remember the story of how *our* ancestors came to America by grace of God and how they gave thanks to God for the food God provided the first winter. It is a custom that reinforces and maintains *our* identity as Americans regardless of when and how one entered America. My suggestion of creating a pan-Asian custom above (Asian New Year) was in the hope of helping to form a common identity among various Asian-American groups, as well as to remind American society in general of the diverse society we all share. Josiah's reinvention of Passover functioned to reinforce and maintain the identity of all 'Israelites', regardless of when and how they came to live in Judah, of a common heritage and story in the exodus event. In this sense, Josiah's Passover retrieves the forgotten or overwritten memories of the exodus during the Assyrian domination.

However, Shigeyuki Nakanose's comprehensive analysis of Josiah's Passover reminds us of negative impacts of the reinvention of the Passover celebration.[254] Josiah's reinvention of the Passover was a homogenization of

---

254. Shigeyuki Nakanose, *Josiah's Passover: Sociology and the Liberating Bible* (Maryknoll, NY: Orbis Books, 1993). Nakanose analyzes Josiah's Passover using the following analyses: critico-literary, economic, social, political, ideological, and historical.

5. *The* Realpolitik *of Liminality*

a popular festival. Nakanose agrees with the view of the majority of scholars that the inspiration for Josiah's Passover is to be found in Deut. 16.1-8 (D source). Nakanose concludes that Josiah's Passover is a slight but important modification of the Deuteronomic festival (D source), which was a change or evolution from the festival described in Exod. 12.21-23 (J source). Nakanose says:

> It is indisputable that there is a historical change or evolution of the Israelite religious institution of the Passover festival in the interval between J and D. In this change, the sanctuary, the Temple, assuredly stands as the most important and central component. It was the Deuteronomic legislator who had altered and adapted the Passover ritual to the sacral activities of a sanctuary. Yet Josiah's reform made the Passover a pilgrimage feast that had to be celebrated only in the Jerusalem Temple.[255]

The popular version of the Passover was a tribal or family ritual that reinforced the communal life of the villages. Josiah's Passover forced the peasants living outside of Jerusalem to bring their offerings to the Jerusalem Temple. This reinvention of the Passover festival, changing from a tribal festival to the Jerusalem Temple festival, was done in the name of YHWH, as a mark of a pious and exclusive loyalty to YHWH, and as part of the popular anti-Assyrian policy.[256]

However, the religious reform and the anti-Assyrian policy, according to Nakanose, concealed many benefits the ruling elite harvested at the expense of the poor rural population. The anti-Assyrian policy benefited the few ruling elite:

> By securing the autonomy of Judah and the control of Israel, they intended to promote the centralized mercantilistic economic policy in Jerusalem. So it was with the power- and wealth-seeking interests of the ruling elite in Josiah's reform. We believe that nationalism, the well-known policy of Josiah, came mainly from political propaganda of the ruling elite. Their political gains were skillfully concealed beneath the popular anti-Assyrian policy.[257]

Nakanose argues that the centralization of the cult, of which the reinvention of the Passover festival was part, was an attempt to control the surplus of

---

Then he examines how Josiah's Passover developed and functioned within the socio-religious context of the time. Finally, he examines how the understanding of Josiah's Passover as a socio-religious movement engages with the particular concerns and contexts of base communities in Brazil.

255. Nakanose, *Josiah's Passover*, p. 9.

256. Therefore, Nakanose notes that 'it is hardly surprising...that modern fundamentalist and idealist hermeneutics present Josiah's reform as a religious movement under a pious and exclusive loyalty to Yahweh' (*Josiah's Passover*, p. 92). Nakanose also assumes that Josiah's policy was anti-Assyrian.

257. Nakanose, *Josiah's Passover*, p. 73. Nakanose also makes the mistake of employing the concept 'nationalism' without any qualification.

the Judeans' production. He suggests that 'Josiah's reform seemed to be basically projected for aggrandizing the surplus for the state and the ruling elite of Jerusalem'.[258] The Jerusalem priests benefited, while the country Levite priests in Judah and non-Israelite priests in Israel suffered when Josiah destroyed sanctuaries outside of Jerusalem.[259] But it was the rural peasants who suffered the most due to the centralization of the cult because: (1) it made religious activities more expensive since they had to travel to Jerusalem and (2) it created a religious vacuum and brought about a deterioration in the social life of village communities.[260] Nakanose argues that the negative impacts on the rural population caused by Josiah's Passover need to be viewed with the understanding that 'the reform represented an attack on the rural population and on many aspects of its social life. Josiah's society appears to be on the track of an urban concentration movement rather than on the track of an egalitarian social movement.'[261]

The reinvention of the Passover was to increase the efficiency of extracting agricultural surpluses from the peasants. When the power of Assyria declined significantly, the time was ripe under Josiah 'for the urban patricians of Jerusalem to transform the Passover festival into a sacred mechanism of the Temple cult for their own advantages'.[262] Nakanose explains:

> By grafting the Passover festival onto the temple cult, the state tried to acquire the surplus of the extended families and to neutralize their sociopolitical cooperation system. It was a function of the mercantilistic system. The erosion of the tribal system could lead, given the control of the entire socioeconomic system to the ruling elite, to an expansion of their profits.[263]

Thus, Nakanose reminds us of the negative impacts on the rural population caused by the centralization of the cult and the reinvention of the Passover festival, concealed underneath the propaganda of royal ideology and the anti-Assyrian policy.

Kong-hi Lo argues that the Passover was turned into a pilgrimage festival as part of a cultic centralization that attempted to consolidate the people of 'Israel' and to resist the Egyptians.[264] Lo contends that the Passover functioned

---

258. Nakanose, *Josiah's Passover*, p. 51.
259. Nakanose assumes that Josiah took control of the northern territories during the decline of Assyria's power.
260. Nakanose, *Josiah's Passover*, p. 64.
261. Nakanose, *Josiah's Passover*, p. 64.
262. Nakanose, *Josiah's Passover*, p. 106.
263. Nakanose, *Josiah's Passover*, p. 110.
264. By 'Israel', Lo means the Israelites living in Judah and in Samaria, but this does not include the 'people' of Samaria who were settlers from other parts of the Assyrian empire. Lo summarizes his conclusion as follows: 'In short, the ideas of cultic centralization might have been designed for King Josiah to (re)define the ethnicity of Israel as a

5. The Realpolitik of Liminality 239

as a means of communication *en masse* of the ideas and purposes of cultic centralization. In other words, the required pilgrimage to Jerusalem to observe the Passover served as the means of disseminating Josiah's policies. Lo compares the function of the Passover with that of the mass media: 'the festival activities (2 Kgs 23.21-23; cf. 23.1-4) could be regarded as King Josiah's mass media'.[265] Lo reasons that if Josiah did not have 'the festival activities' as means of dissemination of his policies, 'it would have been more difficult for the redactor or King Josiah nationally to communicate and carry out the ideas of the cultic centralization to the people of Judah and the people of Samaria'.[266] He argues that one of the main functions of cultic centralization is 'to help define and consolidate the people of "Israel".'[267] Lo draws an idealistic portrayal of the Passover as a pilgrimage festival that functions to consolidate the Israelites:

> When the people, old and young, walked together, sang together, and discussed their faith and life together, they were getting consolidated. The feeling of togetherness, as one people, walking toward one place for one God, was supposed to grow in the people's hearts during their pilgrimage.[268]

Then, Lo continues, it was during the celebration of the Passover that the book of the law was read to disseminate Josiah's policies: 'The ideas of cultic centralization—one God, one people, one land, one temple, and one

nation, to consolidate all the people of Israel, to gain control over all the people through monotheistic Yahwism, to clarify the territory of Israel and its capital, and to get the people ready to reject Egyptian imperialism' ('Cultic Centralization in the Deuteronomistic History', p. 280).

265. Lo, 'Cultic Centralization in the Deuteronomistic History', p. 249. Hayim Tadmor warns against the temptation for a modern person exposed to modern media to understand royal inscriptions as having been 'read aloud to a large and varied contemporary audience' ('Propoganda, Literature, Historiography', p. 332). Tadmor reminds us that royal inscriptions and other official documents were limited to the hegemonic class (see also Coote and Coote, *Power*, who agree with this assessment). Lo's view of the Passover as a direct forum for propaganda is suspect.

266. Lo, 'Cultic Centralization in the Deuteronomistic History', p. 249. Here 'the people of Samaria' seems to mean the 'Israelites' in Samaria rather than the 'foreign' settlers in Samaria.

267. Lo, 'Cultic Centralization in the Deuteronomistic History', p. 11. Here the people of 'Israel' means the people of 'Greater Israel', which includes the people of Judah and the Israelites in Samaria.

268. Lo, 'Cultic Centralization in the Deuteronomistic History', p. 259. According to Lo, the pilgrimage was supposed to start at home when the family would gather around to talk about the lessons of the festival as described in Deut. 6. Lo's analysis suffers from understanding the scenes described in 2 Kgs 23.1-4, 21-23 (and passages in Deuteronomy that are related to the three festivals) as realistic descriptions of these gatherings. Lo did not consult Nakanose's work; thus his story suffers from a lack of socio-economic analysis of the Passover. The Passover is primarily seen as a forum for propaganda.

king—were, thus, disseminated by means of the narration of the book of the law/covenant'.[269]

Lo also suggests that the Passover, with its strong motif of exodus, was carried out as part of the strategy to resist the Egyptians. Lo assumes the Assyrians' withdrawal from Palestine and argues that the Egyptians took control of this area.[270] Therefore, Lo argues that Josiah used the Passover, which is anti-Egyptian in nature, to prepare his people for a future clash with Egypt. He concludes as follows:

> The emphatically anti-Egyptian motif in Deuteronomy, especially in the Deuteronomic rule of Passover, could be King Josiah's preparation of the people to resist the coming Egyptian imperialism. The exodus event is presumably dramatized in annual Passover celebration. When the people eat unleavened bread, they would know that they do so because their ancestors were saved by Yahweh from Egypt in a hurry. Egypt became a place where the Israelites should not return.[271]

Lo points out that Deut. 16.1-8 stresses 'cultic centralization and exodus motif in regulation of the first annual festival'.[272] He credits this emphasis to Josiah's policy of centralization and 'building of animosity against Egyptians'.[273] He further claims that all the ritual elements of the Passover (information gathered from Deuteronomy, not Kings) can be explained by the historical memory of the exodus (particularly the deliverance by YHWH and the evil suffered by the Israelites at the hand of the Egyptians) that helps to consolidate the Israelites and to raise anti-Egyptian sentiments.[274]

After the anti-pilgrimage to Samaria, in which Josiah defeats the memory of the past evil of the northern kingdom, Josiah institutes a pilgrimage festival to Jerusalem through reinvention of the Passover festival, in order to consolidate the various groups living in Judah and to stop the Israelite Judeans (descendants of former immigrants or refugees from the North) from going back to Samaria. As a pilgrimage to Jerusalem, it is embedded in the matrix of the Semitic Combat Myth, and more specifically in the Zion theology that envisions Jerusalem as the center of the world, with all peoples obligated to make a pilgrimage to Jerusalem. Josiah was trying to consolidate the native Judeans and the Israelite Judeans into one people, united under one god, one

---

269. Lo, 'Cultic Centralization in the Deuteronomistic History', p. 264.
270. Lo, 'Cultic Centralization in the Deuteronomistic History', p. 279. I have argued in Chapter 4 that although Egypt controlled the *via maris* in cooperation with Assyria, Egypt was in no position to nor did it desire to control inland Palestine states such as Judah and the province of Samerina.
271. Lo, 'Cultic Centralization in the Deuteronomistic History', p. 279.
272. Lo, 'Cultic Centralization in the Deuteronomistic History', p. 256.
273. Lo, 'Cultic Centralization in the Deuteronomistic History', p. 273.
274. Lo, 'Cultic Centralization in the Deuteronomistic History', pp. 261-62.

cult, and one dynasty. It was an attempt to inscribe their own identity and destiny apart from imperial forces. Josiah was in competition with the politically organized people of Samaria, who continued to worship YHWH next to other gods, for the allegiance of the Israelite Judeans, who may have wanted to go back to the province of Samerina.

Summary

I have read the story of Josiah intercontextually with Asian Americans' efforts to write 'a history of their own'. Josiah's people was located in a political, ideological landscape not of their own making during the Assyrian domination; it was during this time that their history and culture were overwritten by the Assyrians—more likely through the process of acculturation than coercion. I examined the possibility that Josiah's court may have responded to ethnic sentiments that became prominent during the Sargonid Dynasty of the Neo-Assyrian Empire; this needs further investigation. Josiah's kingdom was located in a political, ideological landscape shaped by the Neo-Assyrians where they were viewed as Others. Josiah's kingdom was no more than a petty state situated at the margin of the ancient Near East, which was unified by the Neo-Assyrian Empire and lasted as a structural characteristic until the collapse of Jerusalem and beyond. Josiah's kingdom was not a significant factor in the economic, political equation of the western region of the unified ancient Near East. Josiah and his people were located in a landscape not of their own making where they experienced the *Realpolitik* of liminality. In light of Asian-Americans' experience of the *Realpolitik* of liminality in North America, I have explored how Judah experienced the *Realpolitik* of liminality in history and how this reality is illustrated in the text.

Asian Americans are familiar with identity politics in which they are viewed as the Other. They have experienced the *Realpolitik* of liminality, the danger of being in a political, ideological landscape not of one's own making, throughout their history in North America. They have been victims of violence and exploitation, collectively as well as individually, in the land they called their home because, in part, of the racialized landscape of North America where they are viewed as aliens. The LA Riots, the Japanese Internment, and the Chinese Exclusion Act are prominent historical examples that remind Asian Americans that they are only a step away from experiencing the *Realpolitik* of liminality. There are also many individual victims of injustice that remind one again of the positionality of Asian Americans in North America. Josiah and his people, too, had experienced the *Realpolitik* of liminality. They had experienced first hand the might of Assyria during the Assyrian domination of the West. Their fate was connected to the whim of larger political forces. Their experience of the danger of being located in a political, ideological landscape not of their own making is best illustrated by the way the story of Josiah is framed within two accounts of death. On the one side, the account of Amon's death illustrates what could happen if the *status quo* is maintained, and, on the other side, the account of Josiah's death illustrates what could happen if the *status quo* is disturbed. There is no safe ground for the 'others'. They can be victims of the *Realpolitik* of liminality whether they follow the script of the empire or choose not to.

In spite of being firmly rooted in the hegemony imposed by Assyria and other imperial forces, Josiah and his court ignored Assyria and other imperial forces and attempted, in part, to write 'a history of their own' when they composed DH. The story of Josiah can be understood as an attempt to write 'a history of their own' independent from the framework of the imperial powers. Thus there is no mention of Assyria or Egypt. It was a subversive strategy to give the agency to the colonized—to imagine one's own history and destiny apart from the empire, an alternative view of the world. I have attempted to inform this study by examining how Asian Americans are writing 'a history of their own' outside of the framework of the nation constructed by Euro-Americans. They are doing this by reframing their history, without always referencing the national history of the US, by recovering their inscriptions of the past, by mapping sites of pilgrimage to remember their past, and by creating Asian-American cultures that view the Asian-American community as a unique American group. These are ways of writing a history that helps to form an Asian-American identity that is separate from the national identity and to inscribe their subjectivity. I have utilized these insights in reading the story of Josiah. DH, in part, was written to consolidate various groups of people living in Josiah's kingdom, rather than to reunify the divided kingdom or to attract the northerners to Judah. It might have been an attempt to discourage the Israelite Judeans (descendants of the northern immigrants/refugees) who wanted to return to Samaria after the 'retreat' of Assyria from that region. DH was written with the 'Israelites' as the subject of YHWH's history, independent from the empires. The story of Josiah shows that the lost 'inscriptions' were discovered, 'inscriptions' which initiated the project of recovering and rewriting 'a history of their own'. The story shows how Josiah attempted to recover what had been overwritten by the cultural patterns of the Neo-Assyrian Empire. Josiah's 'campaign' to the province of Samerina can be understood as a ritual, a pilgrimage to places of 'wrong doing' as a reminder to the Israelite Judeans not to go back to Samaria. Josiah reinstituted the Passover as a means of recovering for the Judeans an identity of their own. Josiah was trying to consolidate the native Judeans and the Israelite Judeans into one people, united under YHWH, practicing one cult, and ruled by one legitimate dynasty.

5. *The* Realpolitik *of Liminality*

In my effort to decolonize Josiah, I have read the story of Josiah intercontextually with the story of Asian Americans from the place of liminality. I have read the story of Josiah in conversation with the experience, aspirations, and history of Asian Americans so that Asian Americans can see themselves in the story of Josiah. It was not, however, my intention to make the story of Josiah a 'safe' text for Asian Americans. The story of Josiah has been 'unsafe' for, among others, the people of the province of Samerina who must have felt 'unhomely' in their own land due to the politics of identity in Josiah's kingdom. The story of Josiah as an illustration of an attempt to write 'a history of their own' may be used to affirm the effort of Asian Americans to construct their own subjectivity by writing 'a history of their own', but it can also be 'unsafe' when it is used to homogenize various groups into one community, thereby making those who are left out in the standard Asian-American history and identity feel 'unhomely' in their own land. We must keep in mind that politics of interpretation go hand in hand with politics of identity.

Reflections

Martin Noth's Deuteronomistic History Hypothesis and the double redaction theory of Cross are modern day *monuments* that have the backing of two centuries of modern biblical scholarship and the support of a countless number of first-rate scholars embedded in academic institutions around the world. There is no denying that they cast a long shadow and it is under the shadow of these *monuments* that we find Josiah securely situated. Perhaps there is, in the spirit of Qohelet, nothing new to add under the sun to the scholarship on DH in general and on King Josiah in particular. Of course, there are modifications and refinements and elaboration on the *monuments* that change slightly how one reads Josiah just as changes in lighting affect the appearance of a painting. But there is nothing 'new' on Josiah that does not reference itself to the *monuments*.

It was not my attempt in this study to go around or to deny the solidity of the *monuments*, as if that was possible. Perhaps I also have not added anything new under the shadow of the sun. It was in the spirit of postcolonialism that I undertook my work and proclaimed: 'If there is nothing new under the sun, perhaps it is time to look beneath the shadow of the moon'. I wanted to engage not only the knowledge garnered by mainstream scholarship 'under the sun' but also to reap insights and knowledge from those who are searching 'under the shadow of the moon'. I chose to engage those scholars who chose to be in the space of liminality (Thirdspace, counterspace, the margin)—'under the shadow of the moon'—where new possibilities and relations are open and the hierarchy of the center and the periphery is thwarted. Many Asian Americans in particular are aware of and experience their lived space as being 'under the shadow of the moon', where they experience the *Realpolitik* of liminality—the danger of living in a space where they are viewed as 'different' from those who construct the hierarchy of the center and the periphery.

My critique of the *monuments* and reading of King Josiah applied the historical imagination and used the tools of the critical historian. But my critique and reading were informed also by the experience, expressed with honesty and in its complexity, of those who have lived as the Other, as the colonized, as not at home in their own land, as interstitial beings—for me, the experience of being Asian American in North America. I was not shy about using the experience of Asian Americans as a critical tool to draw attention to the connection between Western imperialism and the production of Western knowledge—what is happening under the shadow of the sun—and how it maintains the hierarchy of the West and the rest—what is happening under the shadow of the moon. I hope my study would help to bring King Josiah out from under the shadow of the monuments, but, more importantly, I hoped to encourage new light to be cast on King Josiah and the monuments themselves.

BIBLIOGRAPHY

Ahlström, G.W., *The History of Ancient Palestine: From the Palaeolithic Period to Alexander's Conquest* (Minneapolis: Fortress Press, 1993).
Albertz, R., *A History of Israelite Religion in the Old Testament Period.* I. *From the Beginning to the End of the Monarchy* (trans. John Bowden; Louisville, KY: Westminster/John Knox Press, 1994).
Alfrink, B., 'Die Schlacht bei Megiddo und der Tod des Josias (609)', *Bib* 15 (1934), pp. 173-84.
Althann, R., 'Josiah', in *ABD*, III, pp. 1015-18.
Anderson, B., *Imagined Communities: Reflections on the Origin and Spread of Nationalism* (New York: Verso, 1991).
Ankersmit, F., 'Historiography and Postmodernism', *History and Theory* 28 (1989), pp. 37-53.
Appleby, J., E. Covington, D. Hoyt, M. Latham, and A. Sneider (eds.), *Knowledge and Postmodernism in Historical Perspective* (London: Routledge, 1996).
Appleby, J., L. Hunt, and M. Jacob, *Telling the Truth about History* (New York: W.W. Norton, 1994).
Ashcroft, B., 'On the Hyphen in Post-colonial', *New Literature Review* 32 (1996), pp. 23-32.
Ashcroft, B., G. Griffiths, and H. Tiffin, *Post-Colonial Studies: The Key Concepts* (London: Routledge, 2000).
Ashcroft, B., G. Griffiths, and H. Tiffin (eds.), *The Empire Writes Back: Theory and Practice in Post-colonial Literature* (London: Routledge, 1989).
— *The Post-colonial Studies Reader* (London; New York: Routledge, 1995).
Auld, A.G., Review of Keith Whitelam, *The Invention of Ancient Israel*, *Expository Times* 108 (1996), pp. 25-26.
Bakhtin, M., *The Dialogic Imagination* (ed. M. Holquist; Austin: University of Texas Press, 1981).
—*Speech Genres and Other Later Essays* (ed. C. Emerson and M. Holquist; Austin: Texas University Press, 1986).
Bartlett, J.R., Review of G.W. Ahlström, *The History of Ancient Palestine*, *PEQ* 127 (1995), pp. 70-71.
Barrick, W.B., *The King and the Cemeteries: Toward a New Understanding of Josiah's Reform* (Leiden: E.J. Brill, 2002).
Batto, B.F., *Slaying the Dragon* (Louisville, KY: Westminster/John Knox Press, 1992).
Begg, C.T., 'The Death of Josiah in Chronicles', *VT* 37 (1987), pp. 1-8.
—'The Death of Josiah: Josephus and the Bible', *ETL* 64 (1988), pp. 157-63.
—Review of Gary N. Knoppers, *Two Nations under God*, *RelSRev* 20 (1994), pp. 328-29.
Berquist, J.L., 'Critical Spatiality and the Construction of the Ancient World', in Gunn and McNutt (eds.), *'Imagining' Biblical Worlds*, pp. 14-29.

Bhabha, H.K., 'DissemiNation: Time, Narrative, and the Margins of the Modern Nation', in *idem* (ed.), *Nation and Narration*, pp. 291-322.
—'Interrogating Identity: The Postcolonial Prerogative', in D.T. Goldberg (ed.), *Anatomy of Racism* (Minneapolis: University of Minnesota Press, 1990), pp. 183-209.
—'Introduction', in *idem* (ed.), *Nation and Narration*, pp. 1-7.
—*The Location of Culture* (London: Routledge, 1994).
—'The Postcolonial and the Postmodern: The Question of Agency', in *idem*, *The Location of Culture*, pp. 171-97.
Bhabha, H.K. (ed.), *Nation and Narration* (London: Routledge, 1990).
Biran, A., and J. Naveh, 'An Aramaic Stele Fragment from Tel Dan', *IEJ* 43 (1993), pp. 1-98.
—'The Tel Dan Inscription: A New Fragment', *IEJ* 45 (1995), pp. 1-18.
Boehmer, J., 'König Josias Tod', *ARW* 30 (1933), pp. 199-203.
Bolin, T., 'History, Historiography, and the Use of the Past in the Hebrew Bible', in Kraus (ed.), *The Limits of Historiography*, pp. 113-40.
Boyarin, D., *A Radical Jew: Paul and the Politics of Identity* (Berkeley: University of California Press, 1994).
Breisach, E., *Historiography: Ancient, Medieval, and Modern* (Chicago: University of Chicago Press, 2nd edn, 1994).
Brennan, T., 'The National Longing for Form', in Bhabha (ed.), *Nation and Narration*, pp. 44-70.
Brettler, M.Z., *The Creation of History in Ancient Israel* (London: Routledge, 1995).
Bright, J., *A History of Israel* (Philadelphia: Westminster Press, 2nd edn, 1972).
—*A History of Israel* (Philadelphia: Westminster Press, 3rd edn, 1981).
—*A History of Israel* (Introduction and Appendix by W.P. Brown; Louisville, KY: Westminster/John Knox Press, 4th edn, 2000).
Brinkman, J.A., *Prelude to Empire: Babylonian Society and Politics, 747–626 B.C.* (Philadelphia: The Babylonian Fund, University Museum, 1984).
Brock, R.N., 'Interstitial Integrity: Reflections toward an Asian American Woman's Theology', in R.A. Badham (ed.), *Introduction to Christian Theology: Contemporary North American Perspectives* (Louisville, KY: Westminster/John Knox Press, 1998), pp. 183-96.
Campbell, A.F., 'Martin Noth and the Deuteronomistic History', in McKenzie and Graham (eds.), *The History of Israel's Traditions*, pp. 31-62.
Campbell, A.F., and M.A. O'Brien, *Unfolding the Deuteronomistic History: Origins, Upgrades, and Present Text* (Minneapolis: Fortress Press, 2000).
Carter, P., *The Road to Botany Bay: An Essay in Spatial History* (London: Faber & Faber, 1987).
Chakrabarty, D., 'Postcoloniality and the Artifice of History', in Ashcroft, Griffiths, and Tiffin (eds.), *The Post-Colonial Studies Reader*, pp. 383-88.
—'A Small History of Subaltern Studies', in Schwartz and Ray (eds.), *A Companion to Postcolonial Studies*, pp. 467-85.
Chan, S., *Asian Americans: An Interpretive History* (Boston: Twayne, 1991).
Cho, E.S., 'Josianic Reform in the Deuteronomistic History Reconstructed in the Light of Factionalism and Use of Royal Apology' (PhD dissertation, The Graduate Theological Union, 2002).
Christensen, D.L., 'Zephaniah 2.4-15: A Theological Basis for Josiah's Program of Political Expansion', *CBQ* 46 (1984), pp. 669-82.

Claburn, W.E., 'The Fiscal Basis of Josiah's Reforms', *JBL* 92 (1973), pp. 11-22.
Clark, K., and M. Holquist, *Mikhail Bakhtin* (Cambridge, MA: Harvard University Press, 1984).
Clifford, J., 'Diasporas', *Cultural Anthropology* 9 (1994), pp. 302-38.
Clines, D.J.A., 'The Postmodern Adventure in Biblical Studies', in Clines and Moore (eds.), *Auguries*, pp. 276-91.
Clines, D.J.A., and S.D. Moore (eds.), *Auguries: The Jubilee Volume of the Sheffield Department of Biblical Studies* (JSOTSup, 269; Sheffield: Sheffield Academic Press, 1998).
Cogan, M., *Imperialism and Religion: Assyria, Judah and Israel in the Eighth and Seventh Centuries B.C.E.* (SBLMS, 19; Missoula, MN: Scholars Press, 1974).
—'Judah under Assyrian Hegemony: A Re-examination of Imperialism and Religion', *JBL* 112 (1993), pp. 403-14.
Coggins, R.J., 'History and Story in Old Testament Study', *JSOT* 11 (1979), pp. 36-46.
Coogan, M.D., *Stories from Ancient Canaan* (Philadelphia: Westminster Press, 1978).
Coogan, M.D., J.C. Exum, and L.E. Stager (eds.), *Scripture and Other Artifacts: Essays on the Bible and Archaeology in Honor of Philip J. King* (Louisville, KY: Westminster/John Knox Press, 1994).
Coote, R., 'The Deuteronomistic History' (unpublished manuscript, 1999).
Coote, R., and M.P. Coote, *Power, Politics, and the Making of the Bible* (Minneapolis: Fortress Press, 1990).
Coote, R., and D.R. Ord, *In the Beginning: Creation and the Priestly History* (Minneapolis: Fortress Press, 1991).
Coote, R., and K.W. Whitelam, *The Emergence of Early Israel in Historical Perspective* (The Social World of Biblical Antiquity, 5; Sheffield: Almond Press, 1987).
Cross, F.M., *Canaanite Myth and Hebrew Epic: Essays in the History of the Religion of Israel* (Cambridge, MA: Harvard University Press, 1973).
Cross, F.M., and D.N. Freedman, 'Josiah's Revolt against Assyria', *JNES* 12 (1953), pp. 56-58.
Cryer, F.H., 'On the Recently Discovered "House of David" Inscription', *SJOT* 8 (1994), pp. 1-19.
Dalley, S., *Myths from Mesopotamia: Creation, the Flood, Gilgamesh, and Others* (Oxford: Oxford University Press, 1989).
Daniels, R., *Asian America: Chinese and Japanese in the United States since 1850* (Seattle: University of Washington Press, 1988).
Davies, G., *Megiddo* (Cambridge: Lutterworth Press, 1986).
Davies, P.R., 'Biblical Studies in a Postmodern Age', *Jian Dao* 7 (1997), pp. 37-55.
—'The Future of "Biblical History"', in Clines and Moore (eds.), *Auguries*, pp. 126-41.
—*In Search of 'Ancient Israel'* (JSOTSup, 148; Sheffield: JSOT Press, 1992).
—'Method and Madness: Some Remarks on Doing History with the Bible', *JBL* 114 (1995), pp. 699-705.
—'What Separates a Minimalist from a Maximalist? Not Much', *BARev* 26 (2000), pp. 24-27, 72-73.
Dever, W.G., 'Histories and Nonhistories of Ancient Israel', *BASOR* 316 (1999), pp. 89-105.
—'Save Us from Postmodern Malarkey', *BARev* 26 (2000), pp. 28-35, 68-69.

—'The Silence of the Text: An Archaeological Commentary on 2 Kings 23', in Coogan, Exum, and Stager (eds.) *Scripture and Other Artifacts*, pp. 143-68.
—'Syro-Palestinian and Biblical Archaeology', in G.M. Tucker (ed.), *The Hebrew Bible and its Modern Interpreters* (Philadelphia: Fortress Press, 1985), pp. 31-74.
DeVries, S.J., Review of Gary N. Knoppers, *Two Nations under God*, *Int* 50 (1996), pp. 293-95.
Dietrich, W., 'Martin Noth and the Future of the Deuteronomistic History', in McKenzie and Graham (eds.), *The History of Israel's Traditions*, pp. 153-75.
Donaldson, L.E. (ed.), 'Postcolonialism and Biblical Reading: An Introduction', *Semeia* 75 (1996), pp. 1-14.
—*Postcolonialism and Scripture Reading* (Semeia, 75; Atlanta: Society of Biblical Literature, 1996).
Doi, J., 'The Lake Pilgrimage: Dissonant Memories, Sacred Journey', in J. Iwamura and P. Spickard (eds.), *Revealing the Sacred in Asian and Pacific America* (London: Routledge, 2003), pp. 273-89.
Edelman, D.V. (ed.), *The Fabric of History: Text, Artifact and Israel's Past* (JSOTSup, 127; Sheffield: JSOT Press, 1991).
Elat, M., 'The Political Status of the Kingdom of Judah within the Assyrian Empire in the 7th Century B.C.E.', in Y. Aharoni (ed.), *Investigations at Lachish: The Sanctuary and the Residency* (Tel Aviv: Gateway, 1975), pp. 61-70.
Eph'al, I., 'On Warfare and Military Control in the Ancient Near Eastern Empires: A Research Outline', in H. Tadmor and M. Weinfeld (eds.), *History, Historiography and Interpretation: Studies in Biblical and Cuneiform Literature* (Jerusalem: Magnes Press, 1983), pp. 88-106.
Evans, C.D., 'Judah's Foreign Policy from Hezekiah to Josiah', in Evans, Hallo and White (eds.), *Scripture in Context*, pp. 157-78.
Evans, C.D., W.H. Hallo, and J.B. White (eds.), *Scripture in Context: Essays on the Comparative Method* (Pittsburgh: Pickwick, 1980).
Evans, R.J., *In Defense of History* (New York: W.W. Norton, 2000).
Eynikel, E., *The Reform of King Josiah and the Composition of the Deuteronomistic History* (Leiden: E.J. Brill, 1995).
Fales, F.M. (ed.), *Assryian Royal Inscriptions: New Horizons in Literary, Ideological, and Historical Analysis* (Rome: Instituto per l'Oriente, 1980).
—'The Enemy in Assyrian Royal Inscription: "The Moral Judgment"', in Nissen and Renger (eds.), *Mesopotamien und seine Nachbarn*, pp. 425-35.
—'A Literary Code in Assyrian Royal Inscriptions: The Case of Ashurbanipal's Egyptian Campaigns', in *idem* (ed.), *Assyrian Royal Inscriptions*, pp. 169-202.
Feldman, L.H., *Josephus, Jewish Antiquities, Books IX–XI* (LCL; Cambridge, MA: Harvard University Press, 1978).
Finkelstein, I., 'State Formation in Israel and Judah', *NEA* 62/1 (1999), pp. 35-52.
Finkelstein, I., and N.A. Silberman, *The Bible Unearthed: Archaeology's New Vision of Ancient Israel and the Origin of its Sacred Texts* (New York: Free Press, 2001).
Forsberg, S., *Near Eastern Destruction Dating as Source for Greek and Near Eastern Iron Age Chronology: Archaeological and Historical Studies: The Case of Samaria (722 B.C.) and Tarsus (696 B.C.)* (Uppsala: Uppsala University Press, 1995).
Foskett, M.F., 'The Accident of Being and the Politics of Identity', in Liew (ed.), *The Bible in Asian America*, pp. 135-44.
Foucault, M., *The Archaeology of Knowledge* (New York: Pantheon Books, 1972).
—'Of Other Spaces', *Diacritics* 16 (1986), pp. 22-27.

—*The Order of Things* (New York: Pantheon Books, 1970).
—*Power/Knowledge* (New York: Pantheon Books, 1980).
—'Questions on Geography', in idem, *Power/Knowledge*, pp. 63-77
Frame, G. (ed.), *Rulers of Babylonia from the Second Dynasty of Isin to the End of Assyrian Domination (1157–612 B.C.)* (The Royal Inscriptions of Mesopotamia, Babylonian Periods, 2; Toronto: University of Toronto Press, 1995).
Frick, F.S., 'Cui Bono?—History in the Service of Political Nationalism: The Deuteronomistic History as Political Propaganda', *Semeia* 66 (1994), pp. 79-92.
Frost, S.B., 'The Death of Josiah: A Conspiracy of Silence', *JBL* 87 (1968), pp. 369-82.
Gallagher, S.V., 'Mapping the Hybrid World: Three Postcolonial Motifs', *Semeia* 75 (1996), pp. 225-40.
Gallagher, W.R., *Sennacherib's Campaign to Judah* (Leiden: E.J. Brill, 1999).
Garbini, G., *History and Ideology in Ancient Israel* (New York: Crossroad, 1988).
Gattung, G., *The Cambridge Companion to Foucault* (Cambridge: Cambridge University Press, 1994).
Geary, P.J., *The Myth of Nations: The Medieval Origins of Europe* (Princeton, NJ: Princeton University Press, 2002).
Gellner, E., *Nations and Nationalism* (Ithaca, NY: Cornell University Press, 1983).
Gitin, S., 'The Neo-Assyrian Empire and its Western Periphery: The Levant, with Focus on Philistine Ekron', in Parpola and Whiting (eds.), *Assyria 1995*, pp. 77-103.
Godley, A.D., *Herodotus* (LCL; Cambridge, MA: Harvard University Press, 1981).
Gordon, R.P., Review of Gary N. Knoppers, *Two Nations under God*, *JTS* 47 (1996), pp. 569-72.
Grabbe, L. (ed.), *Can a 'History of Israel' Be Written?* (JSOTSup, 245; Sheffield: Sheffield Academic Press, 1997).
Graham, M.P., K.G. Hoglund, and S.L. McKenzie (eds.), *The Chronicler as Historian* (JSOTSup, 238; Sheffield: Sheffield Academic Press, 1997).
Grayson, A.K., *Assyrian and Babylonian Chronicles* (Texts from Cuneiform Sources; Locust Valley, NY: J.J. Augustin Publisher, 1975).
—'Histories and Historians of the Ancient Near East: Assyria and Babylonia', *Or* 49 (1980), pp. 140-94.
Green, B., *Mikhail Bakhtin and Biblical Scholarship: An Introduction* (Atlanta: Society of Biblical Literature, 2000).
Gunn, D.M., and P.M. McNutt (eds.), *'Imagining' Biblical Worlds: Studies in Spatial, Social and Historical Constructs in Honor of James W. Flanagan* (JSOTSup, 359; London and New York: Sheffield Academic Press, 2002).
Gyles, M.F., *Pharaonic Policies and Administration, 663 to 323 B.C.* (Chapel Hill: University of North Carolina Press, 1959).
Habermas, J., 'The Critique of Reason as an Unmasking of the Human Science: Michel Foucault', in idem, *The Philosophical Discourse of Modernity* (trans. F.G. Lawrence; Cambridge, MA: MIT Press, 1990), pp. 238-65.
Hall, R.G., 'Circumcision', in *ABD*, I, pp. 1025-31.
Hall, S., 'Cultural Identity and Diaspora', in P. Williams and L. Chrisman (eds.), *Colonial Discourse and Post-Colonial Theory* (New York: Columbia University Press, 1994), pp. 392-403.
—'The Local and the Global: Globalization and Ethnicities', in A.D. King (ed.), *Culture, Globalization and the World-System: Contemporary Conditions for the Representation of Identity* (Minneapolis: University of Minnesota Press, 1997), pp. 19-40.

Hallo, W., 'Biblical History in its Near Eastern Environment: The Contextual Approach', in Evans, Hallo, and White (eds.), *Scripture in Context*, pp. 1-26.
Halpern, B., 'Erasing History: The Minimalist Assault on Ancient Israel', *BRev* 11/6 (1995), pp. 25-35, 47.
—*The First Historians* (San Francisco: Harper & Row, 1988).
—'The State of Israelite History', in Knoppers and McConville (eds.), *Reconsidering Israel and Judah*, pp. 540-65.
Halpern, B., and D.S. Vanderhooft, 'The Editions of Kings in the 7th–6th Centuries BCE', *HUCA* 62 (1991), pp. 179-244.
Handy, L.K., 'Historical Probability and the Narrative of Josiah's Reform in 2 Kings', in S.W. Holloway and L.K. Handy (eds.), *The Pitcher is Broken: Memorial Essays for Gösta W. Ahlström* (JSOTSup, 190; Sheffield: Sheffield Academic Press, 1995), pp. 252-75.
Hastings, A., *The Construction of Nationhood: Ethnicity, Religion and Nationalism* (Cambridge: Cambridge University Press, 1997).
Hayes, J.H., 'The History of the Study of Israelite and Judean History', in Hayes and Miller (eds.), *Israelite and Judaean History*, pp. 1-69.
Hayes, J.H., and J.M. Miller (eds.), *Israelite and Judaean History* (Philadelphia: Westminster Press, 1977).
Heltzer, M., 'Some Questions concerning the Economic Policy of Josiah, King of Judah', *IEJ* 50, pp. 105-108.
Herr, L.G., 'The Iron Age II Period: Emerging Nations', *BA* 60 (1995), pp. 67-86.
Holloway, S.W., Review of Keith Whitelam, *The Invention of Ancient Israel*, *JBL* 117 (1998), pp. 117-19.
Holquist, M., *Dialogism: Bakhtin and his World* (London: Routledge, 1990).
Howard, D.M., Review of Gary N. Knoppers, *Two Nations under God*, *JETS* 39 (1996), pp. 471-73.
Huizinga, J., 'A Definition of the Concept of History', in R. Klibansky and H.J. Paton (eds.), *Philosophy and History: Essays Presented to Ernst Cassirer* (Cambridge: Cambridge University Press, 1963), pp. 1-10.
Iggers, G.G., *Historiography in the Twentieth Century: From Scientific Objectivity to the Postmodern Challenge* (Hanover: Wesleyan University Press, 1997).
Iwamura, J.N., 'The "Hidden Manna" That Sustains: Reading Revelation 2.17 in Joy Kogawa's *Obasan*', in Liew (ed.), *The Bible in Asian America*, pp. 161-79.
Japhet, S., *I & II Chronicles* (OTL; Louisville, KY: Westminster/John Knox Press, 1993).
Jenkins, K., *Refiguring History* (London: Routledge, 2003).
Jenkins, K. (ed.), *The Postmodern History Reader* (London: Routledge, 1997).
Joyce, P., 'First among Equals? The Historical-Critical Approach in the Marketplace of Methods', in S.E. Porter, P. Joyce, and D.E. Orton (eds.), *Crossing the Boundaries: Essays in Biblical Interpretation in Honour of Michael D. Goulder* (New York: E.J. Brill, 1994), pp. 17-27.
Kaiser, W.C., *A History of Israel: From the Bronze Age to the Jewish Wars* (Nashville: Broadman & Holman, 1998).
Kane, H., 'Leaving Home', in L.R. Brown *et al.* (eds.), *State of the World 1995* (New York: W.W. Norton, 1995), pp. 132-49.
Kim, E., 'Home is Where the *Han* Is?', in Wu and Song (eds.), *Asian American Studies*, pp. 270-89.
Kim, J.H., 'At the Tables of an Asian American Banquet', in Liew (ed.), *The Bible in Asian America*, pp. 325-37.

Kim, T.H., 'Assyrian Historical Inscriptions and the Political and Economic Relations among Assyria, the Syro-Palestinian States, and Egypt in the Eighth-Seventh Centuries BCE' (PhD dissertation, The Graduate Theological Union, 2001).

Kim, U.Y., 'God, Apple Pie, and Kim-chi: A Theological Response to Korean-American Predicament' (MA thesis, Emory University, 1997).

—'Uriah the Hittite: A (Con)Text of Struggle for Identity', in Liew (ed.), *The Bible in Asian America*, pp. 69-85.

Kitano, H., and R. Daniels, *Asian Americans: Emerging Minorities* (Englewood Cliffs, NJ: Prentice–Hall, 2nd edn, 1995).

Kitchen, K.A., *The Third Intermediate Period in Egypt* (Warminster: Aris & Phillips, 1986).

Klein, K.L., *Frontiers of Historical Imagination: Narrating the European Conquest of Native America, 1890–1990* (Berkeley: University of California Press, 1997).

Klein, R.W., Review of Gary N. Knoppers, *Two Nations under God*, *JBL* 114 (1995), pp. 302-304.

—Review of Gary N. Knoppers, *Two Nations under God*, *JBL* 115 (1996), pp. 732-34.

Kleinig, J.W., 'Recent Research in Chronicles', *CurBS* 2 (1994), pp. 43-76.

Knoppers, G.N., 'Is there a Future for the Deuteronomistic History?', in Römer (ed.), *The Future of the Deuteronomistic History*, pp. 119-34.

— *Two Nations under God: The Deuteronomistic History of Solomon and the Dual Monarchies. I. The Reign of Solomon and the Rise of Jeroboam* (Cambridge, MA: Harvard University Press, 1993).

— *Two Nations under God: The Deuteronomistic History of Solomon and the Dual Monarchies. II. The Reign of Jeroboam, the Fall of Israel, and the Reign of Josiah* (Cambridge, MA: Harvard University Press, 1994).

Knoppers, G.N., and J.G. McConville (eds.), *Reconsidering Israel and Judah: Recent Studies on the Deuteronomistic History* (Winona Lake, IN: Eisenbrauns, 2000).

Köckert, M. Review of Gary N. Knoppers, *Two Nations under God*, *ZAW* 108 (1996), p. 473.

Kogawa, J., *Obasan* (New York: Anchor Books, 1994).

Kraus, C.S. (ed.), *The Limits of Historiography: Genre and Narrative in Ancient Historical Texts* (Mnemosyne, 191; Leiden: E.J. Brill, 1999).

Kroll, P.W., 'Us and Them', *JAOS* 113 (1993), pp. 457-60.

Kuan, J., 'Asian Biblical Interpretation', in J.H. Hayes (ed.), *Dictionary of Biblical Interpretation* (Nashville: Abingdon Press, 1999), pp. 70-77.

—'Diasporic Reading of a Diasporic Text: Identity Politics and Race Relations and the Book of Esther', in Segovia (ed.), *Interpreting beyond Borders*, pp. 161-73.

—'My Journey into Diasporic Hermeneutics', *USQR* 56 (2002), pp. 50-54.

—'Reading Amy Tan Reading Job', in T. Sandoval and C. Madolfo (eds.), *Relating to the Text: Interdisciplinary and Form-Critical Insights on the Bible* (JSOTSup, 384; London: T. & T. Clark International, 2003), pp. 266-79.

—'Reading with New Eyes: Social Location and the Bible', *Pacific School of Religion Bulletin* 82.1 (2003), pp. 1-3.

Kwok, P., *Discovering the Bible in the Non-Biblical World* (The Bible and Liberation Series; Maryknoll, NY: Orbis Books, 1995).

—'Jesus/the Native: Biblical Studies from a Postcolonial Perspective', in Segovia and Tolbert (eds.), *Teaching the Bible*, pp. 69-85.

Laato, A., *Josiah and David Redivivus: The Historical Josiah and the Messianic Expectations of Exilic and Postexilic Times* (Stockholm: Almqvist & Wiksell, 1992).

Lai, H.M., *Island: Poetry and History of Chinese Immigrants on Angel Island, 1910–1940* (San Francisco: HOC DOI [History of Chinese Detained on Island], 1980).
Lance, H.D., 'The Royal Stamps and the Kingdom of Josiah', *HTR* 64 (1971), pp. 315-32.
Lanfranchi, G.B., 'Consensus to Empire: Some Aspects of Sargon II's Foreign Policy', in H. Waetzoldt and H. Hauptmann (eds.), *Assyrien im Wandel der Zeiten* (RAI, 39; Heidelberger Studien zum alten Orient, 6; Heidelberg: Heidelberger Orientverlag, 1997), pp. 81-87.
Larsen, M. (ed.), *Power and Propaganda: A Symposium in Ancient Empires* (Mesopotamia, 7; Copenhagen: Akademist, 1979).
Lee, J.Y., *Marginality: The Key to Multicultural Theology* (Minneapolis: Fortress Press, 1995).
Lee, R., *Orientals: Asian Americans in Popular Culture* (Philadelphia: Temple University Press, 1999).
Lee, S.H., 'Pilgrimage and Home in the Wilderness of Marginality: Symbols and Context in Asian American Theology', *Princeton Seminary Bulletin* 16 (1995), pp. 49-64.
Lemche, N.P., 'Clio is also Among the Muse! Keith W. Whitelam and the History of Palestine: A Review and Commentary', in Grabbe (ed.), *Can a 'History of Israel' be Written?*, pp. 123-55.
—'Is it Still Possible to Write a History of Ancient Israel?', *SJOT* 8 (1994), pp. 165-90.
Levine, B., and A. Malamat, Review of Keith W. Whitelam, *The Invention of Ancient Israel*, *IEJ* 46 (1996), pp. 284-88.
Liew, T.B. (ed.), *The Bible in Asian America* (Semeia, 90–91; Atlanta: Society of Biblical Literature, 2002).
—'Introduction: Whose Bible? Which (Asian) America?', in *idem* (ed.), *The Bible in Asian America*, pp. 1-26.
Lipschits, O., 'Nebuchadrezzar's Policy in "Hattu-Land" and the Fate of the Kingdom of Judah', *UF* 30 (1998), pp. 467-88.
Liverani, M., 'The Ideology of the Assyrian Empire', in Larsen (ed.), *Power and Propaganda*, pp. 297-317.
Lo, K., 'Cultic Centralization in the Deuteronomistic History: A Strategy of Dominance and Resistance' (PhD dissertation, Chicago Theological Seminary, 2003).
Lohfink, N., 'Recent Discussion on 2 Kings 22–23: The State of the Questions', in D.L. Christensen (ed.), *A Song of Power and the Power of Song* (Winona Lake, IN: Eisenbrauns, 1993), pp. 36-61.
Long, B.O., 'Historical Narrative and the Fictionalizing Imagination', *VT* 35 (1985), pp. 405-16.
Long, V.P., *The Art of Biblical History* (Foundations of Contemporary Interpretation, 5; Grand Rapids: Zondervan, 1994).
Long, V.P. (ed.), *Israel's Past in Present Research: Essays on Ancient Israelite Historiography* (Sources for Biblical and Theological Study, 7; Winona Lake, IN: Eisenbrauns, 1999).
Lowe, L., 'Heterogeneity, Hybridity, Multiplicity: Marking Asian American Differences', *Diaspora* 1 (1991), pp. 24-44.
—*Immigrant Acts: On Asian American Cultural Politics* (Durham: Duke University Press, 1996).
Luckenbill, D.D., *Ancient Records of Assyria and Babylonia* (2 vols.; Chicago: University of Chicago Press, 1926–27).
Malamat, A., 'The Historical Background of the Assassination of Amon', *IEJ* 3 (1953), pp. 26-29.

—'Josiah's Bid for Armageddon: The Background of the Judean–Egyptian Encounter in 609 B.C.', *JANES* 5 (1973), pp. 268-79.

—'The Kingdom of Judah between Egypt and Babylon: A Small State within a Great Power Confrontation', in W. Claassen (ed.), *Text and Context: Old Testament and Semitic Studies for F.C. Fensham* (JSOTSup, 48; Sheffield: JSOT Press, 1988), pp. 117-29.

—'The Last Kings of Judah and the Fall of Jerusalem: An Historical-Chronological Study', *IEJ* 18 (1968), pp. 137-56.

—'The Last Wars of the Kingdom of Judah', *JNES* 9 (1950), pp. 218-27.

—'The Twilight of Judah: In the Egyptian–Babylonian Maelstrom', *SVT* 28 (1955), pp. 123-45.

McConville, J.G., 'The Old Testament Historical Books in Modern Scholarship', *Them* 22 (1997), pp. 3-13.

McDermott, J.J., *What are they Saying about the Formation of Israel?* (New York: Paulist Press, 1998).

McKay, J.W., *Religion in Judah under the Assyrians: 732–609 BC* (Studies in Biblical Theology, Second Series, 26; London: SCM Press, 1973).

McKenzie, S.L., 'The Divided Kingdom in the Deuteronomistic History and in Scholarship on It', in Römer (ed.), *The Future of the Deuteronomistic History*, pp. 135-45.

—*The Trouble with Kings: The Composition of the Book of Kings in the Deuteronomistic History* (Leiden: E.J. Brill, 1991).

McKenzie, S.L., and M.P. Graham (eds.), *The History of Israel's Traditions: The Heritage of Martin Noth* (JSOTSup, 182; Sheffield: Sheffield Academic Press, 1994).

McNutt, P.M., '"Fathers of the Empty Spaces" and "Strangers Forever": Social Marginality and the Construction of Space', in Gunn and McNutt (eds.), *'Imagining' Biblical Worlds*, pp. 30-50.

—*Reconstructing the Society of Ancient Israel* (Louisville, KY: Westminster/John Knox Press, 1999).

Milgrom, J., 'The Date of Jeremiah, Chapter 2', *JNES* 14 (1955), pp. 65-69.

Millard, A.R., J. Hoffmeier, and D.W. Baker (eds.), *Faith, Tradition, and History: Old Testament Historiography in its Near Eastern Context* (Winona Lake, IN: Eisenbrauns, 1994).

Miller, J.M., 'Is it Possible to Write a History of Israel without Relying on the Hebrew Bible?', in Edelman (ed.), *The Fabric of History*, pp. 93-102.

—'W.F. Albright and Historical Reconstruction', *BA* 42 (1979), pp. 37-47.

Miller, J.M, and J.H. Hayes, *A History of Ancient Israel and Judah* (Philadelphia: Westminster Press, 1986).

Mitchell, T.C., 'Judah until the Fall of Jerusalem (c. 700–586 B.C.)', in J. Boardman *et al.* (eds.), *The Assyrian and Babylonian Empires and Other States of the Near East, from the Eighth to the Sixth Centuries B.C.* (The Cambridge Ancient History, 3, Part 2; Cambridge: Cambridge University Press, 1991), pp. 371-409.

Moore-Gilbert, B., 'Spivak and Bhabha', in Schwartz and Ray (eds.), *A Companion to Postcolonial Studies*, pp. 451-66.

Mullen, E.T., *Narrative History and Ethnic Boundaries: The Deuteronomistic Historian and the Creation of Israelite National Identity* (Atlanta: Scholars Press, 1993).

Munslow, A., *Deconstructing History* (London: Routledge, 1998).

Na'aman, N., 'The Kingdom of Judah under Josiah', *Tel Aviv* 18 (1991), pp. 3-71.

Nakanose, S., *Josiah's Passover* (Maryknoll, NY: Orbis Books, 1993).
Naveh, J., 'A Hebrew Letter from the Seventh Century B.C.', *IEJ* 10 (1960), pp. 129-39.
Nelson, R., *The Double Redaction of the Deuteronomistic History* (JSOTSup, 18; Sheffield: JSOT Press, 1981).
—'Josiah in the Book of Joshua', *JBL* 100 (1981), pp. 531-40.
—'Realpolitik in Judah (687–609 B.C.E.)', in W.W. Hallo, J.C. Moyer, and L.G. Perdue (eds.), *Scripture in Context*. II. *More Essays on the Comparative Method* (Winona Lake, IN: Eisenbrauns, 1983), pp. 177-89.
Nissen, H.-J., and J. Renger (eds.), *Mesopotamien und seine Nachbarn: Politische und kulturelle Wechselbeziehungen im Alten Vorderasien vom 4. bis 1. Jahrtausend v. Chr. XXV. Rencontre Assyriologique Internationale Berlin 3. bis 7. Juli 1978* (Berliner Beiträge zum Vorderen Orient, Band 1, Teil 2; Berlin: Dietrich Reimer Verlag, 1982).
Norman, A.P., 'Telling it Like it Was: Historical Narrative on their Own Terms', *History and Theory* 30 (1991), pp. 119-35.
Noth, M., *The Deuteronomistic History* (JSOTSup, 15; Sheffield: JSOT Press, 1981).
Oates, J., 'Assyrian Chronology, 631–612 B.C.', *Iraq* 27 (1965), pp. 135-59.
O'Brien, M.A., 'The "Deuteronomistic History" as a Story of Israel's Leaders', *ABR* 37 (1989), pp. 14-34.
—*The Deuteronomistic History Hypothesis: A Reassessment* (Orbis biblicus et orientalis, 92; Göttingen: Vandenhoeck & Ruprecht, 1989).
Oded, B., 'History vis-à-vis Propaganda in the Assyrian Royal Inscription', *VT* 48, pp. 423-25.
—*Mass Deportations and Deportees in the Neo-Assyrian Empire* (Wiesbaden: Reichert, 1979).
Ogden, G.D., 'The Northern Extent of Josiah's Reforms', *ABR* 26 (1978), pp. 26-34.
Okihiro, G.Y., *The Columbia Guide to Asian American History* (New York: Columbia University Press, 2001).
—*Margins and Mainstreams: Asians in American History and Culture* (Seattle: University of Washington Press, 1994).
Omatsu, G., 'The "Four Prisons" and the Movements of Liberation: Asian American Activism from the 1960s to the 1990s', in Zhou and Gatewood (eds.), *Contemporary Asian America*, pp. 80-112.
Omi, M., and H. Winant, 'On the Theoretical Status of the Concept of Race', in Wu and Song (eds.), *Asian American Studies*, pp. 201-207.
—*Racial Formation in the United States: From the 1960s to the 1990s* (New York: Routledge, 1994).
Oppenheim, A.L., 'Neo-Assyrian and Neo-Babylonian Empires', in H.D. Lasswell, D. Lerner, and H. Speier (eds.), *Propaganda and Communication in World History* (Honolulu: The University Press of Hawaii, 1979), pp. 111-44.
Pallares, J.C., *A Poor Man Called Jesus: Reflections on the Gospel of Mark* (trans. R.R. Barr; Maryknoll, NY: Orbis Books, 1986).
Parpola, S., and R.M. Whiting (eds.), *Assyria 1995: Proceedings of the 10th Anniversary Symposium of the Neo-Assyrian Text Corpus Project Helsinki, September 7–11, 1995* (Helsinki: Neo-Assyrian Text Corpus Project, 1997).
Petersen, D., Review of John Van Seters, *In Search of History*, *CBQ* 47 (1985), pp. 336-40.
Polzin, R., *Moses and the Deuteronomist: A Literary Study of the Deuteronomic History* (New York: Seabury Press, 1980).

—*Samuel and the Deuteronomist: A Literary Study of the Deuteronomic History* (San Francisco: Harper & Row, 1987).
Prior, M., *The Bible and Colonialism: A Moral Critique* (The Biblical Seminar, 48; Sheffield: Sheffield Academic Press, 1997).
Provan, I.W., 'The End of (Israel's) History? K.W. Whitelam's *The Invention of Ancient Israel*. A Review Article', *JSS* 42 (1997), pp. 283-300.
—*Hezekiah and the Books of Kings: A Contribution to the Debate about the Composition of the Deuteronomistic History* (BZAW, 172; Berlin: W. de Gruyter, 1988).
—'Ideologies, Literary and Critical: Reflections on Recent Writing on the History of Israel', *JBL* 114 (1995), pp. 585-606.
Pury, A.de, T. Römer, and J. Macchi (eds.), *Israel Constructs its History: Deuteronomistic Historiography in Recent Research* (JSOTSup, 306; Sheffield: Sheffield Academic Press, 2000).
Rad, G. von, 'The Deuteronomic Theology of History in I and II Kings', in idem, *The Problem of the Hexateuch and Other Essays* (Edinburgh: Oliver & Boyd, 1966), pp. 205-21.
Radovan, Z., '"David" Found at Dan', *BARev* 20/2 (1994), pp. 26-39.
Rainey, A.F., 'Hezekiah's Reform and the Altars at Beer-Sheba and Arad', in Coogan, Exum, and Stager (eds.), *Scripture and Other Artifacts*, pp. 333-54.
—'Manasseh, King of Judah, in the Whirlpool of the Seventh Century B.C.E.', in idem (ed.), *kinattutu sa darâti: Raphael Kutscher Memorial Volume* (Journal of the Institute of Archaeology of Tel Aviv University, Occasional Publications, 1; Tel Aviv: Institute of Archaeology of Tel Aviv University, 1993), pp. 147-64.
—'Stones for Bread: Archaeology versus History', *NEA* 64/3 (2001), pp. 140-49.
Reade, J., 'Neo-Assyrian Monuments in their Historical Context', in Fales (ed.), *Assyrian Royal Inscriptions*, pp. 143-67.
Redford, D., *Egypt, Canaan, and Israel in Ancient Times* (Princeton, NJ: Princeton University Press, 1992).
Renan, E., 'What is a Nation?', in Bhabha (ed.), *Nation and Narration*, pp. 8-22.
Rendtorff, R., 'The Paradigm is Changing: Hopes—and Fears', *BibInt* 1 (1993), pp. 34-53.
Rich, A., *Blood, Bread, and Poetry: Selected Prose 1979–1985* (New York: W.W. Norton, 1986).
Rietz, H.W., 'My Father Has No Children: Reflections on a *Hapa* Identity toward a Hermeneutic of Particularity', in Liew (ed.), *The Bible in Asian America*, pp. 145-57.
Roberts, J.J.M., 'The Davidic Origin of the Zion Tradition', *JBL* 92 (1973), pp. 329-44.
—'Zion in the Theology of the Davidic-Solomonic Empire', in T. Ishida (ed.), *Studies in the Period of David and Solomon and Other Essays: Papers Read at the International Symposium for Biblical Studies, Tokyo, 5–7 December, 1979* (Winona Lake, IN: Eisenbrauns, 1982), pp. 93-108.
Rogers, J.S., Review of Gary N. Knoppers, *Two Nations under God*, *CBQ* 57 (1995), pp. 351-52.
—Review of Gary N. Knoppers, *Two Nations under God*, *CBQ* 58 (1996), pp. 117-18.
Rohe, R., 'Chinese Camps and Chinatowns: Chinese Mining Settlements in the North America West', in J. Lee, I.L. Lim, and Y. Matsukawa (eds.), *Re-Collecting Early Asian America: Essays in Cultural History* (Philadelphia: Temple University Press, 2002), pp. 31-51.
Römer, T.C., 'L'historiographie deuteronomiste (HD): Histoire de la recherche et enjeux du débat', in A. de Pury, T. Römer, and J. Macchi (eds.), *Israël construit son histoire* (Geneva: Labor & Fides, 1996), pp. 9-120.

—'Transformation in Deuteronomistic and Biblical Historiography: On "Book Finding" and Other Literary Strategies', *ZAW* 109 (1997), pp. 1-12.
Römer, T.C. (ed.), *The Future of the Deuteronomistic History* (Leuven: University Press, 2000).
Römer, T.C., and A. de Pury, 'Deuteronomistic Historiography (DH): History of Research and Debated Issues', in de Pury, Römer, and Macchi (eds.), *Israel Constructs its History*, pp. 24-141.
Rose, M., 'Bemerkungen zum historischen Fundament des Josia-Bildes in II Reg 22f', *ZAW* 89 (1977), pp. 50-63.
Rowlett, L., *Joshua and the Rhetoric of Violence: Recent Study of the Deuteronomistic History* (JSOTSup, 225; Sheffield: Sheffield Academic Press, 1996).
Rowton, M.B., 'Jeremiah and the Death of Josiah', *JNES* 10 (1951), pp. 128-30.
Safran, W., 'Diasporas in Modern Societies: Myths of Homeland and Return', *Diaspora* 1 (1991), pp. 83-99.
Said, E., *Culture and Imperialism* (New York: Vintage Books, 1994).
—*Orientalism* (New York: Random House, 1978).
Schniedewind, W., 'The Problem with Kings: Recent Study of the Deuteronomistic History', *RelSRev* 22 (1995), pp. 22-27.
Schwartz, H., and S. Ray (eds.), *A Companion to Postcolonial Studies* (Oxford: Basil Blackwell, 2000).
Segovia, F., 'Biblical Criticism and Postcolonial Studies: Toward a Postcolonial Optic', in Sugirtharajah (ed.), *The Postcolonial Bible*, pp. 49-65.
—*Decolonizing Biblical Studies: A View from the Margin* (Maryknoll, NY: Orbis Books, 2000).
—'Interpreting beyond Borders: Postcolonial Studies and Diasporic Studies in Biblical Criticism' in *idem* (ed.), *Interpreting beyond Borders*, pp. 11-34.
—'Notes toward Refining the Postcolonial Optic', in *idem*, *Decolonizing Biblical Studies*, pp. 133-43.
—'Reading Across: Intercultural Criticism and Textual Posture', in *idem* (ed.), *Interpreting beyond Borders*, pp. 59-83.
—'Toward a Hermeneutics of the Diaspora: A Hermeneutics of Otherness and Engagement', in Segovia and Tolbert (eds.), *Reading from this Place*, I, pp. 57-73.
Segovia, F. (ed.), *Interpreting beyond Borders* (The Bible and Postcolonialism, 3; Sheffield: Sheffield Academic Press, 2000).
Segovia, F., and E.S. Fernandez (eds.), *A Dream Unfinished: Theological Reflections on America from the Margins* (Maryknoll, New York: Orbis Books, 2001).
Segovia, F., and M.A. Tolbert (eds.), *Reading from this Place*. I. *Social Location and Biblical Interpretation in the United States* (Minneapolis: Fortress Press, 1994).
—*Reading from this Place*. II. *Social Location and Biblical Interpretation in Global Perspective* (Minneapolis: Fortress Press, 1995).
—*Teaching the Bible: The Discourse and Politics of Biblical Pedagogy* (Maryknoll, NY: Orbis Books, 1998).
Seow, C.L., 'Ark of the Covenant', in *ABD*, I, pp. 386-93.
—*Myth, Drama, and the Politics of David's Dance* (HSM, 46; Atlanta: Scholars Press, 1989).
Shanks, H., 'The Age of *BAR*: Scholars Talk about how the Field has Changed', *BARev* 27/2 (2001), pp. 21-35.
Shea, W.H., 'Jerusalem under Siege: Did Sennacherib Attack Twice?', *BARev* 25 (1999), pp. 36-44, 74.

Smend, R., 'The Law and the Nations: A Contribution to Deuteronomistic Traditional History', in Knoppers and McConville (eds.), *Reconsidering Israel and Judah*, pp. 95-110.
Soggin, J.A., 'The History of Ancient Israel: A Study in Some Questions of Method', *EI* 14 (1978), pp. 44-51.
Soja, E.W., 'Thirdspace: Expanding the Scope of the Geographical Imagination', in D. Massey, J. Allen, and P. Sarre (eds.), *Human Geography Today* (Cambridge: Polity Press, 1999), pp. 260-78.
—*Thirdspace: Journeys to Los Angeles and Other Real-and-Imagined Places* (Cambridge, MA: Blackwell, 1996).
Spalinger, A., 'Assurbanipal and Egypt: A Source Study', *JAOS* 98 (1974), pp. 316-28.
—'The Concept of the Monarchy', *Or* 47 (1978), pp. 12-36.
—'The Date of the Death of Gyges and its Implications', *JAOS* 98 (1978), pp. 400-409.
—'Egypt and Babylonia: A Survey (c. 620 B.C.–550 B.C.)', *SAK* 5 (1977), pp. 221-44.
—'Psammetichus, King of Egypt: I', *JARCE* 13 (1976), pp. 133-47.
—'Psammetichus, King of Egypt: II', *JARCE* 15 (1978), pp. 49-57.
Sparks, K.L., *Ethnicity and Identity in Ancient Israel: Prolegomena to the Study of Ethnic Sentiments and their Expression in the Hebrew Bible* (Winona Lake, IN: Eisenbrauns, 1998).
Spieckermann, H., *Juda unter Assur in der Sargonidenzeit* (Göttingen: Vandenhoeck & Ruprecht, 1982).
Spivak, G.C., *A Critique of Postcolonial Reason: Toward a History of the Vanishing Present* (Cambridge, MA: Harvard University Press, 1999).
—'Can the Subaltern Speak?', in P. Williams and L. Chrisman (eds.), *Colonial Discourse and Post-colonial Theory: A Reader* (New York: Columbia University Press, 1994), pp. 66-111.
Stern, E., *Archaeology of the Land of the Bible*. II. *The Assyrian, Babylonian, and Persian Periods, 732–332 BCE* (The Anchor Bible Reference Library; New York: Doubleday, 2001).
—'The Eastern Border of the Kingdom of Judah in its Last Days', in Coogan, Exum, and Stager (eds.), *Scripture and Other Artifacts*, pp. 399-409.
Sugirtharajah, R.S., *Asian Biblical Hermeneutics and Postcolonialism: Contesting Interpretations* (The Biblical Seminar, 64; Sheffield: Sheffield Academic Press, 1999).
—*The Bible and the Third World: Precolonial, Colonial and Postcolonial Encounters* (Cambridge: Cambridge University Press, 2001).
—*Postcolonial Criticism and Biblical Interpretation* (Oxford: Oxford University Press, 2002).
—'A Postcolonial Exploration of Collusion and Construction in Biblical Interpretation', in *idem* (ed.), *The Postcolonial Bible*, pp. 91-116.
—'Textual Cleansing: A Move from the Colonial to the Postcolonial Version', *Semeia* 76 (1996), pp. 7-19.
Sugirtharajah, R.S. (ed.), *The Postcolonial Bible* (The Bible and Postcolonialism, 1; Sheffield: Sheffield Academic Press, 1998).
—*Vernacular Hermeneutics* (The Bible and Postcolonialism, 2; Sheffield: Sheffield Academic Press, 1999).
—*Voices from the Margin* (Maryknoll, NY: Orbis Books, 1991).
Sweeney, M., *King Josiah of Judah: The Lost Messiah of Israel* (New York: Oxford University Press, 2001).

Tadmor, H., 'Assyria and the West: The Ninth Century and its Aftermath', in H. Goedicke and J.J.M. Roberts (eds.), *Unity and Diversity: Essays in the History, Literature, and Religion of the Ancient Near East* (Baltimore: The Johns Hopkins University Press, 1975), pp. 36-48.
—'History and Ideology in the Assyrian Royal Inscriptions', in Fales (ed.), *Assyrian Royal Inscriptions*, pp. 13-33.
—'Philistia under Assyrian Rule', *BA* 29 (1966), pp. 86-102.
—'Propaganda, Literature, Historiography: Cracking the Code of the Assyrian Royal Inscriptions', in Parpola and Whiting (eds.), *Assyria 1995*, pp. 325-38.
—'World Dominion: The Expanding Horizon of the Assyrian Empire', in L. Milano, S. de Martino, F.M. Fales, and G.B. Lanfranchi (eds.), *Landscape: Territories, Frontiers and Horizons in the Ancient Near East: Papers Presented to the XLIV Rencontre Assyriologique Internationale Venezia, 7–11 July 1997* (History of the Ancient Near East Monographs, 3/1; Padova: Sargon, 1999), pp. 55-62.
Takaki, R., *A Different Mirror: A History of Multicultural America* (New York: Little, Brown & Company, 1993).
—*Strangers from a Different Shore: A History of Asian Americans* (New York: Penguin Books, 1989).
Talmon, S., 'The New Hebrew Letter from the Seventh Century B.C. in Historical Perspective', *BASOR* 176 (1964), pp. 29-38.
Talshir, Z., 'The Three Deaths of Josiah and the Strata of Biblical Historiography (2 Kings xxiii 29-30; 2 Chronicles xxxv 20-5; 1 Esdras i 23-31)', *VT* 46 (1996), pp. 213-36.
Tan, A., *The Kitchen God's Wife* (New York: Putnam, 1991).
Tappy, R.E., *The Archaeology of Israelite Samaria. II. The Eighth Century BCE* (HSS, 50; Winona Lake, IN: Eisenbrauns, 2001).
Thompson, T.L., *The Historicity of the Patriarchal Narratives: The Quest for the Historical Abraham* (Berlin: W. de Gruyter, 1974).
—'A Neo-Albrightean School in History and Biblical Scholarship?', *JBL* 114 (1995), pp. 683-98.
—Review of Gary N. Knoppers, *Two Nations under God*, *JNES* 57 (1998), pp. 141-43.
Tolbert, M.A., 'Afterwards: The Politics and Poetics of Location', in Segovia and Tolbert (eds.), *Reading from this Place*, I, pp. 305-17.
Tseng, T., 'Beyond Orientalism and Assimilation: The Asian American as Historical Subject', in F. Matsuoka and E.S. Fernandez (eds.), *Realizing the America of Our Hearts: Theological Voices of Asian Americans* (St Louis, MO: Chalice Press, 2003), pp. 55-72.
Tushigham, A.D., 'A Royal Israelite Seal (?) and the Royal Jar Handle Stamps (Part One)', *BASOR* 200 (1970), pp. 71-78.
—'A Royal Israelite Seal (?) and the Royal Jar Handle Stamps (Part Two)', *BASOR* 201 (1971), pp. 23-35.
Umemoto, K., '"On Strike" San Francisco State College Strike, 1968–1969: The Role of Asian American Students', in Zhou and Gatewood (eds.), *Contemporary Asian America*, pp. 49-79.
US Commission on Civil Rights, *Civil Rights Issues Facing Asian Americans in the 1990s* (Washington, DC: US Commission on Civil Rights, 1992).
Vaggione, R.P., 'Over All Asia? The Extent of the Scythian Domination in Herodotus', *JBL* 92 (1973), pp. 523-30.

Vanderhooft, D.S., *The Neo-Babylonian Empire and Babylon in the Latter Prophets* (Harvard Semitic Museum Monographs, 59; Atlanta: Scholars Press, 1999).
Van Seters, J., *Abraham in History and Tradition* (New Haven: Yale University Press, 1975).
—*In Search of History: Historiography in the Ancient World and the Origins of Biblical History* (New Haven: Yale University Press, 1983; repr. Winona Lake, IN: Eisenbrauns, 1997).
Vice, S., *Introducing Bakhtin* (Manchester: Manchester University Press, 1997).
Wagenaar, J.A., 'Crossing the Sea of Reeds (Exod 13–14) and the Jordan (Josh 3–4): A Priestly Framework for the Wilderness Wandering', in M. Vervenne (ed.), *Studies in the Book of Exodus* (Leuven: Leuven University Press, 1996), pp. 461-70.
Weippert, H., 'Die "deuteronomistischen" Beurteilungen der Königsbücher', *Bib* 53 (1972), pp. 301-39.
—' "Histories" and "History": Promise and Fulfillment in the Deuteronomistic Historical Work', in Knoppers and McConville (eds.), *Reconsidering Israel and Judah*, pp. 47-61.
Welch, A.C., 'The Death of Josiah', *ZAW* 43 (1925), pp. 255-60.
—'When was the Worship of Israel Centralised at the Temple?', *ZAW* 43 (1925), pp. 250-60.
White, H., *The Content of the Form: Narrative Discourse and Historical Representation* (Baltimore: The Johns Hopkins University Press, 1987).
—'The Historical Text as Literary Artifact', in *idem, Tropics of Discourse*, pp. 81-100.
—'Historicism, History, and the Figurative Imagination', in *idem, Tropics of Discourse*, pp. 101-20.
—'Interpretation in History', in *idem, Tropics of Discourse*, pp. 51-80.
—*Metahistory: The Historical Imagination in Nineteenth-Century Europe* (Baltimore: The Johns Hopkins University Press, 8th edn, 1993).
—*Tropics of Discourse: Essays in Cultural Criticism* (Baltimore: The Johns Hopkins University Press, 1978).
Whitelam, K.W., *The Invention of Ancient Israel: The Silencing of Palestinian History* (London: Routledge, 1996).
—'Recreating the History of Israel', *JSOT* 35 (1986), pp. 45-70.
Williamson, H.G.M., *1 and 2 Chronicles* (New Century Bible Commentary; Grand Rapids: Eerdmans, 1982).
—'The Death of Josiah and the Continuing Development of the Deuteronomistic History', *VT* 32 (1982), pp. 242-48.
—'Reliving the Death of Josiah', *VT* 37 (1987), pp. 9-15.
Wilson, N.J., *History in Crisis? Recent Directions in Historiography* (Upper Saddle River, NJ: Prentice–Hall, 1999).
Wiseman, D.J., *Chronicles of Chaldaean Kings (626–556 B.C.) in the British Museum* (London: British Museum, 1956).
Wolff, H.W., 'The Kerygma of the Deuteronomic Historical Work', in W. Brueggemann and H.W. Wolff (eds.), *The Vitality of Old Testament Traditions* (Atlanta: John Knox Press, 1982), pp. 83-100.
Wu, J.Y.S., and M. Song (eds.), *Asian American Studies: A Reader* (New Brunswick, NJ: Rutgers University Press, 2000).
Würthwein, E., *Studien zum deuteronomistischen Geschichtswerk* (BZAW, 227; Berlin: W. de Gruyter, 1994).

Bibliography

Yadin, Y., *The Art of Warfare in Biblical Lands in the Light of Archaeological Study*, II (New York: McGraw–Hill, 1963).
—'Beer-Sheba: The High Place Destroyed by King Josiah', *BASOR* 222 (1976), pp. 5-17.
—'The Historical Significance of Inscription 88 from Arad: A Suggestion', *IEJ* 26 (1976), pp. 9-14.
Yamauchi, E., 'The Current State of Old Testament Historiography', in Millard, Hoffmeier, and Baker (eds.), *Faith, Tradition, and History*, pp. 1-36.
Young, R., *Colonial Desire* (London: Routledge, 1995).
—*White Mythologies: Writing History and the West* (London: Routledge, 1990).
Younger, K.L., *Ancient Conquest Accounts: A Study in Ancient Near Eastern and Biblical History Writing* (JSOTSup, 98; Sheffield: JSOT Press, 1990).
—Review of John Van Seters, *In Search of History*, *JSOT* 40 (1988), pp. 110-17.
Yu, H., *Thinking Orientals: Migration, Contact, and Exoticism in Modern America* (New York: Oxford University Press, 2001).
Zaccagnini, C., 'The Enemy in the Neo-Assyrian Royal Inscriptions: The "Ethnographic" Description', in Nissen and Renger (eds.), *Mesopotamien und seine Nachbarn*, pp. 409-24.
—'An Urartean Royal Inscription in the Report of Sargon's Eighth Campaign', in Fales (ed.), *Assyrian Royal Inscriptions*, pp. 259-95.
Zagorin, P., 'Historiography and Postmodernism: Reconsiderations', *History and Theory* 29 (1990), pp. 263-74.
Zhou, M., and J.V. Gatewood (eds.), *Contemporary Asian America: A Multidisciplinary Reader* (New York: New York University Press, 2000).
Zia, H., *Asian American Dreams: The Emergence of an American People* (New York: Farrar, Straus & Giroux, 2000).

INDEXES

INDEX OF REFERENCES

Old Testament		2 Kings		34.6	145, 149
Exodus		17.1-23	2	34.33	145
12.21-23	237	17.5-6	139	35.20-27	219
		17.24	139, 142	35.22	221
Deuteronomy		17.25	139		
6	239	21.19-36	182	*Jeremiah*	
12.1-14	228	21.19-26	217	1.13-14	165
16.1-8	237, 240	21.20-21	217		
		22–23	1, 116,	*1 Esdras*	
Joshua			134, 144	1.25-31	219
3–5	231	22.1–23.25	2		
4	231	23	168	Josephus	
5.1-8	231	23.1-4	239	*Antiquities*	
5.10-12	231	23.3	137	10.73-77	220
21.1-42	129	23.4-14	223, 226	10.74-83	219
		23.8	145, 150	10.74	220
Judges		23.13	199	10.75	221
1.27-33	129	23.15-20	138, 140,	10.76	221
14.3	231		145, 199,		
15.8	231		235	Classical	
		23.20	138	*Herodotus*	
1 Samuel		23.21-23	236, 239	1.95	165
14.6	231	23.21	137	1.104-106	165
17.26	231	23.22	199	1.104	164, 165
17.36	231	23.26-27	199	1.105	163, 164
31.4	231	23.28-30	145, 182,	1.106	164
			217	1.130	165
2 Samuel		23.29-30	219, 221	1.151-53	173
1.20	231	23.29	219	2.151-53	172
6	234			2.157	163
6.17-19	235	*1 Chronicles*		4.1	165
11	230	6.54-81	129		
24	129	21.1-27	129	Inscriptions	
				Prism A	
1 Kings		*2 Chronicles*		II, 113-15	174
11–14	135	33.22-23	217		
13	134	34–35	161		
13.2-5	2	34.6-7	145		

INDEX OF AUTHORS

Ahlström, G.W. 81, 156, 169
Albertz, R. 226
Alfrink, B. 147
Althann, R. 155
Anderson, B. 6, 8, 9
Appleby, J. 48, 60-63, 66, 67, 88
Ashcroft, B. 48, 89, 121, 209
Auld, A.G. 105

Bakhtin, M. 31
Barrick, W.B. 4
Bartlett, J.R. 82
Batto, B.F. 232-34
Begg, C.T. 136, 147
Berquist, J.L. 116, 179
Bhabha, H.K. 13-15, 25, 34, 37
Biran, A. 132
Boehmer, J. 147
Bolin, T. 58
Boyarin, D. 102
Breisach, E. 59, 60, 122, 123
Brennan, T. 13
Brettler, M.Z. 76
Bright, J. 127, 128, 145-47, 169, 171
Brinkman, J.A. 162
Brock, R.N. 39, 40

Campbell, A.F. 3
Carter, P. 118-21
Chakrabarty, D. 89-93
Chan, S. 97, 98, 183, 184, 187, 192
Cho, E.S. 141, 142, 218, 228
Clark, K. 31
Clines, D.J.A. 83, 84
Cogan, M. 214, 223-27
Coggins, R.J. 81
Coogan, M.D. 233
Coote, M.P. 227, 228
Coote, R. 82, 160, 227, 228, 230
Covington, E. 60, 61, 66, 67, 88

Cross, F.M. 2, 133-35, 145, 147, 161, 218, 220

Dalley, S. 233
Daniels, R. 36, 192
Davies, G. 148
Davies, P.R. 79, 83, 85, 87, 102, 129
Dever, W.G. 79, 85, 106, 107
DeVries, S.J. 136
Doi, J. 195, 196
Donaldson, L.E. 23

Fales, F.M. 205, 206
Fernandez, E.S. 27
Finkelstein, I. 130, 131, 148-50, 156-58, 227-29
Forsberg, S. 177
Foskett, M.F. 43
Foucault, M. 70, 72, 73, 114, 119, 144
Freedman, D.N. 134, 145, 147, 161, 218, 220
Frost, S.B. 147

Gallagher, S.V. 117, 214
Garbini, G. 81, 101, 102, 126
Gattung, G. 70-72
Geary, P.J. 12
Gellner, E. 6, 7, 12
Gitin, S. 166, 167, 210, 211
Gordon, R.P. 136
Grabbe, L. 83
Graham, M.P. 1, 161
Grayson, A.K. 162, 212
Green, B. 31
Griffiths, G. 48, 89, 121, 209
Gyles, M.F. 170, 173-76

Habermas, J. 69
Hall, R.G. 230, 231
Halpern, B. 54-56, 77

Hastings, A. 10, 11
Hayes, J.H. 75, 76, 81, 129, 155, 169
Hoglund, K.G. 161
Holloway, S.W. 105
Holquist, M. 31
Howard, D.M. 136
Hoyt, D. 60, 61, 66, 67, 88
Huizinga, J. 56, 57
Hunt, L. 62, 63

Iggers, G.G. 62
Iwamura, J.N. 43

Jacob, M. 62, 63
Japhet, S. 161, 219, 220
Jenkins, K. 61, 67, 74

Kaiser, W.C. 80, 129
Kane, H. 35
Kim, E. 188
Kim, J.H. 42
Kim, T.H. 211-14, 216-18
Kim, U.Y. 37, 43, 230
Kitano, H. 36
Kitchen, K.A. 173
Klein, K.L. 122, 123
Klein, R.W. 136, 137
Kleinig, J.W. 161
Knoppers, G.N. 4, 135-39
Köckert, M. 136
Kogawa, J. 195
Kuan, J. 31, 43-46
Kwok, P. 32-35

Laato, A. 140
Lai, H.M. 193
Lance, H.D. 148
Lanfranchi, G.B. 208-10, 213
Latham, M. 60, 61, 66, 67, 88
Lee, J.Y. 38
Lee, R. 99, 184-86, 188, 189
Lee, S.H. 38
Levine, B. 106-108
Liew, T.B. 42, 43
Liverani, M. 210
Lo, K. 141-43, 238-40

Long, V.P. 68, 79
Lowe, L. 100

Macchi, J. 1
Malamat, A. 106-108, 144, 145, 147, 148, 163, 211, 218
McConville, J.G. 4, 135
McDermott, J.J. 130
McKay, J.W. 223-26
McKenzie, S.L. 1, 3, 4, 161
McNutt, P.M. 130
Miller, J.M. 76, 77, 79-81, 129, 155, 169
Moore-Gilbert, B. 89, 93
Mullen, E.T. 199, 229, 232, 233
Munslow, A. 68, 74

Na'aman, N. 145, 147-49, 151, 155, 157, 158, 162, 163, 166-69, 172, 173
Nakanose, S. 236-38
Naveh, J. 132, 149
Nelson, R. 155, 221
Noth, M. 1, 51-54

Oates, J. 161
O'Brien, M.A. 4
Oded, B. 203
Ogden, G.D. 148
Okihiro, G.Y. 41, 63, 97-99, 123, 124, 183, 187, 192, 193
Omatsu, G. 64, 65
Omi, M. 89
Ord, D.R. 230

Pallares, J.C. 23
Petersen, D. 57
Polzin, R. 4
Provan, I.W. 4, 108, 109
Pury, A. de 1

Radovan, Z. 132
Rainey, A.F. 131, 132, 150, 217
Reade, J. 208
Redford, D. 147, 156, 164, 165
Renan, E. 6
Rietz, H.W. 43

Roberts, J.J.M. 235
Rogers, J.S. 136
Rohe, R. 125
Römer, T. 1
Rowton, M.B. 147

Said, E. 18-21
Schniedewind, W. 4, 5
Segovia, F. 22, 27-31
Seow, C.L. 234, 235
Shanks, H. 83
Shea, W.H. 214
Silberman, N.A. 148-50, 156-58, 227-29
Smend, R. 2
Sneider, A. 60, 61, 66, 67, 88
Soja, E.W. 115, 179
Spalinger, A. 147, 164-66, 168-70, 172, 174, 176, 177
Sparks, K.L. 199-204
Spieckermann, H. 226
Spivak, G.C. 93, 94
Stern, E. 147, 150-54
Sugirtharajah, R.S. 21-27, 37, 39

Tadmor, H. 161, 163, 207, 208, 212, 239
Takaki, R. 94-97, 187, 188, 193
Talmon, S. 149
Talshir, Z. 155, 220, 221
Tappy, R.E. 178
Thompson, T.L. 76, 136

Tiffin, H. 48, 89, 121, 209
Tolbert, M.A. 27
Tseng, T. 94-96, 99, 100
Tushingham, A.D. 148

Umemoto, K, 64

Vaggione, R.P. 165
Van Seters, J. 4, 55-57, 75
Vice, S. 31

Wagenaar, J.A. 232
Welch, A.C. 155, 219, 221
White, H. 68, 69
Whitelam, K.W. 16, 55, 59, 81, 82, 84-86, 103-105, 126, 127, 132, 133
Williamson, H.G.M. 147, 161, 220
Wilson, N.J. 67
Winant, H. 89
Wiseman, D.J. 162, 171
Würthwein, E. 4

Yadin, Y. 147, 150
Yamauchi, E. 77, 78
Young, R. 49, 88, 89, 93, 94
Younger, K.L. 56, 209
Yu, H. 40, 65, 66, 97, 124, 125, 183, 191

Zaccagnini, C. 204-206, 209
Zia, H. 190, 196, 197

www.ingramcontent.com/pod-product-compliance
Lightning Source LLC
Chambersburg PA
CBHW071702160426
43195CB00012B/1548